The Blackwell Companion
to Social Work

Edited by Martin Davies

BLACKWELL
Publishers

Copyright © Blackwell Publishers Ltd 1997
Editorial matter and arrangement © Martin Davies 1997

First published in 1997

2 4 6 8 10 9 7 5 3 1

Blackwell Publishers Ltd
108 Cowley Road
Oxford OX4 1JF
UK

Blackwell Publishers Inc.
238 Main Street
Cambridge, Massachusetts 02142
USA

British Library Cataloguing in Publication Data

A CIP catalogue record for this book is available from the British Library.

Library of Congress Cataloging-in-Publication Data

The Blackwell companion to social work / edited by Martin Davies.
    p.   cm.
    Includes bibliographical references and index.
    ISBN 0–631–19876–8. — ISBN 0–631–19877–6 (pbk.)
    1. Social service — Great Britain.   I. Davies, Martin, 1936–
    HV245.B63   1997
361.3′2′0941—dc20   96–14974
                                                                          CIP

1000988335

Typeset in 9 on 11pt Palatino by Grahame & Grahame Editorial, Brighton
Printed in Great Britain by T.J. Press Limited, Padstow, Cornwall

This book is printed on acid-free paper

Contents

Contributors

Jane Aldgate is Professor of Social Work at Leicester University.

Graham Allan is Reader in Sociology at Southampton University.

Caroline Ball is Senior Lecturer in the Schools of Law and Social Work at the University of East Anglia, Norwich.

Peter Beresford works with Open Services Project in London, and is Principal Lecturer in Social Policy at Brunel University College.

Tim Booth is Professor of Social Policy at Sheffield University.

Gwyneth Boswell is Senior Lecturer in Social Work at the University of East Anglia, Norwich.

Allan Brown is Senior Lecturer in the School for Policy Studies at the University of Bristol.

Juliet Cheetham established and was the first Director of the Social Work Research Centre at Stirling University. She is now Emeritus Professor there.

Jo Connolly is a qualified social worker and Research Associate at the University of East Anglia, Norwich.

Suzy Croft works with Open Services Project in London and is a social worker at St John's Hospice, London. She is a member of the Editorial Collective of the journal, *Critical Social Policy*.

Martin Davies is Professor of Social Work at the University of East Anglia, Norwich.

Lena Dominelli is Professor of Social Work at Southampton University, and President of the International Association of Schools of Social Work.

Dave Evans is Principal Lecturer in Social Work at Suffolk College, Ipswich.

Gillian Harris is Lecturer in Developmental Psychology at Birmingham University, and Principal Clinical Psychologist at the Children's Hospital, Birmingham.

Robert Harris is Professor of Social Work and Pro-Vice Chancellor at the University of Hull.

Martin Herbert is Professor of Clinical and Community Psychology at Exeter University.

David Howe is Professor of Social Work at the University of East Anglia, Norwich, and Editor of the Journal, *Child and Family Social Work*.

Peter Huxley is Professor of Psychiatric Social Work and Director of the Mental Health Social Work Research Unit at Manchester University. He is consulting editor of the *Social Work and Social Sciences Review*.

Adrian L. James is Senior Lecturer in Applied Social Studies at the University of Hull. A qualified probation officer, he is joint editor of the *Journal of Social Welfare and Family Law*.

Chris Jones is Professor of Social Work and Social Policy at Liverpool University.

Bill Jordan is Reader in Social Studies at Exeter University.

Siobhan Lloyd is Lecturer in Sociology/Women's Studies at Aberdeen University, where she is also Head of the Counselling Service.

Peter Marsh is Reader in the Department

of Sociological Studies at the University of Sheffield.

Audrey Mullender is Professor of Social Work in the Department of Applied Social Studies at Warwick University and is editor of the *British Journal of Social Work*.

Jack Nathan, a qualified social worker and psychoanalytic psychotherapist, is an associate member of the London Centre for Psychotherapy. He is a lecturer at the Maudsley Hospital, and is responsible there for advanced practice teaching.

J. Owusu-Bempah is Lecturer in Psychology in the School of Social Work at Leicester University.

Alison Petch is Professor and Director of the Nuffield Centre for Community Care Studies at the University of Glasgow.

Chris Phillipson is Professor of Applied Social Studies and Social Gerontology at Keele University.

Ian Philp is Professor and Head of the Department of Health Care for Elderly People at Sheffield University.

Peter Raynor is a former probation officer and currently Professor of Applied Social Studies at the University of Wales, Swansea.

Nigel Reigate is a social worker in Norfolk Social Services Department.

Lena Robinson is Lecturer in Psychology at Birmingham University.

Tammie Ronen is Lecturer in the Bob Shapell School of Social Work at Tel Aviv University and President of the Israeli Association for Behaviour and Cognitive Therapy.

Gillian Schofield is Lecturer in Social Work and Deputy Director of the Centre for Research on the Child and Family at the University of East Anglia, Norwich.

Michael Sheppard is Principal Lecturer in Social Work at Plymouth University.

Ian Sinclair is Professor of Social Work at York University.

Nigel Stone is Senior Lecturer in the School of Social Work at the University of East Anglia, Norwich, and a Norfolk probation officer. He is editor of the *Probation Journal*.

June Thoburn is Professor of Social Work and Director of the Centre for Research on the Child and Family at the University of East Anglia, Norwich.

Neil Thompson is Professor of Social Work and Applied Social Studies at Staffordshire University.

Brian Thorne is Director of the University Counselling Service and Professor of Counselling at the University of East Anglia, Norwich.

John Triseliotis is Emeritus Professor and Senior Research Fellow at the International Social Science Institute, University of Edinburgh.

Sir William Utting has been successively a Principal Probation Officer, Director of Social Services, Chief Social Work Officer at the Department of Health and Social Security, and Chief Inspector of Social Services at the Department of Health.

Janet Walker is Professor of Family Policy and Director of the Relate Centre for Family Studies at the University of Newcastle upon Tyne. She is a qualified probation officer.

Lorraine Waterhouse is Professor of Social Work at Edinburgh University.

Jan White is a Lecturer in the Centre for Professional Studies at Bristol University and Family Therapist with Avon NSPCC.

Brian Williams, a former probation officer, is Lecturer in Criminal Justice Studies at the University of Keele.

Introduction

No editorial task has given me greater pleasure than the job of putting together this book.

I have eaten, drunk and slept social work in one form or another ever since the day in 1959 when, as a rather raw sociology graduate from Liverpool, I wandered into the London School of Economics and caught sight of a dusty type-written notice which invited interested persons to present themselves for possible recruitment as probation officers in London. I had not thought of social work as a possible career route until then, but I nevertheless went along for an off-the-cuff interview with an avuncular Deputy Principal, and, before I knew what was happening, I was knocking on doors in Islington, doing 'matrimonials' in Tottenham with formidable women who knew more about sex and violence than I'd ever dreamt of, and giving the Soho stipendiary magistrate the dubious benefit of my experience of human nature each morning before he started to go through his regular list of drifters, prostitutes and thieves.

Over the next year, I met all manner of probation officers: one was an ex-paratroop sergeant who, it was reputed, always found some excuse to throw every young male client over his shoulder onto the floor 'just to show him who was the boss'; another had a cross on his office wall and required his charges to kneel before it before they got down to the business of social casework. Untrained, virginal, but not as nervous as I should have been, I was taught by a range of senior officers how to cope with a caseload of 120, how to perform in court, and how important it was to make friends with lots of local employers in order to ensure that my clients were able to 'lead an industrious life'. (The unemployment rate at the time was, of course, 2.5 per cent.)

From that time to this, I have remained fascinated by the practice of social work – and not least by its seemingly infinite variety of modes. But despite my own best efforts, and those of my colleagues and friends in the world of academic social work, its nature and purpose remain defiantly elusive.

There are, I think, two reasons for this: the first I have written about elsewhere (Davies, 1994) – that too many people fail to differentiate between what social work *is* and what they think it *ought* to be; but the second is more important for the purpose of this book – that social work actually does cover a multitude of virtues which are remarkably difficult to characterize in a conceptually tidy manner.

The Blackwell Companion to Social Work does not aim to present a homogeneous portrait, nor is it always internally consistent. But the reader who perseveres with the text will emerge with a good idea of the range of activities that are practised by social work professionals; she will recognize the importance of political, economic and demographic contexts; and she will realize the importance of an understanding of human behaviour, of an awareness of the nature of human relationships, and of an acceptance that social work has a great deal to do with the interface between vulnerable people, the law and the machinery of the state.

Above all, she will come to understand that those who practise social work are committed to the task of making life more bearable for those whom others might prefer to forget – or choose to condemn. How that objective can be achieved is of course highly debatable – and it is debated in these pages.

'Always remember,' my sixth-form English teacher once said to me, 'Always remember, when you're reading an academic book that it isn't a detective novel. There is no rule that says you must start at the beginning and read all the way through to the end. Indeed,' he went on, 'there is a great deal to be said for reading the last few pages first. That way you can often save yourself a lot of unnecessary time and effort.'

He would, I am sure, have taken it for granted that the sensible reader, faced with a collection of 44 essays, should feel free to scan the list of contents and go directly to those topics, those authors and those sections which feel immediately seductive, or which look as though they might meet an urgent purpose. If the reader likes what she finds, then she will almost certainly be tempted to sample other chapters which, in the first flush of self-indulgent enthusiasm, she has passed over.

The Blackwell Companion to Social Work is designed to be that kind of book. To help the browsing process, my contributors have highlighted five key points; again in contrast with detective story mode, these should enable you to find out 'whodunnit' straightaway: after that, you can go back to read through the material in order to work out *how* it was done.

The reader will decide for herself which chapters work best. I have read all the chapters several times, and I have learnt a great deal that I didn't know

before. Of course, I have an opinion about which contributions I think are the most elegantly crafted – though I'm not going to share my views with you. I know enough about the subjectivity of people's interests and their appreciation of different styles to realize that you, the reader, might have very different ideas of which chapters are the most useful.

One question which all readers of a collection like this might ask themselves is whether the whole is greater than the sum of the parts. Here are 44 essays on, for the most part, familiar topics. Each essay aims to introduce the reader to its subject, and every author hopes that she will be persuaded to explore it more deeply and at greater length. To that end, three questions are posed for readers to think about and discuss with others in a group; and three suggested references are offered to allow the student the opportunity of reading further. But if you, the reader, do what I have done and study the whole book – whether in page-order sequence or not is immaterial – will you find that you have been given a landscape perspective on social work at the millennium? I hope you will. It is not, I think, you will quickly acknowledge, a tidy picture. And it is one that continues to evolve before your eyes. Indeed, during the editorial process itself, the question of whether the work of the probation service is or is not social work has assumed major political significance in the United Kingdom, and, because of that, three of the contributors to the *Companion* have had to write in full awareness that their argument could yet be overtaken by events, with social work in the UK criminal justice system conceivably being squeezed into oblivion by the year 2000.

But there is also a sense of continuity and of commonality in this book. We are writing about a field of human endeavour that is itself 100 years old; and some elements within it have remained remarkably stable. Moreover, social work is almost wholly concerned with meeting human needs of a kind that are common always and everywhere. Changing demographic patterns increase demand; so, too, do developments in medicine; and changes in family structure. Definitions and terminology may evolve; but the nature of the experience of mental illness, of discrimination, of poverty and of interpersonal violence does not.

The Blackwell Companion has been designed to enable the reader to reflect upon the reality of human behaviour in conditions of stress, and to understand how the social worker is charged with the task of making an appropriate response.

Martin Davies
School of Social Work
University of East Anglia
Norwich

Reference

Davies, Martin (1994) *The Essential Social Worker* (3rd edn), Aldershot: Arena.

Part I
Social Work and Society

Introduction to Part I

As a political philosopher with experience as a qualified social worker, Bill Jordan is uniquely positioned to explore and analyse the place of social work in contemporary society. He recognizes both the material and the symbolic significance of the emergence in the twentieth century of social work as a high budget, publicly funded activity in the urban world, and in this anchor-chapter he considers afresh the way in which social work has found itself drawn into programmes of enforcement, gate-keeping and social control. Jordan's analysis takes in not only the impact of the new right in recent years and the past and potential influence of social democracy, but draws our attention to the value of a comparative perspective by taking account of the very different social work scenes in western Europe, the United States, the emerging democracies of eastern Europe and the Third World.

I.1

Social Work and Society
Bill Jordan

The aims of this chapter are:

1 to analyse why social work has developed in some societies and not in others;

2 to explain why social work takes different forms in the various societies in which it has taken root; and

3 to anticipate future developments in social work in post-industrial, postmodern societies, within a changing global environment.

Whereas there were doctors and lawyers, pharmacists and engineers, in Classical Greece and Rome and throughout the medieval period, social workers did not appear until the nineteenth century. There are still no social workers among the Bedouin, the Nuer or the Tikopia, or even in the People's Republic of China, and officially there were no social workers in the centrally planned countries of the Soviet Bloc before the collapse of those regimes in 1989. However, immediately after that cataclysmic change, they sprang up, like caring mushrooms, all over those countries, almost overnight. The first objective of my analysis is to explain the gradual emergence of social work among the developing countries of the Third World and their sudden recent appearance in the post-communist Second World.

Social work does not take identical forms in all the countries where it has developed. In Britain, which was among the first societies to have identifiable

social work activity, it originally manifested itself as voluntary (and predominantly female) work, in the final quarter of the nineteenth century, and it focused on the undesirable social consequences of industrialization and urbanization. However, by the second half of the twentieth century, it had been transformed into a predominantly professional activity, organized mainly in large, hierarchical, public-sector agencies, eventually consolidated into a single 'fifth social service' (Titmuss, 1968). By contrast, in Continental Europe, Australasia and the developing world, social work continued to be done mainly in smaller voluntary agencies or local community associations, with professional staff more closely integrated with volunteers, while in the USA there developed a commercial sector alongside the voluntary one. By the end of the twentieth century, these differences are still recognizable, even though there has been some convergence between the various traditions. Social workers in all the advanced industrialized states are scattered among a range of statutory public bodies, voluntary agencies, community associations and commercial enterprises, working alongside or under the supervision of a number of other professionals, and accountable to a regulatory framework of law and guidance (Jones and May, 1992). The second objective of my analysis is to explain these developments.

Although there are identifiable norms and aspirations of social work that can be recognized in its practice within almost all of these traditions, settings and organizational forms, it continues to evolve and change, along with society itself. Whereas its original practitioners were predominantly Christian, bourgeois, conservative and committed to the upholding of family values and the ethic of hard work and responsibility, some have at various times adopted radical or even quasi-revolutionary ideas (Statham, 1978), challenging the moral basis of capitalism, patriarchy and white supremacy. Such ideas have always originated in wider social movements, and entered social work from society; there has never been a radical challenge generated by the profession itself. In recent years, its evolution has reflected tendencies in the world economy and in national politics towards the fragmentation of the mass solidarities on which welfare states were built, the decline of industrial employment and working-class organization in the advanced economies, the commercialization of welfare provision, the relative weakness of national governments in the face of global market forces, the growth of 'lifestyle politics' at the expense of 'emancipatory politics' and the precariousness of the daily lives of the poor (Giddens, 1991). These 'post-industrial' and 'postmodern' developments focus social work on the assessment and management of risks (Parton, 1994b), on 'partnership' with service users and on business-like management of tasks. The third objective of my analysis is to indicate the likely future trajectory of these changes.

In this introduction, I shall argue that social work arises where communities (either of the traditional type, based on kinship and geographical proximity, or of the twentieth-century compulsory kind, forged by state regulation and coercive collective inclusion, as in the former communist countries) begin to break up under pressure from market forces. Social work is one of the measures

Five Key Points

1 There is a close association between social work and economic individualism, despite the paradox that social work itself represents a form of collective action and provision.

2 This paradox is reflected in many of the tensions to be found in present-day social work.

3 Social work has not been marginalized by the New Right, but has been transformed into a more precise instrument of state power.

4 Voluntary associations are better able than public bureaucracies to be responsive to the specific needs of groups and individuals, though their contribution to effective democratic governance is more debatable.

5 Eventually the costs of enforcement in public-sector bureaucracies will threaten economic efficiency – and social work may start again 'from roughly its late nineteenth century beginnings'.

by which societies seek to protect themselves, and compensate their most vulnerable members in face of socially undesirable consequences of commercial, contractual relations (Polanyi, 1944), and it is the approach to doing this which is furthest from collectivism, and hence most readily reconciled with economic individualism. Hence social work was often the *only* form of social service in the early stages of capitalism in many countries, and always the *least developed* form of social service in those states which adopted totalitarian forms of collectivism, the Soviet bloc command economies.

The close association between social work and economic individualism (or anti-collectivism) is paradoxical, since social work itself represents a form of collective action and provision. It arises where systems of reciprocity, sharing and redistribution (either informal, as in communities and networks, or formal, as in public welfare schemes) begin to break down and are replaced by contractual exchanges, leaving some individuals without protection. It substitutes 'professional friendship' (or 'targeted intervention' in present-day business-speak) for the inclusive membership rights provided by those disintegrating systems, thus seeking to shore up the social relations of disrupted communities, and shield the vulnerable and excluded. There is a contradiction at the heart of social work, because it is spawned by market-orientated economic individualism, yet its values are those of a caring, inclusive, reciprocal community that takes collective responsibility for its members.

I shall argue that this contradiction is reflected in the many tensions evident in present-day social work. As commercial and contractual relations penetrate social work agencies themselves, as practitioners are required to assess service users for individualized packages of care, treatment, training, containment or punishment, and as their work comes under ever more detailed state regulation and surveillance, social work still strives and yearns for the caring, intimate, inclusive, voluntary, negotiated, co-operative, trusting and empowering relationships on which its golden years of expansionism were built. This is not an irrational, backward-looking fantasy; as an organized activity, social work only makes sense if it can be done within just such an ethos, and is only efficient and equitable on just these terms. Yet increasingly, it is actually concerned with rationing public provision, regulating deviant behaviour and arbitrating in antagonistic relationships, on behalf of a beleaguered public power. Social work is the spirit of community (Etzioni, 1993) in the clothes of Hobbesian third-party enforcement – a caring face in the service of Leviathan (Hobbes, 1651). This reflects a contradiction in modern liberal democratic society, as much as in social work itself.

Social workers have always been peacemaking negotiatiors at the front line of conflicts between modern social systems and their perishing and dangerous classes. Like blue-helmeted UN troops serving as peace-keepers in a civil war, their role is ambiguous, and they are often denounced, and sometimes attacked, by both sides. They are open to manipulation and exploitation by the combatants, and their work is always morally compromised. Their future is as uncertain as the search for bargains and compromises amid escalating antagonism.

Communities and Social Care

Social work upholds an ethic of social relations – caring, sharing, inclusive and forgiving – that is borrowed from the traditional terms of membership of the oldest human collectivities. The archaic morality of simple societies of hunter-gatherers left no member unprotected; all activities were shared, all goods held in common, and each vulnerable individual benefited from the redistribution of everything that could be gathered or culled (Polanyi, 1944). Yet it is just when such collective moralities break down that social work appears, as an alternative, individualized version, that tries to restore something of that ethic of social relations, through the offer (or imposition) of a 'professional friend'. And historically it has been a short step from the appearance of charitable visitors to the burgeoning of official, public social work that rations resources and requires standards of behaviour to be maintained. This section aims to show how each step in the evolution of social work – first as substitute social cement and then as low-key social enforcement – has occurred.

'Community' is suddenly the focus of

attention, among political and social theorists (Mulhall and Swift, 1992; Etzioni, 1993) and policy makers, as the limited success and high costs of state-organized social services become apparent. Theorists point out that communities existed before states or markets, and have provided the necessary conditions for all other systems of social relations. Communities are systems of mutual obligation that steer and regulate all other interactions, socializing individuals into norms of trust and co-operation, on which economic and political transactions rely (Wolfe, 1989, 1991). Hence the belated recognition that the gung-ho economic individualism of the New Right in the 1980s – the decade when Margaret Thatcher and Ronald Reagan cut their swathes through the UK's and USA's post-war social institutions – has undermined the basis of economic efficiency as well as distributional equity (Gray, 1994; Jordan, 1995).

Paradoxically, although social work was among the first targets of the New Right's critique (Anderson, 1980; Brewer and Lait, 1980), it has been a sphere of considerable expansion during this period. Although the ideologues of economic individualism denounced social workers' bleeding hearts and open hands (dispensing taxpayers' money), their reforms required more, not less, 'targeted intervention'. This was partly because market forces laid waste traditional communities through unemployment and poverty, and partly because the erosion of compulsory mass solidarities (such as social insurance) required some other form of compensatory protection. Just as the New Right's economic reforms were driven by a crude version of Adam Smith's utilitarianism, so their social policies drew them back into Benthamism (Jordan, 1992). In Margaret Thatcher's Britain, the self-regulating market had to be supplemented by the panopticon state; the atoms activated by economic

individualism must be steered by social engineering. Those who could not survive in the new, competitive environment required individual assessment, and a personalized prescription for re-education, retraining, therapeutic intervention or social care. The New Right expected more, not less, from its professional experts; social workers were to provide a good part of this regulatory and surveillance expertise.

Thus social work has not been marginalized in those countries where the New Right's reforms went furthest, but transformed into a more precise instrument of state power. It is only now that theorists and politicians are raising old questions about its original role in communities, and how it can again help

---

Three Questions

1   How has social work been transformed under the New Right's auspices?
2   How have the priorities in social work practice been determined?
3   Is there a role for social work in the criminal justice system?

---

to provide the moral glue that every society needs if it is to achieve prosperity and harmony (Etzioni, 1993). Hence it is appropriate to look into the roots of community, and its relationship with social work – how the moral obligations that bound members of simple societies are replaced or reinforced by professional and official interventions in family, kinship, neighbourly and community social relations.

As with social work, in the analysis of community it is difficult to separate substantive from normative elements; both run on *morality*, it seems. Human societies are rescued from the perils of murderous conflict, so well captured by Hobbes (1651), primarily through *informal*, self-imposed constraints. Human beings are socialized into these in childhood, and discursively regulate themselves and each other as adults. Human speech appears to be a special code for doing this, allowing groups to restrain internal competition, and achieve forms of co-operation that are inaccessible to animals – such as the maintenance of individual property rights within complex social production, involving long-term investments (Levy, 1992). Meaningful communication is, on many recent micro-sociological accounts, a co-operative accomplishment, involving the shared construction of mutually comprehensible utterances between active participants in an exchange (Goffman, 1969; Sacks, 1972; Heritage, 1984). 'Reality' itself – the external world, with all its opportunities and constraints – has recently been analysed as the product of everyday interactional efforts, through which members of communities strive to improvise the sense of moral obligation, binding commitments and common purposes (Hilbert, 1992).

If morally purposeful communication is the bedrock of all human society (and everything else human beings have achieved), then serious talking about what we owe each other in our everyday relationships is fundamental to all other, more technical, rational or political activity. The basic rule of every social relationship – economic exchange, political accountability, family obligation – is *reciprocity*. The rules of human conduct that are so universal as to be universally unwritten are all about reciprocity: offer visitors a drink; avoid rough bodily contact with strangers; take turns in conversation; trade, don't grab; always remember your mother's birthday. All morality is superstructure on these foundations, and constructed by negotiating (within this framework of reciprocal exchange) over particular situations. Reciprocity is a necessary condition for community and for social work, since no more complex or sophisticated set of obligations can be put

in place without agreements that require negotiation, that are reinforced by interaction and that are interpreted discursively. When the informal regulation of community is in trouble, it makes sense to call in a social worker to discuss the issue in question.

The second essential element in both community and social work is *shared activity*. Despite Sartre's view that hell is other people, human society is based on the assumption that sharing with (some) others gives benefits that outweigh the costs. In every known society, there are fairs, feasts and festivals, usually exceptional rather than everyday events, where large numbers of people celebrate collectively (and often drunkenly). Most societies also have more sober religious rites of collective worship, in which they bind themselves to common moral purposes, and celebrate the totems of their collectivity.

The physical basis of these rites of solidarity is provided by shared resources – churches, village halls, community centres and the like. In political theory, there has been much recent interest in the successful management of 'common-pool resources' (Ostrom, 1990), since it is a notorious axiom of economics that what is not privately owned is overused and becomes degraded (Hardin, 1968). The solution to this problem is good management by community elders, or an elected committee, with a big stake in conserving and improving the facilities. Shared activities promote solidarity and the sense of mutual obligation, which in turn – together with the wise stewardship of the elders – leads to good-quality shared resources, and a more convivial social life.

Here again the connections with social work are obvious. Groupwork methods assume that sharing is a benefit rather than a cost. Residential work implies that people benefit from sharing a common resource, and from the good management of their shared activities. Community work entails the strengthening of local solidarities, and the improvement of shared facilities, under local management. All these methods come into play when the community itself no longer successfully supplies them, or when it can only maintain harmony by excluding specially needy, disruptive or deviant individuals.

Finally, community is concerned with the *redistribution* of goods for final consumption. In every society, production involves co-operation and the postponement of gratification – sowing seeds in the ploughed earth, rather than fighting over who should eat them, and hunting game in teams, rather than running pell-mell after it to see who can be first to catch it. But co-operative production then requires a division of the product into individual shares, since even a communal meal has to be divided up into pieces that fit into an individual mouth. Every society thus has rules about who gets what in the post-production shareout – rules about merit, entitlement and need that form the core of ideas of justice. What is due to each individual, and the rituals of redistribution, are therefore at the heart of each community's collective decision-making processes (Adler and Asquith, 1981).

Social work too is about redistribution for final consumption. It involves decisions about benefits and services for those in greatest need, and about whom the wider community has difficulties in making allocations. Social work is thus involved in social justice, but in a highly discretionary way; it is all about hard cases, that fall outside the general rules of distributional decisions, and require some kind of interpersonal negotiations. Social work begins where community has difficulty in providing.

But here we begin to recognize the fundamental ambiguity of social work that I am seeking to analyse. Part of what social workers seek to do is to strengthen the bonds of inclusive membership, by

practising and nurturing reciprocity, sharing and redistribution, either within 'natural communities', or in the 'artificial' communities of groups, residential and day facilities, therapeutic or training units. But part is concerned with the compulsory enforcement of social obligations, rules, laws and official regulations. The two are not distinct and separate; nearly all social work is *underpinned*, implicitly if not explicitly, by state power. And statutory social work, even of the most coercive kind, relies on the reciprocities and co-operative exchanges of community. A prison welfare officer uses many of the same methods as a worker in a voluntary project.

Yet despite this overlap, there are two quite different things going on here. The spontaneous (or professionally nurtured) morality of a harmonious, inclusive group is a *public good* in one sense. It is available to all, because no one can be excluded from its benefits; it is not in the interests of any one individual to supply it to the rest, because he or she could not demand a price; and it is not depleted (in fact it is apparently enhanced) by such use. In this sense, it is like the air we breathe – free, public and abundant, yet pollutable and perhaps ultimately finite in supply. Social work arises where economic development threatens to pollute and damage this public good. It

Further Reading

1   Jones, A. and May, J. (1992) *Working in Human Service Organisations: A Critical Introduction*, Melbourne: Longman Cheshire.
2   Anheier, H. and Seibel, W. (eds) (1990) *The Third Sector: Comparative Studies in Non-Profit Organisations*, Berlin: de Gruyter.
3   Hirst, P. (1994) *Associative Democracy: New Forms of Economic and Social Governance*, Cambridge: Polity Press.

aims to increase its supply by generating more moral, socially responsible relationships among its service users, and ultimately in wider society.

But social work activity is also a public good in another sense. Like the police force, the army or the fire service, it supplies an official and authoritative system for controlling forces that endanger or jeopardize order, prosperity and co-operation. It is part of the solution to disruptive social conflicts that consists in third-party enforcement. The sovereign territorial state, modernity's answer to the threat of war, sedition, crime, disorder, defection, disease and destitution, provides compulsory and binding remedies to these ills. Social work is the lowest (most detailed, personal) form of enforcement. Its work is necessary because community's morality breaks down under modern conditions.

These two elements coexist uneasily in organized social work. Economic individualism exaggerates the tension between them.

Co-operation, Contract, Citizenship

It is not surprising that the enforcement side of social work grows in a society in which government promotes economic individualism as the mainspring of growth and progress. In such a society, the paradigm for social relations is gainful exchange between bargain-hunting actors in the market, the political forum and in everyday informal interactions. Individuals are seen as rational egoists who can order their diverse preferences and pursue their interests by means of strategies that are orientated towards institutional opportunities and incentives, and each other's strategic behaviour (Hollis, 1994). Such actors will exploit each other and renege on agreements unless they can see good reasons for doing otherwise; the

enforcement of contracts ultimately gives them such reasons. This applies as much to the moral commitments made in families and communities as to the economic contracts of the market place.

Ideally, all such agreements should be self-enforcing, in the sense that no actor can do better by any other strategy, and all gain from the exchanges made (Lyons, 1992). But unfortunately there are always temptations to take unfair advantage, and the law attempts to block this option. Economic individualism argues that society's institutions should promote gainful voluntary exchanges of all kinds (Buchanan, 1986), but provide efficient arbitration in disputes, and retribution for defection. The dominant political agenda of the 1980s, bringing sweeping structural change in most First and Third World countries and the collapse of all communist Second World regimes, pursued its programme from this blueprint.

Two sets of issues now cast doubt on that whole project. The first is whether adequate opportunities and incentives can be given to all for what is seen by policy-makers as socially desirable behaviour. To take a few examples: why should unskilled workers in advanced economies take work that pays less than subsistence wages? Why should parents care for their severely handicapped children, or offspring for their mentally and physically deteriorating parents? Why should battered wives stay married to violent husbands? And why should minorities, discriminated against by powerful majorities, stay loyal to their political systems? If actors are really rational egoists, they will do none of these things. What they will do instead (commit crimes; abandon their children or parents; divorce; or turn to political resistance and subversion) will increase the need for, and costs of, enforcement. Unfortunately, for a variety of reasons (including the globalization of production and exchange, the break-up of traditional communities, the insecurity of male egos attendant on rapid social change, and the xenophobia and racism that accompany recession) all these problems grew in the 1980s and have continued to increase. Market-orientated reforms were simply unable to provide positive incentives and opportunities to counteract them. Hence politicians and officials, including social workers, were driven back on tougher enforcement measures (Jordan, 1995).

The second cluster of problems stems from the assumption that actors are rational egoists. This, of course, is sociologically naïve; systems make actors, just as actors make (or break) systems. Every institutional structure represents the attempt to construct good citizens (Offe and Preuss, 1990). This is why critics of economic individualism accuse its ideologues of a self-fulfilling prophecy; their programme turns people into instrumental bargain-hunters (Wolfe, 1991). But the trouble is that such actors are much more likely to behave strategically, not only in relation to each other, but also to institutional systems. The New Right's programme was supposed to block the 'rent seeking' of social democratic politicians, bureaucrats and trade unions, achieved through the oversupply of public goods and services (Buchanan, 1978; Peacock, 1979). But its own institutions were far from strategy-proof, and the actors it created were more cunning. This applies to the fat cats exercising their share options in the newly privatized monopolies, and to claimants of social assistance, who work while claiming (Jordan, James, Kay and Redley, 1992). It applies even more strongly in the former communist countries of east-central Europe, where new market-orientated services have been created, without a pause for anyone to learn the ethos of social care. The result is that welfare bureaucrats learn game theory before they learn casework or professional ethics, becoming proficient in calculative strategic bargaining that is more appropriate for the trading floor than the social welfare agency.

More fundamentally, the transformation from social democracy or central planning to economic individualism changes the role of the public power itself. Welfare states were solutions to the collective action dilemmas of the inter-war years, when the stalemate between capital and organized labour had led to nationalism, totalitarianism and war. In continental Europe they constructed institutional compromises between the state and corporate bodies, representing the 'social partners', to negotiate over shares of national income. The centrally planned regimes controlled competition by suppressing the profit motive, and allocating all goods and services by political and technocratic processes. Individuals were thus bound into collectivities by compulsory forms of solidarity, such as social insurance and 'full employment' policies. Economic individualism gave each citizen more autonomy and scope for choice, but it also changed the role of the state, which became instead the guarantor of each contract between citizens, and the provider of goods and services where markets failed. In the first instance, therefore, its role was primarily one of enforcement, to punish defectors, fraudsters and violent predators. In the second it was to provide individual citizens with a quality and standard of goods and services in a quasi-contractual way, according to a 'citizens' charter' (Taylor, 1992).

What both these uses of public power overlook is the state's role in promoting co-operation for the common good. Economic individualism fails to recognize the importance of the collective life of society, with its emphasis on individual gain as the motor of development. Part of the function of the public power in a democracy is to create common interests, and to make them recognizable to citizens, for the sake of co-operation and collective harmony. Democracy is not only a way of making collective decisions in a diverse, pluralistic society, by registering voters' preferences. It is also a way of binding citizens to common purposes and mobilizing them for collective action, by overcoming potentially costly conflicts and the socially undesirable consequences of individual and interest-group strategies (Barry, 1991, p. 276). Democratic government is *possible* because people share a common interest in a good quality of life together; it is *necessary* because of their conflicting interests (Ryan, 1983, p. 54). The institutions of government must therefore take intelligent account of potential conflicts of interest, and strive to overcome collective action dilemmas.

Social work can play a small but significant part in all this. In post-war Britain, commentators noted that social work should be informed by the new *democratic* spirit of the welfare state, and should educate service users for citizenship as well as offering them service as fellow citizens (Macadam, 1945, p. 15). But the New Right's policy programme moves as far away from this approach as it is possible to go, with its emphasis on expert individual assessment, targeted intervention, value for taxpayers' money, risk management and the resocialization of the 'underclass'. In its most ambitious, optimistic forms, it is a programme for converting welfare dependants and social deviants into the autonomous, bargain-hunting but self- and family-responsible actors of economic individualist theory. In its pessimistic, neo-Darwinian forms, it is a programme for the surveillance and containment of large groups of citizens, seen as potentially burdensome or threatening, and the treatment or punishment of a smaller group of

'dangerous' individuals (Arnold and Jordan, 1995).

In the USA, these negative policies have been focused on the poor, and especially on lone-parent black families. They reflect a new conviction among comfortable, suburban Americans that (in the words of one of Newt Gingrich's supporters) 'they should be made to get off the welfare cart, and push it'. Benefits and services are to become more conditional upon the demonstration of willingness to work, train and take responsibility for family (Mead, 1986). Punishment is to become more painful, humiliating and deterrent. In this cradle of democracy and liberalism, few forms of coercion are now off limits; executions of juveniles are openly canvassed, and 'orphanages' for the children of welfare mothers who defect on workfare recommended (Gingrich, 1994).

In Britain, this move towards a 'politics of enforcement' has been slower to emerge, but became clearly recognizable from the autumn of 1993, when the Conservative government went 'back to basics', and new measures were announced to raise the price of crime (Howard, 1993), and clamp down on fraudulent welfare claims (Lilley, 1993). Within the subsequent two years, the prison population rose by over 20 per cent, and the government embarked upon a review of the training of probation officers, concluding that they should be taken out of the ambit of social work education, and be given corrections-orientated training instead.

All these policy developments signal problems in the New Right's project. If voluntary and gainful exchanges between bargain-hunting citizens were really available and self-enforcing, expenditure on enforcement should be falling, not rising. Instead, in Britain the increase in public spending on criminal justice has cancelled out the savings on other programmes, especially council housing

(Social Trends, 1994, table 6.21). The Department of Health has recognized the waste of conducting hundreds of thousands of investigations of suspected child abuse, only 20 per cent of which result in any follow-up action, and only 5 per cent in any support for families (Gibbons, Conroy and Bell, 1995). The use of social work for pure enforcement is inefficient, as well as signalling social injustice.

The fundamental problem behind all these phenomena is that social polarization and economic globalization have combined to make poor people much more vulnerable and unprotected. They in turn adopt resistance strategies, aimed at reducing risks, taking opportunistic advantage of 'informal' openings, and gaining revenge on their oppressors. These strategies can include crime, working while claiming, truancy, drug dealing, begging, prostitution, even rioting. They reflect a decline in opportunities and rewards within the formal labour market, and a rise in 'informal' opportunities and pay-offs in the hypercasualized economic relations that have followed from deregulation (Jordan, 1993, 1995, 1996). Government's solution is to raise the price of deviance by enforcement measures, and social work is drawn into these tasks.

Voluntary co-operation is a necessary condition for effective social work, and social work can promote co-operation in wider society. Social work methods seek to create islands of co-operation and agreed partnership, even in such seas of coercion as prisons, closed psychiatric wards or workfare programmes. Social workers hope that these will spill over into their surrounding environment, making wider social relations more harmonious, and increasing the scope for democratic government by consent. Social work values include an anti-oppressive agenda, which focuses on the discriminatory use of power against minority and subordinate groups. This new political context for social work makes its practice particularly difficult and compromised in those countries, such as the USA and UK, where New Right influence on institutional change has been strongest.

Social Work Organizations and Society

The organization of social work has followed paths that varied with the historical traditions and political cultures of nation states (Chapman and Dunsire, 1971). For many, it is the voluntary sector that is the largest employer, and so-called 'intermediate organizations' (nowadays usually working under contract to central or local government) that provide most of the services. This section will explore the reasons for this diversity of institutional development, and why the 'third sector' has been the main provider in so many countries.

Services such as day and residential care can be – and often are – purchased in markets by better-off customers. In this context they are private goods that can be consumed exclusively, for instance, by those who can afford a companion by day, or a live-in care attendant; or they can be consumed collectively, by those who prefer to live in a hotel or club. The issue for public policy about such services is that those who are most likely to need them (people with handicaps or disabilities, or with the frailties of extreme old age) are least likely to be able to afford them. Hence the state is drawn into funding the services and making decisions about who should provide them on its behalf.

In Britain between 1946 and 1979, the local authorities became the main providers of social care. The institutions through which this was developed sprang directly from the Poor Laws (Jordan, 1974), but were modified by the post-war principles of the welfare state. There were some economic arguments for the administrative efficiency of such large public bureaucracies in terms of economies of scale and the reduction of transaction costs (Perrow, 1979). Their capacity to integrate public policy into a single whole was at a premium in the 1970s, when 'social planning' and 'corporate strategies' were in vogue. They were also capable of reconciling a number of different and changing organizational goals, through slow and complex decision processes (Hood and Schuppert, 1990). But during the 'winter of discontent' that led to the election of Margaret Thatcher's first government in 1979, the case for monolithic public agencies was weakened, as strikes threatened a total breakdown of the local infrastructure.

In continental Europe, the organization of social work had developed in quite another way. They had largely retained their basis in voluntary organizations, usually with a denominational Christian, a socialist or a humanist affiliation. In some countries (such as the Netherlands), these had lost their financial independence comparatively recently; in others (such as Germany), they had always been closely integrated with the structures of the state – and notoriously with state 'security' and policy in the Nazi period. Similar organizational forms persisted as important providers in the USA and Canada, in Australasia and in most developing countries, making this the dominant form of social work organization in a global context, despite the presence of social workers also in a wide variety of government agencies (criminal justice, education, social assistance, special employment, health, housing).

The explanation of the success of this organizational form (in competition with the monolithic public agency of the British model, and the commercialization of contractual care in the USA) is often traced to the Catholic 'subsidiarity principle'. This implies that institutional arrangements for any governmental function should devolve tasks to the lowest possible level, and use the 'lightest bureaucratic tackle and the minimum amount of public power to deal with any specific task in hand' (Hood and Schuppert, 1990, p. 101). Although the standard reference on subsidiarity is the Papal Encyclical of Pope Leo XIII, *Rerum Novarum* (1891), there are some specific efficiency arguments in its favour. Unlike the public bureaucracies, which are notoriously unresponsive to the needs of small or specialized groups of service users (because the politicians who sit on their controlling committees heed the preferences of the median voter, and hence respond to widespread needs, such as the home help services), voluntary agencies can focus on particular service users, and occupy 'niches' that are difficult to identify through the political process (Weisbrod, 1977). They are also able to achieve greater flexibility through the terms on which they employ staff (outside the scope of public sector unions), and to attract personnel who are more dynamic and creative than those who seek a typically secure, low-risk, public-service career.

A further argument in favour of specifically confessional or politically committed organizations is that they contribute indirectly to voluntary co-operation and civic engagement. On this analysis, wider society benefits from the political skills and participatory energies that are generated by the committee work and voluntary activity of such agencies. The benefits – 'social capital' (Coleman, 1990) – of a flourishing voluntary sector thus spill over into a society of active citizens, and in turn contribute to a healthy democracy. These arguments are advanced by the socialist writer Paul Hirst in his recent analysis of the associative principle, in which he argues that self-governing voluntary organizations should form the basis of all social service provision (Hirst, 1994).

But none of this explains why commercial organizations have not advanced more rapidly as providers outside the US context. Many organizational theorists attribute this to problems over the specification and enforcement of contracts. As British local authority purchasers who contract with private-sector agencies have discovered, such agreements are difficult to define, especially where needs can be expected to change over a period of time. Alternatively, of course, each individual consumer's needs may be subject to a separate contract, but this involves very high transaction costs. These features have been cited as reasons for 'contract failure' in many countries (Hansmann, 1987; Weisbrod, 1988; Badelt, 1990); public-sector purchasers have found difficulties in monitoring and measuring the performance of commercial providers. There may also have been complaints from service users about quality. All this indicates that for-profit agencies are too opportunistic and sharp to be reliable in this field; like all good rational egoists, they have difficulties in passing up opportunities to cheat.

Voluntary sector agencies may, therefore, be preferred by purchasers, because their values, structures and dependence on the goodwill of a wider public (e.g., for donations), along with a history of partnership with state organizations, make them more reliable, and hence reduce transaction costs.

The success of voluntary organizations is therefore paradoxical; they are less *politically* responsive than public-sector agencies, and often less cost-effective than commercial organizations, but they may solve awkward legitimation problems by acting as a buffer between local government and electorate, and an institutional form that is not too opportunistic and exploitative (Seibel, 1990). The principles of voluntary

organizations make them more trustworthy, thus saving transaction costs, and minimizing the use of public power and bureaucratic administration. Whether they always contribute to effective democratic governance is much more debatable. Hirst's claim to this effect is qualified by the proviso that, in a society that is divided (along ethnic, religious or ideological grounds) into mutually antagonistic groups, this form of organization may merely exacerbate social conflicts (Hirst, 1994, pp. 65–7). Instead of training citizens for public-spirited democratic participation (Tocqueville, 1835–40), it may instead mobilize them for strife (Hobbes, 1651, ch. 22). Instead of spilling over into a culture of civic engagement, trust and co-operation (Putnam, 1993), that benefits the economy as well as democratic processes, it may instead feed into militancy and wasteful struggles, as between gays and Christian fundamentalists, or pro-life and pro-choice activists in the USA.

Furthermore, Hirst also concedes that the associative principle can do little to address the social polarization that divides American and British societies into 'communities of choice' and 'communities of fate'. If economic individualism has allowed better-off families to exit from mass solidarities and form narrower mutualities, based on like incomes and risks, and left the poorest in the worst housing, schools, health facilities and environments (Jordan, 1996), then social welfare organizations are likely to replicate this tendency, and to reinforce these divisions. The associative principle will do little to offset the strong pressures from comfortable majorities to use public power to contain, coerce and punish excluded minorities, to ration assistance and to impose mainstream standards.

Conclusions

I have argued that social work exists in tension between its principles of care, compassion and harmony, and its tasks of assessment, rationing and enforcement. The former are derived from the terms of membership of inclusive communities; the latter from the socially undesirable consequences of modern market economies. Social work appears where archaic community begins to break down, and it aims to restore inclusion and co-operation. But its organized, public functions drive it towards compulsory methods, the isolation of individual 'cases', and an antagonistic relationship with its clientele (Packman, 1986).

Social work makes little sense as a mode of intervention in social relations unless it can find ways of resolving conflicts peacefully, by agreement with minimum coercion and anguish. If what is needed is rigid enforcement of rules, other methods are just as effective – hence perhaps the re-emergence of the issue of training for criminal justice social work in Britain (Jordan and Arnold, 1996). If offenders are to be dealt with simply as rational predators, who need a proportionate punishment both for retribution ('just deserts') and deterrence, there is little point in individualized assessment or the offer of personal befriending and support. It is simply a matter of finding the appropriate 'price' for crime (Cornish and Clarke, 1986). If social work is to return to the field of social justice, it will be through wider movements for mediation and 'restorative justice' that arise elsewhere in society, outside the ambit of the public power.

But equally social work is inescapably involved in certain very ambiguous tasks with society's most deprived individuals, giving assistance and trying to influence behaviour in ways that attempt to reconcile authority and fairness (Jordan, 1990). These face-to-face encounters with the perishing and dangerous classes, on the front line of interpersonal and intergroup conflict, inevitably compromise practitioners with public power. Where this goes so far that conflict becomes endemic in relationships, another option is for public policy to seek new forms of partnership, agreement and participation. In Britain this has been evident in the Children Act, 1989, and the subsequent attempts to move away from care orders and the assumption of parental rights, to more voluntaristic and negotiated methods (Packman and Jordan, 1991).

The scope of such shifts is rather limited in a polarized society, under pressure to economize on public spending. Early evaluation of the Children Act indicate that fewer care orders and place of safety orders do not reflect less statutory intervention. There are said to be more than 200,000 investigations of alleged child abuse each year, a high proportion of which lead to no further action (Gibbons, Conroy and Bell 1995). The fall in court orders does not imply a rise in family support, only an increase in anxious monitoring of situations.

More generally, British public-sector social work has moved away from direct involvement with service users' everyday lives, and towards the management of needs and risks (Parton, 1994a, 1994b). In assessing applicants for packages of care, or contracting with other (commercial or voluntary sector) providers for these, it engages in an arm's-length way, often leaving day-to-day interaction to volunteers or untrained personnel, or to informal networks. Feminists have not been slow to point out that all the latter groups predominantly consist of women, and that the new political economy of care has increased exploitation and oppression of (mainly female) carers (Pascall, 1986). Like men in wider society, public social work agencies have come to care *about* those in need, rather than to care *for* them (Dalley, 1988), and to express this caring through their cheque-books rather than by offers of their time and skill. More accountability to service users turns out to mean more accountancy, as business methods invade practitioner teams. Professionalism consists in delegating tasks to less well-paid workers, or carers who are not paid at all.

It is difficult to foresee a major change in the future direction of social work's development. The British Labour Party has few plans that would alter these trends. Its emphasis on 'community' sounds friendly to social work's aspirations, but it is equally keen to emphasize its commitment to enforcement (being tough on crime, benefit fraud and all other manifestations of underclass resistance). If a majority government seeks to mobilize mainstream interests against minority actions, 'community' becomes part of the problem, rather than part of the solution. Middle-class suburban communities have become defensive enclaves, drawing together to protect themselves from crime; the poor's 'communities of fate', and the beleaguered inner-city ethnic minority communities, achieve solidarity and loyalty by commitment to quite different cultural practices. In such situations, appeals to communitarian sentiments are empty rhetoric.

Even if public-agency social work becomes completely absorbed in assessments for social assistance payments, care packages, training programmes and treatment regimes, the original principles and values of social work will not disappear. They will be kept alive in many unofficial activities and small-scale organizations, and in the everyday practices of ordinary people. In this way they will remain available to collective decision-makers when – at some future date – all semblance of voluntarism and co-operative engagement has drained out of public-sector agencies, and the costs of

enforcement have come to threaten economic efficiency itself. Then the historical wheel will have come full circle, and social work may start again from roughly its late nineteenth-century beginnings.

References

Adler, M. and Asquith, S. (1981) *Discretion in Welfare*, London: Heinemann.

Anderson, D. (1980) *The Ignorance of Social Intervention*, London: Croom Helm.

Arnold, J. and Jordan, B. (1995) 'Beyond Befriending or Past Caring? Probation Values, Training and Social Justice', in B. Williams (ed.), *Probation Values*, Birmingham: Venture Press.

Badelt, C. (1990) 'Institutional Choice and the Nonprofit Sector', in H. Anheier and W. Seibel (eds), *The Third Sector: Comparative Studies in Nonprofit Organisations*, Berlin: De Gruyter, pp. 53–64.

Barry, B. (1991) 'The Continuing Relevance of Socialism', in B. Barry, *Liberty and Justice, Essay in Political Theory 2*, Oxford: Clarendon Press.

Brewer, C. and Lait, J. (1980) *Can Social Work Survive?*, London: Temple Smith.

Buchanan, J. M. (1978) *The Economics of Politics*, London: Institute for Economic Affairs.

Buchanan, J. M. (1986) *Liberty, Markets and the State: Political Economy in the 1980's*, Brighton: Harvester Wheatsheaf.

Chapman, R. and Dunsire, A. (eds) (1971) *Style in Administration*, London: Allen and Unwin.

Coleman, James S. (1990) *Foundations of Social Theory*, Cambridge, Mass.: Harvard University Press.

Cornish, D. B. and Clarke R. V. (1986) *The Reasoning Criminal: Rational Choice Perspectives on Offending*, London: Allen and Unwin.

Dalley, G. (1988) *Ideologies of Caring: Rethinking Community and Collectivism*, Basingstoke: MacMillan.

Etzioni, A. (1988) *The Moral Dimension*, New York: Basic Books.

Etzioni, A. (1993) *The Spirit of Community*, New York: Basic Books.

Gibbons, J., Conroy, S. and Bell, C. (1995) *Operating the Child Protection System: A Study of Child Protection Practices in English Local Authorities*, London: HMSO.

Giddens, A. (1991) *Modernity and Self-Identity*, Cambridge: Polity.

Gingrich, N. (1994) 'Speech during the US Congressional Elections', *The Guardian*, 3 November.

Goffman, E. (1969) *Interaction Ritual*, New York: Doubleday Anchor.

Gray, J. (1994) 'The Great Atlantic Drift', *The Guardian*, 12 December.

Hansmann, H. (1987) 'Economic theory of non-profit organisations' in W. Powell (ed.), *The Non-Profit Sector: A Research Handbook*, New Haven: Yale University Press, pp. 27–42.

Hardin, G. (1968) 'The tragedy of the Commons', *Science*, 162: pp. 1243–5.

Heritage, J. (1984) *Garfinkel and Ethnomethodology*, Oxford: Polity.

Hilbert, R. A. (1992) *The Classical Roots of Ethnomethodology: Durkheim, Weber and Garfinkel*, Chapel Hill: University of North Carolina Press.

Hirst, P. (1994) *Associative Democracy: New Forms of Economic and Social Governance*, Cambridge: Polity.

Hobbes, T. (1651) *Leviathan*, ed. Michael Oakeshott, Oxford: Blackwell (1966 edn), XIII.

Hollis, M. (1994) *The Philosophy of Social Science: An Introduction*, Oxford: Blackwell.

Hood, C. and Schuppert, G. (1990), 'Para-government organisations in the provision of public services; three explanations' in H. Anheier and W. Seibel (eds), *The Third Sector: Comparative Studies in Non-Profit Organisations*, Berlin: de Gruyter.

Howard, M. (1993) Speech to Conservative Party Conference, 23 October.

Jones, A. and May, J. (1992) *Working in Human Service Organisations: A Critical Introduction*, Melbourne: Longman Cheshire.

Jordan, B. (1974) *Poor Parents: Social Policy and the Cycle of Deprivation*, London: Routledge and Kegan Paul.

Jordan, B. (1987) *Rethinking Welfare*, Oxford: Blackwell.

Jordan, B. (1990) *Social Work in an Unjust Society*, Hemel Hempstead: Harvester Wheatsheaf.

Jordan, B. (1992) 'Authoritarian Benthamism' in B. Williams and C. Senior (eds), *Probation After the Criminal Justice Act, 1991*, Sheffield: PAVIC.

Jordan, B. (1993) 'Framing claims and the weapons of the weak', in G. Drover and P. Kerans (eds.), *New Approaches to Social Welfare Theory*, Aldershot: Edward Elgar, pp. 205–19.

Jordan, B. (1995), 'Are New Right policies sustainable? "Back to Basics" and public choice', *Journal of Social Policy*, 24(3), 363–84.

Jordan, B. (1996) *A Theory of Poverty and Social Exclusion*, Cambridge: Polity.

Jordan, B. and Arnold, J. (1996) 'Crime, poverty and probation', in M. Vanstone and M. Drakeford (eds), *Beyond Offending Behaviour*, Aldershot: Arena.

Jordan, B. and James, S., Kay, H. and Redley, M., (1992) *Trapped in Poverty? Labour-Market Decisions in Low-Income Households*, London: Routledge.

Leo XIII (1891) Papal Encyclical *Rerum Novarum*, Rome: Vatican.

Levy, D. (1992) *The Economic Ideas of Ordinary People*, London: Routledge.

Lilley, P. (1993) Speech to Conservative Party Conference, 24 October.

Lyons, Bruce (1992) 'Game theory', in S. Hargreaves Heap, M. Hollis, B. Lyons, R. Sugden and A.

Weale, *The Theory of Choice: A Critical Guide*, Oxford: Blackwell, pp. 93–129

Macadam, E. (1945) *The Social Servant in the Making*, London: Allen and Unwin.

Mead, L. M. (1986) *Beyond Entitlement: The Social Obligations of Citizenship*, New York: Basic Books.

Mulhall, S. and Swift, A. (1992) *Liberals and Communitarians*, Oxford: Oxford University Press.

Offe, C. and Preuss, U. K. (1990) 'Democratic institutions and moral resources', in D. Held (ed.) *Political Theory Today*, Oxford: Polity, pp. 143–71.

Ostrom, E. (1990) *Governing the Commons: The Evolution of Institutions for Collective Action*, Cambridge: Cambridge University Press.

Packman, J. (1986) *Who Needs Care? Social Work Decisions about Children*, Oxford: Blackwell.

Packman, J. and Jordan, B. (1991) 'The Children Act, 1989; looking forward, looking back', *British Journal of Social Work*, 21, 315–27.

Parton, N. (1994a) '"Problematics of government", (post) modernity and social work', *British Journal of Social Work*, 24, 9–32.

Parton, N. (1994b) 'The nature of social work under conditions of (post) modernity', *Social Work and Social Sciences Review*, 5(2) 93–112.

Pascall, G. (1986) *Social Policy: A Feminist Analysis*, London: Tavistock.

Peacock, A. (1979) *The Economic Analysis of Government*, Oxford: Martin Robertson.

Perrow, C. (1979) *Complex Organizations: A Critical Essay*, Glenview, Ill.: Scott, Foresman.

Polanyi, K. (1944) *The Great Transformation: The Political and Economic Origins of Our Times*, Boston: Beacon.

Putnam, R. (1993) *Making Democracy Work: Civic Traditions in Modern Italy*, Princeton: Princeton University Press.

Ryan, A. (1983) 'Mill and Rousseau: utility and rights', in G. Duncan (ed.), *Democratic Theory and Practice*, Cambridge: Cambridge University Press.

Sacks, J. (1972) *Conversational Analysis*, New York: Free Press.

Seibel, W. (1990) 'Organisational behaviour and organisational function: toward a micro–macro theory of the third sector', in K. Anheier and W. Seibel (eds), *The Third Sector: Comparative Studies of Non-Profit Organisations*, Berlin: de Gruyter.

Social Trends (1994) London: HMSO (Central Statistical Office).

Statham, D. (1978) *Radicals in Social Work*, Basingstoke: MacMillan.

Taylor, D. (1992) 'A big idea for the Nineties: the rise of citizens' charters', *Critical Social Policy*, 11, 3, Issue 33, pp. 87–94.

Titmuss, R. (1968) 'Social work and social service: a challenge for local government' in R. Titmuss, *Commitment to Welfare*, London: Allen and Unwin, pp. 85–90.

Tocqueville, A. de (1835–40) *Democracy in America*, ed. J. P. Mayer and M. Lerner (1968), London: Collins.

Weisbrod, B. (1977) *The Voluntary Non-Profit Sector:*

An Economic Analysis, Lexington, Mass.: D. C. Heath.

Weisbrod, B. (1988) *The Non-Profit Economy*, Cambridge Mass.: Harvard University Press.

Wolfe, A. (1989) *Whose Keeper? Social Science and Moral Obligation*, Berkeley and Los Angeles: University of California Press.

Wolfe, A. (1991) 'Market, state and society as codes of moral obligation', in M. Mennell and D. Salée (eds), *The Legacy of Kark Blanyi: Market, State and Society at the End of the Twentieth Century*, New York: St. Martin's Press, pp. 31–49.

Part II
Frameworks

Introduction to Part II

The various functions which social workers perform are influenced by a range of social, political and biological factors – or frameworks. They interact with each other, and different theorists will argue that different frameworks should or do carry greater weight in determining the nature and the objectives of social work practice. Power and the law simultaneously constrain and facilitate the social worker's role; they separately and together have undeniable relevance for the service user. The client's race and gender are bio-psychosocial attributes which have life-defining implications and which are rarely irrelevant in the situations which bring them into contact with the social work service. Families, however defined, however traditional or radical in shape or structure, are the normal locus for child development and, for better or worse, in reality or aspiration, they provide the context in which most people live out their days; even for those living alone or in institutions, the *idea* of family life is never wholly absent. The power of sexual behaviour, inside or outside of families, heterosexual or homosexual, reflects a biological drive affecting human relationships, promoting imbalances of power, but necessary for the survival of the human race; an often unrecognized proportion of social work practice is concerned with the consequences of sexual behaviour or its aberrations.

II.1
Power
Robert Harris

If politics involves the acquisition and deployment of power, and social work is 'one of the most political of all professions' (Yelloly and Henkel, 1995, p. 9), an understanding of power in all its manifestations must be more than normally important for social workers. This essay considers power from a number of perspectives, introducing ideas about power and its regulation, and touching briefly on the popular but complicated concept of 'empowerment'.

Any discussion of social work not underpinned by an analysis of power misunderstands what social work is. Social workers operate at the boundaries of the public and the private. They intervene in families and communities in a manner both supportive and controlling; their power and influence are such that their judgement (for their work seldom entails merely the routine application of law or policy) affects the lives of many. Because social work entails applying social and political theory to a multitude of complex and sometimes insoluble problems, social workers require more than technical competence in pre-ordained areas to pass muster. Professionals who exercise power must, as a policy imperative, be trained in its legitimate exercise as well as its technology: they must know whether, as well as how, to intervene. Hence the study of power is essential for reflective practitioners.

Understanding Power: Some Theoretical Considerations

Power is not simple to define: striking disagreements about it exist (for a flavour of which see Lukes, 1986) and so fundamental is it to social formation that the concept is variously employed. Probably it is not fruitful to spend too long on these differences here, however, and for present purposes to have power is defined as having *the capacity to act in such a way as to control others*. This definition would, however, require qualification in a more substantial text and must not be taken as authoritative.

Even in this oversimplified definition there is a studied ambiguity in the word 'capacity'. Capacity may imply a form of legal authority ('acting in my official capacity . . .') or, simply, ability ('I have the capacity to do this'). These meanings reflect different aspects of social work. Social workers act in an official capacity when they impose power by, for example, supervising a court order or participating in a compulsory mental health admission. In such cases they act as agents of the state, their power derives from legislation, and in accepting the job they are agreeing to exercise it. Hence social workers' power is expressed not only in what they do but in what they are; and they are subject to the very power they are themselves exercising. The fact that it is state power they are enforcing and that they may have reservations about its nature or application helps explain why, though textbooks describe them as 'powerful professionals', they frequently feel decidedly otherwise (Luhmann, 1990, p. 155).

Secondly, social workers exercise personal power in interacting with their clientele. Though it is hard to disentangle this from powers derived from statute this power is best understood by reference to the sociology of class and the social psychology of small group interactions: as one commentator has observed, even in a pluralist heaven the celestial choir sings with an upper-class accent (cited in Bachrach, 1980, p. 37). In this sense social workers have personal power akin to that of professionals like priests, counsellors and other advisers whose activities lack the force of law but who are taken seriously by their clientele because of their perceived prestige:

fictive and illusionary components that become reality as a result of perceptual differences between environment and system, and consequently take effect as reality, enter into the composition of organizational power . . . The holder of power makes more decisions and has more of his or her decisions complied with than he or she could effect in cases of conflict.

(Luhmann, 1990, p. 164)

This second type of power transforms our understanding of the concept. Whereas in a Marxian analysis power tends to be perceived tangibly, as the central state apparatus which, once seized, permits social and political transformation, power in this sense is a process, a part of daily life, differentially distributed but identifiable as a dimension of the micro-politics of professional, bureaucratic or social encounters. And power is interactional: to understand it we must comprehend not only the conduct of the social security official, police sergeant, prison officer or abusing husband but that of the claimant, defendant, prisoner or abused wife, whose behaviour also influences the resolution of any encounter.

Power is also ubiquitous: nearly every interaction from job interview to

Five Key Points

1 Professionals who exercise power (whether legal or personal) must be trained in the legitimacy of its exercise as well as in its technology: they must know *whether*, as well as *how*, to intervene.

2 Power is interactional: to understand it we must comprehend the behaviour of the powerless as well as the powerful.

3 Almost no one is devoid of power, lacking entirely the capacity to influence those with whom they come into contact.

4 The exercise of power is almost always regulated; but regulation is not only a response to power but a form of it, and one which affects the behaviour of its objects, be they clients or professionals.

5 Social workers talk about empowering others, but if power is intrinsic to social work and social workers are carriers not progenitors of power it is not necessarily theirs to surrender, or even share.

courtship ritual entails the bilateral, though not necessarily equal, transmission of power. Almost no one is devoid of power: the condemned prisoner, the hostage, someone who is dying all have control over their mind and behaviour if not their situation, and therefore some capacity to influence those with whom they come into contact. But relatively powerless people may make bad situations avoidably worse: unemployment, homelessness, racism can have psychological consequences which social workers, fearful of being accused of 'psychologizing' structural inequalities, have sometimes been reluctant to address. These consequences in turn have behavioural concomitants which may entail clients making bad situations avoidably worse – and it is at the very least helpful for social workers to encourage their clients to avoid the avoidable. More positively, given that social workers usually work with people who are relatively powerless, it is important that they help them deploy what power they have to maximum effect.

The bilateral character of power means that the outcome of any interchange is unpredictable: individuals engage in multitudinous interactions, and a chance word or hasty intervention in any of them can transform the others for better or worse. It is incorrect, therefore, to believe that any one encounter can be so controlled by a social worker as to be guaranteed to yield a predictable outcome. When the author studied the imposition of social work power on young offenders he concluded that, far from moving towards a nightmare world of social conformity, something always went wrong in practice (Harris and Webb, 1987). This unpredictability is a phenomenon understated in those social work texts which give an overly ordered impression of methods such as task-centred practice: reality is usually more messy than the textbook example (for a more realistic account see Marshall, 1987).

Power is not simply, not even primarily, *repressive* but *generative*. History is littered with instances of the powerless striking back, sometimes in an inchoate way, but a way nonetheless which may create and sustain new modes of interaction. Whether the protests are by prisoners, paupers or peasants, and whether successful or not, life is never the same again. It is, however, characteristic of the power of the powerless to backfire: when one is silenced, when the structures of power exclude one, when one is abused with impunity by officialdom one may feel one has recourse only to violence, which is then turned back, morally and physically, on its immediate perpetrators.

But violence is but one extreme response to power: where there is power

there is always resistance, and without understanding resistance one cannot understand power. The author, writing about child protection social work, identified two modes of resistance (Harris, 1990). Type A resistance is generative in that it justifies the exercise of yet more power. The ideas behind this are normally associated with the French writer Michel Foucault. For example, in *The History of Sexuality* Foucault offers a natural history of solitary adolescent sexuality. The child engages in a masturbatory act, is apprehended and chastised. He repeats the act and suffers further, receiving medical warnings of the consequences of continuation. Deception follows, and the boy stands doubly condemned, his dissimulation signalling even more decisively his moral turpitude; and more control results. And this is precisely the point, for Foucault is enquiring why this solitary act should precipitate the exercise of power in a certain place at a certain time. His answer is that cause and effect have become inverted: it is not the act which causes the imposition of power but the necessity of the imposition of power which causes the prohibition. Power is a necessary and permanent aspect of micro-political existence, and its withdrawal simply creates a vacuum to be filled by a new strategy of power.

The child's 'vice' was not so much an enemy as a support; it may have been designated as the evil to be eliminated, but the extraordinary effort that went into the task that was bound to fail leads one to suspect that what was demanded of it was to persevere, to proliferate.

(*Foucault, 1981, p. 42*)

Type B resistance, on the other hand, comprises situations where resistance is successful and brings about the intended change. The author took the challenge of the Cleveland parents to social workers who removed children from their families following allegations of sexual abuse as an instance of successful resistance, and analysed the socio-political circumstances which made this success possible. Any analysis of pressure group politics generally would equally illustrate that tactical astuteness deployed at the right political moment can increase the chance of, though not in this volatile mutable world guarantee, success.

Regulating Power

If power and resistance are susceptible to analysis at different levels, so is formal regulation. At the level of political theory liberal democracy is intended to prevent the centralization of power by devices such as secret ballots, constitutional restrictions on self-perpetuating legislation and separation of powers. But it has been claimed that liberal democracy merely gives voters a choice of elites in the hope that competition among them and the expectation of alternating government will prevent an excess of power resting with one group. That even this modest expectation implies an unduly optimistic perspective on democratic governance is probably uncontentious (for a lucid discussion see Bachrach, 1980).

Operationally, numerous strategies exist to regulate the imposition of power. These have multiplied in the complex modern state, in which power is characteristically employed diversely by variably accountable instruments of administrative justice. They include increased transparency, checks and balances such as appeals procedures and judicial review, the issuance of guidelines to structure the deployment of professional or executive discretion (see Davis, 1971), advice bureaux such as community law centres, inspections and, in a strategy redolent of the 1960s and 1970s, public participation in decision making (see Pateman, 1970).

In the 1980s and 1990s regulation has taken on different meanings. First, both competition and inspection have been deployed: competition in public-sector services is typified by a move towards a mixed economy embracing private-sector interests or, where this is impractical, the introduction of internal or quasi-markets (Le Grand and Bartlett, 1993). And in order to prevent unregulated competition worsening service quality, minimum quality specifications have been introduced as ground rules for the competition itself. Secondly, centralized policy direction coexists with devolved budgeting and administration, with reductions in the unit of resource (more

---

Three Questions

1 What are the main reasons why social workers should understand power?
2 What if anything is the relevance of such an understanding to the non-directive counselling of non-statutory clients?
3 It is widely believed that it is fundamental to social work for service users to be 'empowered'. What main criticisms, tactical and conceptual, can be made of this view?

---

patients, clients, students processed on reduced *per capita* funding) balanced by quality enhancement strategies. These structures are legitimated by a populist consumerism, defined in terms of choice, and manifested in the Citizen's Charter, consumer involvement in regulatory bodies, league tables, and inspections by organizations such as the Audit Commission.

In social work it has been suggested that one consequence of these developments has been a shift in the professional discourse from the nebulous subtlety of casework to the measurable and verifiable:

[The Social Services Inspectorate] introduced the language of objective measurement, input, output and outcome into the evaluation of quality of care, alongside that of process and subjective experience. Underpinning these two approaches are radically different views about the nature of social action and about knowledge of the social world, one using the language of cause and effect and generalizable laws of behaviour, the other that of meaning and motivation and shared or conflicting norms and beliefs.

(Henkel, 1991, p. 131)

From this it is a short step to concluding that what cannot be measured in these ways will not be done, or will at least be assigned lower priority. For regulation is not only a response to power but a form of it, and if power is indeed generative it will affect the behaviour of its objects, be they clients or professionals. Hence regulation is by no means external to action, and contemporary social work must be defined not primarily by reference to an abstract value base or set of procedures but by the modes of power to which its practitioners are subject, and the manner in which they respond to them. In short the regulation of social work both checks what social workers do and helps define the nature of the enterprise. In this sense while contemporary social work may be heir to its own history it is the child of contemporary politics; and the same analytic mode which helps us understand a power transaction between social worker and client helps illumine the transaction between social work and the state.

Some Concluding Reflections

Power in social work today is most decisively addressed in the concepts empowerment and oppression. Though the literature in this field is increasing in scope and sophistication (see in particular Rees, 1991) it remains very variable, and 'empowerment' by no means has a clear

and agreed purpose, ideology or technology.

In relating empowerment to oppression, for example, one quite angry book (Mullender and Ward, 1991), which draws particularly on the work of Freire, bases its ideology on radical politics and its technology on a form of groupwork termed 'self-directed'. But there is a problem here, for the authors (as 'facilitators') seem simultaneously to abdicate a leadership role and to encourage group members to perceive their oppression in a manner based on their own a priori theorizing. Hence the self-direction is at best qualified, and the method seems designed to promote an alliance between facilitators and clients intended to challenge oppression and define the aetiology of members' problems as political rather than individual:

Service users themselves are helped to analyse, confront and transform the exercise of power on a small and localised scale at first but with the capacity to grow from there, since the analysis need not be unsophisticated.

(Mullender and Ward, 1991, pp. 6–7)

Any tactical awkwardness deriving from this attempt to pursue potentially conflicting client-driven and political agendas is associated with the application not the idea, however, for other empowerment workers have a more client-centred approach; but problems remain. For example, whatever the merits of using education to persuade the dispossessed in South America to embrace one political ideology rather than another as a means of challenging their own oppression, it is not immediately obvious that such a method can be translated appropriately to an advanced western liberal democracy by a state-funded social worker, or that when it is so translated it is best termed empowerment. Nor, if power is indeed intrinsic to social work and social workers are carriers not progenitors of power, is it simple to see how they can actually surrender it to self-direction. While doubtless there is little day-to-day difficulty when the clients are co-operative, what happens to the worker's power when deviant attitudes assume ascendancy? What do the facilitators do when freely chosen but politically incorrect working-class ideologies come to predominate?

An alternative view is that social work has always contained within its cultural tapestry strands of both liberation and constraint, which make a certain ambiguity of focus proper and inevitable, if uncomfortable for its practitioners, charged as they are with working with the dispossessed in an unfair system:

social workers draw for their professional activities from: charity and philanthropy; Christian reformism; the psychiatric and educational services; the Poor Law; social and political radicalism; and state control (for after all, did not the Charity Organisation Society remark in 1927 that 'the only real antidote to Bolshevism is good casework?')
(Harris, 1989, p. 24)

Whether it follows that it is proper to attempt to 'empower' clients by politicizing them, or preferable for social workers to continue to utilize their own power and knowledge to seek a proper philosophy and practice to express and meet the needs of disadvantaged or oppressed people in an affluent liberal democracy is a question of strategic as well as ethical significance. That strict neutrality is impossible few would dispute; that strong partiality is therefore legitimate if not obligatory is altogether more contentious.

References

Bachrach, P. (1980) *The Theory of Democratic Elitism: a Critique*, Lanham, MD: University Press of America.

Davis, K. (1971) *Discretionary Justice: a Preliminary Inquiry*, Urbana: University of Illinois Press.

Foucault, M. (1981) *The History of Sexuality: Volume I: an Introduction* (trans. R. Hurley), Harmondsworth: Penguin Books.

Harris, R. (1989) 'Social work in society or punishment in the community?', in R. Shaw and K. Haines (eds), *The Criminal Justice System: a Central Role for the Probation Service*. Cambridge: University of Cambridge Institute of Criminology.

Harris, R. (1990) 'A matter of balance: power and resistance in child protection policy', *Journal of Social Welfare Law*, 5, 332–40.

Harris, R. and Webb, D. (1987) *Welfare, Power and Juvenile Justice: the Social Control of Delinquent Youth*, London: Tavistock Publications.

Henkel, M. (1991) *Government, Evaluation and Change*. London: Jessica Kingsley.

Le Grand, J. and Bartlett, W. (eds) (1993) *Quasi-Markets and Social Policy*, London: Macmillan.

Luhmann, N. (1990) *Political Theory in the Welfare State* (trans. J. Bednarz Jr.), Berlin: Walter de Gruyter.

Lukes, S. (ed.) (1986) *Power*, Oxford: Basil Blackwell.

Marshall, P. (1987) 'Task centred practice in a probation setting', in R. Harris (ed.) *Practising Social Work: Case Studies from Social Work Education*, Leicester: University of Leicester School of Social Work.

Mullender, A. and Ward, D. (1991) *Self-Directed Groupwork: Users Take Action for Empowerment*, London: Whiting and Birch.

Pateman, C. (1970) *Participation and Democratic Theory*, Cambridge: Cambridge University Press.

Rees, S. (1991) *Achieving Power: Practice and Policy in Social Welfare*, Sydney: Allen & Unwin.

Yelloly, M. and Henkel, M. (eds) (1995) *Learning and Teaching in Social Work: Towards Reflective Practice*, London: Jessica Kingsley.

Further Reading

1 Foucault, M. (1977) *Discipline and Punish: the Birth of the Prison* (trans. A. Sheridan), Harmondsworth: Allen Lane.

2 Graham, K. (ed.) (1982) *Contemporary Political Philosophy: Radical Studies*, Cambridge: Cambridge University Press.

3 Harris, R. and Webb, D. (1987) *Welfare, Power and Juvenile Justice: the Social Control of Delinquent Youth*, London: Tavistock Publications.

II.2
The Law
Caroline Ball

Most social workers are the employees of public bodies, namely local authorities, themselves creatures of statute, which fulfil responsibilities and exercise powers and duties determined by legislation. The law does not, nor could or should it, tell social workers *how* to practice, in terms of how they handle their relationships with clients, but, increasingly, it sets the parameters of social work intervention. The law determines which members of the public will qualify to become social work clients, the range of services to which qualifying individuals may be entitled and the circumstances in which duties or powers have to, or may, be exercised in relation to adult clients or on behalf of children (Howe, 1986). It also, particularly in more recent legislation, sets detailed boundaries to intervention – compare, for example, the minutiae of the provisions for the protection of children in an emergency, in sections 44 and 45 of the Children Act 1989, with the blanket nature of those replaced (Children and Young Persons Act 1969 s. 28). The law also builds in an element of accountability, by providing – through access to the Ombudsman, statutory complaints procedures or judicial review in the High Court – social workers' clients with the means to challenge decisions made by employees of social services departments.

Recognizing the extent to which the law determines, validates and controls social work practice is relatively unproblematic. What is more exercising, and indeed has practical implications, is that social workers and lawyers

enmeshed in aspects of the relationship between their subjects, are working at an interface between what have historically been perceived to be conceptually polarized entities. The law being categorized – or caricatured – as essentially, and impersonally, concerned only with rules, clarity and certainty, whilst the mainspring of social work practice is perceived – or caricatured – as protection of the vulnerable, and a well-intentioned, if woolly, search for remedies for the consequences of disadvantage and the messy unpredictability of failed human relationships. In this chapter the author reflects upon the changing nature of the professional interface, by describing a crucial aspect of it – the way in which law is taught to social work students. A review of the problems that this has presented over the last quarter century, and consideration of recent developments, suggests that, far from continuing to be polarized entities, social work and the law may be reaching a new and possibly even fruitful accommodation.

The Place of Law in Social Work Education

When reporting on the circumstances surrounding the death of Jasmine Beckford, Louis Blom-Cooper (1985) indicated that 'training in legal studies must not be allowed to remain any longer the Cinderella of social work training'. Then, and subsequently in regard to the death of Kimberley Carlile (1987), Blom-Cooper was writing in circumstances in which qualified social workers' lack of knowledge of the statutory framework of child care practice had come dramatically and tragically to public attention. There is little doubt that the publicly pilloried lack of legal competence amongst social workers with child protection responsibilities had dire, if some thought unjust, consequences for the reputation of social work and social workers (Blom-Cooper, 1985 and 1987; Stevenson, 1986; Parton, 1986).

The suggestion that training in legal studies should form an integral part of social work training was not, of course, a new one. As early as 1972, when the Seebohm reorganization of the personal social services was under way, the newly formed Central Council for the Education and Training of Social Workers (CCETSW) made law teaching on courses, awarding the Certificate of Qualification in Social Work (CQSW), the subject of one of its earliest studies of the curriculum. More than a decade before Jasmine Beckford died, a prestigious study group chaired by Professor Nigel Walker, Director of the Institute of Criminology at the University of Cambridge, consulted widely with interested organizations and individuals about social workers' legal knowledge, formed their own conclusions about an appropriate knowledge base and then undertook a review of law teaching on qualifying courses. The Group was somewhat daunted by what they found as compared with their requirements. As Priscilla Young, the first Director of CCETSW, summed up the situation:

The teaching of law to student social workers has long been a matter of concern and controversy among social work educators, students, social workers, and their employers; it has been regarded as among the most important, or among the least important, areas of learning in professional training, according to the point of view adopted. Teaching has therefore been extremely variable in quantity and quality.

Five Key Points

1 Most social workers practise in a statutory setting, exercising powers and duties defined by legislation.
2 In the past research and child abuse inquiry evidence suggested that many social work courses failed to teach students relevant law practice.
3 There was evidence that many social work educators were resistant to including law in the syllabus.
4 Until recently most lawyers teaching under a service arrangement lacked relevant expertise, especially in the legally complex area of child care.
5 By the mid-1990s, reform of child law and changes in social work practice suggest a productive convergence of interest as between lawyers and social workers.

In its report (CCETSW, 1974), the study group identified, and urged courses to address in the academic curriculum, four categories of law for social workers: *professional law* (that part of the law that relates to the professional practice of social workers in various agencies); *general law* (the law affecting the day-to-day life of clients as citizens); *the administration of law* (the work of the legal profession and the structure of courts and tribunals) and *law and society* (the general function of law in society). In order to meet the identified deficit in suitable texts for students, within a year of the report eminent academic lawyer members of the study group had produced books on 'professional law' (McClean, 1975), and on aspects of the other three categories identified by the study group (Zander, 1974). Others followed, as did a debate on several levels about social work and the law, and law teaching on CQSW courses (Bates and Bates, 1975; Alcock, 1977; Grace and Wilkinson, 1978).

How was it, with all this interest, that

more than a decade later, members of the CCETSW convened Law and Social Work Research Group, in a series of studies undertaken in 1986–7, were able to identify that little had changed and that law teaching on CQSW courses was still 'extremely variable in quality and quantity'?

Research Evidence

The group's interlocking studies revealed that whilst many courses were expressing some satisfaction with the range and detail of the law taught, with notable exceptions the perceptions of students coming off the same courses were considerably less positive (Ball et al., 1988). These findings confirming both those of Davies' (1984) survey – in which students, three years after leaving qualifying courses, were identifying law teaching as jointly the least successful subject – in terms of enjoyment, usefulness and the quality of teaching – and Blom-Cooper's (1985) characterization of law teaching as the 'Cinderella' subject in social work education.

The answers are, it is suggested, both ideological and practical in nature. Ideological, in that in the mid-1980s there were still many social work academics whose practice was grounded in therapeutic casework, and who had – whatever guidance CCETSW issued, or requirements as to assessment of law teaching they introduced – a principled belief that law was of secondary importance, in terms of its relevance to professional practice, to almost all other subjects taught on qualifying courses. It followed, and was even articulated, that if, improbably, any legal knowledge was required by students, it could best be looked up as necessary or picked up on practice. At the practical level two linked factors probably hold the key. First, the very real difficulty of identifying and

securing the services of lawyers with an interest and necessary expertise in the subject matter of social workers' *professional law* – that relating to child care, mental illness and people disabled through learning difficulties, age or chronic illness. Secondly, the sheer complexity of the substantive law relating to child care and protection made it not only profoundly unsatisfactory in practice but also singularly hard to teach and to learn. As an eminent former Family Division and Appeal Court judge commented:

I am sure my perspective on the present state of child care law is shared in the broadest sense by everyone who has anything to do with its administration. It is in a state of confusion which is unparalleled in any other branch of the law now or at any other time in the past.

(Ormrod, 1983)

One is led to the inescapable conclusion that at that time, however much CCETSW wished to raise the profile of law teaching on qualifying courses, the low priority given by many social work academics to law teaching, combined with the problem of finding law teachers with the necessary expertise and interest in social work related law, and the sheer daunting complexity of a key area of the substantive law, militated to prevent this happening.

The Law Teachers

The 1988 study showed that the majority of courses relied on service teaching from law departments in the same institution, though for several, generally poorly regarded by students, the law sequence was provided by a series of one-off contributions from lay people and practitioners such as magistrates, justices' clerks and practising solicitors (Ball et al. 1988). Data from the survey suggested that where a service teacher arrangement was used, exceptionally there would be an individual with a real interest in the subject area who could provide students with much valued, high quality, law teaching relevant to social work practice. For the most part, however, as with service teaching on other courses (banking, journalism, planning, etc.), the law teaching on the CQSW course would be given to the most junior member of the law department, who might reasonably hope within a year or two to pass it on to another. Unless there was close liaison between the social work and law lecturers – and the evidence suggests that there was little – this posed very real problems in regard to the delivery of a coherent law sequence relevant to social work practice. First, because the law lecturer might have very little idea of the nature of social work practice, and secondly because when presented with an outline of the law relevant to that practice, the topics included would for the most part be dauntingly unfamiliar.

A newly graduated lawyer in the mid-1980s would be very unlikely to have any knowledge of any social work relevant legislation such as the Mental Health Act 1983, the National Assistance Act 1948 or the Chronically Sick and Disabled Persons Act 1974. As an undergraduate he or she might or might not have taken an option in family law, but in so far as teaching CQSW students was concerned, family law studied for a law degree would be of little help, since in regard to children it would only cover the private and not the public law. The junior law teacher would, therefore, be most unlikely to have wrestled with that area of the law with which social workers in child and family work most need expertise – the, at that time, complex jumble of separate legislation relating to child care and protection. In providing a course for CQSW students, the law lecturer was faced with a dilemma hard to resolve without informed and interested co-operation from the social

work lecturers. Where this was not forthcoming, the rest of the law syllabus, if based on CCETSW guidance, must have provided a welcome answer. Social workers' 'professional law' might be unknown territory, but the new law lecturer would, as an undergraduate, have studied many of the topics mentioned in the other categories in *Legal Studies in Social Work Education* (CCETSW, 1974), such as the legal system, criminal law, housing, and even that part of family law relating to marriage and divorce. As a consequence it was very often these topics rather than 'professional' law which constituted the entirety of the law syllabus on social work qualifying courses.

Three Questions

1 What breadth of legal knowledge do competent social work practitioners need?
2 Is law best taught to DipSW students by law lecturers with an interest in social work practice, or social work lecturers with an understanding of the relevant legislation?
3 Is there an identifiable body of 'social work law'?

Students' Perceptions

It is hardly surprising that, when canvassed for their perceptions of the relevance of the law teaching on their qualifying courses, only 31 per cent of respondents to a 1987 CCETSW survey questioning two-year qualified social workers expressed the view that the law teaching they had received as students had been relevant or very relevant to their subsequent practice; 28 per cent rated it as fairly relevant, and 37 per cent as not relevant or useless (see table II.2.1). Law teachers with an interest in 'professional' social work law, and courses with a commitment to ensuring that the subject

Table II.2.1   Perceptions of the relevance of law teaching: students leaving qualifying courses in
1985 and 1994.

Perception	1985	1994
Relevant/very relevant (fairly relevant, 1985)	175 (62%)	456 (84%)
Not relevant/useless	109 (38%)	90 (16%)
Total responding	284 (100%)	546 (100%)

was taught in a way which gave it relevance for social work practice, certainly existed, but they appeared to be in the minority.

As with its predecessor (CCETSW, 1974), when *The Law Report* (Ball et al., 1988), based on the interlinked studies referred to above and making suggestions about a syllabus for the law sequence on qualifying courses, was published, a conference and subsequent healthy debate (Stevenson, 1988; Braye and Preston-Shoot, 1990; Vernon et al., 1990) followed, as did new books on social work law written by members of the study group (Ball, 1989; Vernon, 1990) and others. So far the parallels with the position in the mid-1970s are inescapable, but this time things turned out differently.

A Further Law Teaching Initiative

In 1990 CCETSW set up the Law Improvements Project (LIP) as one of three initiatives funded by Government to improve the quality of social work education though elaborating curricula and producing models of good practice. The LIP Group was commissioned to give guidance on the law context of the DipSW within the framework of the Council's *Rules and Requirements for the Diploma in Social Work* (CCETSW, 1990), and their report, *Teaching, Learning and Assessing Social Work Law* (Ball et al., 1991) sought to provide both curriculum guidance and models of teaching. Following

observations in *The Law Report* (Ball et al., 1988) particular emphasis was laid on the linking of teaching in college and on placement. The report was widely circulated and appeared well received. It may or may not have had an impact on what follows, although it seems likely that, without the key developments elaborated below, it might well have suffered the same fate as its predecessor in the mid-1970s (CCETSW, 1974).

Changing Perceptions of Social Work and the Law

Early in 1995 the Social Work Law Research Group was given the opportunity to replicate the survey of newly qualified social workers' perceptions of the relevance to practice of the law teaching on their training courses undertaken in 1987. Data were gathered by means of a postal questionnaire, asking questions similar to those posed earlier, to a 27 per cent sample of DipSW and CQSW students who had qualified in 1994. One difference between the 1987 and 1995 questionnaires was that the latter only offered a choice of two categories of relevance instead of three. Even with the 1987 middle category of 'fairly relevant' collapsed upwards into the 'very relevant' and 'relevant' category, the perceptions of the class of 1994 contrast significantly ($p < .001$) with that of their predecessors in 1985 (table II.2.1); indeed, it looks as though there has been a sea change within a relatively short period of time. So where might the explanation lie? Can it be found within the change from CQSW to the DipSW, or a successful search for a coherent conceptual framework for the teaching of law which followed publication of *The Law Report* in 1988 (Stevenson, 1988; Braye and Preston-Shoot, 1990; Ball et al., 1991)? Have social work teachers and students altered radically in nature over the period? Does the linking of law teaching in college and on practice placement make all the difference? All these factors probably play a part, but, it is suggested there are two developments without which the perceived shift in attitude and provision would have been unlikely:

- the statutory framework of a key area of social work practice has altered fundamentally with implementation of the Children Act 1989; and
- the nature of social work itself has changed.

The Children Act Factor

Responsibility for the care and protection of children constitutes one of the major and most onerous statutory duties of local authority social services departments. For this reason knowledge of child care law has tended to be the benchmark by which social workers' legal competence has been judged, and most publicly exposed when lacking (Blom-Cooper, 1985, 1987). Historically, child care law has also, partly owing to the disparate origins of its component strands of legislation, been incredibly complex and hence lacking in that essential of satisfactory law – clarity. Other areas of social workers 'professional law', those relating to mental health, and all aspects of disability, and criminal (including youth) justice, may not provide a framework for intervention with which social workers are entirely at ease, but their interpretation is for the most part

regarded as relatively unproblematic.

It is the author's view that the changed nature of the provision of law teaching on social work qualifying courses, and students' perceptions of the relevance of that teaching to practice are to a very large extent a bonus of the comprehensive reform of child care law which took effect with implementation of the Children Act 1989. From what has been said earlier, it would be reasonable to assume that this conclusion is reached on the basis of the clarity of the Children Act provisions in regard to the public law. Clarity is undoubtedly an important factor, but it is only one. There are, it is suggested, other characteristics of the Act which are probably of no less, and may even be of greater significance. They are not apparently connected, in that they relate on the one hand to the extent to which, on the basis of research undertaken into all aspects of social work decisions in child care cases (DHSS, 1985; Ball, 1990; Freeman, 1992), the Act's provisions seek to underpin good child care practice, and on the other to the bringing together of the public and private law relating to children within a single Act. The former influencing the extent to which social work teachers of child care (if not all practitioners) feel in tune with the law, and the latter bringing the public law relating to children, which was formerly not within the curriculum of most law undergraduates, into mainstream law

Further Reading.

1   Freeman, M. D. A. (1992) *Children, their Families, and the Law: Working with the Children Act*, London: Macmillan.
2   *Law for Social Workers in England and Wales* (1995) London: CCETSW.
3   Stevenson, O. (1988) 'Law and social work education: a commentary on the law report', *Issues in Social Work Education*, 1(8), 37–45.

school teaching. As we have seen, the past mismatch between the needs of social work students and the expertise of service teachers from law departments was identified by the authors of *The Law Report* as one of the most intractable obstacles to the provision of relevant law teaching for social work students (Ball et al., 1988). Now that the law is easily accessible and comprehensible, and knowledge of the public law provisions more widespread amongst law graduates, there should be a corresponding increase in the pool of law academics competent and willing to teach child care law to social work students. The relative simplicity of the provisions also makes it possible and desirable for child care social work tutors to weave the relevant legal provisions into practice teaching.

The Changing Nature of Social Work Practice

It is impossible to escape the conclusion that, if child care law has been dramatically changed by reforming legislation, so too, insidiously, within the last decade has the very nature of social work practice altered almost out of recognition. Such is the bombardment of statutory demands on social services departments, that there is little latitude for the high level of informal 'helping' that was a feature of practice only ten years ago. It is not suggested that this change improves social work practice or gives personal satisfaction, but it does provide an explanation for the changed attitude to the relevance of law to practice discerned amongst practitioners – whose practice is now almost solely related to fulfilling statutory obligations. This makes it hard, in a way that it clearly was not in the past, for client group specialists in college, or practice teachers on placement, to deny that an understanding of the law is an essential ingredient of competent social work practice. Also on

the positive side, the introduction of legislation which establishes the rights of both adult service users and children to make representations or complain about the way in which they have been treated by the social services department, are seen by many social workers as an appropriate means of empowering clients (Connolly, 1996).

Looking Forward

Whether the relationship between social work and the law will continue to develop in a way that allows beginning practitioners to leave qualifying courses with a confident and appropriate understanding of the legal context of their practice, only time will tell. For the time being, however, it does seem as though Blom-Cooper's (1985) wish has been met, and that, as social work education moves into the twenty-first century legal studies are no longer 'the Cinderella of social work training'. Indeed, it is possible that the same changes that have taken Cinders out of the educational kitchen may be representative of a shift which has radically altered the whole interface between social work and the law. In the light of current experience it would seem at least arguable that the influence of social work and law academics who have, and promote, a sympathetic interest in each others' professional expertise, together with the increasing numbers of lawyers who have everyday experience of working with social workers – whether in local authority legal departments or as solicitors receiving instructions from guardians ad litem when representing children – means that there is an emerging caucus in each profession with a real understanding of each others' roles and practice dilemmas. The emergence of 'social work law' as a sphere of academic activity as recognizably distinctive as, say, banking or planning law, suggests that, however dissimilar the professional roles of social workers and lawyers, the notion that social work and the law are 'polarized entities' belongs to the past and not to the twenty-first century.

References

Alcock, P. (1977) 'Law in society: problems of course construction for social work students', *The Law Teacher*, 11(1), 11–17.

Ball, C. (1989) *Law for Social Workers: an Introduction*, Aldershot: Wildwood House (3rd edn, 1996).

Ball, C. (1990) 'The Children Act 1989: origins, aims and current concerns', in P. Carter, T. Jeffs and M. Smith (eds), *Social Work and Social Welfare 2*, Milton Keynes: Open University Press.

Ball, C., Harris, R., Roberts, G. and Vernon, S. (1988) *The Law Report: Teaching and Assessment of Law in Social Work Education*, London: CCETSW.

Ball, C., Preston-Shoot, M., Roberts, G. and Vernon, S. (1995) *Law for Social Workers in England and Wales: Guidance for Meeting the DipSW Requirements*, London: CCETSW.

Ball, C., Roberts, R., Trench, S. and Vernon, S. (1991) *Teaching, Learning and Assessing Social Work Law*, London: CCETSW.

Bates, S. and Bates, M. (1975) 'The legal education of social workers', *Social Work Today*, 5(23), 10–12.

Blom-Cooper, L. (1985) *A Child in Trust: The Report of the Panel of Inquiry into Circumstances Surrounding the Death of Jasmine Beckford*, London Borough of Brent.

Blom-Cooper, L. (1987) *A Child in Mind: Protection of Children in a Responsible Society: the Report of the Commission of Inquiry into the Death of Kimberley Carlile*, London Borough of Greenwich.

Braye, S. and Preston-Shoot, M. (1990) 'On teaching and applying the law in social work: it is not that simple', *British Journal of Social Work*, 20(4), 333–53.

CCETSW (1974) *Legal Studies in Social Work Education*, CCETSW, Paper 4.

CCETSW (1990) Paper 30, Second Edition.

Connolly, J. (1996) 'Scaling the wall', *Community Care*, 11–17 July, 26–7.

Davies, M. (1984) 'Training: what we think of it now', *Social Work Today*, 15(20), 12–17.

DHSS (1985) *Social Work Decisions in Child Care: Recent Research Findings and their Implications*, London: HMSO.

Freeman, M. (1992) *Children, their Families and the Law: Working with the Children Act*, London: Macmillan.

Grace, C. and Wilkinson, P. (1978) *Negotiating the Law; Social Work and Legal Services*, London: Routledge.

Howe, D. (1986) 'Welfare Law and the Welfare Principle in Social Work Practice', *Journal of Social Welfare Law*, May 1986, 130–43.

McClean, J. D. (1975) *The Legal Context of Social Work*, London: Butterworth.

Ormrod, R. (1983) 'Child care law: a personal perspective'. *Adoption and Fostering*, 7(4), 10–12.

Parton, N. (1986) 'The Beckford report: a critical appraisal', *British Journal of Social Work*, 16, 511–30.

Stevenson, O. (1986) 'Editorial', *British Journal of Social Work*, 16, 502–10.

Stevenson, O. (1988) 'Law and social work education: a commentary on *The Law Report*', *Issues in Social Work Education*, 8(1).

Vernon, S. (1990) *Social Work and the Law*, London: Butterworth (3rd edn, 1996).

Vernon, S., Harris, R. and Ball, C. (1990) *Towards Social Work Law*, London: CCETSW.

Zander, M. (1974) *Social Workers, their Clients, and the Law*, London: Sweet & Maxwell.

II.3
Gender
Audrey Mullender

It is not possible to understand the personal or social world without taking a gendered perspective. We are not able as professionals to intervene appropriately or justly in people's lives unless we perceive the ways in which women are disadvantaged by an unequal dispersal of power, and in which both men and women are constrained by over-rigid and falsely dichotomized role and relationship expectations. Nor is a gender analysis sufficient without an understanding of the overlaps between sexism and other forms of social oppression; the charge that early feminism represented only the interests of middle-class, middle-aged, white, able-bodied, heterosexual women contained too large a grain of truth to allow for complacency. The organization and practice of social work itself tends both to replicate and compound all these tensions for its practitioners and service users.

We need to develop not just a gender analysis in social work, but a gender power analysis. The gender analysis highlights men and women's differing needs and strengths, whilst the gender power analysis places this in a wider socio-political context. A gendered perspective acknowledges that the majority of service users, informal carers and staff in the lower grades are female, while the majority of senior managers are men (Social Services Inspectorate, 1991). A gender power perspective exposes the fact that social work, like society, is run largely to male priorities, derived from male thought processes, within male operational systems (Fawcett, 1994).

Despite major advances this century, underpinned by sex discrimination and other legislation, women in Britain still lack equal access to power and social influence – and women who are black, and/or lesbian, and/or disabled or poor or older find their choices doubly or multiply constrained. Women still suffer discrimination in relation to education, employment, income, the performance of tasks in the home, access to services to share the care of children and other dependants, and social attitudes and expectations throughout all stages of life (see Pascall, 1986, for a social policy consideration of all these issues and Bryan et al., 1985, for a black women's perspective). Women are also frequently in danger both in public spaces and in the privacy of their own homes from sexual violence (Kelly, 1988). It is important for social work, in every sphere of practice, to encompass these realities.

Child Care

There is a tendency for child care social workers to perceive women predominantly in terms of their responsibility for child rearing. The women with whom social workers typically intervene are already shouldering enormous burdens – the majority of lone parents are women; women disproportionately live in poverty, which in turn causes health problems (Payne, 1991); startlingly high numbers of women are surviving or enduring abusive relationships (Kelly,

1988; Mooney, 1994). Many women feel that social work intervention only adds to their problems instead of providing practical assistance or helping them feel more able to cope.

we got to talking about the way that women are treated as clients – about how women are 'done to' rather than having any sort of power in their own lives and that social work actually perpetuates that and makes it worse . . . It's got to be your fault because your kids don't go to school or it's got to be your fault because you've not enough food in the house.

(Donnelly, 1986, pp. 18 and 24)

The social worker quoted above jointly set up a group for women on child care caseloads; it started from women's own perspectives on their problems – isolation, poverty, lack of access to jobs – and eventually grew large and confident enough to run its own women's centre.

Such awareness of women's agendas is still rare in social work and, indeed, in some respects the position of women is becoming worse. Prevailing political attitudes take a harshly condemnatory attitude towards single mothers, particularly if they are black (Bryan, 1992), for example, and lesbian mothers have to fight to prove themselves as competent parents – including in the eyes of some social workers (Brown, 1992, p. 214). Concepts introduced into child care as a result of the Children Act 1989 – of shared parental responsibility and children's right to contact with both parents – have rebounded on women, driving many into continued or renewed danger from men who abuse them and/or their children (Mullender and Morley, 1994). Women voicing their fears in court are being classed as 'implacably hostile' to their male ex-partners, and they can face prison if they refuse to allow contact to take place. Far from women being empowered to keep themselves or their children safe, they are not even being heard or believed.

The recognition that most sexual

Five Key Points

1 Gender must be on the agenda in all matters relating to the organization and practice of social work.
2 Women have traditionally been discriminated against by society and its institutions, including social work.
3 Women's needs and experiences of life are different from men's.
4 Groups and organizations established by women for women and run to women's agendas are the best means of empowering women.
5 Men, too, both as professionals and as service users, need to be challenged to rethink their traditional roles and assumptions.

violence is perpetrated by men on women and children means both that some male workers in health, welfare and educational settings are likely to be posing a current threat as actual or potential abusers (Pringle, 1992/3) and that male workers are, arguably, less appropriately able to take on disclosure and major areas of counselling work with survivors (Frosh, 1988). A gender power analysis offers not only the most convincing view of the causes of widescale abuse (Driver and Droisen, 1989), but also a model for understanding reactions to abuse cases (Campbell, 1988). Investigative and protective work with abused children – high profile and high cost – neither names nor raises awareness of patriarchal power in the family, in society or its institutions, including the child protection agencies themselves (Hudson, 1992). The avoidance of challenge to male authority and male responsibility can be seen in family dysfunction (as opposed to male abuse) theories, in accusations that mothers 'fail to protect' and in attempts to teach children to take charge of keeping themselves safe. Meanwhile, invaluable therapeutic work with child and women survivors of sexual violence – offered by women along feminist lines, and rarely by the child protection agencies – remains under-resourced, and only recently has information been collated on where such services can be found (Broadcasting Support Services, 1994). Even more ignored are the support needs of mothers of abused children (Hooper, 1992; Dobbin and Evans, 1994), traditionally suspected of collusion and still treated punitively by child care agencies and the courts (Mullender and Morley, 1994).

Community Care – The Role of Carers

Considerations of gender in community care began with a focus on women as carers:

in practice community care equals care by the family, and in practice care by the family equals care by women.
                    (Finch and Groves, 1980, p. 494)

Although there are also significant numbers of male carers, they are mainly husbands and mainly elderly (OPCS, 1992). The person who organizes life around caring for a dependent parent, child, sister or brother is still far more likely to be a woman and she may still have to give up her work, leisure or health to do so (Ungerson, 1987). The idea that informal carers should have attention paid to their own needs for practical and emotional support has been pursued by carers' organizations inspired and run largely by women (Briggs and Oliver, 1985). They are challenging a situation where the more effort carers put in the less likely they are to receive help because they are seen to be doing a good job and fulfilling their expected social role. Minority ethnic carers (McCalman, 1990), and lesbian and gay partners who care, are amongst the most neglected groups.

Low-paid carers in residential homes are almost all women and they are assumed to be suitable for the work purely on account of their gender. This can block training, support and promotion (Phillipson, 1988). The fact that gender interacts with race and class to affect women's quality of life, life chances and ascribed social roles can also be seen in respect of the caring occupations. Many black women, for example, carry a double burden of caring, acting both as low-paid care or nursing staff *and* as key family and community supports.

It is not only as carers but also as service users that women have particular needs in the adult care field, in every specialism from substance misuse (Ettorre, 1992) to AIDS care (Doyal, 1993). Some of the major areas of relevant practice will now be explored.

Women and Mental Health

Women use mental health services more than men (Andrews et al., 1994), yet psychiatric hospitals lack mother and baby units, treatments are inappropriate and key causative experiences are ignored. Amongst the largest groups of women patients are survivors of childhood and/or adult abuse, but traditional diagnostic techniques do not engage with these issues. Work in the USA (cited in Andrews et al., 1994) found that virtually all histories of childhood and adult sexual and physical assaults were missed by psychiatrists. Whilst not denying the depression and anxiety that these experiences can cause, it is clearly unhelpful to blame the victim by labelling her as sad or mad, whilst failing to attend to the real issues.

Women themselves have begun to voice their discontent and to reject the traditional labels and inadequate responses (Barnes and Maple, 1992; MIND, 1994; Good Practices in Mental Health, 1994). Recent criticisms have moved beyond sex-bias in diagnosis

(Broverman et al., 1970) to the institutional level revealing, for example, widespread sexual harassment and sexual violence, not only by male therapists, (Teevan, 1991) but also by male service users in mixed institutions (MIND, 1992). There is a growing movement towards women finding their own, more effective and less damaging solutions to psychological distress outside mainstream services (Women in MIND, 1986) – chiefly through women-only, empowering groups. Workshops on agoraphobia or tranquillizer use, eating disorders or depression, events aimed specifically at black, working-class and/or lesbian women, groups to develop creativity or body-awareness can all help (Ernst and Goodison, 1981; Krzowski and Land, 1988). Many women nation-wide find healing and raised awareness in alternative therapies, groupwork, campaigning or community activities.

Women with Learning Difficulties

Once we begin to consider women-only groups as a source of strength, the possibilities open up for innovative and constructive intervention with women in every field of practice. There is now, for example, a national network of women service users, women staff and women researchers called Women in Learning Difficulties (WILD) which produces a newsletter and held its first conference in June 1994. Women-only self-advocacy groups give women with learning difficulties more confidence to voice their own agendas and talk about their lives, as in People First's 'Women First' group. Similarly, the Powerhouse is a group of disabled and non-disabled women working to raise awareness and to offer refuge, in Beverley Lewis House in London, for women with learning difficulties who have been threatened or abused. McCarthy (1991) and Williams

(1992) offer a vital analysis of the traditional denial to women with learning difficulties of sexual knowledge and sexual choices (including reproductive rights), which increases their vulnerability to assault and exploitation – including in care settings – and excludes them from basic human rights.

Disabled Women

Physically disabled women, similarly, have particular needs as women, over and above those they have as disabled

---

Three Questions

1   What is my gender power analysis of what I am doing or reading (i.e., are there men or male-dominated institutions here wielding personal, organizational or social power unfairly over women) and how does this integrate with my understanding of other oppressions?

2   What difference does it make, to me and to them, that the person or people I am working with is/are male or female, and that I am male or female?

3   What can I do to empower women colleagues and service users to have greater safety, more choices and higher self-esteem, and to challenge men to take responsibility for their own actions and feelings and the impact these have on other people?

---

people (Lonsdale, 1990). Being female and being disabled is a double oppression which can compound feelings of powerlessness, rejection and invisibility (Begum, 1992). 'Normality' and 'attractiveness' are tied up in socially constructed ideas of female body image. Whereas women generally are subsumed under the categories of wife and mother, disabled women struggle to be regarded as sexual beings, and as capable of parenting (Campion, 1995, chapter 6). Similarly, disabled women may not be recognized as being at risk of sexual violence, yet they may be more vulnerable both in their own homes (London Borough of Hounslow, 1994) and in care and educational settings. In one disability equality group, every member had had experiences of abuse; for example, one woman had been taken daily to school by taxi and had been indecently assaulted by the driver as he lifted her in and out.

Disabled women are beginning to organize themselves for change. The Greater London Association of Disabled People produces a newsletter entitled *Boadicea* and has held a conference on women's safety issues. Just as social workers are being challenged to see civil rights for disabled people, rather than psychological adjustment to a limited social role, as the route to progress, so there is a need to perceive disabled women – whatever their race, class, sexuality or age – as powerful and vocal, not as a depersonalized group of victims.

Older Women

Older women, though present in society in large and growing numbers, are doubly marginalized, on the grounds both of age and of gender. The domestic and sexual roles through which they were defined, albeit as inferior, earlier in their lives are now deemed to be over and they are rendered socially invisible. (See, for example, Macdonald with Rich, 1983, pp. 14–17, which also engages with the social ostracism of lesbianism; and Greer, 1992, chapter one). The challenge to social work is not to collude with dismissive ageist attitudes (Ford and Sinclair, 1989). The physical and/or mental frailty which brings social workers into the lives of a proportion of older women adds the negative connotations of dependence and disability (Stevenson, 1986), while

poverty disproportionately results from pay and pension inequities along gendered lines (Stevenson, 1986; Crawley, 1994), but none of these should dictate the end of choices, dignity or respect.

Older women can tell the fascinating story of a revolution in opportunities for women; they have lived through – and often participated in – a social struggle for forms of help which they themselves were told they had no right even to request (Hughes and Mtezuka, 1992, pp. 231–2). Women's groups in settings where large numbers of older women receive services, such as residential establishments and day centres, would be enthralling and empowering – and could help older women to access services run by younger women which have not always catered for them as well as they might (Hughes and Mtezuka, 1992, p. 221).

Criminal Justice

Theories of male power and control underpin mainstream practice with perpetrators of sexual violence, which now works to hold men responsible for their behaviour and accountable for their actions (Morrison, Erooga and Beckett, 1994, p. xvii; Mullender, 1996, chapter nine). Male tendencies towards domination have also been perceived in inner-city riots – viewed as an 'explosion of lawless masculinity' (Campbell, 1993, back cover), cutting across women's attempts to hold communities together – while disaffected young men offend to gain peer group status, control of the urban space, and no-cost access to high performance cars. Though the atmosphere in male-dominated probation services may not be conducive to challenging male power, there *are* examples of gender awareness in intervention with male offenders (Bensted et al., 1994) and of women's agendas being clearly voiced by women staff

(Perrott, 1994). There is also a gender power analysis of responses to women's offending – statistically far less significant than that of men but seen, as a consequence, as doubly deviant (Heidensohn, 1987) – more than doubly so for black or lesbian women – and leading to more interventive or punitive sentences. Women's offending is measured in relation to norms of domestic and sexual roles and behaviour (Worrall, 1990, p. 163), rather than real causes such as poverty (Carlen, 1988), male coercion or relative powerlessness both in daily life and in the court system.

Methods and Settings of Intervention

Women are most easily empowered through women-only groups which value each woman's contribution and focus on women's lived experience of socially constructed expectations and ways to challenge them (Pence, 1987; Butler and Wintram, 1991). They also free women from taking responsibility for men's feelings and communication difficulties in groups. Discussion starts from women's individual experiences and uses these to draw out broader institutional, cultural and social aspects of the ways in which women are consistently denied equal choices and control. Women (or girls) recognize, together, that abuse and exploitation are not their personal fault but are endemic in a society dominated by male agendas, which devalues women and their contribution. This leads to decisions to take relevant action for change. Similar principles have been applied to modes of organizing work settings resulting in the collective, non-hierarchical lines favoured in women-only organizations such as Women's Aid and Rape Crisis.

Meanwhile, more traditional methods and settings also need to adapt to a gendered agenda. It is now beginning to

be recognized, for example, that couple and family work (including court welfare work) is neither safe nor productive where there is the threat of violence (Mullender, 1996, chapter seven). Groupwork is giving greater consideration to the gender mix of members and facilitators (Brown and Mistry, 1994). Special efforts have been highlighted which could improve promotion prospects for women in social services departments (Social Services Inspectorate, 1992), including promotion for black women (Watt and Cook, 1989).

Challenges to Men

It is not only women who need to change. The challenge to men is arguably greater, especially as they have more to lose in status and power terms (Cockburn, 1991). In social work education and practice, men can usefully come together in groups to work on the emotional barriers to the feminine in themselves – to feelings and vulnerabilities – which drive them towards aggressive competitiveness and, at the same time, keep women and gay men oppressed (*Working with Men* newsletter). Men need to consider how they can better support women colleagues – at every level from campaigning for crèches and sharing the care of dependants, to tackling harassment and sexist remarks – and be part of a more appropriate service for

Further Reading

1 Dominelli, L. and McLeod, E. (1989) *Feminist Social Work*, Basingstoke: Macmillan.
2 Hanmer, J. and Statham, D. (1988) *Women and Social Work: Towards a Woman-Centred Practice*, Basingstoke: Macmillan.
3 Langan, M. and Day, L. (1992) *Women, Oppression and Social Work*, London: Routledge.

women and children and a more confrontational stance with abusive or exploitative men.

Conclusion

We live in a society where there is no such thing as gender balance. Achieving equality in numbers – in organizations, on committees, between group members or facilitators – cannot of itself achieve equity since women carry less social influence, and often less organizationally ascribed authority – in short, less power – than men. There is no form of social work intervention and no setting for social work practice where gender does not have a central relevance. Women-only organizations have led the way in helping women feel stronger, more in control of their lives, and more able to make choices. Women's agendas have posed a challenge to men, too, to stop being the problem and become part of the solution. Gendering the agenda in social work, and tackling the issues of power, will improve both the employment context and the commissioning and delivery of every type of service.

References

Andrews, C., Nadirshaw, Z., Curtis, Z. and Ellis, J. (1994) *Women, Mental Health and Good Practice*, Brighton: Pavilion Publishing.

Barnes, M. and Maple, N. (1992) *Women and Mental Health: Challenging the Stereotypes*, Birmingham: Venture Press.

Begum, N. (1992) 'Disabled women and the feminist agenda', in H. Hinds, A. Phoenix and J. Stacey (eds) *Working Out: New Directions for Women's Studies*, London: Falmer Press.

Bensted, J., Brown, A., Forbes, C. and Wall, R. (1994) 'Men working with men in groups: masculinity and crime', *Groupwork*, 7(1), 37–49.

Briggs, A. and Oliver, J. (1985) *Caring: Disabled Relatives*, London: Routledge.

Broadcasting Support Services (1994) *Survivors' Directory 1994: Support Services for Survivors of Sexual Violence in Britain and Ireland*, Manchester: Broadcasting Support Services.

Broverman, I., Broverman, D., Clarkson, F., Rosenkrantz, P. and Vogal, S. (1970) 'Sex-role stereotypes and clinical judgements of mental health', *Journal of Consulting and Clinical Psychology*, 34, 1–7.

Brown, A. and Mistry, T. (1994) 'Group work with "mixed membership" groups: issues of race and gender', *Social Work with Groups*, 17(3), 5–21.

Brown, H. C. (1992) 'Lesbians, the state and social work practice', in M. Langan and L. Day (eds), *Women, Oppression and Social Work: Issues in Anti-Discriminatory Practice*, London: Routledge.

Bryan, A. (1992) 'Working with black single mothers: myths and reality', in M. Langan and L. Day (eds), *Women, Oppression and Social Work: Issues in Anti-Discriminatory Practice*, London: Routledge.

Bryan, D., Dadzie, S. and Scafe, S. (1985) *The Heart of the Race: Black Women's Lives in Britain*, London: Virago.

Butler, S. and Wintram, C. (1991) *Feminist Groupwork*, London: Sage.

Campbell, B. (1988) *Unofficial Secrets*, London: Virago.

Campbell, B. (1993) *Goliath: Britain's Dangerous Places*, London: Methuen.

Campion, M. J. (1995) *Who's Fit to be a Parent?*, London: Routledge.

Carlen, P. (1988) *Women, Crime and Poverty*, Buckingham: Open University Press.

Cockburn, C. (1991) *In the Way of Women: Men's Resistance to Sex Equality in Organizations*, Basingstoke: Macmillan.

Crawley, B. (1994) 'Older women: policy issues for the twenty-first century', in L. Davis (ed.), *Building on Women's Strengths: A Social Work Agenda for the Twenty-First Century*, Binghamton, New York, USA: Haworth.

Dobbin, D. and Evans, S. (1994) 'Staying alive in difficult times: the experience of groupwork with mothers of children who have been sexually abused', *Groupwork*, 7(2), 117–24.

Donnelly, A. (1986) *Feminist Social Work with a Women's Group*, Norwich: University of East Anglia Social Work Monographs.

Doyal, L. (1993) *Aids: A Feminist Agenda*, Brighton: Falmer.

Driver, E. and Droisen, A. (1989) *Child Sexual Abuse: Feminist Perspectives*, Basingstoke: Macmillan.

Ernst, S. and Goodison, L. (1981) *In Our Own Hands: A Book of Self-Help Therapy*, London: The Women's Press.

Ettorre, E. (1992) *Women and Substance Abuse*, Basingstoke, Macmillan.

Fawcett, J. (1994) 'Promoting positive images: the role of groupwork in promoting women managers within organisations', *Groupwork*, 7(2), 145–52.

Finch, J. and Groves, D. (1980) 'Community care and the family: a case for equal opportunities?', *Journal of Social Policy*, 9(4), 487–511.

Ford, J. and Sinclair, R. (1989) 'Women's experience of old age', in P. Carter, T. Jeffs and M. Smith (eds), *Social Work and Social Welfare Yearbook 1, 1989*, Buckingham: Open University Press.

Frosh, S. (1988) 'No man's land?: the role of men working with sexually abused children', *British*

Journal of Guidance and Counselling, 16(1), January, 1–10.

Good Practices in Mental Health (1994) *Women and Mental Health: An Information Pack of Mental Health Services for Women in the United Kingdom*. London: GPMH (Publications Dept., 380–4 Harrow Road, London W9 2HU.

Greer, G. (1992) *The Change: Women, Ageing and the Menopause*, Harmondsworth: Penguin.

Heidensohn, F. (1987) 'Women and crime: questions for criminology', in P. Carlen and A. Worrall (eds), *Gender, Crime and Justice*, Buckingham: Open University Press.

Hooper, C.-A. (1992) *Mothers Surviving Child Sexual Abuse*, London: Routledge.

Hudson, A. (1992) 'The child sexual abuse "industry" and gender relations in social work', in M. Langan and L. Day (eds), *Women, Oppression and Social Work: Issues in Anti-Discriminatory Practice*, London: Routledge.

Hughes, B. and Mtezuka, M. (1992) 'Social work and older women: where have older women gone?' in M. Langan and L. Day (eds), *Women, Oppression and Social Work: Issues in Anti-Discriminatory Practice*, London: Routledge.

Kelly, L. (1988) *Surviving Sexual Violence*, Cambridge: Polity Press.

Krzowski, S. and Land, P. (eds) (1988) *In Our Experience: Workshops at the Women's Therapy Centre*, London: The Women's Press.

London Borough of Hounslow (1994) *Domestic Violence – Help, Advice and Information for Disabled Women*, London: London Borough of Hounslow.

Lonsdale, S. (1990) *Women and Disability: The Experience of Physical Disability Among Women*, Basingstoke: Macmillan.

Macdonald, B. with Rich, C. (1983) *Look Me in the Eye: Old Women, Aging and Ageism*, London: The Women's Press.

McCalman, J. A. (1990) *The Forgotten People: Carers in Three Minority Ethnic Communities in Southwark*, London: King's Fund.

McCarthy, M. (1991) 'The politics of sex education', *Community Care*, 21st November, 15–17.

MIND (1992) *Stress on Women*, London: MIND (pack).

MIND (1994) *Eve Fights Back: Report on MIND's 'Stress on Women' Campaign*, London: MIND.

Mooney, J. (1994) *The Hidden Figure: Domestic Violence in North London*, London: London Borough of Islington, Police and Crime Prevention Unit.

Morrison, T., Erooga, M. and Beckett, R. C. (1994) *Sexual Offending Against Children: Assessment and Treatment of Male Abusers*, London: Routledge.

Mullender, A. (1996) *Rethinking Domestic Violence: The Social Work and Probation Response*, London: Routledge.

Mullender, A. and Morley, R. (eds) (1994) *Children Living with Domestic Violence: Putting Men's Abuse of Women on the Child Care Agenda*, London: Whiting and Birch.

Office of Population Censuses and Surveys (OPCS) (1992) *General Household Survey: Carers in 1990*, London: Government Statistical Service.

Pascall, G. (1986) *Social Policy: A Feminist Analysis*, London: Tavistock.

Payne, S. (1991) *Women, Health and Poverty: An Introduction*, Hemel Hempstead: Harvester Wheatsheaf.

Pence, E. (1987) *In Our Best Interest: A Process for Personal and Social Change*, Minneapolis, Minnesota, USA: Minnesota Program Development Inc.

Perrott, S. (1994) 'Working with men who abuse women and children', in C. Lupton and T. Gillespie (eds), *Working with Violence*, Basingstoke: Macmillan.

Phillipson, J. (1988) 'The complexities of caring: developing a feminist approach to training staff in a residential setting', *Social Work Education*, 7(3), 3–6.

Pringle, K. (1992/3) 'Child sexual abuse perpetrated by welfare personnel and the problem of men', *Critical Social Policy*, 12(3), 4–19.

Social Services Inspectorate, Department of Health (1991) *Women in Social Services: A Neglected Resource*, London: HMSO.

Social Services Inspectorate, Department of Health (1992) *Promoting Women: Management Development and Training for Women in Social Services Departments*, London: HMSO.

Stevenson, O. (1986) *Women in Old Age: Reflections on Policy and Practice*, Nottingham: University of Nottingham, School of Social Studies.

Teevan, S. (1991) *Women Who Are Abused by Their Therapists*, London: MIND.

Ungerson, C. (1987) *Policy is Personal: Sex, Gender and Informal Care*, London: Tavistock.

Watt, S. and Cook, J. (1989) 'Another expectation unfulfilled: black women and social services departments', in C. Hallett (ed.)*Women and Social Services Departments*, Brighton: Harvester Wheatsheaf.

Williams, F. (1992) 'Women with learning difficulties are women too', in M. Langan and L. Day (eds), *Women, Oppression and Social Work: Issues in Anti-Discriminatory Practice*, London: Routledge.

Working With Men, newsletter (and other publications) available from 320 Commercial Way, London SE15 1QN.

Women in MIND (1986) *Finding Our Own Solutions: Women's Experience of Mental Health Care*, London: MIND.

Worrall, A. (1990) *Offending Women: Female Lawbreakers and the Criminal Justice System*, London: Routledge.

II.4
Race
J. Owusu-Bempah

Never let the fox into the henhouse to feed the chickens.

(An African proverb)

UNESCO (1967), emphasizing the similarities between human groups, has declared: 'All men living today belong to the same species and descend from the same stock'. This renders the notion of 'Race', as applied to *homo sapiens*, baseless and meaningless. Notwithstanding, the belief that humanity comprises different racial groups continues to dominate the thinking and behaviour of reactionaries and liberals alike. Race has acquired a social reality (racism) manifest in the ways the presumed inherent worth of the 'races' is all too often used as a basis for formulating policies and differentially allocating power and resources. The stubborn belief in 'racial differences' shows that understanding the nature of race or racism requires a multi-level analysis, rather than a simple, reductionist approach. Racism must be studied as something more than a biological notion or a psychological phenomenon – racial antipathy. In short:

In order to undermine racism it is not sufficient that biologists should expose its fallacies. It is also necessary that psychologists and sociologists should demonstrate its causes. The social structure is always an important factor . . .
(*UNESCO, 1967, statement 10*)

The institution of social work is a microcosm of the social structure. Thus, understanding the influence of race on social work should aid understanding its dynamics in the wider society. Historically, social work has been influenced by race theories, beliefs and assumptions. These, in turn, have generally biased and distorted social workers' perceptions, assessments and treatment of black service users and their needs . This paper discusses some of the ways in which race continues to influence social work today. It uses social workers' preoccupation, in recent years, with black children's self-concept, their putative 'negative self-identity', as an illustration of their insensitivity to the adverse structural (socio-politico-economic) circumstances facing black service users; they tend to use race in various ways as the ultimate explanation for black people's problems and needs (Owusu-Bempah, 1994).

Professional interest in the self-concept arises from the belief that self-knowledge permits the comprehension of one's future and place in the world. It is believed that individuals' conceptions of themselves influence their aspirations and behaviour. Amongst social workers the interactionist views of Cooley (1902) and Mead (1934) about the self-concept provide the major rationale for this belief. These theorists' ideas have spawned literature suggesting that they are pertinent to the study and understanding of the nature of black people's self-concept and psychological functioning. Cooley's idea of 'the social looking-glass self' which presents the social environment as analogous to an undistorted mirror through which we receive feedback about ourselves, is claimed to be especially applicable. Clark and Clark's (1939, 1947) misidentification studies and subsequent studies based upon them have reinforced this view. Consequently, social work continues to be influenced by the myths and assumptions about black people's self-concept (Owusu-Bempah, 1994).

In social work, nowhere is the notion of race more perceptible than in the child care system. The literature in this area is replete with claims that black children (over-represented in the system) have more psycho-social developmental problems than other children. These problems are commonly attributed to 'self-hatred' which, in turn, is explained in terms of racism and the children's lack of awareness of the 'black culture'(e.g., ABSWAP, 1983; Small, 1991). For obvious reasons, the latter explanation is particularly favoured by the Children Act 1989. Although it is yet unknown what the best explanation of the problems is, the accepted solution is to 'work on' the children's self-identity. Writers and practitioners still insist on the 'need' to improve the self-identity of black children (e.g., Maxime, 1993a), losing sight of the inherent racism of such practice. Ironically, some advocate it as a necessary anti-racist strategy for social work even with black adults (e.g., Thompson, 1993). According to Coleman (1994), some SSDs have taken these suggestions seriously and have established special clinics to 'repair the damaged self-identity' of black children in their care.

Unsurprisingly, programmes used to achieve this are also race-based. They include providing the children with information about their 'black' cultural background, including information about black historical figures and/or counselling them to identify with 'the black community' and to take pride in their 'blackness' (e.g., Maxime, 1991a, 1993b; Banks, 1993; Coleman, 1994). It is claimed that this will neutralize the damaging effects of the racist feedback

Five Key Points

1 To understand the notion of 'race' and its influence on social work, we need to start with an examination of the social structure.

2 Race continues to dominate social work theory and practice.

3 Social work training and practice with black service users must be grounded in tested theories about race, and not in racial myths, assumptions and stereotypes or folklore.

4 Black social work service users suffer discrimination on the grounds of 'race'.

5 Racism damages the life chances of black people more than it does their self-esteem.

they receive from the white community about themselves, their 'racial group' and 'culture'. This claim is unwarranted. If the white community is the pathologizing agent, then it is this agent, those whose nocuous attitudes and behaviour they are victims of, which must be neutralized. Providing therapy to these children is sheer victim-blaming. Historically, biological or genetic factors have been evoked to justify the plight of black people. Today psychological (e.g., self-identity) or cultural factors provide the excuse. These children cannot be expected to find comfort in whatever explanation is offered for their difficulties, if it remains at the level of the individual (the child or the family) and fails to undertake to tackle the racism in the larger society, if it leaves the culprit free to carry on victimizing them; and it matters not a hoot the skin colour of its proponents.

The programmes assume that the children experience 'identity crises' because they have favourable attitudes to white people and the white community. For example, Maxime (1991b) described a ten-year-old black girl as psychologically disturbed, simply because she preferred 'a white family placement as black ones were all too poor' (p. 103). Describing this girl's choice as astute, based upon reality, would be more helpful. Likewise a black child who keeps white company is often seen as having an identity crisis. A satisfactory explanation for why the efforts of black children, living in a predominantly white community, to broaden their social milieu should be regarded as symptomatic of psychological disturbance (Howitt and Owusu-Bempah, 1994) is yet awaited.

The programmes also equate 'non-affiliation' with one's 'racial group' with psychological damage. It may be rather helpful to regard such behaviour as an example of what Erikson (1968) termed: 'negative identification'. According to Erikson, developing a coherent identity requires repudiation as well as identification. That is, he regarded negative identification (or shifting identities) as a normal and important factor in personality development, and so must not be interfered with unnecessarily. Thomas's (1995) notion of 'identity by proxy' supports this view. This notion proposes that pretending to be white ('identity by proxy') is a psychological manoeuvre which some black children engage in to preserve their *real self*, to protect their psychological integrity against racism. This implies that 'misidentification' or group rejection is not a sign of psychological disturbance; rather it appears to be a source of strength. Furthermore, it suggests that the identity crises which black children are often reported to experience may be caused by adults' (notably social workers' and therapists') reactions (or actions) to these types of tricks which the children employ in order to mitigate the general racial antipathy they encounter daily. That is, describing these children as having identity problems and 'treating' them potentially robs them of their protective shield against racism.

Because race is endemic in these programmes they confuse self-identity with 'racial identity'. Self-identity refers to an individual's sense of uniqueness – what sets a person apart from everyone else; 'racial identity' relates to group identity, a racial reference group. They also equate one's personal identity with one's culture (e.g., Coleman, 1994). A stark distinction between the two is that the latter is shared with other members of one's culture; the former, simply, is a unique personal property. Perhaps due to this confusion, black people are also presented as a culturally homogenous group, as belonging to a single, monolithic culture shared by all black people, regardless of their national or ethnic origins. It is hard to imagine where such a culture might exist. This illusory posture regarding the homogeneity of black people is likely to diminish the efficacy of these programmes (or any practice) in meeting clients' individual needs.

Children of 'mixed-race' parentage receive particular attention from social workers. It has become almost axiomatic amongst social workers (and therapists) that they can develop a healthy personality only by identifying with 'the black community' – any sign of identification with their white side is automatically seen as symptomatic of dire psychological disturbance. Programmes to deal with this putative disturbance involve, explicitly or implicitly, denying their white side, a process which many of the children find psychologically painful, damaging and undesirable (Tizard and Phoenix, 1993). This assumption is also puzzling. If it is acceptable for these children to identify with their black side, what is problematic about their identification with, or attachment to, their white side? Who should decide which aspects of themselves should be significant to them, the children or those who want them to see themselves as black? Which 'racial' side of their inheritance they feel comfortable with is largely determined by their own experiences and the subjective meanings to them. Briefly, denial of the 'black' label, or group rejection, is not necessarily symptomatic of a personality disturbance. There exists no evidence to suggest a relationship between black children's attitudes to their race and their self-esteem. On the contrary, research shows that black children learn to compartmentalize their racial attitudes and prevent them from influencing self-evaluation (Rosenberg, 1979, 1989; Thomas, 1995) – neither racial preference nor racial attitude seems to be a predictor of a person's self-esteem. It is undeniable that racism is hurtful to black children (and adults). However, it is not their self-worth, but rather their life chances which are damaged by it. Of course, this in turn is likely to affect their psychological functioning, depending upon the person's comparison-group or aspirations. Nevertheless, our efforts should be directed towards improving the children's life chances rather than their self-concept.

There is evidence to support the above view. For example, Wilson (1987) and Tizard and Phoenix (1993) have reported that African-Caribbean children and those of 'mixed-race' parentage living with their families do not have the identity problems commonly associated with their counterparts in care. They suggest also that children of 'mixed-race' parentage living with their families are as psychologically stable as their counterparts, black and white. Such evidence suggests also that the self-identity of black children in care is no more damaged than that of other children in care, a fact acknowledged by therapists working with these children (e.g., Coleman, 1994). Yet, others have reported 'very high rates of psychological disturbance and feelings of rejection amongst both black and white children in care' (Tizard and Phoenix, 1993, p. 33). We may wonder, then, why the issue of

identity problems does not arise for white children (Owusu-Bempah, 1994). A simple explanation for this is that race theories hold that white people (including children), by virtue of being white, are superior in all aspects of humanity. It would, therefore, be schismatic to attribute any form of weakness to them, *vis-à-vis* black people.

Why does race continue to be so significant in social worker–black service user relationships, to the virtual exclusion of structural factors? One possible explanation is that the mythologies concerning race are deeply rooted in (pseudo) science such that they are embraced by social institutions, including

---

Three Questions

1 What is the 'black culture', and how significant do you consider it to be to black service users?
2 Consider some of the covert ways in which 'race' is used in social work to disadvantage black service users.
3 Ashley Montagu (1974) has described Race as 'man's (sic) most dangerous myth'. To what extent does this myth endanger social work in a multi-ethnic society?

---

social work. Another explanation relates to subjugation and control. In psychology, Bhavnani (1994) has described IQ (historically inextricably linked with race) as a mode of domination, an apparatus for attaching various labels to people for the purpose of control. In social work, as in other social institutions, race has historically served this purpose, and continues to do so (Chase, 1980; Littlewood and Lipsedge, 1989; Owusu-Bempah, 1990). It is now 'politically incorrect' to espouse overt racist theories to explain why black service users deserve second-class services, or should be controlled. Invoking 'black inferiority' under the guise of such an abstract, virtually meaningless psychological concept as (negative) self-identity serves this purpose safely. It does so even more safely and effectively because, as the literature reveals, it has the sanction and active support and co-operation of black social workers and therapists. A third explanation is that the traditional social work model was designed to equip practitioners with tools for detecting pathology, weaknesses and deficiency in clients. Hence, social work training, today, is designed to restrict practitioners' vision and perspective by narrowing interests to 'what is wrong with black service users' rather than 'what is wrong with the system, and how has it contributed to the creation and maintenance of their problems?' Added to the fact that the 'black race' has, for centuries, been synonymous with mental, cultural and moral degeneracy, it is not surprising that social work continues to problematize black service users.

What kind of framework is needed for social work, at least, to minimize the invidious and insidious impact of race upon it? What social work model is needed to provide appropriate services in a multi-ethnic society in the approaching century? Such a framework requires a multi-level – educational, institutional, professional and personal – approach to race (i.e., racism). Regarding education and training, MacDonald (1990) has charged social work training with being 'all too often cluttered by unsubstantiated ideas of dubious utility' (p. 539). We need to acknowledge that race exemplifies such unfounded ideas, whose utility is to limit understanding of the structural causes of black service users' problems and needs and how best to address them. That is, social work educators and writers must cease to provide students and practitioners with groundless ideas about race. Instead, they must ensure that their curricula and writings contain tested theories or views about race, and that

invidious distinctions about peoples are not propagated in texts or classrooms under any pretext. Likewise, training programmes 'de-skill' and 'disempower' practitioners wishing to work effectively with black service users through their over-emphasis on race (as distinct from racism) and 'black cultural awareness'. This must cease.

Institutionally, the focus of social services departments has been on describing and explaining 'what is (congenitally) wrong with black service users'. Pollard (1989) provides an alternative approach. Pollard distinguishes between 'alterable' and 'static' variables. 'Alterable variables' relate to factors in a person or the environment which can be somehow manipulated to enhance their functioning. These are contrasted with 'static variables' which represent factors that are not easily changed and which only classify or label people. This would be a more productive approach to understanding and helping black service users generally than the current fad which concentrates on static variables within the individual, such as 'race', to the virtual exclusion of external or environmental factors (alterable variables). In the case of children in care, for example, the 'alterable variables' approach would: (a) identify those children who seem to be thriving in the system and determine what factors are associated with their general well-being; (b) seek to identify those factors within the system which deleteriously affect, as well as those which enhance, their functioning. Alterable factors within the system include institutional policy and practices, as well as the attitudes and behaviour of professionals and carers.

Recently, white social workers have been over concerned with understanding the 'black culture'. However, understanding a culture is not the same as respecting it. Instead, social workers should begin to examine and understand their own feelings about black service users' *cultures*. They also need to extend their knowledge of the structural causes of black service users' problems and the part they, as beneficiaries, play in those problems in order to counterbalance the barriers to providing them with appropriate services. They need to examine their own cache of cultural, professional, class and gender, etc., baggage which often interferes with their perceptions, assessment and treatment of black clients. This applies to black social workers as much as it does to white social workers.

Many claim that within the context of professional or helping relationships, black clients are best served by black professionals. Others, however, dispute this claim (e.g., Owusu-Bempah, 1989, 1990; Fernando, 1988). In therapy, for example, it has been noted that being black does not automatically ensure a therapist's success in working with black clients. Besides, many black service users do not perceive black social workers as 'black', owing to their professional status. O'Brian, a black male social worker, was made (painfully) aware of this fact by a black male service user:

Sir, . . . You see, you are in a position of authority . . . You live in a different Britain to the one me and my family live in.

(O'Brian, 1990, p. 4)

To many black service users, having a black skin does not necessarily make a person 'black'. Rather, a 'black' person or professional is one who not only empathizes with their circumstances, but also can formulate problems consistent with their needs. A 'black' professional has a social-change outlook rather than a problem-solving philosophy; their focus is more on the system than on the service user. They are also able to distinguish between what is a *real* problem and what is merely a system-induced problem. Many of the problems facing black service

users are system-induced, and have nothing inherently to do with their 'race' or skin colour. In short, social work practitioners, managers and educators need to recognize and acknowledge that the important factors impinging adversely upon black service users are structural – social, political and economic – rather than biological (race). Race, a red (or perhaps black) herring, only helps to deflect attention from these factors. We must not ignore Race, but, at the same time, we must not let it dominate social work – we must always be mindful of its destructive power.

References

ABSWAP (1983) *Black Children in Care*, London: The Association of Black Social Workers and Allied Professions.

Banks, N. (1993 'Identity work with black children', *Educational and Child Psychology*, 10, 43–6.

Bhavnani, K. (1994) 'Shifting the subject', in K. Bhavnani and A. Phoenix (eds), *Shifting Identities, Shifting Racism: A Feminism and Psychology Reader*, London: Sage, pp. 19–39.

Chase, A. (1980) *The Legacy of Malthus: The Social Cost of the New Scientific Racism*, Urbana: University of Illinois Press.

Clark, K. B. and Clark, M. (1939) 'The development of the consciousness of self and emergence of racial identity in Negro pre-school children', *Journal of Social Psychology*, 10, 591–9.

Clark, K. B. and Clark, M. (1947) 'Racial identification and preference in Negro children', in T. M. Newcomb and E. L. Hartley (eds), *Readings in Social Psychology*, New York: Holt, Rinehart and Winston, pp. 602–11.

Coleman, J. (1994) 'Black children in care: A crisis of identity', *The Runnymede Bulletin*, No. 279, October, 4–5.

Further Reading

Bulhan, H. A. (1985) *Frantz Fanon and the Psychology of Oppression*, Boston: Boston University Press.

Chase, A. (1980) *The Legacy of Malthus: the Social Costs of the New Scientific Racism*, Urbana: University of Illinois Press.

Montagu, A. (1974) *Man's Most Dangerous Myth: the Fallacy of Race*, New York: Oxford University Press.

Cooley, C. H. (1902) *Human Nature and Social Order*, New York: Scribner.

Erikson, E. (1968) *Identity: Youth and Crisis*, London: Faber.

Fernando, S. (1988) *Race and Culture in Psychiatry*, London: Tavistock/Routledge.

Howitt, D. and Owusu-Bempah, J. (1994) *The Racism of Psychology: Time for Change*, Hemel Hempstead: Harvester Wheatsheaf.

Littlewood, R. and Lipsedge, M. (1989) *Aliens and Alienists: Ethnic Minorities and Psychiatry* (2nd edn), London: Unwin Hyman.

MacDonald, G. (1990) 'Allocating blame in social work', *The British Journal of Social Work*, 20, 525–46.

Maxime, J. E. (1991a) *Black Pioneers: Workbook Two of Black Like Me Series*, London: Emani Publications.

Maxime, J. E. (1991b) 'Some psychological models of black self-concept', in S. Ahmed, J. Cheetham and J. Small (1991), *Social Work with Black Children and their Families*, London: Batford/British Agencies for Adoption and Fostering, pp. 100–16.

Maxime, J. E. (1993a) 'Therapeutic importance of racial identity in working with black children who hate', in V. Verma (ed.), *How and Why Children Hate: A Study of Conscious and Unconscious Sources*, London: Jessica Kingsley.

Maxime, J. E. (1993b) 'The importance of racial identity for the psychological well-being of black children', *Association of Child Psychology and Psychiatry Review & Newsletter*, 15(4), 173–9.

Mead, G. H. (1934) *Mind, Self and Society*, Chicago: Chicago University Press.

Montagu, A. (1974) *Man's Most Dangerous Myth: the Fallacy of Race*, New York: Oxford University Press.

O'Brian, C. (1990) 'Family therapy with black families', *Journal of Family Therapy*, 12, 3–16.

Owusu-Bempah, J. (1989) 'Does colour matter?', *Community Care*, 26 January, 18–19.

Owusu-Bempah, J. (1990) 'Toeing the white line', *Community Care*, 1 November, 16–17.

Owusu-Bempah, J. (1994) 'Race, self-identity and social work', *The British Journal of Social Work*, 24, 123–36.

Pollard, D. S. (1989) 'Against the odds: a profile of academic achievers from the urban underclass', *Journal of Negro Education*, 58, 297–308.

Rosenberg, M. (1979) 'Group rejection and self-rejection', *Research in Community and Mental Health*, 1, 3–20.

Rosenberg, M. (1989) 'Old myths die hard: the case of black self-esteem', *Revue Internationale de Psychologie*, 2, 355–65.

Small, J. (1991) 'Ethnic and racial identity in adoption within the United Kingdom', *Adoption and Fostering*, 15, 61–9.

Thomas, L. (1995) 'Psychotherapy in the context of race and culture: an inter-cultural therapeutic approach', in S. Fernando (ed.), *Mental Health in a Multi-ethnic Society: A Multi-disciplinary Handbook*, London: Routledge, pp. 172–90.

Thompson, N. (1993) *Anti-Discriminatory Practice*, London: Macmillan.

Tizard, B. and Phoenix, A. (1993) *Black, White or Mixed Race? Race and Racism in the Lives of Young People of Mixed Race Parentage*, London: Routledge.

UNESCO (1967) *Statement On Race and Racial Prejudice*, Paris: UNESCO.

Wilson, A. (1987) *Mixed Race Children: A Study of Identity*, London: Allen and Unwin.

II.5
Family
Graham Allan

Politicians and other pundits frequently lament the perceived decline of contemporary social institutions. Of all such institutions, 'the family' is probably the one which is most routinely seen as being under greatest threat. There is, of course, nothing new in this. Certainly since the early days of industrialization in the early nineteenth century, the apparent decline of acceptable family life has been a focus of much political rhetoric and debate. Cries to 'strengthen the family', to preserve 'family values' and to ensure that the next generation is presented with the right family role models seem to be present in all eras, though their detailed form varies according to the moral panics being stoked at the time (Gittins, 1993).

Clearly, moral rhetoric and political ideology can be influential in shaping legislative action which directly impinges on the material welfare of different families. For example, the regulations governing welfare benefits and tax advantages can have a direct impact on family organization. Equally the state's actions in 'policing' and monitoring the behaviour of families through its various agencies, including social work, health visiting and other services, help shape the boundaries of what constitutes acceptable family relationships (Donzelot, 1979). Yet past claims about the family's demise have clearly been mistaken. Not only has historical analysis demonstrated that contemporary family dilemmas – be these domestic violence, child abuse or family dissolution – are not new but, as importantly, families continue to be seen by those involved as arenas in which

personal security and emotional satisfaction can be expected, if not always delivered.

The confusion in much of this public rhetoric centres upon change in family organization being seen as inherently pathological. Romantic visions of the past are glorified, so that change – almost any change – gets defined as undermining and damaging. Yet precisely because family relationships are both personally and socially significant, family organization cannot be expected to remain static. Any social institution which is central to the workings of a society, and of course thereby closely integrated to other key aspects of economic and social structure, must alter as those other aspects are themselves modified under new conditions. Dominant family forms cannot remain constant and still be institutionally crucial. From a sociological angle, this is the key to understanding family life: family organization is inevitably shaped by the wider social and economic formation, even if ideologically the family is presented as being separate and apart – a cosy private domain located in an increasingly threatening public world.

The reality of changing family forms has become very apparent in late twentieth-century Britain, as elsewhere in the western world. There have been three very obvious areas of change, in particular. Firstly, there have been rapid changes in patterns of coupledom and family formation. Aside from gay couples now being more accepted, the growth in cohabitation has been quite remarkable.

According to the data available, relatively few people cohabited outside of marriage until the early 1970s. The typical pattern was one of youthful marriage following a formal engagement which often involved an element of sexual knowledge but stopped well short of living together. By the late 1980s, cohabitation had not only become the dominant form of engagement in that most couples did cohabit prior to marriage, but moreover a fifth of unmarried women aged 18–49 who were not married were cohabiting (General Household Survey, 1993). From being a stigmatized form of coupledom, cohabitation had become a normal phase, receiving social approval rather than opprobrium.

One reason for these changes in family formation patterns lies in the second major shift which has occurred in the last third of the twentieth century: the rapid growth in levels of marital separation and divorce. Legislative change has fostered this, but the root causes go far deeper, reflecting – and in turn encouraging – fundamental changes in the ways people define a satisfactory and acceptable marriage. While the reality of marriage has not altered as radically as popular literature sometimes suggests, there has been considerable movement in the ideological basis of coupledom. What Cancian (1987) usefully calls 'marital blueprints' have developed to emphasize the expectation of intimacy and mutual fulfilment through the quality of the couple relationship itself. A failure in this regard within a relationship is increasingly recognized as grounds for reconsidering its future (Giddens, 1992).

In turn the high prevalence of divorce has played its part in encouraging cohabitation. Not only have divorcees been more likely than others to cohabit, but more importantly the high levels of divorce, particularly amongst those who married young, have led to a popular conception that cohabitation is a wise 'apprenticeship' before the full commitment of marriage (despite some contrary evidence; Haskey, 1992). Equally high levels of divorce amongst those marrying young has had an impact on the outcomes of pre-marital pregnancy. For those choosing to give birth, there is far less social encouragement and/or pressure than there was for the prospective parents to marry. This is the third of the three major areas of change mentioned above. In 1982, 14 per cent of all mothers, and 52 per cent of teenage mothers, were unmarried. Ten years later, these figures had risen to 31 per cent and 84 per cent respectively (Birth Statistics, 1992). By any standards this is a mammoth demographic shift in a single decade. It reflects the changed social vision there is about the place of marriage (and divorce) within society and altered images of what individuals, and especially women, should be striving for in constructing their personal lives.

Because of these and other associated changes in family patterns, new approaches to analysing family life needed to be developed. In the past, social science discourses – and perhaps especially social work ones – were often based around some notion of 'the normal family'. While the relationships, domestic roles and kinship responsibilities of these 'normal' families were not static, they were nonetheless characterized by what now seems a curious sense of stability. This was best captured by the notion of the family or domestic cycle through which families typically passed: marriage; child bearing; child rearing; the 'denuded' family once children had left home; and the death of one of the spouses. In the late twentieth century such images of 'normal' families seem quite out of place (Finch, 1987). What has emerged is a far higher degree of diversity in family patterns and a far greater variation in the pathways different families follow. This has had repercussions for how we define 'normal' families. Thus, with increases in cohabitation, in childbirth outside marriage (which in about 50% of cases involve cohabiting partners, though there is no data on the stability of these partnerships), in divorce, and in remarriage and step-family formation, there can be no assumed or standard familial pathway. Recognizing that these factors can affect people's experiences in both childhood and adulthood, it is evident that over the course of their lives different people follow quite distinct family pathways. So it is reasonable to talk of 'family course' or 'family pathway' but it is not so sensible to think in terms of structured, patterned family careers that are common for the majority of people in the way that the notion of 'family cycle' implies. Yet in recognizing this, it is also important to be aware that different pathways have real implications for the family issues and problems which people face and certainly influence future family decisions. There is no suggestion of anarchy or randomness in this; family life may not follow a tidy scheme, but earlier household and family structures still impact on later experiences.

As suggested earlier, 'the family' appears at nearly all times to be seen as potentially under threat, in need of protection and strengthening. From this perspective, many of the issues which have rightly concerned social and other welfare workers in the late twentieth century should be recognized as matters which indicate less a fall in public and private standards and more the emergence of new definitions and discourses about the way family relationships should be ordered. In analysing the emergence of these 'problems', it becomes apparent that demographic change and family organization are only part of the process. What also matters is the interplay of moral, political and professional responses to the difficulties families of different forms face.

In a brief chapter like this, it is not possible to examine these processes in

Five Key Points
1 The experience of family life is now far more diverse than it once was.
2 In recent years there have been radical shifts in patterns of family formation and dissolution.
3 Changes in family and domestic relationships need to be understood in the context of other social and economic changes.
4 Poverty continues to be the normal experience for the increasing numbers of lone-parent families.
5 Economic and political factors influence the processes through which 'families with problems' become defined as 'problem families'.

any depth. Many of the 'family problems' with which social workers routinely have to grapple – child abuse, marital breakdown, domestic violence, family support for elderly people – are discussed elsewhere in this book. These will not be considered here, important though they are. Instead the rest of this chapter will focus on one particular 'problem': the growth of lone-parent families and the development of different understandings of these families. Examining the 'social construction' of lone-parent families will illustrate some of the means by which aspects of family life become problematized.

Lone-parent Families

The numbers of lone-parent families have increased substantially in recent years, following the trends outlined above. In 1971 there were approximately 600,000 lone-parent families, containing about one million dependent children. By 1992 the number of lone-parent families had increased to 1.4 million, with 2.3 million children estimated to be living in them (Haskey, 1994). Notwithstanding changes in divorce legislation, it seems probable that these trends will continue some time into the future. It needs remembering too that these figures are 'snapshots'. What they represent is the number of adults and children in lone-parent families at a given time. Others will have experienced living in lone-parent families, but now be independent or part of step-families through (re)marriage or cohabitation.

Now just as family life in general has become less uniform, so the experiences of lone-parent families are also varied (Crow and Hardey, 1992). Many factors influence the circumstances in which they operate. However, a great deal of research has shown that the single most common characteristic of such families is poverty. Material disadvantage is the norm; only a minority of lone-parent families have sufficient resources to manage comfortably. In particular, female-headed lone-parent families, which comprise 90 per cent of all such families, are especially likely to be experiencing financial hardship. Thus some 70 per cent of all female-headed lone-parent families are dependent on state support for their main income, with others being close to the state benefit level despite having earnings or other means of support (Millar, 1992). The reasons for this are various, but include the low level of women's earnings, especially for those women with few qualifications; the pattern of mothers in Britain re-entering the labour force in a part-time capacity; and the inadequate supply of cheap child care provision, both for pre-school children and for school-age children outside school hours.

However it is not only financially that lone-parent families are materially disadvantaged. They are also disadvantaged in terms of housing. For example, they tend to occupy housing of inferior quality and to live in less desirable areas. Thus, not only are lone-parent families less likely to be owner-occupiers, they also tend disproportionately to live in flats rather

than houses and in older rather than newer property. In addition, they are more likely to be in less secure accommodation and more frequently to be sharing accommodation with relatives and friends. As Crow and Hardey (1991, p. 47) note: 'In both a tenurial and a geographical sense, lone-parent households are concentrated in the poorer parts of the urban system'.

Social concern for lone-parent families has a long history, much of it less than progressive. The welfare of children in such families is a recurring theme, but so too is the burden of support which the state bears. In the immediate post-war period, welfare measures aimed at increasing social participation and citizenship rights, including the development of health, education and income support services, covered lone-parent families just as much as any other family and household forms. However, there was a sense in which lone-parent families were seen as pathological and in need of extra support. A metaphorical red light flashed in the minds of social welfare professionals in their dealings with lone-parent families, warning them that special support and provision might be necessary.

With the increased incidence of lone-parent families, this potentially stigmatizing professional benevolence has become less marked. The red light no longer flashes so regularly. There is a greater acceptance of the 'normality' of lone-parent families and a recognition that many of the problems they confront are created by poverty rather than personality defects or family disorganization. Yet given the overriding concern with reducing levels of state expenditure in the 1980s, it is not surprising that attempts were made to redefine the 'problem' of lone-parent families in this period. The high dependence of lone mothers on state benefits and state housing, the increasing numbers of divorces and births to single mothers, and the apparent failure of non-married fathers to accept financial responsibility for their children resulted in the state seeking ways to limit its commitments. State benefit regulations were altered in an effort to encourage lone mothers to enter employment, but most importantly greater pressure was mounted on non-residential fathers to ensure they made sufficient financial contribution to their children's needs. The Child Support Agency was created in 1993 to police this and enforce compliance by aberrant fathers, thereby reducing the costs which the state bore in providing financial support to lone-parent families.

At the same time, the notion of 'underclass' began to gain acceptance. Although not restricted to lone-parent families, common conceptualizations certainly incorporated some of these families into the term, in particular young unmarried mothers and those who had been dependent on state support long-term. Aspects of racism were also involved here, not only because American usage of the term emphasized black inner-city residents as members of the underclass, but also because young black women were perceived as particularly likely to bear children outside marriage or, indeed, a stable cohabitation. Like the earlier notions of 'cultures of poverty' and 'cycles of deprivation' (Rutter and Madge, 1976), the concept of 'underclass' highlights the idea that children lacking the benefits of a 'normal' family environment come to be socialized into dysfunctional patterns of behaviour and hold sub-cultural values at odds with those of the mainstream. These discrepant values and behavioural patterns, instilled into the next generation thereby supposedly perpetuating the underclass, are seen as a principal cause of poverty. While this underclass thesis has been heavily criticized in academic research, the main issue here concerns the ways in which public visions of particular family forms and particular family problems are

modified within a changing socio-political climate.

So, while in Chester's (1977) terms, the lone-parent family is now far more socially accepted as a 'variant' family form instead of a 'deviant' one, a tension nonetheless remains. Some lone-parent families are still seen as deviant. And, with no coincidence whatsoever, they happen in the main to be those with the fewest resources and those experiencing the greatest hardship. Such families have been shown to be disadvantaged in a variety of ways. For example, the

Three Questions

1 What impact has the growth of cohabitation had on social work practice?
2 How can the processes of divorce and step-family formation be best managed from the viewpoint of children?
3 What role does state action, including the activities of social welfare professionals, play in shaping domestic life?

correlation between poverty and health is now firmly established (Townsend, Davidson and Whitehead, 1988). So too evidence that children in poor material

Further Reading

1 Gittins, D. (1993) *The Family in Question: Changing Households and Familiar Ideologies* (2nd edn), Basingstoke: Macmillan.
2 Hardey, M. and Crow, G. (eds) (1991) *Lone Parenthood: Coping with Constraints and Making Opportunities*, Hemel Hempstead: Harvester Wheatsheaf.
3 Phoenix, A., Woollett, A. and Lloyd, E. (eds) (1991) *Motherhood: Meanings, Practices and Ideologies*, London: Sage.

circumstances consistently under-perform educationally (David, 1993). It is not surprising then that these families are also likely to be seen as 'problem families' in the sense of being known to social services and being in need of higher levels of support.

Conclusion

The point of this chapter has been to highlight the changes that are occurring in family life. As the social and economic basis of society alters so too does the structure and organization of domestic and reproductive relations. With the various shifts there have been over the last generation the complexity of family relationships has undoubtedly increased. This in turn is reflected in popular imagery and language about family patterns. As indicated above, new ideas evolve about what is appropriate for families and what is problematic. Yet not all these new complexities receive the same public or official concern. Thus some lone-parent families have continued to be problematized. Yet other family matters which generate equal levels of personal concern and potentially have equal impact on children's development are left largely outside public action.

Think in particular here of the growth in step-families. A good deal of research has pointed to the complex dynamics inherent in step-families (Robinson and Smith, 1993). For children in particular, the advent of a new 'parent' can raise all manner of emotional tension, resentment and ambiguity. To develop successfully, these relationships require considerable investment and understanding. Yet the state apparently regards the formation of step-families as unproblematic, if anything viewing them as 'solutions' to the problems of divorce and lone parenthood. Thus there are relatively few official services provided for people

entering step-families, even at the level of protecting the interests of children. These families are defined as 'normal' and as quite capable of meeting their own needs without additional support. In many respects the 'problem families' continue to be defined as those in poverty who rely on state welfare benefits and public housing. Caught in a vortex of material disadvantage, there is an ever-present tendency to redefine their problems in terms of their own personal inadequacies, despite all that is known about the difficulties of sustaining family well-being with inadequate resources.

References

Birth Statistics, (1992), Office of Population and Census Surveys, Series FM1, No. 21.

Cancian, F. (1987) *Love in America: Gender and Self-Development*, Cambridge: Cambridge University Press.

Chester, R. (1977) 'The one-parent family: deviant or variant?', in R. Chester and J. Peel (eds), *Equalities and Inequalities in Family Life*, London: Academic Press.

Crow, G. and Hardey, M. (1991) 'The housing strategies of lone parents', in M. Hardey and G. Crow (eds), *Lone Parenthood: Coping with Constraints and Making Opportunities*, Hemel Hempstead: Harvester Wheatsheaf.

Crow, G. and Hardey, M. (1992) 'Diversity and ambiguity among lone-parent households in modern Britain', in C. Marsh and S. Arber (eds), *Families and Households: Divisions and Change*, Basingstoke: Macmillan.

David, M. (1993) *Parent, Gender and Educational Reform*, Cambridge: Polity.

Donzelot, J. (1979) *The Policing of Families: Welfare versus the State*, London: Hutchinson.

Finch, J. (1987) 'Family obligations and the life course', in A. Bryman, B. Bytheway, P. Allat and T. Keil (eds), *Rethinking the Life Cycle*, Basingstoke: Macmillan.

Giddens, A. (1992) *The Transformation of Intimacy*, Cambridge: Polity.

Gittins, D. (1993) *The Family in Question: Changing Households and Familiar Ideologies* (2nd edn), Basingstoke: Macmillan.

Hardey, M. and Crow, G. (eds) (1991) *Lone Parenthood: Coping with Constraints and Making Opportunities*, Hemel Hempstead: Harvester Wheatsheaf.

Haskey, J. (1992) 'Pre-marital cohabitation and the probability of subsequent divorce', *Population Trends*, 68, 10–19.

Haskey, J. (1994) 'Estimated numbers of one-parent-families and their prevalence in Great Britain in 1991', *Population Trends*, 78, 5–19.

Millar, J. (1992) 'Lone mothers and poverty', in C. Glendinning and J. Millar (eds), *Women and Poverty in Britain: The Nineties*, Hemel Hempstead: Harvester Wheatsheaf.

Robinson, M. and Smith, D. (1993) *Step-by-Step: Focus on Stepfamilies*, Hemel Hempstead: Harvester Wheatsheaf.

Rutter, M. and Madge, N. (1976) *Cycles of Disadvantage*, London: Heinemann.

Townsend, P., Davidson, N. and Whitehead, M. (1988) *Inequalities in Health*, Harmondsworth: Penguin.

II.6
Sexuality and Sexual Relations
Siobhan Lloyd

Consider any of these scenarios:

- a social work team in which one member embarks on a sexual relationship with another;
- a family centre worker who is invited to attend a parents' night out at a local pub where the entertainment is a stripper;
- a field social worker who discloses sexual attraction to a long-standing client;
- a residential unit for older children, many of whom have been sexually abused by a trusted adult, where a staff member believes that physical affection between adults and children should be encouraged;
- a newly qualified social worker practising in a psychiatric hospital where a patient continually makes explicit sexual overtures;
- a day care worker who is accused by a centre user of being 'a raving poof';
- a worker in a youth project who discovers two under-age young people in bed together during a weekend camping trip;
- a practice teacher who becomes attracted to a student on placement;
- a residential home for older people in which a resident makes a complaint that a staff member is overly interested in helping with bathing

With more information our reaction to each situation might be influenced by a number of factors including an understanding of the power relationships involved between the two parties, the gender of a client and social worker, their sexuality, whether a behaviour is consensual, coercive or potentially abusive, or consideration of the consequences of disclosure of a relationship or potential relationship. In the absence of a professional code of ethics for social work some of the situations sketched out above might be reacted to in a way which leaves either the worker or client feeling vulnerable, exposed, victimized or further abused. The organizational response to each situation might have some similar consequences for both parties. The fact that social workers in training and practitioners of many years' standing are now looking at these sorts of issues is itself something of a transformation.

Times have indeed changed. When I first became a social work educator and trainer in the early 1980s issues relating to sex, sexuality and sexual relationships were scarcely on the training agenda. I can clearly remember my sense of panic when a student group who were nearing the end of their course asked for a day workshop on the theme of sexuality. There was little in the way of training material; there was virtually no literature. When preparing this paper I relocated the outline for that day and the reading list which was distributed to students. I was horrified to see that one of the items on that list was an article by a then-respected residential social worker who has since been exposed as a paedophile (Righton, 1977). Now there is a more comprehensive body of knowledge on topics relating to sexuality and social work and, hopefully, a heightened awareness among social workers, whether newly qualified or of longer standing, of the centrality of the issues for social workers as human beings and professional workers.

What has been the impetus for this change? Firstly, there is a recognition that sexuality like gender, class, ethnicity and creed are defining characteristics for any individual and that they all have significance too for the nuts and bolts of social work practice. By implication, therefore, an acknowledgement of their significance and their interrelatedness is crucial for social work training, as is an examination of the ways in which they can be abused, misused and exploited. A second motivating force has been the raising of the profile of child protection and, more specifically, the 'discovery' of the sexual abuse of children within families and by the child care system itself. This has ensured that the issue of exploitative sexuality will remain on the public agenda, despite any efforts to discredit the testimony of survivors of that abuse of trust and power. In this context it is vital to acknowledge the part played by adult survivors of sexual abuse through the women's movement in bringing the issue to the attention of the public, policy-makers and politicians through their courageous breaking of the silence surrounding the issue since the early 1980s.

Social work shows an historical preoccupation with sexual contagion. The common image of the poor in the nineteenth century as licentious and 'enjoying' a sexual freedom and corruption which was not available to the middle classes is one manifestation of this view. Another was the interpretation of breakdown in the family unit as arising from a lack of moral stability including 'incest, promiscuity, pederasty and prostitution' (Hart, 1979, p. 24). People became clients because their sexual behaviour was seen as different from and a threat to what was perceived as 'proper'

Five Key Points

1 An acknowledgement of issues relating to a social worker's own sexuality is an important component in good social work practice.
2 Social workers have the responsibility for maintaining sexual boundaries in a social work relationship.
3 Training on issues relating to sex, sexuality and sexual relationships is crucial in social work education.
4 Sexually abusive behaviour occurs in a myriad of ways in social work organizations.
5 In order to be able to hear issues relating to clients' sexuality, social workers need to be educated in matters sexual, sensitive in their response and aware of areas of potential difficulty.

conduct. One could argue that the same issues, albeit with a different focus, are just as prevalent within social work today. We need look no further than the moral panic surrounding single motherhood, HIV and AIDS, and teenage sexuality for evidence of this.

Consider, for example, the situation of women with learning difficulties. The Mental Deficiency Act 1913 labelled them mentally 'deficient, idiots, imbeciles and feeble minded, legitimising their detention in single sex institutions, separated from family and friends' (Williams, 1992, p. 152). This course of action was double-edged, since it reflected not only the need to protect the women from the outside world but to protect that world from the moral threat they were seen to represent. The 'problem' of the sexuality of women with learning difficulties was therefore resolved by segregation and institutionalization. Present-day community care policies can be seen to carry on this line of thinking in a rather different way, with examples of local authorities and health care trusts applying to the courts for the right to sterilize women with learning difficulties. The 'caring' rationale offered in defence of these actions by the state is that it offers protection to the women from the trauma of pregnancy and the responsibilities of child rearing and that it is an effective form of contraception. So here the granting of rights in two areas – decarceration – and the right to have intimate relationships – is paid for by the denial of rights to reproduce and to parent.

A very different example relates to the sexual preference of staff working in residential care. Heterosexual women are seen to be able to care for both sexes, young and old, because 'the act of caring renders them asexual' (Aymer, 1992, p. 192). Lesbians, on the other hand, archaically labelled potentially moral corrupters, find themselves in a curious position where their caring role neutralizes this concern. This is not the case for gay men, especially in situations where they are caring for young people or children and their sexuality immediately calls into question their 'fitness' for care work in relation to their perceived potential to abuse those in their care. The ultimate sanction by social work employers is, of course, the sacking of a gay person on the grounds of 'being a danger to children' (Brown, 1992, p. 208). The sexual double standard operating here clearly denies the extent of abuse perpetrated by heterosexual men in residential care (Parkin, 1989).

Another area in which sexual preference may become an issue relates to the process of 'coming out' whether it is by client, social worker or social worker in training. For example, some young people who have difficulty in coming to terms with their sexuality exhibit behavioural problems which lead to them coming into care. If the young person is gay they will need sensitive work and support. They may experience victimization by other children or staff,

compounding an already fragile sexual identity. If staff have not looked at the issue in training they may believe that there is something 'wrong' with being lesbian or gay and refer the young person for treatment; or they may not give the best support possible to the young person for fear of being labelled gay themselves. A more openly supportive response would be for a worker to challenge homophobic remarks or to heed the words of one worker who points out:

Some workers jump straight to safe sex. They don't ask 'are you sure he loves you' or 'what are you feeling towards him?' If there is training it is always slanted towards HIV/AIDS – thus compounding stereotypes.

(Sone, 1993, p. 18)

Coming out as a gay social worker can itself be fraught with tension and, as gay workers have testified, the issue exposes the reality that 'some parts of equal opportunities policies are sold short of others' (Sone, 1993, p. 18).

Sexuality is a significant part of all our lives. We may want to debate the usefulness of assuming that there is one sexuality when the concept is so differently expressed between cultures, from one person to another and at various points in history. Any discussion of the centrality of sexuality and, by implication of the nature of sexual relationships and sex itself, needs to begin with an exploration of what sexuality entails. Wright (1996), in a sensitive paper relating to working with men and boys on issues relating to sexuality, notes that it can be variously seen as being synonymous with sexual orientation or 'being sexy' or relating to the frequency of genital (usually penetrative) sexual intercourse. She has identified five different but related themes which are helpful in locating sexuality and its relationship to sex and gender. First, there is its biological and physical base. Sexuality includes the act of having sex, responding to sexual stimuli and fantasy and relating to other people. As such, the sexual response is physiological and located in the body's reactions. Secondly, there is the question of the function of sexual activity in any relationship, whether it is a casual encounter, a long-term partnership, consensual or not. Not only can it be a way of expressing intimacy, love and affection, but it can be used as 'a way of gaining power, paying the rent or inflicting pain' (Wright, 1996, p. 132). This takes us into the arena of sexual abuse and exploitation. Thirdly, there is the question of the way in which we manage and deal with feelings in sexual relationships. A knowledge of psychology and human relationships can help here, as can the knowledge that childhood experiences can have a hugely adverse effect on adult behaviour. This is most obvious in working with adult survivors of childhood sexual abuse. Fourthly, an understanding of the relationship between sexuality, power and gender is vital. For example, the continued equating of masculinity with power and femininity with submission has implications for the sexual expression of feelings of vulnerability and aggression. Coupled with this is the question of sexual orientation and its implications for the individual, especially when the choice of sexual partner can lead to social stigmatization or suspicion. Sexuality and identity are influenced by the cultural context in which they are constructed and this varies between classes, generations, and across ethnic and religious backgrounds.

From this it can be seen that sexuality has implications for all aspects of our lives and that it can be the vehicle for great pleasure or extremes of pain and abuse. This has a number of significant consequences for social workers. It is essential that they have an understanding of their own sexuality, no matter how confused or unsettled it feels. It means recognizing the extent to which it has

been affected by their own history and the personal significance of gender, class, religion and ethnicity. Understanding ourselves is vital to the process of understanding others and in the area of sexuality this has particular significance when social workers are called by their clients to respond to a range of issues including sexual orientation, sex education, sexual exploitation, prostitution, sexual abuse, rape, problem pregnancies and becoming sexually active.

A further complexity is that sex, sexual relationships and sexuality are features of both the private and public domain, though in the latter there is often still a

---

Three Questions

1   What professional boundaries in relation to sexuality have you encountered in your practice?
2   What would you do if you became aware of a sexual attraction towards a colleague, or a client?
3   What work are you aware you need to do in the area of sex, sexuality and sexual relationships in order to enable you to practise more effectively?

---

reluctance to acknowledge its presence. Pringle (1995) develops this theme in his discussion of 'organization sexuality'. He suggests that

sexuality constructs its existence in organisations in a variety of ways, through sexual meetings, sexual liaisons, sexual relationships, affairs, gossip, rumour, innuendo, myth as well as sexual harassment.

(Pringle, 1995, p. 33)

Organization sexuality operates across all welfare contexts. It can manifest itself in a host of ways, including the sexual abuse perpetrated by staff on service users or service users on one another or in the sexual harassment of peers. There are, however, significant difficulties in defining organization sexuality in areas which are less clear-cut. Take the example of a social work manager having a relationship with a member of staff. It is a potential minefield to determine at what point in the development of the relationship it has the potential to be seen (or to become) abusive in an organizational sense. We might debate whether this is when the relationship becomes sexual, when professional boundaries have been crossed, when they continue to work together or when their relationship has implications for line management decisions. We might also want to check out any differences in our responses if the manager was a woman and the staff member male, or vice versa. What would our reactions be if the workers were gay and would these be different if the social workers were peers within an agency? Obviously not all workplace liaisons are potentially abusive but the point remains that social workers need to have an awareness of the power relationships within their organizations and the way in which personal relationships between workers can be impinged upon by them.

Turning to the vexed question of sexual abuse within the care system, there is increasing evidence, largely from the United States, that this may be at a higher level than previously thought (Finkelhor and Williams, 1988). Residential care, foster care, day care and nursery care have all been investigated but there has been little work carried out in Britain. There are two reasons for service users to expect the highest of standards in these contexts of care. First, when children are entrusted to care provided or purchased for their safety, they have an undeniable right to an assurance that they will be as safe as humanely possible. The same applies to adults in similar circumstances. Secondly, care systems should alleviate the adversity already experienced by

service users, not compound that adversity. Finally, as Pringle (1995) chillingly attests, if an abuser operates within the welfare system it is likely that he or she will gain access to large numbers of children or adults to abuse, and some abusers will deliberately gravitate to welfare work. Police checks will identify only a small number of abusers since, in common with sexual abuse in other contexts, the abuse is more likely to go unreported and the abuser undetected (Margolin, 1991).

Russell (1993) argues that there are two prevailing myths regarding the abuse of clients which persist within all helping professions. The first, that *'our professionals don't abuse'* is, of course, no longer sustainable within social work, as the profession struggles to come to terms with disclosures and inquiries into the sexual abuse of children in residential, day and foster care. The second is portrayed in the assertion that *'of course we talk about it'*. This, argues Russell, is profoundly misleading because the words which are used fail to represent the myriad of experiences and behaviour which constitute abuse. One need look no further than the term 'sexual abuse' – now almost anodyne in itself but representing a continuum of behaviour with sexual glances at one end and gross invasions of the body and psyche at the other (Hall and Lloyd, 1993).

In the final analysis all social workers, whether they are in training, new to social work or of many years' standing have a responsibility to work on their own issues around sex, sexual relationships and sexuality if they are to practise in a responsible and ethical manner. Such work may have an educational component. It will also entail a high level of self-awareness, being comfortable with the language of sexual expression and being able to talk explicitly about sex. This will inevitably mean that long-held views are challenged and open to change but, equally importantly, it means that the social worker will become more self-aware and, in turn, more open to others who are struggling to express doubt, distress and anxiety in relation to sexual matters.

towards ensuring that clients are less likely to experience abuses of power in therapeutic work with social workers. If this happens clients will also have more of an assurance that they will be heard on issues relating to their own sexuality and sexual relationships.

Further Reading

1 Langan, M. and Day, L. (eds) (1992) *Women, Oppression and Social Work: Issues in Anti-discriminatory Practice*, London: Routledge.
2 Pringle, K. (1995) *Men, Masculinities and Social Welfare*, London: UCL Press.
3 Russell, J. (1993) *Out of Bounds: Sexual Exploitation in Counselling and Therapy*, London: Sage.

In relation to what is 'appropriate professional behaviour' Russell (1993) has the final word: it is behaviour where

- the social worker sets and takes responsibility for clear boundaries with the client;
- the social worker does not exploit the client either covertly or overtly for his or her own gratification;
- the client's needs are the dominant focus of the relationship and work; and
- the social worker has an awareness of the intentions implied in communications with the client and an understanding of how this is understood by the client.

None of this will be easy. It is likely to be fraught and messy at times. It may cause acute distress and it may well have implications for the social worker's own intimate relationships. Hopefully, however, the breaking of silence on matters relating to sex, sexuality and sexual relationships and the training which follows will go a considerable way

References

Aymer, C. (1992) 'Sexuality in residential care', in M. Langan and L. Day, *Women, Oppression and Social Work*, London: Routledge, pp. 186–201.

Brown, H. C. (1992) 'Lesbians, the state and social work practice', in M. Langan and L. Day, *Women, Oppression and Social Work: Issues in Anti-Discriminatory Practice*, London: Routledge, pp. 201–19.

Finkelhor, D. and Williams, L. M. (1988) *Nursery Crimes: Sexual Abuse in Day Care*, London: Sage.

Hall, L. and Lloyd, S. (1993) *Surviving Child Sexual Abuse. A Handbook for Helping Women Challenge their Past* (2nd edn), Brighton: Falmer Press.

Hart, J. (1979) *Social Work and Sexual Conduct*, London: Routledge.

Hearn, J. and Parkin, W. (1987) *'Sex' at 'Work': The Power and Paradox of Organisation Sexuality*, Brighton: Wheatsheaf.

Langan, M. and Day, L. (eds) (1992) *Women, Oppression and Social Work: Issues in Anti-discriminatory Practice*, London: Routledge.

Margolin, L. (1991) 'Child sexual abuse by non-related caregivers', *Child Abuse and Neglect*, 15, 213–21.

Parkin, W. (1989) 'Private experiences in the public domain: sexuality and residential care organisations', in J. Hearn, P. Sheppard, G. Tancred-Sheriff and G. Burrell, *The Sexuality of Organisation*, London: Sage, pp. 110–25.

Pringle, K. (1995) *Men, Masculinities and Social Welfare*, London: UCL Press.

Righton, P. (1977) 'Sex and the residential social worker', *Social Work Today* 8(19).

Russell, J. (1993) *Out of Bounds: Sexual Exploitation in Counselling and Therapy*, London: Sage.

Sone, K. (1993) 'Coming out at work', *Community Care*, 7 October, 18–19.

Williams, F. (1992) 'Women with disabilities are women too', in M. Langan and L. Day, *Women, Oppression and Social Work: Issues in Anti-discriminatory Practice*, London: Routledge, pp. 14–25.

Wright, C. (1996) 'Sexuality, feminism and work with men', in K. Cavanagh and V. E. Cree (eds), *Working with Men. Feminism and Social Work*, London: Routledge, pp. 128–47.

Part III
The Human Life Cycle

Introduction to Part III

Developmental psychology is not static, and the chapters on infancy and childhood both reflect the vibrancy of research and theory building characteristic of the field. Adolescence is a time often thought to be turbulent, though Martin Herbert suggests that we should not exaggerate its disruptive impact; Lena Robinson's chapter introduces us to the additional problems facing black children as they adapt to the conflicting pressures caused by being a minority group in a multi-cultural society. The process of partnership and parenting dominates interpersonal relations in maturity, and in the twenty-first century the process of ageing is likely to last a long time. Ian Philp even suggests the horrific possibility of interfering with the process of intrinsic ageing to the extent that 'put simply, we could live for seven hundred years, but the last six hundred would be spent in a state of advanced dementia'.

III.1
Infancy
Gillian Harris

The period of infancy is usually defined by developmental psychologists as being the first two years of life. There are many focal points of study in this particular field, but perhaps one of the most interesting questions we can ask about infants is; how and when do they become social beings? When do they begin to recognize others; and when does the first relationship form between the infant and caregiver?

One of the main problems, however, with studying infants is that it is difficult to measure their skills and preferences. We cannot rely on verbal response, or even upon controlled motor movements in the early months. Research carried out on early developmental preferences has, therefore, to rely upon certain assumptions. These are, that the infant will turn, or orient, towards pleasing, or familiar, stimuli; that the infant will preferentially look at pleasing, or familiar, stimuli; that the infant will modify its sucking response to experience pleasant, or familiar, stimuli; and that when the infant is bored with (or has habituated to) a known stimulus, it will preferentially respond to a novel stimulus. Most studies of new-born infants rely upon these methodologies.

Early Development

The infant is born with certain innate preferences, and these are usually for salient stimuli within the environment that have survival value. The most salient stimuli are those that are linked with other humans, in that infants are relatively helpless for many years and must attract another to care for them. New-born infants have specific perceptual preferences, for speech-type sounds, and for visual stimuli which, if grouped together, comprise face-type configurations (Goren, Sarty and Wu, 1975). New-born infants also prefer sweet-tasting solutions. This means, of course, that the neonate prefers stimuli associated with the caregiver; human speech, the human face and, of course, breast milk – which is sweet.

Following birth and even in some cases, prior to birth, there is a period of very rapid learning, a period in which the infant learns to identify known tastes, smells, sounds and faces. The new-born infant shows a preference for the mother's voice (Decasper and Fifer, 1980), shows a preference for the mother's face (Bushnell, Sai and Mullin, 1989) and a preference for the smell of the mother's milk (Cernoch and Porter, 1985). This does not mean that the infant recognizes the mother, but that the infant prefers things that are familiar. Innate neonatal preferences can also be modified very rapidly by learning if this modification has survival value. If an infant is given bitter-tasting milk from birth, then because the bitter taste is associated with a positive calorie intake, then the infant will learn to like it, even though infants usually find bitter tastes aversive.

Although the infant seems to prefer the known properties of the mother, this does not mean that a relationship has formed. There is no evidence to support the idea of early 'bonding' between infant and mother; despite the findings by Klaus et al. (1972) which seemed to support the 'bonding' hypothesis. More recent studies do not support the idea that early contact between infant and mother has a beneficial effect upon mothering behaviour in the long-term (Svejda, Campos and Emde, 1980).

Given the dangers of the birth process it would give the infant no advantage to become attached to the biological mother at, or immediately after, birth. In fact, the new-born infant does not appear to show any signs of specific pleasure in the mother's presence, or distress at separation from her. This absence of early attachment means of course that the first relationship does not have to be with the biological mother; it does not even have to be with a female adult. Research has shown that men can, and do, react to and interact with infants in the same manner as women, especially where they have had experience in caregiving (Field, 1978). Infants can form an attachment to their fathers even if they do not form an attachment to their mothers. In extended families, infants might form an attachment to family members other than the main care provider (Schaffer and Emerson, 1964). The function of the early preference shown by the infant for the caregiver seems to be to give the appearance of social intent, to make the caregiver feel that the infant does recognize them. As a result, the caregiver is more likely to feel attached to the infant, and to provide care.

Social-cognition and Attachment Formation

In order to decide whether or not an attachment has formed between infant and caregiver we must observe and measure infant behaviours; but which behaviours are likely to indicate that an attachment has formed?

Five Key Points

1 Following birth, there is a period of very rapid learning.
2 There is no evidence to support the idea of early 'bonding' between infant and mother.
3 A 'fear of strangers' response is not usually observed before about ten months. At the same age the child can remember sustained patterns of interaction specific to each caregiver.
4 Infants of ten months or so show separation distress, are more discriminatory in affect, smile more at the people with whom they are familiar and are more wary of strangers. They are social beings.
5 Attachment formation, infant to caregiver, is dependent on consistent and reciprocal interactions occurring across time – usually between three and twelve months.

One affiliative behaviour, smiling, is present from birth. The neonate will smile in response to various internal and external stimuli that are found pleasing. The smile gradually becomes more discriminatory over time until it is only observed as a response to social stimuli – that is other people. Eventually, the smile is reserved only for familiar people. This only tells us, however, that the infant can discriminate between those who are known, and those who are not known.

A better indicator of attachment is thought to be distress at separation, a behaviour not observed until about six months, when the infant will cry if left by the primary caregiver. Similarly, discriminatory responses, which are fear responses directed towards a stranger, are not usually observed until the infant is around ten-months old. This 'fear of strangers' response is less marked if the 'stranger' looks familiar to known caregivers, behaves in a positive manner to the infant or if the caregiver behaves in a positive manner towards the 'stranger'.

This is possibly because the infant is able, at this age, to match internal representations of known adults with the external representation of the stranger, and find a mismatch (Kagan, 1976). We could say, that at this age, the infant is able to not only recognize, but also to recall images of absent caregivers. This means in effect that the infant has achieved person permanence; the child is aware that the caregiver continues to exist when out of the sight of the infant, and has an existence separate from that of the infant.

We would expect that the concept of person permanence would be attained at about the same age as object permanence; the understanding that objects continue to exist when out of sight of the infant. It was thought that infants did not attain object permanence until the age of eighteen months (Piaget, 1952). But the task that infants were asked to do in this study was quite complex and mapped onto other abilities that possibly do not develop until the second year. If we look at research studies carried out on purely perceptual tasks (Baillargeon, Spelke and Wasserman, 1985) then the infant seems to be able to understand that objects do continue to exist, even though they can no longer be seen, and that the objects have certain immutable properties in that one cannot pass through another. In a far simpler task (Hood and Willets, 1986), six-month-old infants were observed to reach out for objects in the dark that they had observed in the light. Infants do then seem to develop the concept of object permanence at and around the time at which they develop person permanence. We might also say that, to be able to form an attachment to someone, it is necessary to be able to sustain a memory of them in their absence. Research studies certainly do suggest that infants retain some memory for events which are experienced as early as ten months (Fivush, 1994).

Infants of ten months are also able not only to recognize familiar caregivers, and

this would include siblings, but to remember sustained patterns of interaction specific to each caregiver. Infants can play quite elaborate social games with familiar others; games of give and take, games of hide and look. During these games, the infant is able to predict the partner's behaviour, to attempt to elicit such behaviour and to respond to it appropriately. Caregivers usually also respond in quite a specific way to the infants, not only do they engage in specific 'games', but all adults and 'experienced' children use a unique form of speech and behavioural mannerism when interacting with infants and young children. The speech style, sometimes termed 'motherese', uses lots of exaggerations of pitch and speed, with many questions, imitations, repetitions and extensions of the infant's own utterances. This speech style acts mainly as an attentional marker for the infant. When someone uses such a speech style then the infant is more likely to react to them, and interact with them. The behaviours which accompany this speech style, such as exaggerated facial expression and extensive eye contact, also serve to engage and maintain the infant's attention within the dyadic interaction (Gleitman et al., 1984). In this way the infant learns, not how to talk, for that ability is innate, but how to structure social interactions with others. The infant's learns what to expect from others. When strange adults use this familiar style of interaction then infants are likely to be less wary of them; if strangers address or behave to them in the usual 'adult' style of interaction then the infant will be more wary of them (Kaye, 1982). The infant is also able, from the age of ten months, to use the caregiver as a source of information, that is they can engage in social referencing (Feinman and Lewis, 1983). And although we might say that an infant of this age is not fully aware of another's mind state, infants are able to interpret the adult's emotional expression. If an adult smiles at, or behaves positively towards, a stranger then the infant will be less wary of that stranger.

Attachment Classifications

Infants of ten months or so show separation distress, are more discriminatory in affect, smile more at the people with whom they are familiar and are more wary of strangers; and these are all behaviours which we would expect to observe between adults where an emotional bond has formed. It is assumed, therefore, that by this age infants are likely to have formed attachments, and that attachment behaviour between infant and caregiver can be measured. There is one standardized measure of infant—adult attachment that is most frequently used in research studies; the procedure is called the 'strange situation', and was first devised by Mary Ainsworth (Ainsworth et al., 1978). It is usually carried out when the infant is mobile, at about 14 months, and entails monitoring of the infant's behaviour during a series of manoeuvres in which the mother (or father) and a 'stranger' alternately leave the room and return. The infant is left at one point with the stranger, and at a second point, entirely alone. Separation, reunion and exploratory behaviours are specifically noted. The infant's behaviour in this situation tends to fall into one of three categories; two of which are deemed insecurely attached, one of which is deemed securely attached. The securely attached infants explore the strange environment with some confidence, and there is a difference between the ways in which they respond to the parent and to the stranger. The secure infant shows some distress on separation, and shows pleasure at reunion with the parent; but not so with the stranger. Insecure avoidant infants tend to ignore the

parent. Insecure anxious infants, however, tend to be very clingy towards the parent in the strange situation and do not explore the environment. They also become extremely distressed at separation from the parent and rather ambivalent and angry upon reunion.

In the original studies approximately 66 per cent of a sample of children were observed to be securely attached, 20 per cent avoidantly attached, and 12 per cent ambivalently attached, when observed with the mother.

It has been suggested that this behaviour, shown by the infant, merely reflects differences in infant temperament. However, an infant can display insecure behaviour with one parent but secure behaviour with the other (Sroufe, 1985). This is not to say that

---

Three Questions

1 How and when do attachments form?
2 What methods have developmental psychologists used to observe infant behaviour?
3 How do patterns of attachment appear to affect infant behaviour?

---

infant temperament does not play any part in determining the relationship between infant and caregiver, but that it does not explain all of the behavioural differences observed in the 'strange situation'. Cultural differences have, however, been observed in the percentages of infants who fall into the three categories (Grossman and Grossman, 1981). Therefore, differences in child-rearing methods, or expectations about the achievement of autonomy, will affect the mode of interaction in the infant–parent dyad and hence the attachment category attributed to that relationship.

We can gain some insight into how and when this first attachment relationship is formed, by observing the behaviour of the parents towards infants who are given different attachment classifications. Observations carried out in the home showed that a mother's behaviour towards her infant could explain the infant's responses to her (Ainsworth, Blehar and Waters, 1978). Mothers of infants that were rated as securely attached behaved in a consistent and sensitively responsive manner towards their infants. Mothers of insecurely attached children behaved in either a rejecting, or in an inconsistent fashion towards their infants. It could be said then, that the infants respond to the mothers' behaviour towards them. Those infants who are treated consistently and responsively become securely attached and discriminating in affect. Those infants whose mothers reject them show avoidant behaviour (an absence of attachment). Those mothers who are inconsistent in their behaviour to their infants have anxiously attached children, that is children who cannot predict what the attachment figure's behaviour towards them is going to be.

Attachment formation, infant to caregiver, would seem to be dependent upon consistent and reciprocal interactions which occur across time. The process does not seem to start before the age of three months, and is possibly complete by the end of the first year. It has been suggested, most notably by Bowlby (1953), that an attachment to a primary caregiver must form within the first two years of life for the subsequent optimal mental health of the child. However, in single case studies of children deprived of the opportunity to form attachments in the first six years of life (Clarke and Clarke, 1976), subsequent attachments have been observed to foster parents. If there is a critical period for attachment formation then it would appear to be quite a long one. In normal family life, infants usually form a hierarchy of attachments to available family members or caregivers; and this

hierarchy seems to serve a protective function for the infant. The availability of multiple caregivers also means that the likelihood of forming a secure attachment with at least one available caregiver is increased.

We might conclude then, that infants do not become truly social beings until the end of the first year of life, and that the ability to form attachments is based upon the acquisition of specific stages in cognitive development, and upon the availability of a consistent reciprocal interaction with another.

Further Reading

1   Field, T. (1990) *Infancy*, Cambridge, Mass.: Harvard University Press.
2   Schaffer, H. R. (1990) *Making Decisions about Children*, Oxford: Blackwell.
3   Sluckin, W., Herbert, M. and Sluckin, A. (1984) *Maternal Bonding*, Oxford: Blackwell.

References

Ainsworth, M. D. S., Blehar, M. and Waters, E. (1978) *Patterns of Attachment*, Hillsdale, NJ: Erlbaum

Baillargeon, R., Spelke, E. S. and Wasserman, S. (1985) 'Object permanence in 5-month-old infants', *Cognition*, 20, 191–208.

Bowlby, J. (1953) *Child Care and the Growth of Love*, Harmondsworth: Penguin Books.

Bushnell, I. W. R., Sai, F. and Mullin, J. T. (1989) 'Neonatal recognition of the mother's face', *British Journal of Developmental Psychology*, 7, 3–15.

Cernoch, J. M. and Porter, R. H. (1985) 'Recognition of maternal axillary odours by infants', *Child Development*, 56, 1593–8.

Clarke, A. M. and Clarke, A. D. (1976) *Early Experience: Myth and Evidence*, London: Open Books.

DeCasper, A. J. and Fifer, W. (1980) 'Of human bonding; newborns prefer their mothers' voices', *Science*, 208, 1174–6.

Feinman, S. and Lewis, M. (1983) 'Social referencing at ten-months; a second order effect on infants' responses to strangers', *Child Development*, 54, 753–71.

Field, T. (1978) 'Interaction behaviours of primary

versus secondary caretaker fathers', *Developmental Psychology*, 14, 183–4.

Fivush, R. (ed.) (1994) *A Special Issue of Memory – Long Term Retention of Infant Memories*, Hove: LEA.

Gleitman, L., Newport, E. and Gleitman, H. (1984) 'The current status of the motherese hypothesis', *Journal of Child Language*, 11, 43–79.

Goren, C., Sarty, M. and Wu, P. (1975) 'Visual following and pattern discrimination of face-like stimuli by newborn infants', *Pediatrics*, 56, 544–9.

Grossman, K. and Grossman, K. (1981) 'Parent–infant attachment relationships in Bielefeld', in K. Immelman (ed.), *Behavioural Development: The Bielefeld Interdisciplinary Project*, New York: Cambridge University Press.

Hood, B. and Willets, P. (1986) 'Reaching in the dark to an object's remembered position; evidence for object permanence in 5-month-old infants', *British Journal of Developmental Psychology*, 4, 57–66.

Kagan, J. (1976) 'Emergent themes in human development', *Scientific American*, 64, 186–96.

Kaye, K. (1982) *The Mental and Social Life of Babies*, London: Methuen.

Klaus, M. H., Jerauld, R., Kreger, N., McAlpine, W., Steffa, M. and Kennel, J. H. (1972) 'Maternal attachment – importance of the first post-partum days', *New England Journal of Medicine*, 286, 460–3.

Piaget, J. (1952) *The Origin of Intelligence in the Child*, New York: Basic Books.

Schaffer, H. R. and Emerson, P. E. (1964) 'The development of social attachments in infancy', *Monographs of the Society for Research in Child Development*, 29, 3.

Sroufe, L. A. (1985) 'Attachment classifications from the perspective of infant–caregiver relationships and infant temperament', *Child Development*, 56, 1–14.

Svejda, M. J., Campos, J. J. and Emde, R. N. (1980) 'Mother–infant "bonding"; a failure to generalize', *Child Development*, 51, 775–9. Thomas, A. and Chess, S. (1977) *Temperament and Development*, New York: Bruner/Mazel.

When social workers think about childhood from infancy to adolescence, they need to be aware of the specific features of the period which tend to mark certain stages, such as developing language or coping with the first demands of school. But they also need to be aware of the continuous tasks, such as building self-esteem or defining an identity, which flow from birth through infancy, childhood, adolescence and, some would argue, continue to evolve in adult life (Sugarman, 1986). Although social workers must be familiar with both kinds of evidence of healthy development, it is often the relationship-based areas of development which social workers are best placed to observe and assess because of their perspective on the child in her social context – the family, the playgroup, the school and the community.

Dependency and Autonomy in Pre-school Children

The early attachment relationships which are established during infancy develop and change focus during the toddler and pre-school years. Fahlberg (1991) suggests that in the first year of life the parent needs to do whatever will build the child's *trust*. Understanding this process is helpful in thinking about how the development of a secure attachment leads to the child's experience of the attachment figure as a secure base (Bowlby, 1969). During the second year, in the context of the child's experience of security, the

parent needs to respond in whatever way will make the child feel more *capable* (Fahlberg, 1991). The task of this period is to begin the move from the *dependency* of infancy to a gradual sense of *autonomy*. This development is a challenge to both the child and the parent. The toddler often goes through a phase of assertive or oppositional behaviour as she learns the power of saying 'mine' and 'no'. Assertiveness can be associated with pleasure and also with anxiety. As the sense of a *psychological* separation from the parent develops, the child can become anxious and apprehensive about *physical* separation and become clingy. Behaviour at this stage is neither consistent nor apparently rational. The child who one day is demanding the freedom to put on her own shoes and gaining obvious pleasure from her new-found abilities, the next day may be refusing to walk and be demanding to be spoon-fed. The lesson to be learned most vividly from toddlers, but which is relevant throughout childhood, is that although children's development may be seen as broadly following in stages, a child's anxiety and uncertainty about the implications of progress are likely to mean frequent regressions before the drive to move forward reasserts itself. This pattern results from the fact that all developments in childhood are associated to some degree with a sense of loss. As soon as you can walk, you gain the freedom to pick up the toy you have your eye on but you lose the regular physical comfort of being carried around. Once you can feed yourself, you can control the speed at which you eat and enjoy the sensation of smearing the food around your face but there is a risk that your mother or father may go in the next room and watch television.

The challenge for the child at each point is to come to terms with the element of loss and to learn age- and stage-appropriate ways of getting their needs met. The challenge for parents in this period is to allow the child some flexibility and regression while giving appropriate encouragement to the child to enjoy and develop new skills. The child who likes to be cuddled may learn to bring a book or toy to the parent in such a way as to require the parent to pick her up and hold her on a lap. The child is therefore allowed to be cuddled while exploring new items of interest. Communication which leads to needs being met, however, takes a sensitive receiver as well as a competent expression of need. If the child's request to be picked up is rejected because 'she's a big girl now', she may try lying on the floor and screaming. This is even less likely to get her needs met and important lessons fail to be learned about age-appropriate behaviour.

Parents who get into difficulties at this stage have often been unable to cope with the challenge to their *control* which a three-year old may represent. Parents who are feeling under stress in other areas of their lives are even less likely to feel comfortable with the idea that a small child appears to be openly defying them. Dunn's research (1988) showed that the majority of two–three-year olds persisted in demands or did what they had just been told not to do. What is more, although many children were simply angry and defiant, a good number would be actually smiling at the parent and teasing them as they defied them. For most parents, such behaviour is immediately recognizable as part of a common and temporary phase but some children may be at risk because of what

Five Key Points

1 Pre-school children gradually move from the dependency of infancy to a sense of autonomy and self-efficacy.
2 By the age of three, children have a sophisticated understanding of others' feelings and are already learning about the social world.
3 By the time children start school, they need to have many skills. Social workers need to be able to identify children who are not negotiating the tasks of the pre-school period successfully.
4 Between the ages of five and eleven, children refine their sense of self, expand their knowledge of the social world and develop standards of behaviour and strategies for ensuring conformity with the dominant culture.
5 Cognitive, emotional, behavioural and social development proceed together and affect each other. Problems in one area of development, such as language delay or being bullied at school must be put in the context of all areas of development if the behaviour is to be understood.

parents attribute to the child and to the behaviour (Bugental et al., 1989). The impact of parental attributions may mean that defiant behaviour is seen as confirmation that a child is responsible for parenting failure and is *constitutionally* a bad or difficult child. In this context, normal developmental processes of assertiveness are seen as *persecutory* and as beyond the influence or control of the parent. If the behaviour is perhaps further linked, for example, with a previous child who died or an absent parent whom the child is felt to resemble, then the *meaning* of the child's behaviour will contribute to a further distortion in the parental response (Reder and Duncan, 1995). Research has also shown that where parents resort to persistently negative responses to the child, the child becomes more stressed and is often more persistently negative to the parent (Bugental et al., 1989). Where parents are unpredictable and punitive, the child can appear to be frozen and be physically immobilized by anxiety.

Although defiant behaviour is usually an important expression of the child's growing ability to see themselves as a separate person, there is evidence that serious behaviour problems, or *conduct disorders*, in pre-school children may persist into middle childhood (Richman et al., 1982). Behaviour, therefore, needs to be examined in the light of the other important processes of this period in order to distinguish between normal development, of which there is a wide range, and the problems which need to be recognized and helped.

Development of Social Understanding

From birth, the child is learning lessons about how the world works. Early connections are made which help the child feel safe and allow her to postpone satisfaction. Even young babies are able to learn after a while that they can stop crying as soon as they hear the parent's footsteps on the stairs, because they can predict that a cuddle or a bottle or both is going to happen next. The parent who says at the point that the child stops crying, 'she didn't really need me' or even 'she is being a nuisance deliberately', misses the chance to help the baby learn that lesson. Looking for patterns in relationships and social behaviour, starting to learn the rules, is a critical part of the early experiences of children. The sound of the footstep starts to represent in a symbolic sense the beginning of the feed. This predictability, the reciprocity between parent and child and the development of trust in symbols are important elements in developing

language. Once a comprehension of language is developed, the mother can say, 'Now we are going shopping', and the child will piece together a whole picture from getting a coat on, walking down the road, shopping, having some sweets and so on. Gradually the child will understand, 'We are going shopping *after* I've done the washing up', and will survive the wait. Once the child is able to put her own thoughts into words, she will be able to ask 'When going to see Grandad?' and be told, 'When Mum gets home from work'. The likelihood that events follow each other starts the child on the way to understanding that two and two always make four, that life has patterns which can be relied on.

Predictability in the young child's world enables her to develop that feeling of competence which emerges from a capacity to produce an impact on her world. The two-year old climbs into her chair after seeing her Dad put her lunch in the dish and anticipating what comes next. But predictability also brings mastery of her feelings. Piaget, who is best known for his work on cognitive development, believed that the *link between cognitive and emotional development* during childhood was fundamental. Wolff summarizes Piaget's views thus:

Affectivity constitutes the energetics of behaviour, the motives from which intelligent action springs. Feeling states, on the other hand, depend on the individual's perceptions and comprehension and these form part of his or her intelligence. Affective and cognitive development proceed together.
(Wolff, 1989, p. 115)

A key part of what we think of as the secure base effect of attachment, an *emotional* connection, is to free the child to *think*, to explore and to find out about her environment. The child's *ability to play* is used as part of the assessment of the quality of a child's attachments (Ainsworth, 1978). In everyday life, the child who is preoccupied about getting emotional needs met and fears separation, will find it hard to be interested in the leaf which floats by or the sound of the rain. The child has a natural awareness of stimuli from birth which, if needs are met in a way which can be described as 'good enough' to use Winnicott's expression (Winnicott, 1965), will continue through childhood and will lead to learning. To a large extent the environment merely has to facilitate that process. This facilitative environment depends on the nature of the available relationships more than it does on the nature of the available toys. The significance of the child being able to *play* is that it enables the child to explore the physical world of wooden bricks or saucepan lids and use them symbolically as beefburgers and plates. When socio-dramatic play begins and the child learns to role play the parent who feeds the baby or gets cross, she safely explores social situations which give pleasure or cause anxiety and develops her ability to see the world through the eyes of others.

Learning about the social world initially requires the child to learn from the patterns of relationships which she, herself, experiences; the impact others have on her and the impact she has on them. But a sophisticated operator within the social world needs also to learn about *how other people feel and how other people think*. This area has attracted a considerable amount of research as children's capacity to comprehend the subtleties of 'other minds' has emerged as far more sophisticated than had been thought. This sophistication has important survival value for the child since communication of needs, practical and emotional, relies on some degree of understanding of how certain kinds of communications will be received and an ability to predict reactions. These lessons are learned with parents, grandparents, brothers and sisters. Increasingly, children start to become skilled observers of relationships *between* other family members and to learn lessons from them. The child is then likely to move into relationships with other children. Within the peer group, the child learns a whole new set of rules and the skills needed to establish relationships and negotiate within them.

Judy Dunn has led the field in studying this area of development, by observing young children in their own homes rather than testing their capacities in laboratory conditions (1988, 1993). She found that within what she called 'the drama of their everyday world', children are highly motivated and emotionally involved, and therefore much more skilled in negotiating and learning about how the

---

Three Questions

1 What might be the impact of abuse and neglect in early childhood on a child's self-esteem and identity?
2 What is the importance of peer group relationships for healthy development in childhood?
3 What are the factors which might enable the child to be resilient and to make good developmental progress at home and at school in spite of adversity?

---

world works than had been thought by writers like Piaget. In her research, she found that by the age of three, children were demonstrating an *understanding of other's feelings*, 'the causes of pain, distress, anger, pleasure and displeasure, comfort and fear in others as well as in themselves. They joke, play with, and tell stories about these feeling states in self and other' (1988, p. 170). Out of this early responsiveness, she suggests, comes 'the foundations for the *moral* virtues of caring, considerateness and kindness'.

Children of this age are also demonstrating an *understanding of others' goals and intentions*. Dunn suggests that an understanding of feelings and intentions leads to 'an interest in transgressions of acceptable or expected behaviour and an understanding of social rules and family relationships'. Children's use of humour, jokes and teasing can be seen in this context as important evidence of the child's growing ability to use their understanding of adults and other children to anticipate and have an impact on other people in their lives.

The ability to lie, which seems to develop between the age of two and four (Lewis et al., 1989), can also be seen as an indicator of social knowledge. Telling a successful lie for the first time is important evidence to the child that the adult cannot know or control her thoughts (Garbarino et al., 1992). Lies which protect self, 'I didn't take the biscuit' and lies which protect others, 'That's a lovely dress' and lies just for fun, such as the 'tooth fairy', are common in adult interactions and rely on a knowledge of the etiquette of social interaction. The inability to lie is just as pathological as compulsive lying. Again, like defiance in toddlers, behaviours which many adults find hard to tolerate in children can be an important part of learning.

Dunn and other researchers have made a strong case for rejecting Piaget's notion that young children are 'egocentric', in the sense of lacking the ability to understand and take into account the feelings of others. However, it is the case that children, and particularly children facing stressful situations, are often egocentric in the sense of holding themselves responsible for much of what happens to them. *Magical thinking*, as it is often called, is not of course unique to childhood. A bereaved adult may feel, 'If I hadn't been angry with my partner that day, he may not have had that car accident'. Nevertheless, a sense of omnipotence can be particularly striking in children between the ages of four and seven or eight, who are still trying to make sense of their world (Jewett, 1993).

Social workers need to be constantly alert to the ways in which children blame themselves for the separation of parents, for parental illness and, most commonly, for the abuse which they have experienced. Because this is often a dark secret, the child may act out in her behaviour the feelings of shame and guilt rather than putting them into words.

Developing and Refining a Sense of Self

Much of the process of social learning derives from and contributes to the child's developing sense of self. The emotional significance of attachment to parents and the tension which follows between dependence and autonomy in a world of more powerful and more competent others motivates the child to find a place for herself in the social world. The child's sense of 'self-efficacy' (Dunn, 1988) develops as the child finds the skills to operate within relationships. The child learns to oppose others where necessary, negotiate where necessary and co-operate where necessary. The *self-esteem* which is derived from early attachments and security should during this phase evolve through increasing competence.

For children whose experience of early relationships has not included developing a sense of trust and attachment which provides a secure base, self-esteem may be fragile. Children who live in families where there are frequent changes either in the physical environment or in the relationships and the emotional climate, do not experience the reassuring and predictable patterns which encourage them to go on to the next stage and develop a sense of self-efficacy. This becomes particularly important when we consider what is needed for the child to make a successful transition to school.

If we consider what Bentovim says a child needs to have achieved by the age of five, we can see how significant these early learning experiences will be for the child's successful move into school. He suggests that the five-year old should:

- Be emotionally ready to learn;
- have a clear idea of herself as a person;
- have the ability to relate to other children;
- have the ability to control and postpone urgent needs; and
- have the ability to use initiative to find gratification in play and activities which are socially acceptable. (Bentovim, 1972, p. 580)

These, Bentovim concludes, are 'many of the skills necessary for eventual adult independent existence'.

The primary-school years from five to eleven have often been seen as a relatively quiet phase developmentally compared with the dramatic changes from birth to five and during adolescence. This is also reflected in Freud's labelling of this period as 'latency' within his psycho-sexual model of development. More recently, it has come to be seen as a period of *consolidation* of much of the learning about self and relationships which we now know has been initiated in the pre-school years.

Collins (1984) suggested that the four key tasks of the development of *self-concept* in middle childhood are:

- Developing a relatively stable and comprehensive understanding of the self;
- refining one's understanding of how the social world works;
- developing standards and expectations of one's own behaviour;
- developing strategies for controlling or managing one's behaviour.

The emphasis on developing a sense of self has important implications for much of social work practice with this age group. We know, for example, from research on the psychology of adoption, that adopted children are particularly curious about their origins around the age of eight or nine (Brodzinsky, 1992). Children in foster care also need to make sense of where they fit and can feel very unsettled by change of home and change in school. The highest breakdown rates in foster care are for the five- to eleven-year olds, rather than for adolescents as one might expect (Berridge and Cleaver, 1987). Children in middle childhood are well able to talk about their situation and they need to have their feelings about their situation listened to carefully if their anxieties are to be recognized.

Although each of Collins' key tasks has connections with Dunn's work on pre-school children, the impact of the school environment, the increased distance from parental control of day-to-day life and the intensity of peer group relationships during this period create a significant shift in the child's development. Specifically, they require the child to move even further towards understanding what is required and expected by the wider society. What is more, they place the emphasis on the child understanding the standards of others and then establishing her own. The specific nature of these standards and expectations will inevitably be very culturally specific. Some societies, for example, encourage individualism, expect children to express their individual needs and are inclined to favour children who are assertive. In others, the most important lesson for children to learn is that where there is a conflict, what is in the best interests of the family or the

Further Reading

1 Bee, H. (1995) *The Developing Child*, New York: HarperCollins.
2 Dunn, J. (1988) *The Beginnings of Social Understanding*, Oxford: Blackwell.
3 Howe, D. (1995) *Attachment Theory for Social Work Practice*, Basingstoke: Macmillan.

village or the community must take priority over the child's individual wishes. What is important is for a child to learn the rules which are appropriate to their particular culture. Of course, children are regularly exposed to conflicting cultures, most obviously children from ethnic minority families or minority religions. For many of these children, the challenge will be the need to understand both social worlds, learn to operate in both and to that extent incorporate both identities. Although adolescence is regularly seen as the stage of establishing identity, Maxime (1986) suggests that it is during the period from seven to twelve that children are developing an understanding of the meaning of their racial identity.

Sense of self during this period will also include significant areas such as the development of gender identity. We know that by the age of two, children are choosing stereotypical toys and are already associating certain tasks with men and women. Given the child's need to register patterns in the social world, this is not perhaps so surprising. Two-year olds are also able to label themselves and others by gender, although it is not till about five that a child understands that gender is constant regardless of other external changes such as clothing or hair-style (Bee, 1995). Cross-cultural research has found that stereotyping by gender on certain characteristics, such as aggressions, strength and cruelty for men and weakness, gentleness and appreciativeness for women, is almost universal and that for many children these stereotypes become more fixed between the ages of five and eight (Williams and Best, 1990).

What is apparent from Collins' list of tasks is that it emphasizes *cognitive skills*, rather than emotional development. However, we know that an *understanding* of the self must be linked with *affective* qualities, such as self-esteem and the ability to form emotionally satisfying

relationships with friends as well as family members. When we think of the social skills required to enable a child to make friends, the ability to be appropriately assertive while also being appropriately concerned for the other child's feelings, the ability to negotiate and co-operate, it is not hard to see the complex interconnections between the cognitive skills, the emotional qualities and the child's behaviour. It is the emotional intensity of the child's social world which leads to the distress felt about all kinds of bullying. Making sense of self in relationships and coping with the rule breakers who cultivate conflictual rather than co-operative relationships forces the child to draw on both cognitive and emotional strengths to protect the self-esteem. Children who have not experienced healthy relationships during the pre-school period find this process of negotiation very stressful and often lack the necessary skills.

Conclusion

This account of childhood has focused on some of the key processes of emotional, social and cognitive development, knowledge of which enables the social worker to go beyond the description of a child's behaviour and to acquire an understanding of the meaning behind it. Working sensitively with children in order to understand their needs and take into account their wishes and feelings would not be possible without developing an ability to see the world through the child's eyes.

References

Ainsworth, M. D. S., Blehar, M., Waters, E. and Wall, S. (1978) *Patterns of Attachment*, Hillsdale, NJ: Erlbaum.

Bee, H. (1995) *The Developing Child*, New York: HarperCollins.

Bentovim, A. (1972) 'Handicapped pre-school

children and their families', *British Medical Journal*, 3, 579–81.

Berridge, D. and Cleaver, H. (1987) *Foster Home Breakdown*, Oxford: Basil Blackwell.

Bowlby, J. (1969) *Attachment and Loss: Vol 1. Attachment*, New York: Basic Books.

Brodzinsky, D., Schechter, M. and Henig, R. (1992) *Being Adopted: The Lifelong Search for Self*, New York: Doubleday.

Bugental, D. B., Mantalya, S. M. and Lewis, J. (1989) 'Parental attributions as moderators of affective communication to children at risk from physical abuse', in D. Cicchetti and V. Carlson (eds), *Child Maltreatment*, New York: Cambridge University Press.

Collins, W. A. (ed.) (1984) *Development during Middle Childhood: The Years from Six to Twelve*, Washington, DC: National Academy Press.

Dunn, J. (1988) *The Beginnings of Social Understanding*, Oxford: Blackwell.

Dunn, J. (1993) *Young Children's Close Relationships: Beyond Attachment*, Newbury Park, California: Sage.

Fahlberg, V. (1991) *A Child's Journey Through Placement*, London: BAAF.

Garbarino, J., Stott, F. M. and Faculty of the Erikson Institute (1992) *What Children Can Tell Us?*, San Francisco: Jossey-Bass Inc.

Jewett, C. (1993) *Helping Children Cope with Separation and Loss*, London: Batsford in association with BAAF.

Lewis, M., Stanger, C. and Sullivan, M. (1989) 'Deception in three year olds', *Developmental Psychology*, 25 (3), 439–43.

Maxime, J. (1986) 'Some psychological aspects of black self-concept', in S. Ahmed, J. Cheetham and J. Small (eds), *Social Work with Black Children and Their Families*, London: Batsford/BAAF.

Reder, P. and Duncan, S. (1995) 'The meaning of the child', in P. Reder and C. Lucey, *Assessment of Parenting*, London: Routledge.

Richman, N., Stevenson, J. and Graham, P. (1982) *Pre-School to School: A Behavioural Study*, London: Academic Press.

Sugarman, Leonie (1986) *Life-Span Development: Concepts, Theories and Interventions*, London and New York: Methuen.

Williams, J. E. and Best, D. L. (1990) *Measuring Sex Stereotypes: A Multination Study*, Newbury Park: Sage.

Winnicott, D. (1965) *The Maturational Processes and the Facilitating Environment*, New York: International Universities Press.

Wolff, S. (1989) *Childhood and Human Nature*, London: Routledge.

III.3
Adolescence
Martin Herbert

Somewhere between the immaturity of childhood and the hoped-for maturity of adulthood lie the six or seven years referred to as adolescence. That there is (and is bound to be in contemporary society) a stage of transition from 'irresponsibility' to 'responsibility' has been widely, but not universally, accepted. Some cultures, notably pre-literate ones, had 'rites of passage' that took children directly from their childhood to adult status.

Some theorists reject the notion of adolescence as a distinct stage of development. They repudiate the idea that at puberty every child somehow takes on a qualitatively different personality or engages in radically different developmental tasks more or less overnight. Rather the child grows by imperceptible degrees into a teenager, and the adolescent turns by degrees into an adult.

Others disagree. The confusion over the boundaries defining adolescence is revealed by the metaphors applied to it: the 'in-between stage', and 'that no-man's land between childhood and adulthood'. It has also been referred to as a 'tunnel' into which young people disappear, displaying certain kinds of character. They are then 'lost to sight' for a few years. According to this metaphor you never know what is going to emerge at the other end – a daunting prospect for parents and teachers (if true) when they've put so much time, effort and affection, into preparing the children in their care for adulthood.

It is generally agreed that adolescence begins in biology (the variable time of onset of puberty) and ends in culture (the even more variable point at which young people are deemed 'responsible' and 'independent' by society). Whatever the boundaries, the fact is that many parents await their child's approaching adulthood with a sense of gloomy foreboding. They anticipate the adolescent years as something to be endured rather than enjoyed, to be confronted rather than shared. It is often the case that they are apprehensive that they may 'lose' the closeness, the affection and the degree of parental control they feel to be important in the relationship with their son or daughter. If parents expect the worst they are quite likely to get it – indeed, they contribute unwittingly to a self-fulfilling prophecy.

Of course, adolescence can be traumatic for some young individuals and disruptive for their parents, but it is by no means necessarily so. The truth of it is that adolescence does not deserve quite its gloomy reputation. The popular (and professional) notion that adolescence is different from the whole of development which precedes it, and the whole of development which follows it, is of relatively recent origin. Among the early proponents of this view was G. Stanley Hall in his 1904 treatise on the subject: *Adolescence: Its psychology and its relationship to physiology, anthropology, sociology, sex, crime, religion and education.* His belief, that adolescence is necessarily a stage of development associated with emotional turmoil and psychic disturbance, was to become so deeply rooted, reinforced by a succession of psychoanalytically-orientated writers, that it persists to this day. This 'storm and stress' conceptualization (built on eagerly by journalists in sensational items about feral teenage hooligans and vandals) has filtered down to street level as a veritable 'demonological' theory of adolescence. Certainly the psychiatric profession – with its biased sample of clinic-attending youngsters – has tended to take a jaundiced view of adolescence. Attention was drawn to neurotic – or psychotic – like features: hysteria, regression, mood swings and disintegration.

Hutter in the 1930s described adolescence in Alice in Wonderland terms as a period of development 'in which normally abnormalities so often happen it is abnormal that everything passes normally'. Anna Freud writing in the 1950s, on 'Adolescence' in the journal *Psycholanalytic Study of the Child* said it was 'abnormal' if a child kept a 'steady equilibrium during the adolescent period . . . The adolescent manifestations come close to symptom formation of the neurotic, psychotic or dissocial order and merge almost imperceptibly into . . . almost all the mental illnesses.' As a final illustration of the medical view of adolescence as pathology, and one which almost brings us up to date, we have van Krevelen writing in the 1970s that 'adolescence is a period of life, which by its disintegrative character may seem a psychosis in itself . . . it is difficult to discern in this stage a pathological process from normal development'.

In the 1960s the eminent child psychiatrist Gillespie wrote that 'the astonishing contrasts and contradictions which are so characteristic of adolescence produce so strong an impression of instability as to lead sometimes to a mistaken suspicion of a schizophrenic illness'.

The evidence based on small-scale investigations and large-scale surveys of 'run-of-the-mill' adolescents rather than

Five Key Points

1 Adolescence, while not without its difficulties, can be negotiated by children with intuitive, sensible parents and reasonably benign socio-economic backgrounds with relatively little fuss.
2 Most adolescents are attached to their homes, and continue to depend on the emotional support, goodwill and approval of their parents.
3 The serious problems of adolescence affect only a small minority.
4 Some 10–15 per cent experience serious psychological problems. Although relatively minor delinquent activities are common in adolescence, they are also transitory.
5 Failure at school has significant consequences for the well-being of adolescents.

only the impressions of clinicians who mainly see disturbed or deviant young people (Rutter, 1979; Coleman, 1980; Elkind, 1980; Herbert, 1987a; Nielsen, 1987) is that adolescence, while not without its difficulties, can be negotiated by children with intuitive, sensible parents and reasonably benign socio-economic backgrounds with relatively little fuss. If approached in the right frame of mind adolescence can be a period of relatively harmonious relationships – or at least as harmonious as any other stage of development. This requires an acceptance of the essential continuity of important aspects of the personality from childhood, through adolescence, and on to adulthood. The 'changeling' phenomenon – in the sense of some radical transformation – is highly unusual. Nevertheless, transition and change are features of adolescence, and an understanding of these processes (discussed in counselling sessions when more severe difficulties do arise) can be of benefit to harassed young people and their parents, especially if they 'normalize' the adolescent context by repudiating some of the popular myths – especially the notion that the problems necessarily exist because the client is a member of a distinct and potentially dangerous species.

Take the 'storm and stress' view of adolescence: this phase, while certainly not immune from its share of pain for those growing up (and for those guiding the growing-up processes) is not disproportionately characterized by severe emotional disturbance. Although there may be problems, their overall significance and extensiveness have been exaggerated. Psychological problems are probably a little commoner during adolescence than during middle childhood, but the difference is not very great: some 10–15 per cent of adolescents do experience significant psychological problems, but these figures are close to rates at other stages of development (Graham and Rutter, 1973).

The generation gap is another popular conception that does not live up to expectations. What, in any event, constitutes a gap? Labels are misleading and even dangerous because they suggest distinctions that are absolute rather than matters of degree. If anything, it could be said that the generations are drawing together rather than apart (see Eisenberg, 1995). Adolescents and their parents tend to agree on the important issues more than do parents and their parents (grandparents). People have been led to believe that the 'distancing' of young adults from their parents means that they may not be able to communicate with their children when they get older. Distancing is not, however, a typical pattern. Most adolescents are still attached to their homes in a positive way, and they continue to depend upon the emotional support, goodwill and approval of their parents.

The family continues to be of critical importance to them as it was in earlier, less mature years; indeed, concern and

supervision (as long as it is not oppressive, or too intrusive) can be demonstrated to be vital during a phase when youngsters are experimenting with life. Emotional (i.e., personal) support is important as the young person deals with changes in body image (during the 'growth spurt'), changes in hormonal activity and the increasing challenge of more complex developmental (e.g., academic and social) tasks (see Herbert, 1987b).

It is exceptional for teenagers to feel torn between their two 'worlds' of parents and peers, certainly on the more important issues of life. There are most likely to be differences of opinion on minor issues such as hair-style, fashion, social habits and privileges, where parental views are likely to be rejected in favour of the standards of their offspring's friends. Where major issues are concerned, it seems that only a minority of adolescents radically depart from their parents' views; there is little evidence that secondary or higher education in itself causes dramatic changes in the political attitudes that young people absorb from their parents. A majority of adolescents share their parents' attitudes towards moral and political issues, and are prepared (by and large) to accept their parents' guidance on academic, career and personal issues. Although the evidence is meagre, it does appear that rebelliousness and alienation are more likely in teenagers who, in spite of considerable maturity, remain economically or in other ways, dependent on their parents – such as students in higher education (Rutter, 1979).

Another popular belief about adolescence is that a crisis over personal identity occurs, producing all or some of the symptoms of stress: anxiety, depression, a sense of frustration, conflict and defeatism. The development of identity doesn't always proceed smoothly, but what evidence we have calls into question the belief of Erikson, that adolescents usually suffer a crisis over their identity. Most teenagers actually have a positive but not unrealistically inflated self-image and this view of themselves tends to be fairly stable over the years (Coleman, Herzberg and Morris, 1977).

Although adolescents have become more accepting in their attitudes to pre-marital sex, this does not imply, as the media like to suggest, a massive rise in casual sexual relationships. Young people, and particularly girls, continue to emphasize the importance of love and stable emotional attachment in pre-marital sex, although intended marriage or an engagement is not so often seen as a prerequisite of such relationships. The emphasis tends to be on a stable relationship with one sexual partner at a time – so-called 'serial monogamy' (Rutter, 1979). Girls do, however, display more conservative attitudes to these issues than boys. Most youngsters wish to get married and have children. Certainly a committed relationship is generally thought to be essential for the rearing of children, and, although a majority would wish such a long-standing commitment to take the form of marriage, a substantial minority reject such a view (Schofield, 1973; Rutter, 1979). An American study, by Sorensen in 1973, indicated that a majority of teenagers expect sexual fidelity after marriage, even though they do not expect it before then. There is no evidence that this view has changed.

It is important to remember that children do not face the 'hurdles' of adolescent development all at one time. Different challenges (e.g., sexuality, new relationships, changes in body and self-image, identity and independence issues) are spread out over several years. Children have strengths; they generally bring forward into maturity their positive attributes. They don't suddenly lose these characteristics which most parents have so assiduously nurtured. They also develop new intellectual, social and emotional capacities. They are capable of more flexible, abstract problem solving. Of course, they may wish to flex their intellectual 'muscles' and give their parents an argument. Their idealism may cause them to make unflattering comments about their parents' world-weary opinions.

Having said all this, it is obvious to anyone working in the social, health or educational services that there are some very real problems in adolescence, as there are for every other stage of development. Fortunately, the serious, as opposed to day-to-day difficulties, affect a relatively small minority. At that day-to-day level parents are going to face difficulties – some of which are unique: the child's reactions to the new demands

---

Three Questions

1 When does adolescence begin and end?

2 How does adolescence differ for males and females?

3 Why has the incidence of attempted suicide in adolescence risen so much?

---

of rapid physical change and sexual maturity. There is also the challenge (often an ambiguous one in our society) to be 'grown up'. Others are continuations of earlier difficulties. What puts particular pressure on parents is their perception of some of the awful risks their children may confront at this age: unwanted pregnancies, the exploitation of *naïveté* and innocent emotions, sexually transmitted disease, not least AIDS. Then there are the dangers of experimenting with drugs or the implications of youthful showing off (such as reckless driving in cars and, especially motor bikes). The point is that parents who have fostered a good relationship and honest lines of communication with their children are best placed to sensitize them to danger and strengthen their resolve not to overstep the bounds of reasonable behaviour and risk taking (Herbert, 1987b).

Having emphasized the need to 'normalize' the concept of adolescence (a lengthy stage of life best differentiated in casework into early, middle and late adolescence because of the different changes and challenges arising) there are particular age-related (i.e., raised incidence) problems which may beset the young person, his/her parents and the social worker who may become involved.

Emotional and Behavioural Problems

Contrary to received wisdom, adolescence is not usually characterized by severe emotional disturbance. Still there is a substantial minority of parents who will need to help their children themselves, and if the problems show no signs of being alleviated they should seek expert guidance. There is a paradox in all of this in the sense that, just as it was being appreciated that most adolescents did not suffer from psychological disorders, the evidence began to accumulate that since the late 1940s there has been a dramatic rise in psychosocial problems in teenagers. These include suicidal behaviour, delinquent activities, alcohol and substance abuse, depression and eating disorders, and they have occurred at a time of general improvements in living conditions and physical health. A closer look at the nature of psychological disorders is required.

The term psychological disorder refers collectively to a large and mixed bag of disorders ranging from depression, anxiety, inhibition and shyness to non-compliance, destructiveness, stealing and aggression. In essence, these problems represent exaggerations, deficits

(deficiencies) or disabling combinations of feelings, attitudes and behaviours common, at one time or the other, to most young people. Aggression, shyness and a combination of low self-esteem and poor concentration are examples of each category.

There is a distinction between those difficulties which primarily lead to emotional disturbance or distress for the young people themselves (e.g., anxiety, phobic fear, shyness, depression, feelings of inferiority and timidity) and those which mainly involve the kinds of anti-social behaviour (e.g., aggression, lying, stealing and disobedience) which disrupt the well-being of others, notably those in frequent contact with the young person. (These conduct disorders, as they are known, are dealt with later).

The first category, referred to by psychologists as 'emotional disorders', are manifested by about 2.5 per cent of pre-adolescent children. Their prevalence increases somewhat by adolescence, and we find that boys and girls are about equally prone to them. For most children these kinds of problems manifest themselves briefly at certain periods and then become minimal or disappear completely. We know as a result of longitudinal studies (which follow up people from infancy to adulthood) that, for the most part, young people who suffer from emotional disorders become reasonably well-adjusted adults. In a sense these difficulties are the emotional equivalent of 'growing pains'. They come and go; nevertheless they sometimes persist, and can reach levels of intensity which cause all-round suffering.

At the age of 11 children exhibit an increase in fear. Among 11- and 12-year olds, worries connected with school are nearly half as many again as worries about home matters. In Britain, 11 is that awkward age in a youngster's life when the change from junior to senior school is being made. It may not be coincidental that it is also the age at which phobias about school are at a high peak. Abnormal fears (phobias) involve an intense dread in the presence of an object or situation often amounting to panic; and although the object may be individual to the adolescent, certain forms are common, for example, dread of open or closed spaces, height, water and so on. Some definitions of phobia emphasize the incapacitating or restrictive effect of a phobia, in contrast to the more common fears which most of us endure.

There are various types of phobia. For example, some teenagers have a persistent fear of, and compelling desire to avoid, a social situation (say, a party) in which they are exposed to possible scrutiny by others and fear that they may act in a manner that will cause embarrassment or humiliation. In the case of agoraphobia, the young person has an intense fear of, and thus avoids, being alone or in public places. Behavioural psychotherapy (see Herbert, 1987a, 1991) is particularly effective in treating fear-based problems.

There are children and teenagers whose behaviour is notable for their fundamental inability or unwillingness to adhere to the rules and codes of conduct prescribed by society at its various levels: family, school and, indeed, the community at large. Conduct problems cover a lot of territory, including as they do seriously anti-social acts as well as what is only moderately troublesome behaviour. Although conduct problems can create misery for everyone concerned with the younger child, the disturbance can often be contained within the home or classroom – although often at great cost. As children grow older those problems that involve a persistent defiance of authority, together with a refusal or inability to show self-restraint, become more serious in their implications. They extend more and more beyond the confines of the child's life at home and school. The reverberations of the child's

misdemeanours may eventually lead to the danger not only of being labelled 'conduct-disordered', but also of earning the designation 'juvenile delinquent' if he or she infringes the law, is apprehended and found guilty. It is clear from self-reports of delinquent-type behaviour that large numbers of young people engage in delinquent acts for several years before they receive a police caution or are found guilty of offences.

The number of young people committing detected and adjudicated crimes in the United Kingdom and the United States has increased markedly. What was once an almost completely male preserve now includes substantial numbers of female offenders. The average age for the first court appearance of juveniles is lower, and there is a marked trend towards more violent offences.

The term 'juvenile delinquent' is merely an administrative term, not a clinical diagnosis. It has to be recognized that relatively minor delinquent activities (e.g., petty thefts, vandalism) are surprisingly common in adolescence. Such activities tend to be transitory. However, there is a small but hard core of adolescents who habitually break the law. Delinquency is perhaps the most noteworthy of all activities as an adolescent manifestation, reaching a peak at 15 years for boys and 14 years for girls. By their twenties most of the former offenders have gradually become broadly law-abiding members of the community. Behavioural cognitive methods (individual and group) have had an

Further Reading
1   Coleman, J. (1980) *Nature of Adolescence*, London: Methuen.
2   Herbert, M. (1987) *Living with Teenagers*, Oxford: Basil Blackwell.
3   Rutter, M. and Smith, D. J. (1995) *Psychosocial Disorder in Young People: Time Trends and their Causes*, Chichester: John Wiley.

encouraging success rate with conduct and delinquent disorders (see Hollin, 1991; Webster-Stratton and Herbert, 1994).

Psychiatric Disorders

There certainly are serious but relatively rare psychiatric disorders, such as schizophrenia and anorexia or bulimia nervosa, whose onset is particularly associated with the teenage years. It is fairly typical, in the transition from childhood to adulthood, to experience an upsurge of moodiness and feelings of misery. Adolescents are often tormented by low self-esteem, worries about the future, and fears about such matters as attending school or participating in social activities. These problems are usually relatively mild and might be viewed as developmental problems.

Depression and suicide

However, the feelings of misery and inner turmoil give way, in some adolescents, to more serious moods of depression – a sense of helplessness and powerlessness, of events being out of or beyond control. Some teenagers even entertain ideas about committing suicide. The milder form of depression may show itself as a lack of physical energy and well-being. In its more severe manifestations, adolescents tend to be irritable and bad-tempered, and, when it is at its worst, they sleep poorly, show a lack of appetite, and are always dejected, apathetic and lifeless. They cease to strive and to use their full effectiveness in whatever sphere of activity they find themselves.

The apathy of a young person with poor health is often mistaken for laziness. If a child is to be successful at school, good health is vital; it provides the basis for the stamina demanded by hours of concentration in the classroom. Regular attendance at school depends upon it, and

effective learning, in turn, depends upon reasonably consistent presence at lessons. High rates of non-attendance at school are often a significant indicator that all is not well with the young person.

Depression is a common feature of suicide, which, in adolescents, is usually associated with emotional and behavioural problems related to psychological and social stress. Suicide rates rise sharply during the teens so that it comes to rank among the half-dozen most common causes of death among older adolescents (the figures are still well below those for adults, and only a minute fraction of the suicide rate in old age). Attempted suicide is very much a late adolescent phenomenon, the peak being among 15–19-year olds. There has been a tenfold increase in such incidents since the 1960s among adolescent boys and a fivefold rise for girls. Nevertheless, the rate of attempted suicides for adolescent girls far exceeds that for boys. No one seems able to explain the surge in the statistics. It does not seem to be related to drug abuse or to too liberal prescribing of tablets by doctors. It may be associated with increased use of alcohol, and it is most likely linked in some way with the increasing prevalence of marital discord, childhood separations, unemployment and criminality.

Teenagers sometimes have fantasies about their own death which involve their 'ending it all' and yet surviving the event by 'attending' their own funeral where they are able to savour the grief and guilt displayed by errant parents or boyfriends/girlfriends. These fantasies indicate how, in some adolescents, the finality of death is not fully appreciated, or at least not while in a depressed or hysterical state, and not at the time when the gesture (and, often, more than a gesture) of suicide is contemplated. The cliché that suicide is often a cry for help is true despite its banality. Threats of suicide should not be treated lightly and not dismissed with the words 'If s/he really meant it s/he would do it, not threaten to do it'. Many individuals who have threatened to commit suicide do in the end carry out their threat. In cases of adolescent depression the disorder may be masked and sometimes the outward and visible sign of the problems takes the form of 'acting out' delinquent activity.

Anorexia nervosa

A problem particularly (but not only) associated with adolescent girls, it occurs in pre-pubertal children, is anorexia nervosa. The anorexic girl deliberately restricts her food intake; indeed, she does not want to eat at all, because she believes she is fat and wishes to lose weight. The word 'anorexia' means loss of appetite. However, the absence of hunger or appetite is not a crucial feature of anorexia nervosa. Nevertheless, the teenager will characteristically act as if she had lost her appetite.

Anorexia nervosa is essentially about weight rather than eating. The really central feature of the disorder is a body weight which is abnormally low for the age, height and sex of the person accompanied by a distorted perception by the sufferer of her body. There is a further crucial feature: the individual's attitude to her weight. What makes life difficult for parents and other would-be helpers is that someone with anorexia nervosa will not always be open or truthful about her feelings and will frequently resist help. If she is, she is likely to say that she is ashamed of her body and very frightened of the thoughts of being heavier. She may suffer in various ways through being thin, but compared with putting on weight it is seen as the lesser evil.

Drug Misuse and Abuse

Drug abuse is relatively infrequent among younger schoolchildren, but not as rare as it used to be; it certainly becomes more common during the years of adolescence. Fortunately, most youngsters who try drugs or misuse substances (e.g., glue sniffing) out of curiosity do not continue to use or misuse them regularly. Those who take drugs tend to do so infrequently and give them up altogether after a year or so. The key factor in drug taking is opportunity – the availability of drugs and people to tempt and 'prompt'. Users have generally been exposed to drugs by their peers or by people (not infrequently family members) whose values incline towards non-conformity or even deviance. Rebelliousness, low self-esteem, a poor sense of psychological well-being (including depression) and low academic aspirations are among characteristics commonly found in adolescent drug users. The boredom and hopelessness of unemployment also play their part.

Educational Failure

Mass formal education has created serious problems for the life goals of adolescents with educational disabilities. For academically successful adolescents, school is a bridge between the world of childhood and the world of adulthood. For children unwilling or unable to learn, school is a place where the battle against society is likely to begin. Failure in a success-orientated world has significant consequences for the well-being of adolescents, not only at school, but in other facets of their lives. There is a strong association between emotional disturbance and under-achievement at school – a perennial matter of concern to both teachers and parents. Emotionally disturbed adolescents tend to distract and harass their teachers, and disrupt and anger their more conscientious fellow students.

A sense of failure very often manifests

itself in an obstinate façade behind which the student hides. There is a vicious circle of self-fulfilling prophecy at work. Tell teenagers often enough that they are fools, criticize them whatever they do, even if it is commendable within their own capabilities, and in the end they are likely to become extremely demoralized and even give up. Why should they work hard when all their efforts, good and bad, are condemned? Their confidence will be destroyed and once again they may retreat behind a mask of stupidity and 'don't care' laziness – signs of what, clinically, is referred to as 'learned helplessness'.

Young people who do well at school tend to enjoy good health, have average or above-average intelligence and well-developed social skills. They are likely to have a good opinion of themselves, the ability to gauge accurately their effect on others, and to perceive correctly the quality of others' approaches and responses to themselves. Early-maturing boys and girls also have many advantages in terms of capability and self-confidence.

Doubtless there will be times when parents' assistance is brushed aside, their advice resisted, and their guidance interpreted as interference. But times of rapid transition *are* recognized as times when people are open to help, if sensibly and sensitively proffered. Contrary to widely held myths about adolescence, teenagers *are* susceptible to the right sort of intervention despite their famous reticence and prickliness. Their minds, at this age, are probably as open as they will ever be. But, are parents' minds open or closed?

Wise parents have no wish to emerge as victors of battles of will or confrontations with their children. Rather they wish to *win through*, in the task of supporting them in their journey through adolescence to maturity. A realistic, and optimistic (that does not mean Utopian!) view of adolescence *plus* a sound

knowledge of what is happening physically and emotionally to teenagers, will allow parents to remain rock-solid while their youngster finds his or her adult status. Parents can survive, indeed, enjoy adolescence, by letting the occasional waves of discontent, criticism and rebellion break around them – without breaking them!

References

Adelson, J. (ed.) (1980) *Handbook of Adolescent Psychology*, New York: John Wiley.

Coleman, J. C. (1980) *The Nature of Adolescence*, London: Methuen.

Coleman, J. C., Herzberg, J. and Morris, M. (1977) 'Identity in adolescence: present and future self-concepts', *Journal of Youth and Adolescence*, 6, 63–75.

Eisenberg, N. (ed.) (1995) *Social Development*, London: Sage.

Elkind, D. (1980) 'Strategic interactions in early adolescence', in J. Adelson, (ed.), *Handbook of Adolescent Psychology*, New York: Wiley.

Erikson, E. (1968) *Identity: Youth and Crisis*, New York: Norton.

Freud, A. (1958) *Adolescence: Psychoanalytic Study of the Child*, New York: International Universities Press.

Gillespie, W. H. (1968) 'The psychoanalytic theory of child development', in E. Miller (ed.), *Foundations of Child Psychiatry*, Oxford: Pergamon Press.

Graham, P. and Rutter, M. (1973) 'Psychiatric disorders in the young adolescent: a follow-up study', *Proceedings of the Royal Society of Medicine*, 66, 1226–9.

Hall, S. (1904) *Adolescence: Its Psychology and its Relations to Physiology, Anthropology, Sociology, Sex, Crime, Religion and Education*, vols I and II, New York: D. Appleton & Co.

Herbert, M. (1987a) *Conduct Disorders of Childhood and Adolescence*, Chichester: Wiley.

Herbert, M. (1987b) *Living with Teenagers*, Oxford: Basil Blackwell.

Herbert, M. (1991) *Clinical Child Psychology: Behaviour, Social Learning and Development*, Chichester: John Wiley.

Hollin, C. R. (1991) 'Cognitive behaviour modification with delinquents', in M. Herbert *Clinical Child Psychology: Behaviour, Social Learning and Development*, Chichester: John Wiley.

Hutter, A. (1938) 'Endogene en functionelle psychosen bei kindern in den pubertatscjahren', *A. Kinderpsychiat*, 5, 97–102.

Nielsen, L. (1987) *Adolescent Psychology: A Contemporary View*, London: Holt, Rinehart and Winston.

Patterson, G. (1982) *Coercive Family Process*, Oregon: Castalia.

Rutter, M. (1979) *Changing Youth in a Changing Society*, The Nuffield Provincial Hospitals Trust.

Schofield, M. (1973) *The Sexual Behaviour of Young Adults*, London: Allen Lane.

Sorensen, R. C. (1973) *Adolescent Sexuality in Contemporary America*, New York: World Publishing.

van Krevelen, D. A. (1971) 'Psychoses in adolescence', in J. G. Howells (ed.), *Modern Perspectives in Adolescent Psychiatry*, Edinburgh: Oliver and Boyd.

Webster-Stratton, C. and Herbert, M. (1994) *Troubled Families: Problem Children*, Chichester: John Wiley.

III.4
Nigrescence
Lena Robinson

The field of child development research is based largely on white middle-class children which is assumed (or defined as) normative and generic to all children. The behaviours and patterns of development in non-white children are then viewed comparatively against this 'norm' and defined as 'exceptions' or 'deviations' from the norm. Black psychologists (mainly in the USA) have presented alternative perspectives on black child development. However, the research of black scholars, who have unique insights into the problems of minority children, has been largely neglected by mainstream developmental psychology (Spencer, 1982).

The issues discussed in this chapter are offered as the beginning steps towards an understanding of black identity development. The topic of black identity has been of genuine concern to psychologists and social workers for decades. Low self-esteem, self-hatred, and a negative racial identity have been the characteristics traditionally attributed to black children. A review of the psychological literature shows that there are different perspectives on the identity development question, which have produced contradictory conclusions.

One body of research which dominated the psychological literature from the early 1940s and through the 1950s is the black self-hatred thesis. Another body of research – developed in the USA – focuses on models of psychological nigrescence (i.e., the process of the psychology of becoming black). This chapter argues that the model of

psychological nigrescence is more relevant to the psychological life experiences of black people in Britain than the more traditional psychological theories. It will enable us to gain a better understanding of the difficulties experienced by some black children in Britain.

The term 'black' in this chapter has been used to describe people from South Asian, African and Caribbean backgrounds. Black identity has been discussed extensively in the social science literature using various terms and measures. According to Looney (1988) 'Black identity deals specifically with an individual's awareness, values, attitudes, and beliefs about being Black . . .' (Looney, 1988, p. 41). It can also be viewed as 'an active developmental process which is exposed to various influences within and without, and [which] can be selective and/or adaptive' (Maxime, 1986, p. 101). We will use these definitions as our 'operating definition' in our discussion of black identity development.

For more than 50 years, psychologists have attempted to study children's racial attitudes using doll preference studies. The early work by Clark and Clark (1940) led to numerous studies on children's preferences for objects, usually dolls, representing various skin colourations and facial features (e.g., Milner, 1975, 1983; Davey, 1987). These studies found that children showed a preference for white dolls over black ones. Since the late 1960s several studies have contradicted the above studies, showing many black children making more black preference choices than white preference choices (Clark, 1982; cf. summary in Davey, 1987). A number of arguments have been put forward to explain this discrepancy. Cross (1985) indicated that racially symbolic assessments and direct assessments tap different dimensions of children's self-concept, reference group orientation and personal identity, respectively (see Cross, 1985 for a detailed review). Some researchers have criticized the methodology (Wilkinson, 1980; Baldwin, 1979). Others have noted the failure of researchers, and interpreters of researchers, to recognize the developmental constraints of white preference behaviour (Spencer, 1988).

Whatever the explanation, the conclusions of research showing that children may show preferences for the white dolls (or other white stimuli) cannot be ignored. Some contemporary studies show that many black children continue to make white preference or anti-black racial evaluations (Gopaul-McNicol, 1988; Powell-Hopson, 1985). According to Fairchild (1988): 'These trends . . . are not surprising. The mass media, schools, and other institutions, reinforce the negative values attached to the color black and to black people' (1988, p. 74). There is a 'glorification of things white, and derogation of things black' (1988, p. 74).

Models of Black Identity Development

From the mainstream psychological research literature on black identity examined in the above section, I want to move the focus to a perspective that has largely been ignored by traditional Eurocentric psychology – the research on the psychology of nigrescence. The literature on black self-hatred suggests the operation of a basic Eurocentric position in psychology and social science,

---

Three Key Points

1. The conclusions of research showing that many black children continue to make white preference or anti-black evaluation cannot be ignored.
2. Nigrescence models are useful as they enable us to understand the problems of black identity confusion.
3. Social workers need to take an active approach in helping black children build positive self-images of themselves.

---

at least where the issues of race and racial differences are concerned (Baldwin, 1976).

Nigrescence models tend to have four or five stages – and the common point of departure is not the change process *per se* but an analysis of the identity to be changed. These models are useful as they enable us to understand the problems of black identity confusion and to examine, at a detailed level, what happens to a person during identity change. Perhaps the best-known and most widely researched model of black identity development is Cross's (1971, 1980, 1991) model of the conversion from 'Negro' to 'black'.

Cross suggests that the development of a black person's racial identity is often characterized by his/her movement through a five-stage process, the transformation from Pre-encounter to Internalization–commitment. The five stages are:

1   *Pre-encounter.* In this stage the person is likely to view the world from a white frame of reference (Eurocentric). The black person accepts a 'white' view of self, other blacks and the world. The person has accepted a deracinated frame of reference and because his or her reference point is usually a white normative standard, he or she develops attitudes that are very pro-white and anti-black. The person will also deny that racism exists.

2   *Encounter.* In the second stage some

shocking personal or social event makes the person receptive to new views of being black and the world. The person's Eurocentric thinking is upset by an encounter with racial prejudice and precipitates an intense search for black identity. The Encounter stage involves two steps: first, experiencing and personalizing the event – the person realizes that his or her old frame of reference is inappropriate, and he or she begins to explore aspects of a new identity; the second part is portrayed by Cross 'as a testing phase during which the individual [first] cautiously tries to validate his/her new perceptions' (Cross, Parham and Helms, 1991, p. 324), then definitively decides to develop a black identity.

3 *Immersion–Emersion.* This is the period of transition in which the person struggles to destroy all vestiges of the 'old' perspective. This occurs simultaneously with an intense concern to clarify the implications of the new-found black identity (Cross, 1978). An emotional period ensues where the person glorifies anything black and attempts to purge his or herself of their former world-view and old behaviour. The person tends to denigrate white people and white culture. Hence, the demonstration of one's blackness is given high priority – for example, black clothes and hairstyles, linguistic styles, attending all black functions, reading black literature. The person does not feel secure about his/her blackness. He/she can be vicious in attacks on aspects of the old self that appear in others or her/himself, and he/she may even appear bizarre in his/her affirmation of the new self.

4 *Internalization.* In this stage, the person focuses on things other than himself/herself and his/her ethnic or racial group. He/she achieves an inner security and self-confidence with his/her blackness. He/she feels more relaxed, more at ease with him/her self. The person's thinking reflects a shift from

how one's friends seē him/her (Am I Black enough?) towards confidence in one's personal standards of blackness. The person also exhibits a psychological openness and a decline in strong anti-white feelings. The person still uses 'blacks as a primary reference group [but] moves toward a pluralistic and nonracist perspective' (Cross, 1991, p. 326).

This stage and the fifth stage, *Internalization–commitment*, are characterized by positive self-esteem, ideological flexibility and openness about one's blackness. In the fifth stage the person finds activities and commitments to express his/her new identity.

There is an extensive empirical literature that confirms Cross's model of black identity development (see Cross, 1971; Hall, Cross and Freedle, 1972). Although Cross's identity development model has been developed with African American samples in the USA, it is argued by various authors (e.g., Sue and Sue, 1990; Maxime, 1986) that other minority groups share similar processes of development. In Britain, Maxime (1986) has used Cross's model in the understanding of identity confusion in black people. However, she points out that 'difficulty in maintaining a positive sense of racial identity' does not apply to all black people 'most of whom possess the survival skills necessary for the development of a positive racial identity' (Maxime, 1986, p. 101).

Parham (1989) has expanded Cross's nigrescence model. He integrates Cross's (1971) model into three developmental stages – adolescence, middle adulthood and late adulthood. However, he omits 'childhood' and argues that it is during adolescence and early adulthood that a person might first experience nigrescence, and after this first experience, the likelihood of experiencing nigrescence is present for the rest of a person's life. An assumption of Parham's extension of Cross's model is that manifestations of black identity in childhood reflect parental and/or societal views of race.

Ponteretto (1989) disagrees with Parham and argues that 'the development of racial identity begins ... in early childhood' (1989, p. 265). He argues that 'recent ethnic socialization research in developmental, child, and social psychology supports the position that children (particularly older children) have a greater sense of their ethnic identity than had been previously thought' (1989, p. 265). Ponterotto (1989) suggests 'incorporating developmentally specific, yet parallel, research tracts for the developmental stages posited by Parham (plus adding one for children)' (1989, p. 266). I support this view and consider that Cross's model of nigrescence offers a framework for understanding the racial identity development of children – in particular older children.

Social Work Implications

How does one rear a black child to have a positive identity in a predominantly white society? Social workers, who work with black children, should attempt to answer this question.

Discrimination can have damaging effects on the psychological adjustment and self-esteem of young children and adolescents. In particular, through racial prejudice the black child in Britain is subjected to derogatory views and negative self-images not only projected by the media, but also by teachers, parents and the wider society. Early in life, the child acquires knowledge of how the black person is viewed in society.

Social workers need to take an active approach in helping black children build positive self-images of themselves. Maxime (1986) considers that a preventative approach is preferable to a 'crisis intervention model' (Maxime, 1986, p. 112). Social workers need to be aware that raising children in a white-dominated society places special ·

Three Questions

1 Is the black child merely a white child who 'happens' to be painted black?
2 Some theorists believe that minorities go through stages of racial identity. Why would you need to consider this possibility in working with black children?
3 How does one rear a black child to have a positive self-image in a predominantly white society?

pressures on the black parent. Comer and Pouissant (1992) propose various ways in which black parents can promote racial pride in their children. They suggest that parents 'can discuss color and race-related issues in a natural way' (1992, p. 17). Thus, when parents are teaching children about colours and body parts and functions, they can describe the child's arm as 'brown' or 'black'. 'When the question of color arises later, it can be discussed in a positive, relaxed manner because [parents] have not previously ignored or overdramatized it' (1992, p. 17). Other important tools in combating poor racial identity are talk (open acknowledgement of racial issues), positive modelling, and reinforcement of a child's cultural heritage (blackness) (Powell-Hopson and Hopson, 1990). These techniques could be employed by social workers involved in working with

Further Reading

1 Cross, W. E. (1992) *Black Identity: Theory and Research*, Philadelphia: Temple University Press.
2 Phinney, J. S. and Rotheram, M. J. (eds) (1987) *Children's Ethnic Socialization: Pluralism and Development*, London: Sage.
3 Powell-Hopson, D. and Hopson, D. S. (1990) *Different and Wonderful: Raising Black Children in a Race-conscious Society*, New York: Prentice Hall.

black children and adolescents who experience difficulty in maintaining a positive black identity. Social workers need to also understand and analyse their own biases, assumptions, values and feelings before any help can be given to the children under their care.

References

Baldwin, J. A. (1979) 'Black psychology and black personality', *Black Books Bulletin*, 4(3), 6–11.

Baldwin, J. A. (1979) 'Theory and research concerning the notion of black self-hatred: a review and reinterpretation', *Journal of Black Psychology*, 5, 51–78.

Clark, K. and Clark, M. (1940) 'Skin color as a factor in racial identification of Negro preschool children', *Journal of Social Psychology*, 11, 159–69.

Clark, M. L. (1982) 'Racial group concept and self-esteem in Black children', *Journal of Black Psychology*, 8, 75–88.

Comer, J. P. and Pouissant, A. F. (1992) *Raising Black Children*, New York: Plume Books.

Cross, W. E. (1971) 'The Negro to Black conversion experience: towards the psychology of Black liberation', *Black World*, 20, 13–27.

Cross, W. E. (1978) 'The Thomas and Cross models of psychological nigrescence: a literature review', *The Journal of Black Psychology*, 5(1), 13–31.

Cross, W. E. (1980) 'Models of psychological nigrescence: a literature review', in R. L. Jones (ed.), *Black Psychology* (2nd edn), New York: Harper & Row.

Cross, W. E. (1985) 'Black identity: rediscovering the distinction between personal identity and reference group orientation', in M. B. Spencer, G. K. Brookins and W. R. Allen (eds), *Beginnings: The Social and Affective Development of Black Children*, Hillsdale, NJ: Erlbaum.

Cross, W. E. (1991) *Shades of Black: Diversity in African American Identity*, Philadelphia: Temple University Press.

Cross, W. E., Parham, T. A. and Helms, J. E. (1991) 'The stages of black identity development: nigrescence models', in R. L. Jones (ed.) *Black Psychology* (3rd edn), Berkeley, CA: Cobb & Henry.

Davey, A. G. (1987) 'Insiders, outsiders and anomalies: A review of studies of identities – a reply to Olivia Foster-Carter', *New Community*, 13(3), 477–80.

Fairchild, H. (1988) 'Glorification of things white', *Journal of Black Psychology*, 14(2), 73–4.

Gopaul-McNicol, S. (1988) 'Racial identification and racial preference of black preschool children in New York and Trinidad', *Journal of Black Psychology*, 14(2), 65–8.

Hall, W. S., Cross, W. E. and Freedle, R. (1972) 'Stages in the development of a black identity', *ACT Research Report*, 50, Iowa City: Research and Development Division, American Testing Program.

Jackson, B. (1975) 'Black identity development', in L. Golubschick and B. Persky (eds), *Urban Social and Educational Issues*, Dubuque, IA: Kendall/Haunt.

Looney, J. (1988) 'Ego development and black identity', *The Journal of Black Psychology*, 15(1), 41–56.

Maxime, J. (1986) 'Some psychological models of black self-concept', in S. Ahmed, J. Cheetham and J. Small (eds), *Social Work with Black Children and their Families*, London: Batsford.

Milner, D. (1975) *Children and Race*, Harmondsworth: Penguin.

Milner, D. (1983) *Children and Race: Ten Years On*, London: Ward Lock Educational.

Parham, T. A. (1989) 'Cycles of psychological nigrescence', *The Counselling Psychologist*, 17(2), 187–226.

Ponteretto, J. (1989) 'Expanding directions for racial identity research', *The Counselling Psychologist*, 17(2), 264–72.

Powell-Hopson, D. (1985) 'The effects of modeling, reinforcement, and color meaning word associations on doll color preferences of Black preschool children and white preschool children', unpublished doctoral dissertation, Hofstra University.

Powell-Hopson, D. and Hopson, D. S. (1990) *Different and Wonderful: Raising Black Children in a Race-conscious Society*, New York: Prentice Hall.

Spencer, M. B. (1982) 'Preschool children's social cognition and cultural cognition: a cognitive developmental interpretation of race dissonance findings', *Journal of Psychology*, 112, 275–86.

Spencer, M. B. (1988) 'Self-concept development', in D. T. Slaughter (ed.), *Black Children in Poverty: Developmental Perspectives*, San Francisco: Jossey-Bass.

Sue, D. W. and Sue, D. (1990) *Counselling the Culturally Different*, New York: Wiley.

Wilkinson, D. (1980) 'Play objects as tools of propaganda: characterizations of the African-American male', *Journal of Black Psychology*, 7(1), 1–16.

Partnership and Parenting
Janet Walker

At night returning, every labour sped,
He sits him down the monarch of a shed;
Smiles by his cheerful fire, and round surveys
His children's looks, that brighten at the blaze;
While his lov'd partner, boastful of her hoard
Displays her cleanly platter on the board.

Oliver Goldsmith, 1728–74
The Traveller

Writing in the eighteenth century, Goldsmith captured a comfortable vision of partnership and parenting. Despite vast economic and social transformations in the following two centuries, it continues to provide a template for family relationships. It is a deceptively simple portrayal of complex intimate bonds between adults and between parents and their children. This spectre of warmth, well-being and domestic contentment exalts a model of partnership in which paternal and maternal roles are complementary, clearly defined and delineated within an economic union which creates a supportive adult alliance and kinship networks: men work primarily outside the home to maintain and support their wives and offspring, while women primarily provide the physical and emotional sustenance within it. It provides a powerful image of stability and permanence, of predictable events and transitions commonly associated with the move from childhood, through adolescence to adulthood: completing education, entering paid employment, finding a partner, getting married and starting a family.

Parents are frequently judged against this idealized construction of partnership and child rearing, and when they fail to meet expectations, are held responsible for a variety of social problems including crime and delinquency, violence and abuse, and educational failure and unemployment. None of these is particularly unique to the late twentieth century, but changing patterns of partnership and parenting in postmodern industrial societies have been blamed for an apparent rejection of moral values and personal responsibility, and for the emergence of a benefit-dependent underclass (Murray, 1990; Dennis, 1993), thus justifying the search for ways of preventing further deterioration. Since the Second World War, social interventions have been designed with the aim of buttressing and supporting families in crisis, legitimizing public intrusion in the essentially private domain of family life, and creating difficult dilemmas and contradictions for social workers. These are reflected in successive reforms in legislation relating to children, child support and marriage breakdown (Walker, 1991).

A number of facts have heightened concerns that, far from being the stable building block of contemporary society, family life is a crumbling edifice:

- marriage rates have reached an all-time low: marriage is occurring later and less often;
- almost a third of all births occur outside marriage;
- 40 per cent of marriages end in divorce;
- 20 per cent of families with dependent children are headed by a lone parent; and
- 8 per cent of dependent children live in step-families. (Utting 1995)

Fears that the consequences of family change, if left unchecked, could be disastrous for individuals and for society have put families, and parents in particular, under progressive scrutiny. Today the mood is changing from one of blaming and policing families, to one in which there is a growing demand for policies which reflect the realities of modern living and underpin rather than undermine families, and for the provision of specialist services to support parents to discharge their responsibilities, particularly at times of stress and transition. There is a deepening desire to understand the shifting shapes of adult and marital relationships (Clulow, 1995), and to carefully assess their impact on the quality of parenting (Etzioni, 1993; Brannen and O'Brien, 1995).

Let us consider three key questions:

1   What are the realities of modern partnerships?

2   How do these relate to the process of parenting and the obligations it implies?

3   What are the concerns?

Changes in marriage have been considerable and significant. When Goldsmith commented on family life, the choice of marital partner was less a matter of mate selection and more a matter of suitable arrangements being made.

Although the connection between romantic love and life-long partnership through the institution of marriage was acknowledged, love and companionship were secondary considerations. The affective bond between parents was represented by procreation and child rearing. Social historians (Anderson, 1995) have used the terms 'differentiated' and 'complementary' to describe the 'traditional' marriage. Modern marriages, by contrast, are described as 'symmetrical' or 'companionate': a strong emotional bond from which personal emotional benefits are derived is no longer viewed as a bonus, but, increasingly, as the key aspiration. This is demonstrated by three surveys: in 1955 couples described the most important aspects of marriage as 'fulfilling the roles of breadwinner and homemaker'; by 1970, 'comradeship, doing things together' was held to be the most important component in making a happy marriage. To achieve this, 'husbands and wives liking each other' was considered critical (Gorer, 1955, 1971). In 1990, respondents in a Gallup poll specified, in rank order, a number of qualities considered to be important in a marriage partner: being faithful, caring and loving; having a sense of humour; understanding and tolerance; unselfishness; being prepared to listen; kind; hard-working; home-loving; fun to talk to; sexually responsive; and good looking/physically attractive (Clulow, 1993). With such high expectations it is hardly surprising that marriage rates have fallen and divorce rates have risen so dramatically.

The move from a model of partnership based on social and economic considerations to one based on a companionate relationship has its origins in the domestic world of the middle classes which emerged during the industrial revolution (Reibstein and Richards, 1992). Central to that period was the notion of domesticity, given additional expression in the 1960s and

1970s in public images of closeness in intimate relationships and shared lives. The emphasis on personal fulfilment and individualism in the 1980s and 1990s has further changed the ways in which young adults view and form partnerships and approach parenthood.

Since satisfaction with married life appears to decline almost from the wedding day (Mansfield, 1995), young people are more likely now to postpone marriage in favour of living together (Kiernan and Estaugh, 1993). By the beginning of the twenty-first century some 80 per cent of marrying couples will have cohabited, compared with just 25 per cent in the so-called Swinging Sixties. Most cohabitation is short term – up to two years – and many relationships end by breaking up rather than in marriage. Cohabitation is not new: before legal marriage became widely acceptable in the nineteenth century, and when divorce was not an option for dealing with unhappy marriages, couples opted to live together claiming some status (albeit dubious) through 'common law'. What is new, however, is cohabitation as a prelude to marriage, a stage in the process of partnering.

Although marriage remains a majority practice, it is more commonly a transition experienced at a later age. Most couples now enter marriage having experienced earlier sexual relationships: a trend upward which has been evident for a hundred years. Yet despite this liberal attitude towards sexual behaviour outside marriage, facilitated by vastly improved methods of birth control, paradoxically perhaps, companionate marriage appears to demand a far greater commitment to sexual exclusivity and fidelity than was evident in more traditional marital partnerships. As a consequence, deep tensions emerge: sexual freedom prior to marriage is not only tolerated but frequently encouraged, while monogamy is emphasized as the distinguishing feature of the marital relationship. Thus, while modern

Five Key Points

1 There is a long tradition behind the idealized construction of partnership and child rearing in which maternal and paternal roles are complementary and clearly defined.

2 The reality is often very different.

3 There has been a move in the model of partnership from one based on social and economic considerations to one based on a companionate relationship.

4 The growing incidence of divorce and the consequential increase in multiple family transitions have profound implications for children.

5 Some commentators believe that the more emphasis is placed on companionate marriage, the more it is likely to fail, and there is a growing demand for policies which reflect the realities of family life, and for the provision of services designed to support parents in times of stress and transition.

marriage reasserts Christian values, the expectations of the relationship are substantially greater than in the past and centre on individualism rather than familism, affording more opportunity for pursuing personal interests and developing other friendships. Involvement in extra-marital affairs has become more rather than less prevalent, for women as well as for men. Adulterous relationships are more likely now than in times past to threaten the stability and durability of marriage since tolerance of such behaviour has substantially diminished.

Marriage would appear to contain a basic conundrum: mutual dependence, intimacy and sexual exclusivity have to be balanced within a culture which emphasizes personal growth and getting ahead – the 'we'/'me' dilemma. There is a renewed emphasis on privacy and relative separateness from societal and kinship obligations, increased expectation of emotional companionship and equality, and a positive focus on sexuality beyond its function in procreation (Morgan, 1992). Within this conception, marriage remains *the* central adult relationship, and elements of more traditional expectations mingle somewhat uneasily with more modern ideals: in a British Social Attitudes Survey in 1992, a third of respondents agreed that a husband's job is to earn money, and a wife's job is to look after the home and family. Despite the push for equality, and the fact that over 60 per cent of married mothers are in paid employment (OPCS, 1994), gender divisions of labour remain evident in the large majority of households. Visions of equal partnership promote arguments for equal parenting, but increased freedoms in conjugal arrangements often conflict with constraints inherent in parenthood.

Starting a family appears to present the greatest single challenge to companionate partnerships. Although there has been an increase in lone motherhood – some 30–40 per cent of children are conceived out of wedlock – shotgun marriages seem to be a thing of the past. Nevertheless, many parents marry by the time the child is born, and many who do not are cohabiting and register the birth jointly. The transition into marriage confirms a recognized status on the mother and on her child, but becoming a parent takes on a new significance for both partners within any couple relationship. Although it is possible for men and women to contract an equal partnership in cohabitation or marriage while they have only themselves to consider, when there are children the situation radically alters (Clulow and Mattinson, 1989). As parenthood reasserts traditional divisions of labour between the sexes, stresses emerge. In a study by Mansfield and Collard (1988), husbands described their experience of becoming fathers as watching changes in their wives, rather than as something which gave them a

sense of direct involvement in the transition to parenthood. While psychological literature has moved away from a belief in the exclusivity of the mother–child relationship towards the realization that children can and do form multiple attachments, fathers taking an equal share in parenting tasks turns out to be more difficult than some couples anticipate. Fathers' engagement is inspired by curiosity and a wish to have contact with their children whereas motherhood has a significantly wider meaning (Björnberg, 1995). Furthermore, whereas having a baby inevitably disrupts mothers' working patterns, few men can or do shift their work routines to accommodate children. Couples who successfully manage the transition to parenthood with minimum disruption in their own relationship either have differentiated roles already, or effectively renegotiate and adapt their partnership to embrace the demands of bringing up children. Believing that their partnership is important to their success as parents enables husbands and wives to face, articulate and manage the issues of conflict between being a person, a partner and a parent (Mansfield et al., 1996). For others, the birth of a baby heightens existing conflicts, or significantly lowers personal, emotional satisfaction with the partnership, particularly as men appear to adjust more slowly to parenthood than women (Cowan and Cowan, 1992). This disjunction is more pronounced for couples who have been together longer before having children. This is particularly significant since the current trend to delay marriage usually means that parenthood is similarly delayed, the more so because many married couples decide to leave a substantial time gap between marriage and pregnancy. When children arrive, opportunities for time alone become fewer and less spontaneous, sex becomes less frequent, and arrangements for combining paid work, housework and child care often cause acute strain. Support from family and friends, and sharing concerns with other couples experiencing similar stresses have been shown to be especially important in managing the transitions (Mansfield et al., 1996).

Parenthood, then, is not always the joy it is commonly made out to be. While parenthood requires no particular form of relationship or family structure, parenting denotes expectations about behaviours, tasks and commitments, and is a challenging task (Pugh et al., 1994). Bowlby (1988) has suggested that 'engaging in parenthood is playing for very high stakes'. As patterns of family life and expectations of marriage are shifting dramatically society is placing a high value on good parenting, and children are perceived to be the innocent victims of change (Walker, 1995). One of the most profound challenges in family life in recent decades is that the meaning of parenthood is being transformed alongside the reconstruction of marital relationships. Saporiti (1989) has suggested that the balance of advantages a woman receives from her children (economic, social and psychological) and the resources she invests in them (material, emotional and opportunity costs) is more and more to her disadvantage. Moreover, although women and men agree on the importance of emotional support and companionship, women are much more likely than men to feel disappointed in this respect. If the filing of divorce petitions is taken as a yardstick, then women are three times more likely than men to make the first public move to end the relationship. This choice can complicate commitment, carrying with it a burden of responsibility that neither partner can disown (Clulow, 1995).

Most divorces occur between five and nine years of marriage, the period in which couples are most likely to become parents. If patterns in the 1990s continue in to the twenty-first century, 25 per cent of children will experience their parents'

divorce before they are 16. Since remarriages of divorced people doubled between 1971 and 1991, and these are more likely to break down than first-time marriages, increasing numbers of children will face repeated disruption and the 'loss' of several parental figures from the household. Such children are especially vulnerable and the most adversely affected by family transitions (Cockett and Tripp, 1994).

Until the twentieth century, divorce was not a feature of daily life although there were probably just as many unhappy marriages. Economic, social and emotional constraints served to keep couples locked into intensely unsatisfactory and often violent

---

Three Questions

1 How does *your* experience of childhood, partnership and parenting measure up?

2 How does a child's perspective on parenting vary at different ages?

3 What difficulties do absent fathers encounter when they no longer share in day-to-day parental activities?

---

relationships, with death as the only merciful release. In the nineteenth century, two in every five children lost their father and almost the same proportion their mothers by the age of 15. Some 25 per cent would have lost both. Step-parents were just as much a feature of Victorian life as they are today, as was living in a lone-parent household. For those children, however, the loss of a parent was absolute, and the complexities of post-divorce parenting arrangements unknown. Divorce has profound effects on parenting. In assessing the consequences for children, a number of factors demand consideration: the way in which children are prepared for the divorce (and most are not); arrangements for continued contact with each parent and day-to-day living arrangements; the transition from two-parent to lone-parent (or step-parent) households; the number of disruptions; and, most critically, the quality of relationships between all those involved. It is impossible and unwise to generalize about the effects on children since much depends on their experiences in the family pre-divorce; the process of splitting up; their age and stage of development; and their gender (Schaffer, 1990; Burghes, 1994). The most distressed children, however, are those caught up in their parents' battles.

As families merge into step-families they face a range of pressures, but enduring parental conflict, child poverty and father absence are the three outcomes of separation and divorce causing the most concern, and it is the latter which casts the spotlight on what has been termed 'parenting deficit' (Etzioni, 1993): mothers stay with children, while fathers live apart and come to occupy a decidedly secondary parental relationship compared with mothers. Popular wisdom suggests that fathers consciously or unconsciously drop out of their children's lives after divorce because they lose interest, stop caring and abandon their responsibilities. Reforms in family law have sought to reinforce fathers' responsibilities: the provisions of the Children Act 1989; the Child Support Act 1991; and the Family Law Act 1996 emphasize the importance of co-operative parenting irrespective of marital status or living arrangements, stressing a pro-contact ideology which permeates the legal and welfare system and is firmly enshrined in social work practice.

Growing research evidence, however, demonstrates the difficulties fathers encounter when they no longer share in day-to-day parental activities, and conjugal and parental roles become disentangled (Simpson, McCarthy and Walker, 1995). Since post-divorce family relationships are dynamic and subject to change, new parental relationships have to integrate with new forms of old relationships, and there are rarely blueprints for how these should operate. The absence of clear cultural norms defining appropriate step-parent (particularly stepfather) responsibilities may contribute to the difficulties 'blended' families experience. Men and women have to renegotiate and redefine parental roles when parenting does not go hand in hand with marital partnership, and they are open to a complex set of influences. The shift away from 'home', 'wife', 'children' and the consequent domestic supports challenges a powerful hegemonic masculinity (Cornwall and Lindisfarne, 1994).

Changes in role divisions are reflected both in work patterns and in changes in the process, expectations and experience of partnership and family life. What emerges is parenting based less on authority, gender division and marital status, and more on the quality of relationships between adults and between parents and children. Although children derive real benefits when parents work together in the upbringing of children, particularly after separation and divorce, the development of an active father role can be problematic given a relative lack of role models beyond those associated with differentiated or complementary family structures.

Some commentators (Richards, 1995) believe that the more emphasis is placed on companionate marriage, the more it is likely to fail, and privatized marriages are the hardest kind to help: couples are reluctant to disclose their problems; others are reluctant to intrude (Clulow, 1995). Most parents do not report problems they experience, and professional assistance and support would appear to be in short supply unless children are formally identified as 'in trouble' or 'at risk'. Government departments, statutory and voluntary agencies have focused attention on programmes which promote good interpersonal relationships and enhance parenting skills: preparation and prevention in preference to crisis management, in the knowledge that people's capacity to sustain partnerships in adult life is significantly influenced by the models of partnership they internalize as children.

References

Anderson, M. (1995) 'Today's families in historical context', Paper given to Church of England/Joseph Rowntree Foundation Seminar, London.

Björnberg, U. (1995) 'Family orientation among men: fatherhood and partnership in a process of change', in J. Brannen and M. O'Brien (eds), *Childhood and Parenthood: Proceedings of the International Sociological Association Committee for Family Research Conference 1994*, London: Institute of Education, University of London.

Bowlby, J. (1988) *A Secure Base: Clinical Applications of Attachment Theory*, London: Routledge.

Brannen, J. and O'Brien, M. (eds), (1995) *Childhood and Parenthood: Proceedings of the International Sociological Association Committee for Family Research Conference 1994*, London: Institute of Education, University of London.

Burghes, L. (1994) *Lone Parenthood and Family Disruption: The Outcomes for Children*, London: Family Policy Studies Centre.

Clulow, C. (ed.) (1993) *Rethinking Marriage: Public and Private Perspectives*, London: Karnac Books.

Clulow, C. (ed.) (1995) *Women, Men and Marriage: Talks from the Tavistock Marital Studies Institute*, London: Sheldon Press.

Clulow, C. and Mattinson, J. (1989) *Marriage Inside Out: Understanding the Problems of Intimacy*, Harmondsworth: Penguin.

Cockett, M. and Tripp, J. (1994) *The Exeter Family Study: Family Breakdown and its Impact on Children*, Exeter: University of Exeter Press.

Cornwall, A. and Lindisfarne, N. (1994) 'Dislocating masculinity: gender, power and anthropology', in A. Cornwall and N. Lindisfarne (eds), *Dislocating Masculinity: Comparative Ethnographics*, London and New York: Routledge.

Cowan, C. and Cowan, P. (1992) *When Partners Become Parents*, USA: Basic Books.

Dennis, N. (1993) *Rising Crime and the Dismembered Family*, London: Institute of Economic Affairs Health and Welfare Unit.

Etzioni, A. (1993) *The Parenting Deficit*, London: Demos.

Gorer, G. (1955) *Exploring English Character*, London: Cresset Press & Criterion Books.

Gorer, G. (1971) *Sex and Marriage in England Today*, London: Nelson.

Kiernan, K. and Estaugh, V. (1993) 'Cohabitation: extra-marital childbearing and social policy', Occasional Paper 17, London: Family Policy Studies Centre.

Mansfield, P. (1995) 'What goes wrong in the relationship between parents', Paper given to the Joseph Rowntree Seminar, London.

Mansfield, P. and Collard, J. (1988) *The Beginning of the Rest of Your Life*, London: Macmillan.

Mansfield, P., Collard, J. and McAllister, F. (1996) *Person, Partner, Parent*, London: Macmillan.

Morgan, D. (1992) 'Marriage and society: understanding an era of change', in J. Lewis, D. Clark and D. Morgan (eds), *Whom God Hath Joined Together*, London and New York: Tavistock/Routledge.

Murray, C. (1990) *The Emerging Underclass*, London: Institute of Economic Affairs.

Office of Population Censuses and Surveys (1994) *1992 General Household Survey*, London: HMSO.

Pugh, G., De'Ath, E. and Smith, C. (1994) *Confident Parents, Confident Children: Policy and Practice in Parent Education and Support*, London: National Children's Bureau.

Reibstein, J. and Richards, M. (1992) *Sexual Arrangements: Marriage and Affairs*, London: Heinemann.

Richards, M. (1995) 'The companionship trap', in C. Clulow (ed.), *Women, Men and Marriage: Talks from the Tavistock Marital Studies Institute*, London: Sheldon Press.

Saporiti, A. (1989) 'Historical changes in the family's reproductive patterns', in K. Boh, M. Bak, C. Clason, M. Pankiatova, J. Qvortrup, G. B. Sgritta and K. Waerness (eds), *Changing Patterns of European Family Life*, London: Routledge.

Schaffer, R. (1990) *Making Decisions about Children: Psychological Questions and Answers*, Oxford: Blackwell.

Simpson, B., McCarthy, P. and Walker, J. (1995) *Being There: Fathers After Divorce*, Newcastle upon Tyne: Relate Centre for Family Studies, Newcastle University.

Utting, D. (1995) *Family and Parenthood: Supporting Families, Preventing Breakdown*, York: Joseph Rowntree Foundation.

Walker, J. (1991) 'Intervention in families', in D. Clark (ed.), *Marriage, Domestic Life and Social Change*, London and New York: Routledge.

Walker, J. (1995) 'Parenting in the 1990's', *RSA Journal*, vol. CXLIII, no. 5456, Jan./Feb.

Further Reading

1 Acock, A. C. and Demo, D. H. (1994) *Family Diversity and Well-Being*, Thousand Oaks, CA: Sage.

2 Brubaker, T. H. (ed.) (1993) *Family Relations: Challenges for the Future*, Newbury Park, CA: Sage.

3 Harding, L. F. (1996) *Family, State and Social Policy*, Basingstoke, Macmillan.

III.6
Late Life Ageing
Ian Philp

Late life ageing is shaped by the accumulation of life events and the proximity of death.

Although it is tempting to consider late life ageing as that which occurs towards the end of life, it is becoming increasingly recognized that late life ageing is profoundly influenced by earlier life experience. For example, a substantial body of research from the Medical Research Council Epidemiology Unit in Southampton suggests that early life nutritional experience, including as an embryo, affects health status in late life (Barker, 1992). Therefore, late life ageing needs to be considered as part of the complete life course.

Rembrandt's self-portraits in late life reflect this. His method of building up the foreground from the background until a clear and unique portrait emerges is one reason why his paintings of old age resonate. His method is analogous to late life ageing; the production of a complex and unique individual emerging from layer upon layer of background experience.

As long life increases exposure to life events, there is a tendency for late life ageing to be characterized by increasing diversity amongst individuals in relation to their health, functioning, relationships, standards of living, attitudes and perceived quality of life.

Although death is the ultimate leveller, late life ageing is not. We need, therefore, to avoid the temptation to make general assumptions which are too simplistic to explain late life ageing.

Furthermore, the world is changing at an accelerating pace, so the 80-year olds of 20 years from now will have lived in very different times from the 80-year olds of today, or 20 years ago, whose lives were dominated by the cataclysmic events of two world wars. One of the most obvious changes is the greying of the population which is occurring in both the developed and developing worlds. However, the expectations of older people for improved material and health status may have as much impact on late life as the proportionate increase in the number of older people in the population.

Societies are also becoming more heterogeneous with widening differences (sometimes referred to as inequalities) in health and income which persist into later life.

To a large extent, then, late life ageing reflects the life-long influence of many external events on the individual. This process is described as extrinsic ageing.

Intrinsic ageing, on the other hand, refers to the ageing processes which are independent of external events which, to a large extent, are programmed by genetic control. The genetic basis of ageing is illustrated by the 'disposable soma' theory (Kirkwood, 1995). This states that the human body is simply a vehicle for the transmission of genetic material. Ultimately, the human body is disposable, having served its role in the transmission of genetic material. In late life, it is of greater evolutionary advantage for the human to support 25 per cent of his or her gene pool in his or her grandchild, than 50 per cent in his or her child. Much human attitude and behaviour can, therefore, be explained from this perspective, including differing societal attitudes to old age which, on the one hand, include idealized views of old people in grandparenting roles and, on the other hand, discrimination against old people in relation to life-saving interventions (Giallombardo and Homer, 1994). The most graphic illustration of an ambiguous attitude to old age is the apocryphal tale of a native American tribe which, in times of plenty, venerates its elders and, in times of famine, eats them (Eric Midwinter – personal communication).

An important determinant of intrinsic ageing is the limitation of the number of times different cells of the body can replicate. This is referred to as the 'Hayflick Limit', although the theory can be traced back to the nineteenth century (Weismann, 1891). Replication is necessary to repair worn out cells. In theory, it may be possible to alter the mechanisms which limit cell division, creating immortal cells, and extending life expectancy. However, interference with intrinsic ageing may extend life of poor quality if other ageing changes persist. Put simply, we could live for 700 years, but the last 600 would be spent in a state of advanced dementia.

In fact, advances in medical science are increasing our ability to modify extrinsic rather than intrinsic ageing, but there remains the prospect of molecular and genetic treatments becoming available which would fundamentally alter late life ageing.

The overall impact of recent health and social care systems on late life ageing is debated. Some have argued that the net effect has been the 'survival of the unfittest' (Isaacs, 1972), whereby people who would otherwise have died are saved for a life of disability. Others argue that the net effect has been to extend healthy active life which could lead to the compression of the period of disability into the last few years of life, prior to

Five Key Points

1 Late life ageing is shaped by the accumulation of life events and the proximity of death.
2 Old people vary in health, functioning, relationships, standards of living, attitudes and their perceived quality of life.
3 Advances in medical science are increasing our ability to modify extrinsic rather than intrinsic ageing.
4 Life expectancy for humans limited by intrinsic ageing is reckoned to be about 120 years.
5 Despite the many losses which accompany late life ageing, many older people achieve a sense of integrity.

natural death from old age (Fries, 1980).

The balance of epidemiological evidence suggests that modern health and social care systems are helping to extend both healthy active life and disability-associated life prior to death. The combined effect, therefore, extends overall life expectancy (figure III.6.1).

Perhaps because extrinsic factors are predominant in the ageing process, we have yet to see life expectancy increase to the extent that compression of morbidity can occur as we get close to the limit of human life. Life expectancy for humans limited by intrinsic ageing is reckoned to be about 120 years.

A common misperception about ageing is that ill health and disability in later life are an inevitable feature of growing old. Although some features, such as deafness, poor vision, arthritis, a decline in fitness, failing memory and loss of teeth are common, they are not inevitable in old age. The phenomenon of 'successful' ageing has been described, based on studies of cohorts of middle-aged people who have been followed over time into later life (Rowe and Kahn, 1987). Most of these people experience 'usual' ageing, characterized by a decline

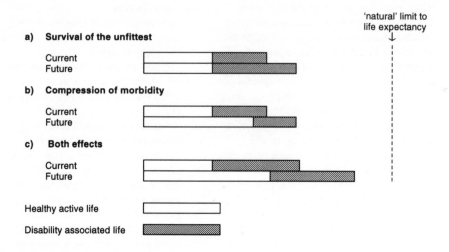

Figure III.6.1   Ageing trends.

in a number of body functions, but some experience very little age-associated decline. Others experience greater than usual decline, described as 'pathological' ageing.

The importance of these studies is that they point to the challenge for disease prevention which could modify usual ageing towards successful ageing for future cohorts of elderly people. These studies also show that usual ageing changes are less dramatic than popular conceptions of ageing, which, for example, equate ageing with dementia. Only about 20 per cent of people aged 85 plus experience dementia, an example of pathological ageing, although most experience mild memory loss (usual ageing) and a small proportion experience no memory loss (successful ageing). These clinical findings are corroborated by autopsy examination of the brains of older people where a minority have extensive numbers of neurofibrillary tangles and plaques (the hallmark of Alzheimer's Disease); most have a few, and a minority have none.

Public health goals may be directed towards promoting successful ageing, but health and social care practitioners will continue to work with older people whose ageing process is usual or pathological. A preoccupation with successful ageing could lead to discrimination against older people with disease and disability.

Disease in late life often comes to attention in non-specific ways including falls, confusion, immobility and failure to thrive. These presentations can be precipitated by a wide range of events, from a urinary infection to a change of environment, but there is usually a background of longer term problems and a complex interplay of physical, psychological and social factors. Treatment strategies themselves may add to the problem. The term 'iatrogenesis' is used to describe illness induced by treatment and is fairly common in older people. The physiological reserve of the older person may be small, so that he or she may function adequately most of the time, but with a minimal threat a critical threshold may be breached causing dysfunction. A chain-reaction may be set up where dysfunction in one area leads to multiple failures of organs, systems, overall functioning and perhaps death.

For these reasons, rapid response to crises in older people may be rewarded by restoration of the older person to a state of acceptable health and functioning. However, repeated crises will reduce physiological reserve further and create a vicious cycle of increasing frequency of crisis and further decline in physiological reserve.

Much of health and social care practice is, therefore, concerned with caring for this type of frail older person, living close to the edge of incapacity. Fragmentation of health and social care systems, and exclusion of older people from access to acute care services undermines our ability to respond to the dynamic needs of older people, and leads to an increased reliance on long-term care services or family care to support an increasingly disabled population of older people. Policy trends in health and social care for elderly people in the United Kingdom are worrying in this respect.

A medical model of ageing which embraces the concepts of disability and disease inevitably reinforces the perception of ageing as a process of decline. A perception of decline in late life extends to the psychological and social as well as physical features of late life ageing, characterized by loss of health, autonomy, financial status and the comfort of family, friendship and marital relations. Yet the experience of late life ageing for many people is not dominated by decline, but by accomplishment and satisfaction with life.

A theoretical basis for a positive view of late life ageing is provided by the work of Eric Erikson on psychological ageing.

Each stage of life, from infancy to old age is characterized by a psychological battle between successful and unsuccessful ageing. In old age, the battle is between integrity and despair. Integrity is characterized by a sense that life was worthwhile, life's mission is complete, and death, while not welcome, is not

feared. Despair is accompanied by a fear of death, or death may be desired because life is seen as worthless.

With increasing longevity, there may be a stage beyond integrity, given that years of life may follow the milestone when life's mission is perceived to have been accomplished (Erikson et al., 1986). In spite of the many losses which accompany late life ageing, many,

---

Three Questions

1 What ethical concerns are raised by the potential of genetic therapy to intervene in the ageing process?

2 If the goals of public health are to reduce disability-associated life prior to death, would resources be withdrawn from disabled older people?

3 How will social work for older people change when the 'me' generation reach old age?

---

perhaps most, older people achieve a sense of integrity. Perhaps the fundamental task of social work with old people should be to promote this goal. Recent work on 'life strengths' (Kivnic, 1991) provides a systematic approach for doing so.

There is much still to be studied about late life ageing, and how it is changing

---

Further Reading

1 Erikson, E. H., Erikson, J. M. and Kivnic, H. Q. (1986) *Vital Involvement in Old Age: the Experience of Old Age in Our Time*, New York: Norton.

2 Fries, J. F. (1980) 'Ageing, natural death and the compression of morbidity', *New England Journal of Medicine*, 303, 130–5.

3 Isaacs, B. (1972) *Survival of the Unfittest: a Study of Geriatric Patients in Glasgow*, London: Routledge & Kegan Paul.

with time, and amongst individuals and cultures of great diversity. New horizons from genetics to psychology are appearing, which could change the course of late life ageing. We can be sure of very little, except that the challenge to better understand late life ageing will remain a fascinating and worthwhile endeavour.

References

Barker, D. J. P. (ed.) (1992) *Fetal and Infant Origins of Adult Disease*, London: British Medical Journal.

Erikson, E. H., Erikson, J. M. and Kivnic, H. Q. (1986) *Vital Involvement in Old Age: The Experience of Old Age in Our Time*, New York: Norton.

Fries, J. F. (1980) 'Ageing, natural death and the compression of morbidity', *New England Journal of Medicine*, 303, 130–5.

Giallombardo, E., Homer, A. (1994) 'Resuscitation: a survey of policies', *Journal of the British Society of Gerontology, Generations Review*, 4(3), 5–7.

Isaacs, B. (1972) *Survival of the Unfittest: a Study of Geriatric Patients in Glasgow*, London: Routledge & Kegan Paul.

Kirkwood, T. B. L. (1995) 'The evolution of ageing', *Reviews in Clinical Gerontology*, 5, 3–9.

Kivnic, H. Q. (1991) *Living with Care, Caring for Life: the Inventory of Life Strengths*, School of Social Work, University of Minnesota, Minneapolis.

Medical Research Council, A Healthy Old Age, Autumn 1994, no. 64.

Rowe, J. W., Kahn, R. L. (1987) 'Human ageing: usual and successful', *Science*, 237, 143–9.

Weismann, A. (1891) *Essays Upon Heredity and Kindred Biological Problems*, vol. 1, Oxford: Clarendon Press.

Part IV
Reasons for Social Work

Introduction to Part IV

Social work in the modern state, unlike education and health, neither universally provides for nor is universally taken up as a service by all citizens. It is selective. And the reasons for its use are almost always to do with disadvantage of one kind or another. Chris Jones argues that poverty is not sufficiently recognized as a common factor among most of the recipients of social work, and this is likely to be because the precipitating variable that brings the social worker into play often has the dimensions of a personal crisis: a criminal conviction, a psychiatric breakdown, a family upheaval, allegations of child abuse, the diagnosis of disability in a developing child, or the recognition that the inexorable process of bodily ageing has reached the point when an elderly person can no longer survive unaided. Social workers in each of these fields become knowledgeable about the relevant specialist disciplines impinging upon their work – psychology, medicine, sociology and the law. They develop high quality expertise in their own right. The service they provide varies in its range and retains an essential flexibility. Interdisciplinary relations – for example, with the police, doctors, nurses and therapists – become an integral part of the working process.

When Alvin Schorr, the distinguished American sociologist was invited to provide an outsider's view of contemporary personal social services in Britain he opened his chapter on clients with the following observation:

The most striking characteristics that clients of the personal social services have in common are poverty and deprivation. Often this is not mentioned, possibly because the social services are said to be based on universalistic principles. Still, everyone in the business knows it. One survey after another shows that clients are unemployed or, to observe a technical distinction, not employed – that is, not working and not seeking work. Perhaps half receive income support, as many as 80 per cent have incomes at or below income support levels.

(*Schorr, 1992, p. 8, emphasis added*)

That this stark characteristic of social work's client population is often not mentioned says much about social work's relationship to the poor and the particularity, even peculiarity of British social work as a state agency dealing with the poor. Ask any new cohort of students on a professional social work course who are the clients of social work and you are likely to be offered a list of people and conditions such as the elderly, single parents, those with disabilities, mental health problems, children and families. The words poverty and the poor are rarely heard. That common reality appears to be lost behind an array of categories. Yet, just as Schorr observed, survey after survey reveals that poverty and deprivation are the most striking common characteristics of social work's client population. It has always been so

since the origins of modern social work created by the Charity Organisation Society (COS) in Victorian Britain.

The research evidence is compelling. In the mid-1980s Becker and MacPherson (1988) discovered that nine out of ten clients were dependent on state benefits, of whom the majority were dependent on means tested benefits. This corroborated the findings of Strathclyde's Social Work Department which noted in 1982/3 that 90 per cent of all its referrals had social security as their main source of income (Becker, Macpherson and Falkingham, 1987).

Impoverishment is a key variable in determining involvement with the personal social services. The Department of Health's report (1991) on children coming into care noted that one in ten of children aged between 5 and 9 years in families dependent on state benefits were admitted into care, compared with 1 in 7,000 for children in the same age group living in families not on income support. The data on all the major client groups of the personal social services, from the elderly, to people with disabilities, embracing the disproportionate numbers of women and black people who are in contact with social work agencies, reveal the centrality of poverty.

Despite the evidence that the vast majority of clients are in poverty, Becker and Silburn observed that:

for many years social workers have been uneasy about their role and responsibility vis-à-vis people in poverty. This is the more curious as so much of the originating impulse behind organised philanthropy was precisely a concern about the welfare of the poor, and so many of the techniques and skills that are now of the essence of professional social work were originally evolved within 19th century agencies such as the Charity Organisation Society, for whom the relief of poverty was a fundamental concern. But in our own time, this historic connection has become severed, and today many social workers, their managers and educators are reluctant to acknowledge the inescapably close professional contact they have with some of the poorest in the land.

(Becker and Silburn, 1990, p. 8)

Historical analysis is valuable in helping us to understand the particular relationship between social work and poverty and in shedding light on the manner in which modern social work relates to its impoverished client populations. From its modern origins in the COS, British social work has determinedly argued for a distinctive approach to the problems of poverty and the poor. In particular, it has sought to carve out a role and practice which separates it from the state agencies which are specifically responsible for the administration and distribution of financial relief to the poor. Up until 1948 this focused on the relationship between social work and the Poor Law and since that time, its relationship with the social security system. Common throughout has been the dominant argument that social work should not be involved in any significant manner with financial relief, and that what financial powers it did have under child care legislation, such as in the provision of moneys under Section One (England and Wales) or Section 12 (Scotland) to prevent children from being admitted into care have been scrupulously regulated in order to prevent social service agencies from being perceived by clients as relief-giving bodies.

Despite the prevalence of financial hardship and material poverty amongst all sections of the client populations, the position taken by social work with respect to financial relief was based on a clear and well-articulated perspective on the

Five Key Points

1 Poverty remains overwhelmingly the most common problem confronting social work's diverse client population.

2 Irrespective of specialisms and other divisions, social work is an activity which is overwhelmingly concerned with the lives and conduct of the most impoverished sections of the population.

3 Since Victorian times, British social work has understood poverty predominantly as a consequence of psychological inadequacy rooted in either the individual or family rather than as a social or political problem.

4 The history of social work reveals a profession with ambiguous and paradoxical attitudes towards its impoverished clients.

5 Individualism and familialism within social work theory and practice have enfeebled the profession as a critic of enduring inequality and the systemic reproduction of poverty in Britain.

poor and the causes of poverty. Namely, the problem of poverty was not a problem about the manner in which society distributed or managed its resources to ensure that all people could live free from want. Inequality and its associated poverty was not the problem, rather these were wholly natural and understandable features of societies. As Patrick Colquhoun noted in his *Treatise on Indigence* published in 1806:

Poverty is the state and condition in society where the individual has no surplus labour in store, and, consequently, no property but what is derived from the constant exercise of industry in the various occupations of life; or in other words, it is the state of everyone who must labour for subsistence. Poverty is therefore a most necessary and indispensable ingredient in society, without which nations and communities could not exist in a state of civilisation.

(cited Rose, 1971, p. 47)

Such a perception of poverty as necessary and inevitable informed the early social workers' perception of the problem of poverty. This concern was not unconditional compassion for the plight of those living without adequate resources. Rather it was a concern that destitution and dependency was a destructive and potentially destabilizing condition that was both politically and economically threatening to the ongoing development of British society.

Unlike their social work equivalents of today, the leaders of the COS were significant in shaping elite attitudes to poverty and the poor, and were forthright in asserting their perspective on the problem of poverty and the poor (Jones, 1983). For them, the problem of poverty was primarily located within the poor themselves. The monthly journal of the COS, stated this clearly:

There can be no doubt that the poverty of the working classes of England is due, not to their circumstances (which are more favourable than those of any working population of Europe); but to their improvident habits and thriftlessness.

If they are ever to be more prosperous, it must be through self-denial, temperance and forethought.

(Charity Organisation Review, *1881, vol. 10, p. 50*)

Throughout the writings of the leading members of the Society, Charles Loch, Helen and Bernard Bosanquet and Octavia Hill, it was stressed time and again that social work's task must avoid any materialistic strategy of financial relief and be focused on improving the character of the poor to ensure that they adopted as their own, values of thrift, sobriety, self-reliance and independence. If this was done they argued, destitution could be prevented, poverty be made tolerable and social harmony and stability achieved. Lack of resources was decidedly rejected as being the problem of poverty, for as Helen Bosanquet argued:

I speak confidently, with full knowledge of all the difficulties of a small income, when I say that there are comparatively few families in London through whose hands there had not passed in the course of a year sufficient money and money's worth to have made a life free at any rate from hunger, and cold, and with much in it of good.

(Bosanquet, 1902, pp. 101–2)

For these social work pioneers, the problem was not insufficient material resources within the working-class poor but rather their morality. The 23rd *Annual Report* of the COS succinctly summarized this perspective:

Speaking broadly and after all due deductions made, one may say that character is the key to circumstances, he therefore, that would permanently mend circumstances must aim at character. All that can be done externally to improve circumstances should be done, but there will be no lasting betterment without internal change.

(1891, p. 9)

This idealistic perspective which accords primacy to character and morality rather than material circumstances has been a decisive influence in the development of British social work, both in its practice and in its understanding of poverty and the poor. It is from this perspective that social work has emphasized the value of its strategy which concerns itself with the character and behaviour of the poor rather than material relief. While it does not entirely neglect material conditions, nor the necessity for financial assistance to be offered in some instances, it has entailed the development of a social work practice and perspective on the poor which places primacy not on material circumstances but on values and attitudes and thus determined its essentially individualistic and moralistic orientation. When social work does offer material assistance, not only is it carefully supervised and specifically targeted – it is not uncommon for social workers to spend any money provided for clothes or food on behalf of the client – it is almost always conditional. Handler (1968) provided the following example whereby a social worker refused financial help to a family for two months:

During this time, it was made plain that this lever was being used until more co-operative efforts were forthcoming. The [child care] officer wanted a better work effort from the husband and a change in attitude as to what the family thought was owing to them from the welfare state.

(Handler, 1968, p. 486)

He concluded by noting:

That the operative principles in the Children's Departments today are remarkably similar to those of the Charity Organisation Society, founded about one hundred years ago. The close supervision of the spending of money is little different from the old system of relief in kind; poor people cannot be trusted to spend money that isn't 'theirs'.

(Handler, 1968, p. 487)

More specifically, social work's tendency towards individualism and familialism and the concomitant assumptions about the moral or character frailties of clients, has generated an ongoing sense of paradox and uncertainty about its perspectives on the poor and impoverished. Even at the time of the COS and through to the current period social work texts carry a sense of genuine concern and compassion about the difficulties and circumstances of clients. Social work's claim to be considered as a caring liberal occupation has not been spurious. In the case of the COS, for example, once clients had met the strict criteria imposed to determine eligibility for social work assistance (rather than the harsh embrace of the Poor Law), charity workers provided a supervised package of financial and material resources which often resulted in substantial improvements in their circumstances. The COS was determined to offer help which would permanently improve the condition of their clients which involved

the co-ordination of resources provided by relatives, neighbours and former employers that would allow the client to regain independence (examples included provision of sewing machines, tools and equipment). Ironically, contemporary social work, with all its restrictions and procedures with respect to offering financial assistance is often less forthcoming. Nevertheless, as Becker and Silburn (1990) noted in their survey of poor clients, many social workers invest considerable effort to maximize the welfare benefits of their clients and search through charitable resources to alleviate some of their acute hardships. Certainly, many of the social work texts which

---

Three Questions

1 Why are social workers so uneasy about their role and responsibility *vis-à-vis* people in poverty?

2 Are there any differences between the COS's concept of 'undeserving poor' and the concept of 'underclass' popularized by the new right in the 1990s?

3 What would a social work practice look like which took a more critical social perspective on poverty and inequality in contemporary society?

---

describe and inform practice portray empathy and compassion for client problems.

Yet the familialist and individualistic foci and the resistance within mainstream social work to consider the systemic social reproduction of poverty and inequality in contemporary society leaves its mark on social work's ambiguous attitudes to the poor. Simultaneously, it is possible to discover social work texts expressing concern and compassion for clients and warning social workers that clients are not to be trusted. In the discussions on the place of material assistance to clients there is a significant historical continuity in social work texts which warn social workers of the manipulative and grasping behaviour of clients. In an anonymously authored article in the *Charity Organisation Review* which provided guidance to charity workers on 'How to Take Down a Case', the author was concerned that new workers should be particularly attendant to the 'different manners' of the working class:

It must be recollected that the poor differ from the more educated in their standards or morals, their code of honour, and their public opinion. To some the legal tie of marriage seems of little importance. Rent is often held of less obligation than other debts. Early marriages and large families are common, and no stigma attaches to those responsible for them. Chivalry is sometimes conspicuously absent. Wives are sent to the relieving officer or to apply for charity while their husbands loaf and smoke at home.

(Anon, 1895, p. 143)

The insistence on charity workers making a home visit was also informed by similar concerns. A Miss Hunt of Gloucester COS was reported as 'having insisted on the importance of visiting the homes and giving relief there; then it would be apparent if want was real, especially if the visits were unexpected' (*Charity Organisation Review* 1895, vol. 11, pp. 263–4). In more recent social work texts such notions of clients as being 'different kinds' of people abound. According to an American social work writer 'problem families' are:

Primitive in ego development, they are quickly overwhelmed by outside pressures and anxieties of the moment, and seek the worker out in their pain and panic . . . Over and over again one senses, beneath a hostile veneer, an oral character; a client who never stops demanding . . . The dependency is pervasive and the client sucks from neighbours, shopkeepers, bartenders and news vendors as well as family members and social workers.

(Cited Richan and Mendelsohn, 1973, p. 15)

Elizabeth Irvine, an influential social

work writer of the 1950s and 1960s similarly noted that a 'great number' of clients, 'resemble greedy demanding children, always clamouring for material help, always complaining of unfair treatment or deprivation; this attitude shades into paranoid imagining or provoking of slights and rebuffs' (Irvine, 1954, p. 27).

Especially through the two decades after the Second World War when variants of psychoanalysis dominated much social work thinking and practice, combined with an optimism that the Keynesian welfare state had largely eradicated systemic poverty, social work tended to further marginalize the experience and reality of poverty amidst its client populations. It was common practice during those years for social workers to claim that the material problems and financial hardships with which so many clients sought help from agencies, were in fact not the 'real issue'. Rather client problems of poverty were renegotiated by social workers as 'presenting problems' behind which 'lies not just a lack of money, or even financial mismanagement, but deeper disturbances in family relationships' (Rodgers, 1960, p. 89). Smith and Harris (1972) discovered in their survey of social work agencies, social workers who denied the problems of poverty for their clients. This was exemplified by the social worker who argued that 'it's not a question of poverty but mismanagement or emotional difficulties which make them spend money the wrong way – you can manage [on welfare benefits] but it's not the kind of thing an inadequate person can do.'

It is a testimony to the prevalence, reproduction and potency of these ideologies concerning the causes of poverty that an occupation such as social work, which in its day-to-day activities is immersed in the underbelly of British society and works with some of its most impoverished and disadvantaged members, and yet employs largely compassionate and liberal educated workers, can maintain such a perverse perspective on poverty. As John Clarke (1993) observed, the concern of mainstream social work to focus on individual circumstances and not on systemic and structural factors of deprivation and inequality means in general terms 'that social work has tended to reproduce rather than redress social inequality'. He continued:

This is not to question the compassion, care and concern of individual social workers, or to suggest that individuals have not been helped by the intervention of social workers. But it is important to recognise that the position and role of social work as a social intervention was dominated by pressures to separate the alleviation of individual misery from concerns with structural inequality. This structuring of social work established constraints and limitations on the forms of help and intervention that were available to social workers.
(*Clarke, 1993, p. 18*)

This focus on individual misery and lack of attention to patterns and processes of structural inequality has been a major feature of British social work and was one of the factors which gave rise to social work's fracturing of the poor into supposedly discrete client groups (Jones, 1983). It also underlies Schorr's observation that social work rarely draws attention to the poverty of its clients and helps to explain the great attention within social work education to providing theoretical models and perspectives which divert social workers away from addressing in any detail the systemic reproduction of poverty and inequality (Jones, 1996). Within agencies which are structured to deal with cases (individual clients) and not issues, social workers are left struggling to explain damaged lives and sometimes brutalized behaviour – as much a consequence of poverty and stigma as empty purses – which often leaves them embracing commonly held pathologizing and prejudicial views of their clients. These interacting factors go

some way to make sense of Becker's discovery that with respect to poverty awareness, social workers:

As a group . . . appear supportive (especially in comparison to the general public). But as individuals their poverty awareness has tendencies towards hostility and prejudice.
(*Becker, 1988, p. 248*)

One consequence of these processes is that social workers and their agencies have been historically viewed with some suspicion by organizations of poor people. A National Federation of Claimant's Union's handbook, for example, maintained, that social services departments 'are worse than the Social Security – they ask you all sorts of questions about your private life and when they refuse to pay you, there is no right of appeal' (cited Carmichael, 1974, p. 62; see also Bradshaw, 1974).

Many of the important continuities in social work's position with respect to poverty and the poor flow from the understandable refusal of a state welfare activity to take a radical political economy perspective. Any meaningful attention to the systemic reproduction of poverty would demand changes of a revolutionary character in British society and would certainly mean a rapid demise of statutory social work. Despite the predominant pathologization of poor clients social work activity and intervention has not always been wholly negative or repressive.

During the later 1960s and early 1970s

Further Reading
1 Becker, S. and Silburn, R. (1990) *The New Poor Clients*, London: Community Care.
2 Bosanquet, H. (1906) *The Family*, London: Macmillan.
3 Novak, T. (1988) *Poverty and the State*, Milton Keynes: Open University Press.

many social workers influenced by developments in radical social policy, feminist and black scholarship took a far more radical perspective on the enduring poverty of clients. There was less readiness to lapse into crude casework or to dismiss the clients' own definition of their problems as mere presenting problems masking more fundamental relational or psychological definitions. The result with respect to practice was a preparedness to take more seriously the material needs of clients, and some, particularly Labour authorities, exemplified by Strathclyde, sought to maximize the income of their clients through extensive welfare rights work. Social work qualifying courses too began to include welfare rights teaching reflecting this growing interest.

Such work whilst hardly revolutionary did mark an important shift away from much of the earlier pathologizing approaches. It also saw many social workers becoming active in pressure groups such as the Child Poverty Action Group, and an active anti-poverty lobby within the British Association of Social Workers (Holman, 1993, p. 45). Equally significant, social workers especially in voluntary agencies such as the Family Service Units (e.g., Cohen et al., 1992) began to draw upon their close contact with the poor to draw out in graphic detail the corrosive impact of long-term poverty on the lives, aspirations, mental health and relationships of those living increasingly in such conditions. Such insights were especially valuable in challenging the pathologizing of the poor for it revealed not only the corrosive realities of living in poverty but also the strengths and skills of previously discounted people as able and innovative survivors. Moreover, such studies also assisted in exposing the multi-dimensional character of contemporary poverty, its lack of choice and opportunity and the manner in which poverty compounded and even created

the problems of crime, mental ill health and the frailties of ageing and physical disabilities.

Whilst such important work continues and the insights generated are not easily wished away, the profound restructuring of welfare systems and ideology which has taken place since the mid-1970s with the rise of the new right has impacted deeply on social work's relationship to poverty and the poor. Successive Conservative governments since the late 1970s have taken a decisively new position with respect to poverty and the poor which has been characterized by toughness, exclusion and close management (Novak, 1988). It has been a policy change which has impacted on every aspect of state welfare activity from social security through to housing, health and education. In the process a new role has been devised for statutory social work not so much as a provider of services or even as a therapeutic intervention but rather as a front-line service focused on the management of exclusion and rationing of scarce resources.

Conservative governments have sought legitimation for such a revolution in welfare provision and ideology by proclaiming that the previous social democratic welfare system was ineffective and wasteful. Ironically, its message closely mirrored the position of the COS, which had also claimed that state welfare for the poor undermined morality, weakened family obligations and created long-term dependency and generated unfounded expectations of the state as provider in periods of need. Moreover, as with the COS, the new right have reasserted the view that poverty and inequality *per se* are both natural and necessary and that it is quite possible to live honourably in poverty without having recourse to crime or other deviant activities.

The consequences of this policy shift have been awesome. As the Rowntree Report on Income and Wealth (1995) noted, poverty and inequality in Britain has deepened over the past 20 years, and in the midst of most of Britain's major cities there are now significant populations who are living in the most abject Third World conditions.

Likewise, the implications for social work have been severe. Considered by many on the right as the epitome of all that was wrong with the previous welfare regime, social work has survived but in a transformed state. In relation to the poor, social work has become a far more regulated and managed activity with a resultant loss in social workers' autonomy and manoeuvrability. One notable consequence has been the deepening levels of antagonism between social workers and their clients, as state social work has been shifted towards a more regulatory and coercive role (Jones and Novak, 1993).

Nevertheless, irrespective of government policies, social work and poverty are irredeemably linked. It may be mediated by other categories such as ageing, disability, marital status, gender and 'race' but its centrality cannot be denied or wished away. But what is less certain, and the question which has haunted social work from its very origins is that which has remained often unspoken on the lips of many clients: is social work to be an activity which is part of our solution or is it to remain as part of our problem? That remains the question.

References

Adler, M. E. (ed.) (1974) *In Cash or In Kind*, Edinburgh: Social Administration Department, Edinburgh University.
Anon (1895) 'How to take down a case', *Charity Organisation Review*, 11.
Becker, S. (1988) 'Poverty Awareness', in S. Becker and S. MacPherson (eds), *Public Issues Private Pain*, London: Insight.
Becker, S. and Silburn, R. (1990) *The New Poor Clients*, London: Community Care.
Becker, S., MacPherson, S. and Falkingham, F. (1987) 'Some local authority responses to poverty', *Local Government Studies*, 13(3), 35–48.
Bosanquet, H. (1902) *The Strength of the People*, London: Macmillan.
Bradshaw, J. (1974) 'Financial help in social work', in M. E. Adler (ed.) (1974).
Carmichael, K. (1974) 'The relationship between social work departments and the DHSS: the use of the Social Work (Scotland) Act', in M. E. Adler (ed.).
Clarke, J. (1993) 'The comfort of strangers: social work in context', in Clarke (ed.) (1993).
Clarke, J. (ed.) (1993) *A Crisis in Care: Challenges to Social Work*, London: Sage.
Cohen, R., Coxall, J., Craig, G. and Sadiq-Sangster, A. (1992) *Hardship Britain, Being Poor in the 1990s*, London: CPAG in conjunction with FSU.
COS, Charity Organization Society (1891) *23rd Annual Report*, London: COS.
Department of Health (1991) *Patterns and Outcomes in Child Placement*, London: HMSO.
Gibbons, J. (1990) *Family Support and Prevention*, London: HMSO.
Handler, J. F. (1968) 'The coercive children's officer', *New Society*, 3 October.
Holman, B. (1993) *A New Deal for Social Welfare*, Oxford: Lion Books.
Irvine, E. (1954) 'Research into problem families', *British Journal of Psychiatric Social Work*, 9, Spring.
Jones, C. (1983) *State Social Work and The Working Class*, London: Macmillan.
Jones, C. (1996) 'Anti-intellectualism and the peculiarities of British social work education', in Parton N. (ed.), *Social Work, Social Theory and Society*, London: Routledge.
Jones, C. and Novak, T. (1993) 'Social work today' *British Journal of Social Work*, 23, 195–212.
Joseph Rowntree Foundation (1995) 'Income and wealth: report of the JRF inquiry group', *Social Policy Summary*, Feb., York.
Novak, T. (1988) *Poverty and the State*, Milton Keynes: Open University Press.
Richan, W. C. and Mendelsohn, A. R. (1973) *Social Work: The Unloved Profession*, New York: New Viewpoints.
Rodgers, B. N. (1960) 'The administration of the social services and the family caseworker', *Social Work* (USA) 17(4).
Rose, M. (1971) *The English Poor Law*, Newton Abbott: David and Charles.
Schorr, A. (1992) *The Personal Social Services: an Outside View*, York: Joseph Rowntree Foundation.
Smith, G. and Harris, R. (1972) 'Ideologies of need and the organisation of social work departments', *British Journal of Social Work*, 2(1).

Social work within the criminal justice and penal system has been aptly described as the 'Russian front' of the profession (Macdonald, 1994). It is a hard field in which to demonstrate effectiveness with a caseload characterized by a very high incidence of social and personal problems and an 'undeserving' profile. Social work has come under heavy bombardment from the Home Office for obstructing policy emphasizing punishment and enforcement, and also friendly fire from academic allies who scorn the contribution of generic social work to the reduction of crime and argue that the probation service should abandon its social work allegiance and carve a new identity as a 'community justice agency' (Nellis, 1995).

This dispatch from the war zone will argue that, despite past shortcomings, social work is gaining a new coherence, self-confidence, legitimacy and empirical worth in its work with offenders, maintaining a distinctive contribution in criminal justice. Uniquely charged with statutory responsibilities from point of conviction to conclusion of sentence, social workers and probation officers draw on knowledge of why and how people become (and some persist as) offenders, and what has the potential to reduce offending in a way which informs and expands the judicial imagination and which negotiates with, challenges and integrates the offender.

Nellis is right to argue the neglected merits of criminological theory for 'community justice' practitioners. This chapter draws particularly upon control theory and upon John Braithwaite's work on 'reintegrative shaming' and new developments in psychological criminology. Control theory concentrates attention on factors outside of the criminal justice system which influence people in the direction of conformity through incentives and disincentives. Roshier (1989) helpfully identifies a number of seminal human needs (affection, status, stimulation, autonomy, security, money, belief) which offer sources of control: 'their satisfaction can be used to drive us towards conformity, and the threat of their denial can be used to divert us from criminality'. Control theory's usefulness in making sense of probation work has been demonstrated in a survey of some 1,400 young adult offenders (Stewart et al., 1994).

Psychological criminology has shown the scope for enhancing offenders' cognitive and reasoning skills. Reintegrative shaming emphasizes moral education. In place of conventional stigmatization, it proffers 'disapproval dispersed within an on-going relationship with the offender based on respect, shaming which focuses on the evil of the deed rather than on the offender' (Braithwaite, 1993). It's an integral feature of Braithwaite's wider 'republican criminology' which seeks to promote 'dominion' (maximum self-determination within the obligations and responsibility of citizenship) and 'parsimony', the minimum necessary use of penal sanctions and exclusionary institutions. Republican criminologists argue that penal policy cannot stand in isolation but must contribute to the attainment of social policy goals which enhance the individual within a conception of the common good.

The broad task for social work is thus:

to engage offenders in a reintegrative dialogue and offer opportunities for them to participate in constructive responses to the harm caused by offending, including efforts to find alternatives to offending in their own lives. This also involves influencing criminal justice processes towards less coercive and more participatory outcomes.

(*Raynor and Vanstone, 1994*)

Given the 'attrition rate' which eliminates the vast majority of crime-as-committed from social work attention, this account concentrates on work with convicted offenders, though social work agencies also use their special knowledge of offending patterns to make a distinctive contribution in broader crime prevention activity.

The Court Arena

The invitation to the social worker to assist the court in understanding the offence and assessing the offender's culpability, and to share the sentencer's dilemma concerning disposal provides a broad opportunity to place the offence in structural, cultural and biographical context, including the elements of motive, intention, need, choice, temperament and constraints within which the crime occurred. This is not to ignore social work's position of 'structural subordination' within the legal arena nor the power relationships which set boundaries to permissible discourses which package the offender and impose limits upon social workers' influence.

The interplay of offence and offender-centred considerations in the assessment of culpability is complex but the social worker's contribution is to enquire beyond the surface facts in a dialogue

Five Key Points

1   As an indication of offenders' adverse social circumstances: of a sample of probation clients aged 17–23, 80 per cent left school without qualifications; only 17 per cent had lived with their parents all their lives; 67 per cent had a weekly income below £40 (1991). Of a sample of clients aged 18–35, 35 per cent were involved with drug misuse; 46 per cent had an alcohol problem and 21 per cent suffered a mental illness (1991).

2   Intervention should primarily address 'criminogenic' needs but should also acknowledge the pressures and stresses of poverty, deprivation and discrimination.

3   Intensive forms of supervision should be reserved for offenders who present the greatest risk of re-offending.

4   Supervision programmes are likely to be most effective when combining cognitive social learning with the enhancement of 'control' factors in offenders' lives and reintegrative shaming strategies.

5   Work with offenders' families, children and kin networks combines humanitarian work with real prospects of crime reduction.

with the offender who is asked to play an active participatory role, albeit within the inevitable constraints of their predicament. Courtroom processes, whether interpreted as status degradation exercises or bureaucratic production lines, can make it easy for offenders to sustain psychological barriers against shame for wrongful acts. Both offence and offender are 'set apart' and defined as distinctively deviant, impoverishing the richness of the offender's reality. The legalistic language and etiquette are often unfamiliar, incomprehensible, distancing or alienating. The offender's energies and attention are readily invested in the alleged shortcomings or hypocrisy of others within the system, such as the police, advocates, victims or the judiciary, creating barriers against the acceptance of responsibility.

The offender–social worker encounter offers more promising prospects. The sequence of events and judgements entailed in the offence, its prelude and aftermath, can be marshalled and techniques of neutralization can be challenged, thus progressing beyond resort to 'it just happened' coincidence, fatalism, the fudging of accounts for different audiences, the convenient projection of blame on to third parties, or upon the influence of alcohol or drugs. The full extent of the harm and loss inflicted and the consequences of the crime can be faced, including the collateral damage caused to direct and indirect victims and to significant others in the offender's life. Patterns of misbehaviour can be traced to detect common themes, repeated triggers and other connections, which throw light on the likelihood of further repetition and the prospects for avoiding re-offending of this nature. Criminal behaviour can also be placed in a context which reduces culpability in a reasoned and appropriate way. This may, for example, identify the offender's experience as victim, either of crime or of adverse life circumstances, not with a view to gratuitous presentation of 'sad stories' which may engender sympathy for the defendant but to demonstrate the shaping of outlook or the constraint of legitimate opportunity. The offender's values and achievements can be examined, acknowledging areas of their life which unproblematically adhere to consensual norms. In Braithwaite's language, offence and perpetrator are 'uncoupled', revealing the latter's pluralistic dimensions and attaining a richer account of their responsibility and culpability.

'Diversion from custody' was the dominant stance of social work in criminal justice through the 1980s and Nellis has proposed 'anti-custodialism' as his first probation value for the 1990s. The particular social work strength in advising sentencers is to make more visible the potentially harmful impact of imprisonment, both for the defendant and significant others in the offender's life, and to question the value of segregation in shaping the offender's future behaviour. This is no mere tenet of occupational faith but arises from growing research evidence about the relative effectiveness of methods of behaviour change, including the shortcomings of deterrence, and a better understanding of offenders' belief systems. Though this will have little weight in a penal system based on the 'just deserts' approach to punishment or driven by tough-talking, populist assumptions, it remains a viable argument within the broad church of contemporary sentencing culture.

'Last resortism' would be a more accurate if inelegant value term than anti-custodialism, reflecting the social worker's task in balancing the potential reintegration of the offender with concern for public protection. Risk assessment, and the management of unpredictability run throughout good practice, requiring a close reading of past behaviour, active involvement with the offender in gauging their approach to risky situations, awareness of repeat victimization patterns and careful judgement about tolerable hazard. At the less serious end of the danger spectrum, proposals for community supervision should ensure that the most intensive forms of supervision are reserved for offenders presenting the greatest risk of re-offending. This not only husbands resources but ensures that greatest effort is directed towards those who have been proved to respond most promisingly.

Supervising Offenders

The new 'What Works?' literature is still at a somewhat rudimentary developmental stage but is beginning to cluster some key, promising ingredients of more effective supervision in ways which enhance reintegrative shaming's emphasis on the worth of the individual and the reversibility of their deviant identity. The growing consensus favours the following elements of good practice.

Systematic assessment

While a thorough review of factors in offenders' lives associated with their offending might seem a self-evident starting-point, Macdonald's research with a team of probation officers suggested that workers varied considerably in their perceptions of social factors, behaviour problems and cognitive problems among their caseload. In a worryingly large number of cases no behavioural difficulties and/or cognitive problems were mentioned. Only one officer mentioned mental disorder as an associated factor. The most 'popular' factors seemed closely related to social problems, suggesting that subsequent work would be more directed to survival than to change, restricting the scope for helpful intervention.

Addressing criminogenic need

Help consistent with a commitment to reducing offending and harm to others/self should follow what research suggests to be more promising avenues and methods with those who continually offend. Within the broad ambit of cognitive-behavioural work, it has proved possible to enhance offenders' problem-solving, communication and negotiation skills, critical, consequential and moral reasoning, management of emotions, assertiveness, and personal control, for example, by self-instructional

management of anger.

Given the cautious optimism for cognitively-based practice and of encouraging results from innovations such as Mid-Glamorgan's STOP programme (Raynor and Vanstone, 1994), Macdonald felt cause for concern about the rarity with which her probation officers deployed behavioural methods, even those who noted behavioural or cognitive factors as being influential in the aetiology of offending. Only three out of ten officers in the team used behavioural change methods with any regularity, in contrast to the high use of 'counselling'. Initiatives attempting to increase self-esteem (without

---

Three Questions

1 What are the main factors which contribute to the variation in offending rates in society?
2 How can social work practice contribute particularly in the statutory supervision and resettlement of ex-prisoners?
3 Consider the applicability of distinctive social work insights and methods to wider community safety and crime prevention initiatives.

---

simultaneous efforts to reduce anti-social behaviour) or to focus on emotional/personal conflict that have not been linked with criminal conduct yield less promising rehabilitative returns.

Creative professional practice

A rigid 'programmatic' approach to the supervision of offenders, whether in group or individual work, runs the danger of:

• delivering a standardized 'prescriptive' product which can be administered routinely by 'technicians' rather than by

professionals, relegating the participant to the role of homogeneous consumer;
- emphasizing the deficiencies of the individual's reasoning and judgement and ignoring structural shortcomings, and the criminogenic force of poverty and disadvantage;
- neglecting the reality of participants' lives and experiences which can preoccupy their energies and attentions;
- working in isolation from community integration;
- relying upon crime reduction as a measure of effectiveness and failing to address issues of social injustice;
- lacking sensitivity to the different perceptions, experiences and needs of women and black participants;
- focusing unduly on the 'presenting' crime and being insufficiently alert to other offending risks and crime-reductive opportunities, including domestic violence or child abuse;
- loading expectations and requirements with 'restrictiveness' rather than utility in mind; and
- adopting rigid and punitive enforcement procedures.

The troublesome complexity of offenders' lives as revealed by studies of younger people on probation is now well documented (Hagell and Newburn, 1994; Stewart and Stewart, 1993; Pritchard et al., 1992), demonstrating the extent of disrupted family backgrounds, limited financial or housing security, lack of work or training experience, depression and other mental disorder or learning disabilities, problems with drug or alcohol use, anxiety, self-harm and attempted suicide.

In essence, effective supervision demands:

- an open contractual style which acknowledges that consent is continually negotiated rather than a simple outset embarkation point;
- matching between worker style and participant need;
- active participatory methods, thoughtful and reflexive diversity which are compatible with participants' learning abilities and style;
- a commitment to addressing their wider social needs and problems with relevant services;
- realism which acknowledges that we can aspire only to reduce uncertainty about human behaviour;
- 'programme integrity' to avoid drift of focus or other unwitting carelessness;
- phased and purposeful endings which acknowledge what has been gained and identify further sources of non-statutory help; and
- practitioner evaluation and dissemination.

Unless participants sustain a collaborative stake in the enterprise and pace of work, gain an early sense of the rewards and pay-off of a programme of work and believe that their personal circumstances are heeded with respect, motivation and commitment will falter and the energies of both worker and participant will be channelled into enforcement and the prosecution of breach. Appropriate tolerance and sensitivity in the process of enforcement does not imply a 'feeble, blank cheque permissiveness' but a real commitment to maintaining contact, alertness to intervening demands and 'reasonable excuse', and openness to renegotiation and alternative means of dispute resolution other than resort to prosecution.

Anti-discriminatory practice

In the quest to enhance participation and to respect difference, social work practice has latterly given somewhat belated attention to the particular needs of women offenders and, to a lesser extent, black service users. In recognition of the constraints which gender roles place upon women and the reality that service provision is not gender-neutral, practitioners have sought to generate 'women-wise' supervision opportunities and feminist practice (e.g., Wright and Kemshall, 1994). This has contributed to a growth in initiatives to work with men in examining their own gender-based assumptions, the social construction of masculinity and the starkest truth of criminological knowledge, that crime is essentially predatory male misbehaviour.

Early attempts to address anti-racist social work practice with offenders over-simplified the complexities of black life and tended to make 'equal opportunities' into a task for management policy and regulation. Denney (1992) has also identified the difficulties for probation officers in transforming black offenders into 'the "good subject" who can be conceptualized as having the potential to become structured into and identify with probation decisions'. Practice in giving black participants the opportunity to explore their experience, examine their offending and express their interest and options is still at an early stage of development but initiatives such as the Black Offenders' Initiative in Inner London (Jenkins and Lawrence, 1993) shows the potential for empowering participants, enhancing thinking within the agency about black offenders' needs and in developing work on racism and racist motivations for crime with white offenders (Wade, 1994).

Community integration

Integration aims to enhance the satisfactions, attachments, rewards and opportunities which the offender can gain from legitimate means and by reinforcing or rallying links with those whose opinion, regard and affection are important to the offender who

disapproves of their offence and will value lawful activities and achievements. This covers a considerable spectrum of citizenship-building from the pursuit of job or skill training to the encouragement of family communication and problem solving or the provision of access to resources, for example, motor projects which encourage lawful enjoyment of vehicles and can reduce the incidence of car crime.

Support for beneficial family life and relationships and the sustaining or building of wider, positive kinship and friendship ties is not simply a humanitarian role for social work but a proven crime preventative strategy, particularly in the resettlement of discharged prisoners. This does not imply simplistic assumptions, for example about the efficaciousness of women partners in ensuring the future good behaviour of their menfolk; the quality of ties and relationships is crucial and hence the need for skilful and perceptive assessment. Given our knowledge of risk factors in family life which contribute to future delinquency and other behavioural problems, it is remarkable how little has yet been invested in enhancing the parenting skills of offenders and in the provision of advice to families. Promising experimental work with male offenders has demonstrated the potential to improve awareness of fatherhood responsibilities, the setting of boundaries and the constructive use of discipline for children, the handling of conflict constructively, the use of quality leisure

---

Further Reading

1 McGuire, J. (1995) *What Works: Reducing Offending*, Chichester: Wiley.
2 Smith, D. (1995) *Criminology for Social Work*, Basingstoke: Macmillan.
3 Stewart, J., Smith, D. and Stewart G. (1994) *Understanding Offending Behaviour*, Harlow: Longman.

time in family life and, in particular, the guidance of male children in their understanding of masculinity.

Particular reintegrative shaming potential arises from continued reference back to the harm caused by offending, whether to a particular victim or in a more generalizable sense. The process of moral education entails a heightened sense of empathy for victims and sensitivity to the distance between the criminal act and the offender's preferred values. The victim perspective will usually be generated on the basis of deposition details and through the empathetic imagination but in some instances the victim can be brought directly into the process of exploration and reintegration.

Conclusion

This account may appear an over-generalized, idealized credo or a self-seeking apologia as the stable-door may be closing on social work in the criminal justice system. It is not seeking to suggest that social work has a unique proprietorial claim to the pursuit of decency, community cohesion and social justice within the penal system but that it brings a distinctive approach to understanding the problems of offenders and crime in their social context and skills of engagement on which a humane and integrated criminal justice policy must rely.

References

Braithwaite, J. (1989) *Crime, Shame and Reintegration*, Cambridge: Cambridge University Press.

Braithwaite, J. (1993) 'Shame and modernity', *British Journal of Criminology*, 33, 1–18.

Braithwaite, J. (1994) 'Conditions of successful reintegration ceremonies', *British Journal of Criminology*, 34, 139–71.

Denney, D. (1992) *Racism and Anti-Racism in Probation*, London: Routledge.

Hagell, A. and Newburn, T. (1994) *Persistent Young Offenders*, London: Policy Studies Institute.

Jenkins, J. and Lawrence, D. (1993) 'Inner London's black groups initiative', *Probation Journal* 40, 82–4.

Macdonald, G. (1994) 'Developing empirically-based practice in probation', *British Journal of Social Work*, 24, 405–27.

Nellis, M. (1995) 'Probation values for the 1990s', *Howard Journal of Criminal Science*, 34, 19–44.

Pritchard, C. and Cotton, A. (1992) 'Mental illness, drug and alcohol misuse and HIV risk behaviour in 214 adult probation clients', *Social Work and Social Sciences Review*, 3, 150–62.

Raynor, P. and Vanstone, M. (1994) 'Probation practice, effectiveness and the non-treatment paradigm', *British Journal of Social Work*, 24, 387–404.

Roshier, B. (1989) *Controlling Crime*, Milton Keynes: Open University Press.

Stewart, G. and Stewart, J. (1993) *Social Circumstances of Young Offenders Under Supervision*, London: Association of Chief Officers of Probation.

Stewart, J., Smith, D. and Stewart, G. (1994) *Understanding Offending Behaviour*, Harlow: Longman.

Wade, A. (1994) *Working with Racism: Racially Motivated Crime and Probation Practice*, Cambridge: Cambridge University Institute of Criminology.

Wright, L. and Kemshall, H. (1994) 'Feminist probation practice: making supervision meaningful', *Probation Journal*, 41, 73–80.

Mental Illness

Peter Huxley

Client groups may be defined by age or by contact with the criminal justice system, but the mental illness client group knows no such boundaries. Psychiatric patients are defined by contact with psychiatric services, but most mental disorder never reaches the psychiatrist. It is pervasive. In the United Kingdom, it has been estimated that GPs assign a psychiatric diagnosis to six million people each year (1.2 million are over 65, and 300,000 are under 15), compared to cancer which affects two million people and AIDS about 2000. At the beginning of the 1990s mental illness accounted for 71 million working days lost (more than double the 1980 figure); indirect costs, generated through lost productivity, may exceed three billion pounds. Mental illness kills more than four times as many people as die in road accidents, and suicide is the second most common cause of death in young men. However, it is not simply the ubiquitous nature of mental illness which makes it an important reason for social work. Social factors play a crucial role in the causation of mental illness, in the course of the illnesses, and in the outcome of treatment and care.

In 1976, the first study of mental illness in social workers' caseloads by Rickards and colleagues, examined the physical and mental health of clients referred to social workers in an outer-London borough. The research team rated physical and mental health from casenotes and found that 45 per cent exhibited minor or major mental illness. Subsequent studies conducted using screening questionnaires, revealed even

higher rates in cases allocated to social workers, and these results were confirmed using standardized psychiatric assessments, which showed a range of mental illness in social work cases from 53 to 66 per cent (Corney, 1984; Huxley et al., 1988; Huxley et al., 1989). One-third of the disorders were severe psychotic illnesses, and 30 per cent were depressive conditions.

Social workers, like GPs, do not identify all the cases of mental illness presented to them. Huxley et al. (1989) found that recognition varied by diagnosis; social workers identified 100 per cent of the manic patients, but only half of the schizophrenia sufferers and less than half of those suffering from severe or psychotic depression.

One study (Isaac et al., 1986) suggests that the overlap between child care problems and mental health problems is very high. While none of the children entering care in this study sample had parental mental illness as an official reason, 84 per cent of the parents had received psychiatric care at some time. At the other end of the age spectrum a number of studies have shown that rates of mild and severe dementia and depression are between 30 per cent and 40 per cent in the residents of local authority homes for people over 65 (Harrison et al., 1990).

Knowledge about mental illnesses has undergone a major upheaval in the past thirty years. Diagnostic classifications based upon the treated population of patients are no longer regarded as adequate to describe the totality of mental health problems. Research has shown that the diagnostic systems themselves are not very reliable, except in the most crude sense, and diagnostic classifications are poor predictors of outcome and also of the costs of providing services (McCrone and Strathdee, 1993). The discovery of the frequent coexistence of symptoms of anxiety and depression reduces the need to have categorical classifications of disorder for less severe conditions. Epidemiological research shows that the prevalence of mental illness is considerable, and that most people with symptoms consult their family doctor, and the family doctor sees and treats most mental illness. In two books (Goldberg and Huxley, 1980, 1992) we outlined the pathway to specialist psychiatric care in the UK. Subsequent research has confirmed important aspects of this model; and even in societies where the filtering mechanisms are dissimilar, the model acts as a useful template against which to examine local rates.

The model consists of five levels, each one corresponding to a stage on the pathway to psychiatric care. The first level is the prevalence of disorder in the community (the data come from community surveys). The first filter is consultation behaviour or illness behaviour. Most people experiencing symptoms will present them to their family doctor, but the presentation is often of a somatic rather than a psychological complaint. Partly as a result, doctors vary in their ability to detect disorder and the factors which contribute to this variation are described in detail in the first book (Goldberg and Huxley, 1980); their ability to recognize psychiatric problems is the second filter. For cases which are detected, the family doctor decides to treat many of them and to refer the others for specialist psychiatric attention; the referral decision is the third filter. When the patient reaches the psychiatrist (level 4) they are treated as an out-patient, or admitted

(filter 4) to hospital (level 5) (figure IV.3.1 contains the rates at each level expressed per thousand population per year).

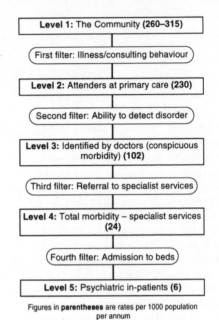

Figures in **parentheses** are rates per 1000 population per annum

Figure IV.3.1   The Goldberg–Huxley Pathway Model

The mental illnesses encountered in community surveys are less severe than those admitted to psychiatric hospitals. Social dysfunction and clinical severity increase at progressively higher levels of the model.

Social and Demographic Factors

A number of social and demographic factors influence the rates of disorder which come to the attention of social workers and other professionals.

Sex ratios

Female rates of mental illness generally exceed male rates (Meltzer et al., 1995), although it should be noted that by including drug dependency and anti-social personality – where male rates greatly exceed female rates – greater parity is found. Jenkins (1985) has shown that if samples of male and female subjects are chosen who are closely comparable from the standpoint of social adjustment the difference in rates disappears.

Social class

Most studies show greater rates for common mental disorders in lower social classes (Meltzer et al., 1995). Brown and Harris (1978) argue that the entire social-class difference among depressed women can be explained on the basis that working-class women have higher rates of severe life events and major social difficulties.

Unemployment

Unemployment has a substantial effect on self-reported physical health, anxiety and depression, and causes a decline in marital support (the number of weeks unemployed is related to the decrease in the quality of the marital relationship). Unemployment causes great financial strain which leaves people more vulnerable to the impact of unrelated life events. The effect of unemployment may be worse for those who have had little social contact outside the work setting. In the OPCS community survey (Meltzer et al., 1995) unemployment was the factor most strongly associated with the rate of mental illness.

Race

While non-whites are over-represented among involuntary hospital admissions (Rosenfield, 1984) and may use more emergency and in-patient services (Hu et al., 1992), the treatments given in hospital (Flaskerud and Hu, 1992), compliance with depot injection clinics (Tunnicliffe et al., 1992) and the prevalence of disorders

Five Key Points

1 Fifty per cent or more of social work clients are suffering from mental disorder.
2 Common disorders can be distinguished from severe disorders and the former more often fail to reach psychiatric care.
3 Rates of mental illness in the community vary according to socio-demographic characteristics and social factors such as life events.
4 In order for people with severe illness to survive in the community effective after-care and continuity of care must be provided.
5 Quality of life measures reflect the social dimensions of severe mental illness, and can be used to assess the outcome of social interventions.

in the community (Meltzer et al., 1995) all appear to be unrelated to ethnicity. Hirschfeld and Cross (1982) found that differences between black and white rates of depression disappeared when social class was controlled.

Life events

A variety of factors make an individual more susceptible to develop symptoms under stress, including: genetically determined emotional reactivity; personality; parental loss and early abuse; and social adversity such as poor housing and unemployment. These factors may act to increase the rate at which adverse life events occur as well as their impact. Good experience of early parenting and a good marital relationship act as protective factors against the rate (and impact) of life events. Goldberg and Huxley (1992) call the process of beginning to experience symptoms 'destabilization', and the process of losing symptoms 'restitution'. It appears to be the case that 'loss' events lead to depression, and 'threat' events lead to the development of anxiety, and combinations of the two to types of mixed anxiety–depression (Brown, 1993). Major life events are not all negative experiences, and some of the most stressful events are culturally accepted as positive experiences, the two most stressful being marriage and moving into a new home. In community surveys, restitution appears to be related to: a decrease in the rate of life events; positive or 'fresh-start' events; the presence of social support which is perceived positively and an absence of physical illness. In treated samples, restitution is associated with: better material circumstances; higher income; low expressed emotion relationships; an absence of negative self-concepts and satisfaction with levels of social support.

Not all problems presented to the social worker are new episodes of common disorder, many are of long-standing psychotic illnesses which are re-occurring for the second or third time. The OPCS survey found a prevalence rate of four per thousand of functional psychosis in the community. Schizophrenia is the major severe mental illness and it affects 1 per cent of the population. The onset is rapid or insidious (about half each), the course is episodic or continuous (also about half each) and outcome over the long-term (more than 30 years) can be moderate or severe disability or full recovery (also about half each). Outcome tends to be better in Third World countries, which is said to be due to better community integration and more rapid return to a useful role.

The rates of admission of severely mentally ill people to psychiatric hospital are higher in areas of high social deprivation (Jarman et al., 1992). One of the major contributory factors to relapse of the illness is the level of expressed emotion in the family home; high-stress homes invariably producing relapse, and low-stress homes only doing so if independent stressful events occur. Schizophrenic patients show heightened levels of arousal which reduce in the presence of non-stressful relatives. A non-stressful social worker may have the same calming influence on the sufferer, and this may help them to maintain the client in the community.

People who develop long-term severe disorders are now cared for in the community where delivering the necessary treatment and continuity of care is much more complicated than in a mental hospital. In the UK a legislative framework has been provided within which care can be focused on severely mentally ill people (DoH, 1994), but the results of this policy are far from clear. Highly publicized tragedies, such as the murder of innocent victims by severely disturbed schizophrenics, suggest that in the mid-1990s the policy is failing many of those it is designed to help (Ritchie et al., 1994). Goldberg and Gater (1991) estimate that in a population of 100,000, there will be 2,600 people who will require planned, prolonged health and social care.

Case management was devised in the USA to provide this continuity of care, and there is a long and substantial history of its use with mentally ill people (Huxley, 1993). When case management was adopted in the UK and transformed into care management, an inappropriate administrative (Challis, 1994), rather than a clinical model (Harris and Bachrach, 1988) was used. Both models include similar components: assessment, case finding, care planning, and monitoring and review, but in the clinical model direct face-to-face work is undertaken by the case manager. Research evidence suggests that this approach is successful with the most severely disabled mentally ill people, and that the administrative model is both unsuccessful and unpopular. A major reason is the need for a close personal working relationship (of a low EE variety) in order to sustain

Three Questions

1 What are the main factors which contribute to the variation in the rates of mental disorder in the community?
2 What are the main factors which contribute to more severe illnesses progressing to in-patient psychiatric care?
3 How can systematic quality of life assessment of mentally ill people become part of the operational practice of social workers?

community living. This long-term clinical case management is also applicable to other client groups such as the older mentally ill person, and emotionally disturbed children and adolescents (Huxley, 1993).

A welcome development in mental health services across the world is the focus upon the outcome of service provision. The fundamental question arises, if patients are no longer cared for in large institutions, or in psychiatric units in general hospitals, how can we be sure that community services provide them with a better quality of life? It is no longer good enough to assert that treatment in the community must be better, there is a need (arising from public accountability of services) to answer this question based upon sound and systematically gathered evidence. Quality of life (QOL) assessment gives social workers a systematic way of assessing the outcome in life domains which have meaning to patients and put their views at the centre of service provision and planning (Oliver et al., 1995). Results of the application of quality of life measures to community services show that community treatment is more popular and can improve mental health and social relationships. However, QOL studies also show: deficiencies in provision especially with regard to meaningful occupation; differences in the quality of residential care and high levels

of poverty (Oliver et al., 1995). Producing a major impact on the life of a schizophrenia sufferer in any of his/her life domains often requires a massive social intervention, which may only have an impact within one or two life domains (this has been called the 'specificity of effects'; Huxley, 1996). QOL assessment offers one opportunity to put the social dimensions of the life of the mentally ill person at the forefront of work on the outcome of care and treatment in the community.

References

Brown, G. W. (1993) 'Life events and affective disorder: replications and limitations', *Psychosomatic Medicine*, 55(3), 248–59.
Brown, G. W. and Harris, T. H. (1978) *Social Origins of Depression*, London: Tavistock.
Challis, D. J. (1994) 'Case management: a review of UK developments and issues', in M. Titterton (ed.), *Caring for People in the Community: the New Welfare*, London: Jessica Kingsley.
Corney, R. (1984) 'The mental and physical health of clients referred to social workers in a local authority department and a general practice attachment scheme', *Psychological Medicine*, 14, 137–44.
DoH (1994) *Key Area Handbook – Mental Illness* (2nd edn), London: HMSO.
Flaskerud, J. H. and Hu, L. T. (1992) 'Relationship of ethnicity to psychiatric diagnosis', *Journal of Nervous and Mental Disease*, 180(5), 296–303.
Goldberg, D. P. and Gater, R. (1991) 'Estimates of need', *Psychiatric Bulletin*, 15, 593–5.
Goldberg, D. P. and Huxley, P. J. (1980) *Mental Illness in the Community: the Pathway to Psychiatric Care*, London: Tavistock.

Further Reading

1 Goldberg, D. P. and Huxley, P. J. (1992) *Common Mental Disorder: a Biosocial Model*, London: Routledge.
2 Oliver, J., Huxley, P., Bridges, K. and Mohamad, H. (1995) *Quality of Life and Mental Health Services*, London: Routledge.
3 Warner, R. (1994) *Recovery from Schizophrenia: Psychiatry and Political Economy* (2nd edn), London: Routledge.

Goldberg, D. P. and Huxley, P. J. (1992) *Common Mental Disorder: A Biosocial Model*, London: Routledge.

Harris, M. and Bachrach, L. (eds) (1988) *Clinical Case Management*, New Directions for Mental Health Services, no. 40, London: Jossey-Bass Inc.

Harrison, R., Salva, N. and Kafetz, K. (1990) 'Dementia, depression and physical disability in a London Borough: a survey of elderly people in and out of residential care', *Age and Ageing*, 19, 97–103.

Hirschfeld, R. and Cross, C. (1982) 'Epidemiology of affective disorders: psycho-social risk factors', *Archives of General Psychiatry*, 3935, 46–50.

Hu, T. W., Snowden, L. R., Jerrell, J. M. and Nguyen, T. D. (1992) 'Ethnic populations in public mental health: services, choice and level of use', *American Journal of Public Health*, 81(11), 1429–34.

Huxley, P. J. (1993) 'Case management, care management and community care,' *British Journal of Social Work*, 23, 366–81.

Huxley, P. J. (1996) 'Quality of life' in K. Muesser and N. Tarrier (eds), *The Handbook of Social Functioning*, London: Addison-Wesley.

Huxley, P., Korer, J., Raval, H. and Jacob, C. (1988) 'Psychiatric morbidity in the clients of social workers', *Journal of Psychiatric Research*, 22(1), 57–67.

Huxley, P. J., Mohamad, H., Korer, J. and Jacob, C. (1993) 'Psychiatric morbidity in social workers' caseloads: a comparison between an inner city area and a suburban area', *Social Psychiatry and Psychiatric Epidemiology*, 28(1), 28–31.

Huxley, P. J., Mohamad, H., Korer, J., Jacob, C., Raval, H. and Anthony, P. (1989) 'Psychiatric morbidity in social workers' clients: social outcome', *Social Psychiatry and Psychiatric Epidemiology*, 24, 258–65.

Isaac, B., Minty, E. B., and Morrison, R. M. (1986) 'Children in care: the association with mental disorder in the parents', *British Journal of Social Work*, 16, 325–39.

Jarman, B., Hirsch, S., White, P. and Driscoll, R. (1992) 'Predicting psychiatric admission rates', *British Medical Journal* 304(6835), 1146–51.

Jenkins, R. (1985) 'Sex differences in psychiatric morbidity', *Psychological Medicine Monograph Supplements*, 12.

McCrone, P. and Strathdee, G. (1993) 'Needs not diagnosis: towards a more rational approach to community mental health resourcing', *International Journal of Social Psychiatry*, 40(2), 79–86.

Meltzer, H., Gill, B., Petticrew, M. and Hinds, K. (1995) *The Prevalence of Psychiatric Morbidity among Adults Living in Private Households*, Office of Population, Censuses and Surveys, London: HMSO.

Oliver, J., Huxley, P., Bridges, K. and Mohamad, H. (1995) *Quality of Life and Mental Health Services*, London: Routledge.

Rickards, C., Gildersleeve, C. and Fitzgerald, R. (1976) 'The health of clients of a social services department', *Journal of the Royal College of General Practitioners*, 26, 237–43.

Ritchie, J., Dick, D. and Lingham, R. (1994) *The Report of the Enquiry into the Care and Treatment of Christopher Clunis*, London: HMSO.

Rosenfield, S. (1984) 'Race differences in involuntary hospitalisation: psychiatric versus labelling perspectives', *Journal of Health and Social Behaviour*, 25, 14–23.

Tunnicliffe, S., Harrison, G. and Standen, P. J. (1992) 'Factors affecting compliance with depot injection treatment in the community', *Social Psychiatry and Psychiatric Epidemiology* 27(5), 230–3.

Warner, R. (1994) *Recovery from Schizophrenia: Psychiatry and Political Economy* (2nd edn), London: Routledge.

Family Breakdown
Jane Aldgate

Prevention and protection are twin aims at any level of social work intervention in child care (Hardiker and Barker, 1995). So it is with social work and family breakdown. The primary role of the social worker is to prevent family breakdown because it is recognized that, all things being equal, children are best brought up in their own families (Department of Health, 1990; Utting, 1995). Under English legislation, social workers have a duty to promote the welfare of children 'in need', who will include children living in families, who through structural problems of living in poverty or experiencing racism, are on the verge of breakdown (Aldgate and Tunstill, 1996; Utting, 1995). If breakdown occurs and, for example, parents divorce or children enter the care system, the prevention of negative consequences and the protection of children's emotional and physical well-being must continue (Triseliotis, 1993; Utting, 1995).

The Social Work Response to Family Breakdown

Family breakdown can occur in several ways. Two circumstances are most commonly associated with social work intervention: where families have broken down through separation of spouses and where children are separated from their parents by entering the care system.

Where parents are divorcing, social workers are most likely to be involved in two ways. Firstly, there is the role in civil court cases of guardians *ad litem*. These are independent social workers whose task is to assess children's needs and advise the court accordingly. They have considerable influence on court decisions about children's residence after divorce. They will also be involved in contested care cases between the local authority and parents (see Department of Health, 1991c).

A second important role for social workers in divorce cases is that of conciliation. Traditionally, in England and Wales, probation officers have offered this service to families within their role of divorce court welfare officers. There are also independent conciliation services where, through direct counselling, social workers help parents to separate as amicably as possible, taking cognisance of the needs of their children (Forster, 1980; Howard and Shepherd, 1987). Sometimes, the divorce court officers combine this role with some brief direct counselling for children, helping them understand the process of family breakdown and their reactions to it.

In social services departments, the most established role for social workers concerns family breakdown where children are admitted to the care system. Here the role is complex and multi-faceted, demanding a considerable repertoire of knowledge and skills (see Thoburn, 1988). Whatever the cause of breakdown, the worker will aim to ameliorate potentially negative effects through direct intervention with children and their families, complemented and underpinned by supporting carers, health professionals, teachers and others to attend to children's developmental needs. The overall aim will be to create permanence for children, either by restoring them to their families or by finding alternative families for them. The philosophy of permanence and continuity should permeate all social work actions (Maluccio et al., 1986; Triseliotis, 1993).

Although the role embraces a duty to do everything possible to make sure children are not further disadvantaged as a result of entering the care system (see Department of Health, 1991a), there is substantial research to show that family breakdown may be compounded by the way the system itself, including social work actions or omissions, can abuse children and their parents (see DHSS, 1985). Arguably, the care system has been bedevilled by its legacy from the Poor Law. It is not accidental that the Children Act 1989 in England and Wales attempted to lay the ghost of stigma by deliberately describing children entering the care system as 'children looked after'. This reframes the role of the social worker as one who is entrusted with responsibility for actively and carefully promoting the children's welfare. This includes a recognition of the importance to children of their parents. As in divorce cases, the law urges that any arrangements are made in voluntary partnership, thereby enabling parents to retain full parental responsibility while their children are being looked after (Department of Health, 1990, 1991a).

The Importance of Attachment and Identity

All forms of family breakdown involve separation and loss for both parents and children (see Aldgate, 1988). In order to counteract the effects of loss, social workers need to be well versed in attachment theory. The works of Bowlby (1971, 1979) and Winnicott (1965), among others, directly inform the social work

role. Social workers need to know that children's reactions to separation will be influenced by factors such as life experiences, patterns of attachment, gender, age and temperament (Aldgate, 1988). Social workers need to understand the impact of loss on children's developing identity (Triseliotis, 1983). The role demands considerable sensitivity to children, time to work with them directly and a repertoire of learnt skills grounded in knowledge of attachment theory and child development (see Aldgate and Simmonds, 1988).

Children often feel the family breakdown is their fault and may be deeply affected by the experience, as Wallerstein and Kelly's (1980) study on the children of divorced parents shows. There may be disturbances in behaviour and problems of concentration at school. Through direct work, using explanations, games and toys, social workers can help children understand why family breakdown occurred and help them come to terms with their feelings about their separation from their parents (see Jewett, 1984; Fahlberg, 1988). Additionally, preparing children for separation can soften the process of admitting them to the care system (see Thoburn, 1988).

Social Work with Parents at Family Breakdown

As children are attached to their parents, so are their parents attached to their children. Work with parents experiencing separation is no less important than work with their children. Indeed, the two are parts of the same whole (Jenkins and Norman, 1972; Millham et al., 1986). It has been known for some time that adults may be deeply affected by separation from their partners and children (Hart, 1976; Hetherington et al., 1978; Hetherington and Clingempeel, 1992) but may find it difficult to resolve their feelings without help. The social work role here is that of enabler and facilitator. At times the role in relation to parents of children 'looked after' can be extremely challenging, especially if children have been removed compulsorily, but as recent child protection research shows, working in partnership in child protection cases is likely to bring about a better outcome for the child (Department of Health, 1995). Similarly, diverting warring spouses from their battle to consider the needs of their children demands a conciliation role that is at once supportive and assertive (Mitchell, 1984).

Parents whose children enter the care system, for whatever reason, need social workers to adopt a strongly supportive role, reassuring them constantly of their importance to their children and recognizing they may need help in their own right. Where parents have abused children, a balance has to be struck between supporting parents and protecting children (Department of Health, 1995).

It has been strongly argued that social work services to parents should be offered in a spirit of partnership (Marsh, 1993), of which the essence is a shared agenda between worker and parent with common aims and understanding from workers about families' problems. Involving parents in essential tasks of information giving and decision making can do much to translate partnership into reality and empower them to take appropriate action to resolve the problems that have led to breakdown (Fahlberg, 1993). In child protection cases, involving parents is part of the assessment of parent–child interaction and can signal what modifications will need to be made if children are to return home. To change parenting behaviour, social workers can employ a range of social casework techniques with individuals (see Thoburn, 1988; Maluccio et al., 1986; Marsh and Triseliotis, 1993). Group support has also been found effective to restore parents' morale (Bullock et al., 1993).

Five Key Points

1   The primary role of social workers in relation to family breakdown is to try to prevent breakdown in the first place. If breakdown cannot be prevented, the social worker's role must be to prevent any further damage to children and to protect them from the potentially negative consequences of that breakdown.

2   Social workers working with children and families experiencing family breakdown through divorce or children coming into the care system need to understand and respond to the effects of severed attachments on children and on parents.

3   Social workers have a duty to preserve continuity of race, culture, language and education for children separated from their parents in the care system. This also includes retaining contact with parents and wider kin so that breakdown will not threaten children's identity and working in partnership with parents in recognition of their importance to children.

4   Social workers are accountable for the welfare of children looked after by them. They have a duty to assess and attend to children's developmental needs so that the care experience does not disadvantage children in any way. Particular attention must be paid to children's health and education.

5   The primary role of the social worker is to promote children's welfare. This is best accomplished by careful planning in partnership with parents and carers and in consultation with children. Family breakdown is best counteracted by early reunification or by the creation for children of a permanent alternative home. Breakdowns of placement only compound the effects of the separation necessitated by entry to the care system.

The Special Needs of Children 'Looked After'

Children who experience family breakdown through admission to the care system need special attention. As Bebbington and Miles (1989) have suggested, many of these children may already have been disadvantaged socially, economically or emotionally. Children who have been abused or neglected or whose early lives have been subject to many disruptions are especially at risk emotionally. Research has suggested that the care system may contribute to the chain of adversity by exposing children to further losses, with concomitant damage to their sense of identity and self-esteem (Department of Health, 1991a). Another extremely vulnerable group are children from ethnic minorities, especially children from mixed-race families (Rowe et al., 1989; Department of Health, 1991a). Black children are at risk because of many factors, including institutional racism in the care system. They have the same needs as other children experiencing family breakdown but these needs may be neglected because of racist attitudes (Barn, 1993).

The social worker has a crucial role in safeguarding the welfare of all children 'looked after'. There are several critical areas of activity involved in this role.

Making clear plans for the purpose and duration of the placement are essential to children's well-being as is early reunification or plans for permanence in foster care or adoption. Preserving continuity in crucial areas of children's lives is part of this work, including the maintenance of contact with parents, except in rare cases where this puts children at risk of significant harm. Further, the social worker has a statutory role to assess children's needs while they are being looked after and implement that assessment. Finally, there is responsibility for effecting reunification or the transition of care leavers to independence. Social workers are assisted in their role by residential social workers and foster carers. Indeed, none of the work of helping children and families could be effected without team enterprise between those organizing and carrying out the caring.

The Care Team

Where children are in residential care, social workers will be supporting specialist residential social workers, but will not have any responsibility for the selection or training of these individuals. The residential social work role should be complementary to that of the field social worker. It is desirable that a strong partnership is effected between the two to share the tasks of formal supervision of children and direct work with parents and children (Kahan, 1994).

A similar partnership obtains between foster carers and social workers. The social work role here is usually divided between specialist workers whose main role is to support carers and the child's social worker. Research shows that neglect of carers can be a major factor in foster home breakdown (Berridge and Cleaver, 1987; Aldgate and Hawley, 1986) and in losing foster carers (Sellick, 1992). There is an uneasy tension inherent in the roles of foster carers and social workers, with carers often feeling they are secondary partners. It has been argued that the only way to resolve this tension is through the full professionalization of foster carers (see Triseliotis et al., 1995). Supporting foster carers is a specialist task. Information on the recruitment, training and support needs of carers has been well documented (Triseliotis et al., 1995).

Planning

Plans made in partnership with parents and in consultation with children are an important feature of any work with 'looked after' children. The reason for family breakdown will influence the nature and extent of planning.

Many breakdowns occur in an emergency, with the social worker forced into a reactive role to find a placement as quickly as possible (see Fisher et al., 1986; DHSS, 1985). Nevertheless, the social worker must as soon as possible attend to making plans with parents and children about the purpose and duration of the period the child is to be looked after (see Department of Health, 1991b; Thoburn, 1988; Marsh and Triseliotis, 1993; Triseliotis et al., 1995). Additionally, social workers must be grounded in knowledge of the relevant law and the social policy contexts in which they operate.

Planning will include assessment of the most suitable placement for children. There can be positive advantages in residential care for older children (Utting, 1995; Berridge, 1985; Kahan, 1994) while foster care is increasingly the preferred alternative for many children. Choice should be made according to the child's needs and the purpose of the placement but the reality of working in the public care sector means that the ideal resource is not always available. Social workers have the difficult task of compromising their choice of placements without compromising children's needs.

Written agreements about the purpose and duration of children's stay and the roles and responsibilities of all the adults concerned are a necessary part of planning. Ensuring these agreements are constructed in a format and language easily accessible to parents is a tangible manifestation of working in partnership with parents (Family Rights Group, 1988; Department of Health, 1991b).

Continuity for Children

In recognition of the importance to children of their families and of the negative outcomes socially and emotionally that can result from children being left without attachments in the care system (DHSS, 1985; Department of Health, 1991a), the law in England and Wales now demands that special attention be paid to continuity of race, culture, language and education for children looked after. Social workers are urged to seek placements with relatives if at all possible. The involvement of extended families in decision making to avoid admission to the care system is also a new but important role for social workers (Marsh and Allen, 1993). This

---

Three Questions

1 How can social workers help children cope with separation and loss?
2 What can social workers do to help parents ameliorate the effects of family breakdown on their children?
3 What issues must social workers address to promote the welfare of 'looked after' children?

---

places considerable responsibility on social workers to preserve links with parents and wider families, prevent further breakdown and make sure placements are appropriate.

Social workers supervising children in the community whose parents have divorced must also pay attention to the retention of continuity with non-resident parents and advise parents accordingly of separating the needs of their children from their own needs (Howard and Shepherd, 1987).

Preventing Further Breakdown

Continuity with the past is important but

preventing further breakdown is equally part of the social work role. Stability of placement is one of the best restorative factors for children (Rowe et al., 1984; Aldgate et al., 1996) as is early reunification with families (Marsh and Triseliotis, 1993; Millham et al., 1986). Other protective factors include the presence of siblings (Wedge and Mantle, 1991) and foster placements with relatives (Berridge and Cleaver, 1987). Unfortunately, as research has shown, the social worker's role in promoting stability in placements has been much neglected, contributing to placement breakdown and the moving of children for administrative convenience (Rowe et al., 1989; Berridge, 1985; Berridge and Cleaver, 1987). Social workers have a clear responsibility to support carers, preserve contact with parents, undertake direct work with children to ensure they understand why they are being looked after and know what is planned for their future. If a change of placement is inevitable, social workers should turn this into a positive experience for children (Fitzgerald, 1983; Aldgate and Hawley, 1986).

Facilitating Appropriate Contact between Children and their Families

A further role for the social worker is to support parents to keep in contact with their children. This applies to social workers in matrimonial supervision cases and to 'looked after' children. Research over the last two decades has identified social work support as a significant factor in preventing the loss of parental contact (Aldgate, 1980; Millham et al., 1986).

The maintenance of contact between children looked after and their families warrants extra attention because of its adverse effect on children's long-term futures both in terms of their social isolation on leaving the care system (Stein and Carey, 1986) and the damage it can do to their identity (Triseliotis, 1983). Consequently, except in exceptional circumstances where it is clear parents will emotionally damage their children through contact, even in cases of abuse the law supports contact to preserve kinship attachments for children.

Two decades of research have identified contact as a significant factor in influencing the return of children to their parents (Aldgate, 1980; Millham et al., 1986). Without social work support, contact can decline remarkably quickly (Millham et al., 1986). There are parallels to this decline in divorce cases (Eekelaar and Clive, 1977). Where the plan is for permanence in an alternative family, contact with birth families seems to enhance the stability of the placement. Further, for older children, the most likely source of permanence on leaving the care system or if placements break down is likely to be with their own families (Thoburn et al., 1986). Research has also found that contact is a protective factor against breakdown of placement (Berridge and Cleaver, 1987). It also provides children with a source of stability against the negative effects of changes of placement which still seem to beset long-term care arrangements. Finally, contact can be an important arena in which to assess parent–child attachments and parenting skills (Fahlberg, 1993).

The barriers to contact have been well documented (Department of Health, 1991a). Social workers are key players in facilitating and maintaining contact, discharging their role by supporting parents, children and carers. They have to recognize and help parents overcome their feelings of failure about the family breakdown; to reassure parents about their important continuing role in their children's lives; to set up placements which are easily accessible to parents; to make sure carers act positively towards parents; to ensure that practical arrangements for visits are convenient for both parents and carers; to ensure parents acquire financial help for travel expenses; to help parents understand and accept the negative reactions of their children.

Assessing Outcomes for 'Looked After' Children

Even if there is a good beginning, research on children looked after has suggested that the system itself can abuse children by neglecting their developmental needs. Children 'looked after' are by definition subjected to corporate parenting, where legal parental responsibility may be with their own families (in voluntary admissions) or shared between parents and the local authority (in compulsory admissions). In all cases, day-to-day responsibility will be delegated to carers with field social workers holding responsibility for the overall case. This has historically led to several problems including the considerable neglect of children's health and educational attainment (see Department of Health, 1991a; Jackson, 1987; Heath et al., 1994). Behaviour problems have also been neglected. Plans for children have not been executed properly so that children have drifted into long-term arrangements (Department of Health, 1991a).

Social workers have a role to assess and take action to ensure children's developmental needs are met. Social workers in at least 13 countries now have access to comprehensive assessment and action schedules, developed by Ward and her colleagues for the UK Department of Health (Parker et al., 1991; Ward, 1995). These schedules make social workers' tasks easier by identifying key areas for action. Significantly, they require social workers to specify who will have responsibility in ensuring outcomes are achieved in areas such as health, educational attainment, contact with

parents and planning. They can be used effectively in conjunction with statutory requirements to review children's progress at set intervals.

Returning Children to their Families

In most cases, 'looked after' children can best be served by social workers by being restored to their families as soon as possible. The importance of early return is shown by what has been called the 'leaving care curve' (Department of Health, 1991a). After an initial period of several weeks, the chances of reunification seem to decline rapidly. The longer children remain looked after, the slimmer are their chances of reunification (Millham et al., 1986).

A critical factor in bringing about reunification is purposeful social work activity (Farmer, 1993). The ingredients of social work are fourfold. There is assessment of what needs to be changed before a child can return; appropriate action to bring about that change through direct intervention with children and their families; preparation of children and parents for transition and support after children have returned (Dartington, 1992). Research provides social workers with predictive factors which may help or hinder a successful outcome (Bullock et al., 1993).

Where children cannot return home,

Further Reading

1 Aldgate, J. and Simmonds, J. (eds) (1988) *Direct Work with Children – A Guide for Practitioners*, London: Batsford.
2 Marsh, P. and Triseliotis, J. (eds) (1993) *Prevention and Reunification in Child Care*, London: Batsford.
3 Thoburn, J. (1994) *Child Placement: Principles and Practice* (2nd edn), Aldershot: Arena.

the social worker has a parallel role in helping children transfer to permanent alternative families (see Thoburn et al., 1986; Thoburn, 1988; Atherton, 1993).

Preparing Care Leavers for Independence

There are currently children looked after who have spent many years of their childhood in the care system. A plethora of research has shown how many leave care with low educational attainment, poor health and ill-prepared for living in isolation in the community (see Department of Health, 1991; Stein and Carey, 1986). The legacy of bad social work practice which has contributed to their demise is scandalous. The assessment and action schedules described above (Ward, 1995) were in part devised to prevent such negative outcomes. The social worker has a role as educator and facilitator, preparing young people for leaving the care system and liaising with housing agencies to help find accommodation. Many young people now receive leaving care grants but these are woefully inadequate to meet their needs. Under English law, social workers can act as befriender to a young person until they are 21 in some circumstances. Unfortunately, the law leaves social workers a measure of discretion in how they fulfil this role but leaving care teams have made some inroads into this neglected area of work. Overall, the aim as with all children, should be to prevent the necessity for remedial action in the first place by attending to the living circumstances which lead to family breakdown (Utting, 1995). The social worker has a critical role to play in that preventive action.

References

Aldgate, J. (1980) 'Identification of factors influencing children's length of stay in care', in J. Triseliotis (ed.), _New Proceedings and Developments in Foster Care and Adoption_, London: Routledge & Kegan Paul.

Aldgate, J. (1988) 'The social worker's role in helping children cope with separation and loss', in J. Aldgate and J. Simmonds, _Direct Work with Children_, London: Batsford.

Aldgate, J. and Hawley, D. (1986) _Recollections of Disruption: A Study of Breakdowns in Long-Term Foster Care_, London: National Foster Care Association.

Aldgate, J., Heath, A. F. and Colton, M. (1996) 'The education of children in and out of care', _Children and Society_, 6, 38–60.

Aldgate, J., Maluccio, A. N. and Reeves, C. (1989) _Adolescents in Foster Families_, London: Batsford.

Aldgate, J. and Simmonds, J. (1988) _Direct Work with Children_, London: Batsford.

Aldgate, J. and Tunstill, J. (1996) _Setting up Services for Children in Need_, London: HMSO.

Atherton, C. (1993) 'Reunification – parallels between new families and reunifying children with their families', in P. Marsh and J. Triseliotis (eds), _Prevention and Reunification in Child Care_, London: Batsford.

Barn, R. (1993) _Black Children in the Public Care System_, London: Batsford.

Bebbington, A. and Miles, J. (1989) 'The background of children who enter local authority care', _British Journal of Social Work_, 19(5), 349–68.

Berridge, D. (1985) _Children's Homes_, Oxford: Blackwell.

Berridge, D. and Cleaver, H. (1987) _Foster Home Breakdown_, Oxford: Basil Blackwell.

Bowlby, J. (1971) _Attachment and Loss_, London: Penguin.

Bowlby, J. (1979) _The Making and Breaking of Affectional Bonds_, London: Tavistock.

Bullock, R., Little, M. and Millham, S. (1993) 'Establish a family support group for parents of children in care or accommodation', in P. Marsh and J. Triseliotis (eds), _Prevention and Reunification in Child Care_, London: Batsford, pp. 106–19.

Dartington Social Research Unit (1992) _Going Home: Returning Children Separated from their Families_, Totnes: Dartington Social Research Unit.

Dartington Social Research Unit (1993) _Going Home_, Dartmouth: Dartmouth Press.

Department of Health (1990) _Principles and Practice in Guidance and Regulations_, London: HMSO.

Department of Health (1991a) _Patterns and Outcomes in Child Placement_, London: HMSO.

Department of Health (1991b) _Guidance and Regulations Volume 2, Family Support, Daycare and Educational Provision for Young Children_, London: HMSO.

Department of Health (1991c) _Working Together under the Children Act 1989, A Guide to Arrangements for Inter-agency Co-operation for the Protection of Children from Abuse_, London: HMSO.

Department of Health (1995) _Child Protection: Messages from Research_, London: HMSO.

Department of Health and Social Security (1985) *Social Work Decisions in Child Care*, London: HMSO.

Eekelaar, J. and Clive, E. (1977) *Custody After Divorce*, Social Science Research Council.

Fahlberg, V. (1988) *Putting It All Together*, London: BAAF.

Fahlberg, V. (1993) 'Working with parents', in P. Marsh and J. Triseliotis, *Prevention and Reunification in Child Care*, London: Batsford, pp. 134–46.

Family Rights Group (1988) *Using Written Agreements with Children and Families*, London: Family Rights Group.

Farmer, E. (1993) 'Going home – what makes reunification work?' in P. Marsh and J. Triseliotis, *Prevention and Reunification in Child Care*, London: Batsford, pp. 147–66.

Fisher, M., Marsh, P. and Phillips, D. (1986) *In and Out of Care – The Experience of Children, Parents and Social Workers*, London: Batsford.

Fitzgerald, J. (1983) *Understanding Disruption*, London: BAAF.

Forster, J. (1980) *Divorce Conciliation*, Edinburgh: Scottish Council for Single Parents.

Hardiker, P. and Barker, M. (1995) *The Social Policy Contexts of Child Care*, London: NSPCC.

Hart, N. (1976) *When Marriage Ends*, London: Tavistock.

Heath, A. F., Colton, M. and Aldgate, J. (1994) 'Failure to escape: a longitudinal study of children in foster care', *British Journal of Social Work*, 24, 241–60.

Hetherington, E. M. and Clingempeel, W. G. (1992) *Coping with Marital Transition: A Family Systems Perspective*, Child Development Research Monograph vol. 57.

Hetherington, E. M., Cox, M. and Cox, R. (1978) 'The aftermath of divorce', in J. H. Stevens jnr. and M. Mathews (eds), *Mother–Child, Father–Child Relations*, Washington DC: National Association for the Education of Young Children.

Howard, J. and Shepherd, G. (1987) *Conciliation, Children and Divorce*, London: Batsford.

Jackson, S. (1987) *The Education of Children in Care*, Bristol: University of Bristol.

Jenkins, S. and Norman, E. (1972) *Filial Deprivation and Foster Care*, New York: Columbia University Press.

Jewett, C. (1984) *Helping Children Cope with Separation and Loss*, London: Batsford.

Kahan, B. (1994) 'Growing up in groups', London: HMSO.

Maluccio, A. N., Fein, E. and Olmstead, K. A. (1986) *Permanency Planning for Children – Concepts and Methods*, London: Tavistock.

Marsh, P. (1993) 'Family unification and preservation – the need for partnership between users and professionals', in P. Marsh and J. Triseliotis (eds) (1993), 39–53.

Marsh, P. and Allen, G. (1993) 'The law prevention and reunification – the New Zealand Development of Family Group Conference', in P. Marsh and J. Triseliotis (eds) (1993), 69–84.

Marsh, P. and Triseliotis, J. (eds) (1993) *Prevention and Reunification in Child Care*, London: Batsford.

Millham, S., Bullock R., Hosie, K. and Haak, M. (1986) *Lost in Care. The Problems of Maintaining Links Between Children in Care and Their Parents*, Aldershot: Gower.

Mitchell, A. (1984) *Children in the Middle, Living Through Divorce*, London: Tavistock.

Parker, R., Ward, H., Jackson, S., Aldgate, J. and Wedge P. (1991) (eds) *Looking After Children – Assessing Outcomes in Child Care*, London: HMSO.

Rowe, J., Cain, H., Hundelby, M. and Keane, A. (1984) *Long-Term Foster Care*, London: Batsford.

Rowe, J., Hundelby, M. and Garnett, L. (1989) *Child Care Now*, London: BAAF.

Sellick, C. W. (1992) *Supporting Short-Term Foster Carers*, Aldershot: Avebury.

Stein, M. and Carey, K. (1986) *Leaving Care*, Oxford: Basil Blackwell.

Thoburn, J. (1988) *Child Placement: Principles and Practice*, Aldershot: Wildwood.

Thoburn, J., Murdoch, A. and O'Brien, A. (1986) *Permanence in Child Care*, Oxford: Basil Blackwell.

Triseliotis, J. (1983) 'Identity and security', *Adoption and Fostering*, 7(1), 22–31.

Triseliotis, J. (1993) 'The theory continuum, prevention, restoration and permanence', in P. Marsh and J. Triseliotis (eds) (1993), 5–23.

Triseliotis, J., Sellick, C. and Short, R. (1995) *Foster Care*, London: Batsford.

Utting, D. (1995) *Family and Parenthood – Supporting Families, Preventing Breakdown*, Joseph Rowntree Foundation.

Wallerstein, J. S. and Kelly, J. B. (1980) *Surviving the Breakup: How Children and Parents Cope with Divorce*, London: Grant McIntyre.

Ward, H. (ed.) (1995) *Looking after Children*, London: HMSO.

Wedge, P. and Mantle, G. (1991) *Sibling Groups and Social Work*, Aldershot: Avebury.

Winnicott, D. W. (1965) *The Family and Individual Development*, London: Tavistock.

IV.5
Child Abuse
Lorraine Waterhouse

Child abuse causes much personal misery for children and parents, raises public concern and requires professional attention. A nationally co-ordinated system of managing child abuse cases has evolved in the UK since the mid-1970s following recommendations made by the inquiry (DHSS, 1982) into the death of Maria Colwell who died while in the care of social services. The system depends on local area review committees to co-ordinate policy and interdisciplinary co-operation. All areas have child protection registers to identify children at risk of harm, hold multidisciplinary case conferences normally led by social work/services to assess child care and formally to identify children in need of registration, and provide local procedural guidelines for different professionals concerned with children's welfare.

Estimates of the incidence and prevalence of child abuse which are based on these registers vary widely, depending on how child abuse is defined, how many cases are identified and how representative they are of the whole child population. There is no mandatory system of reporting or recording confirmed cases of child abuse in the UK. Research into the frequency of abuse depends on registration statistics which are 'not a record of children who have been abused but of children for whom there are continuing child protection concerns and for whom there is an inter-agency protection plan' (Home Office et al., 1991, 6.36).

The National Society for the Prevention of Cruelty to Children (NSPCC) in their

1986 survey of up to 2,000 children, 16 years or younger, placed on child protection registers in eleven local authorities in England and Wales (representing about 9 per cent of the child population) found some 15,000 children were abused (Creighton, 1994); 9,590 children were registered as physically injured by their parents, guardians or carers; a further 6,330 children as sexually abused. These estimates of incidence are based on the largest continuous survey of child abuse in the UK.

The prevalence of child abuse is estimated as between two to four children in every thousand, with one child per thousand under four years of age likely to be severely injured (Creighton, 1994; House of Commons, 1977; Gil, 1970). The rate of reported physical injury to infants under one year appears to be steadily increasing from 1.25 per thousand in 1979 to 1.82 in 1986 (Creighton, 1994, p. 38). The percentage of infants who are seriously or fatally injured, however, is declining. The reported re-injury rate has also fallen. Since 1981 there has been an increase in registrations for sexual abuse, probably owing to increased publicity and information on the problem and its inclusion as a reason for registration (DHSS, 1980). Fisher et al. (1995) found in their study of case conference decision making despite the greater prevalence of child neglect, the child protection system is more sensitive to child physical and sexual abuse.

Children registered for child abuse are in the main young. The average age for registration is seven years with differences found depending on the nature of the abuse. Children who are sexually abused tend to be slightly older (average age of ten years two months) and girls are more likely to be represented (Taylor, 1992, p. 40). Failure to thrive is most commonly found in infants. Cases of reported physical abuse mainly affect primary school age children (average age six years) and more often boys.

Recent research (Gibbons et al., 1995; Pitcairn and Waterhouse, 1993; Creighton, 1994) suggests the majority of children on child protection registers for physical abuse sustain moderate injuries, usually bruising of the body or legs. Less is known about the nature of sexual abuse. Waterhouse, Dobash and Carnie (1994) in a sample of 500 convicted child sexual abusers found a significant proportion of the criminal offences against the children involved a form of sexual intercourse which was sometimes accompanied by violence or threats of violence. This suggests some overlap between different categories of abuse.

Defining and Explaining Child Abuse

There is no absolute definition of child abuse. Official definitions of child abuse usually describe abusive incidents, taking into account whether there is definite knowledge of an intention to harm or knowingly not to prevent harm by any person having care or custody of the child. Harm includes physical injury; physical neglect and failure to thrive, for example, exposure to dangerous circumstances or starvation; emotional abuse where the health and development of the child is threatened and sexual abuse where children under 17 years (England and Wales) have been involved in sexual activities they do not truly comprehend or to which they do not give informed consent.

Five Key Points

1 The management of child abuse depends on a nationally co-ordinated system which seeks to improve professional collaboration and to identify formally children in need of registration.

2 The prevalence for child abuse is estimated as between two to four children in every thousand, with one child per thousand under four years of age likely to be severely injured.

3 Explanations of abuse are complex and depend on models which link social, cultural and personal factors with family relationships.

4 Social workers need to recognize the potential impact of chronic adversity on parental morale and to respond constructively to the concerns of parents and children where abuse is alleged or proven.

5 The three agencies of education, health and social work need to work together with parents to support and protect children in need of child welfare and child protective services.

Defining behaviour as abusive and likely to cause harm to children's health, safety and development gives professionals a duty in law to protect the child. Deciding a threshold where child abuse begins and normal control and discipline end is not easy. Research (Department of Health, 1995) suggests most cases coming to the notice of social work, and other agencies involved in child protection, fall between the extremes and involve children who are in need of support and protection but do not involve serious injury to the child. High public and professional tolerance will reduce the numbers of children requiring investigation, registration and follow-up; low tolerance the converse. Whatever benchmark is employed, universal standards for bringing up children and accepted limits of 'good enough' parenting are likely over time to be affected.

Explanations of abuse have evolved from an initial concentration on single factors, for example, the presence of distinguishing psychological characteristics in parents of abused children to complex models of the interrelationship between multiple factors. Gelles (1987a) and Browne (1988) in their models of the causes of family violence stress the importance of an interaction between psychological, cultural and social factors and family relationships. Families already facing adversity, for example, inadequate housing and unemployment, where poor parent and child relationships routinely feature are considered more likely to resort to aggression in child upbringing. Psychological studies (Sears, Maccoby and Levin, 1957) concerned with parental style and the sociability of the child suggest that highly punitive and highly permissive parents tend to have children who are aggressive. Parents who are aggressive to their children may, in turn, provoke aggression contributing to a cycle of mutually antagonistic interaction. Parents who are highly permissive may fail to provide sufficient positive controls and support to children who, in turn, may develop insufficient self-control.

The psychological status of abused children may shed further light on factors contributing to child abuse and the importance of parent–child interaction. Several studies (Roberts and Taylor, 1993; Pitcairn and Waterhouse, 1993) find that abused children score highly on standardized behavioural check-lists (Rutter, 1967; Richman, Stevenson and Graham, 1984) which are found to have considerable predictive value in discriminating children with neurotic or anti-social behavioural disorders.

Pitcairn and Waterhouse (1993) in a study of parents whose 43 children were registered for physical abuse in three Scottish local authorities report parents,

especially mothers, routinely to admit failing to discipline their children when they knew they should. Day-to-day interaction between parents and their children was characterized by an absence of positive, pro-active limits and controls rather than sustained and systematic aggression. Parents, especially mothers, frankly described poor parenting skills relying mainly on shouting and hitting as the only means to exert influence over their children's behaviour at home.

The Rowntree Inquiry into Income and Wealth (Hills, 1995) describes a cycle of 'poor parenting' in the poorest council estates in the country resulting not from poverty alone but from high rates of family break-up; lack of understanding of the needs of children; social isolation; and universally high rates of unemployment among youth, many of whom were already parents. Five times the number of children were on 'at risk' registers from the poorest estates as in other parts of the same city (Hills, 1995, p. 35). A similar pattern in referrals to registers is noted by Clark (1993) in Australia and Gough (1993) in Scotland, causing them to question whether registration is a means of merely identifying and monitoring rather than positively assisting some of the most disadvantaged families.

By comparison, explanations of reported sexual abuse concentrate on the misuse of power by adults (mainly men) over children (more often girls), and have been highly influenced by feminist writing which examines the influence of gender on relations between men, women and children. Growing concern about sexual misconduct by women against children (especially boys) raises questions about the comprehensiveness of this explanation to account for different types of abuse by different perpetrators. The study of sexual abuse raises questions about what constitutes normative sexual development and the likelihood of untoward sexual experience in childhood and adolescence. Increased recognition is being given to the possibility of young people sexually abusing children younger than themselves. Accounts of men convicted of sexual offences against children suggest abusing behaviour may start young. This suggests there may be a need for new explanations of normal and abnormal sexuality.

Responding to Child Abuse

Public inquiries into the apparent failure of the state to protect children from the consequences of child abuse have been highly influential in determining the nature of professional responses to allegations of child abuse (Parton, 1985). Inquiry findings have given rise to central government guidance which places an emphasis on the investigation and surveillance of abuse, especially by social workers who have duties in law to protect children from harm. Uncertainty about the function of social work as support for or policing of families may account for some of the difficulties which families on the receiving end of child abuse investigations experience.

Brown (1986) found that parents involved in child protection investigations feared their children would be removed from them and taken into public care. This may be a serious misperception when other studies of child care decision making (Vernon and Fruin, 1986) suggest that social workers are reluctant to admit children to public care and instead adopt a 'wait and see' policy in the hope that admission to care may be avoided. Cleaver and Freeman (1992) point to the futility and detriment to children of energies diverted from parents and professionals working collaboratively on problems to covering up family troubles.

The need for open communication is further reflected in Farmer's study (1993) where considerable mismatch arose between the views of parents and social workers. Parents sometimes questioned the legitimacy of child protection intervention creating from the outset a gulf-inhibiting communication between parents and social work services. Parents found the investigatory procedures stigmatizing, and attributing of blame to themselves as failing parents. While social workers may see registration as one means by which to obtain scarce resources for children, Brown (1986) discovered parents remain unaware or unconvinced that a major part of social work intervention could be preventive and enabling rather than reactive and policing.

Three Questions

1   In what way do definitions of 'good enough parenting' vary over time and place?
2   What are the main explanations for child abuse?
3   What problems face the social worker in the search for a good balance between the provision of support for families and the protection of children at risk of abuse?

Magura and Moses (1984) found recipients of child protection services cited material deprivation as the major deleterious influence on their children's daily care, poverty contributing to parental anxiety, stress and depression. More recent studies (Department of Health, 1995) confirm that the majority of children on child abuse registers are children in need of child welfare services, only some of whom will prove in need of continuing protection for their personal safety. Predicting which children need protective as well as child welfare services remains a challenge.

Fisher et al. (1995) note the lack of attention paid in case conferences to the emotional environment in which the child grows up. This outlook may seriously inhibit parents seeking help and accurate professional understanding of parent–child relations. There is also a serious risk that social workers will miss the chance to support parents by focusing narrowly on alleged abuse rather than including the pressing, albeit mundane, daily concerns of parents.

The Children Act 1989 in England and Wales and the comparable Act of 1995 in Scotland emphasize partnership between families and professionals. Procedural guidance which stresses detection and monitoring without sufficient attention to support and follow-up may serve in some instances to drive a wedge between parents and professionals to the detriment of children. The child's interests must come first but this can only be meaningful if the climate of professional intervention allows for an objective and comprehensive appraisal of the child's needs and for these needs to be matched to resources with parental agreement whenever possible.

Social workers need to recognize the potential impact of chronic adversity on parental morale and motivation in bringing up children and to respond constructively to the concerns of parents and children. This is not to suggest that physical, sexual or psychological harm to children should be ignored: on the contrary, taking children and parents seriously is likely to improve assessment and to put resources where they count. Children on child protection registers have a strong claim on and need for comprehensive and interdisciplinary children's services. Social work, health and education working together will improve abused children's life chances.

References

Brown, C. (1986) *Child Abuse Parents Speaking: A Consumer Study*, Bristol: School for Advanced Urban Studies, University of Bristol.
Browne, K. D. (1988) 'The naturalistic context of family violence and child abuse', in J. Archer and K. D. Browne (eds), *Human Aggression: Naturalistic*

Further Reading

1   Browne, K., Davies, C. and Stratton, P. (eds) (1994) *Early Prediction and Prevention of Child Abuse*, Chichester: John Wiley.
2   Department of Health (1995) *Child Protection: Messages from Research*, London: HMSO.
3   Stainton Rogers, W., Hevey, D., Roche, J. and Ash E. (eds) (1992) *Child Abuse and Neglect: Facing the Challenge*, London: B.T. Batsford in Association with the Open University.

Approaches, London: Routledge.
Clarke, R. (1993) 'Discrimination in child protection services', in L. Waterhouse (ed.), *Child Abuse and Child Abusers: Protection and Prevention*, London: Jessica Kingsley.
Cleaver, H. and Freeman, P. (1992) 'Parental perspectives in suspected child abuse and its aftermath', in D. Gough (ed.), *Child Abuse Interventions. A Review of the Literature*, London: HMSO.
Creighton, S. J. (1994) 'The incidence of child abuse and neglect', in K. Browne, C. Davies and P. Stratton (eds), *Early Prediction and Prevention of Child Abuse*, Chichester: John Wiley and Sons.
Department of Health (1995) *Child Protection: Messages from Research*, London: HMSO.
DHSS (1980) Child Abuse: Central Register Systems, LASSL (80)4, HN (80)20.
DHSS (1982) *Child Abuse. A Study of Inquiry Reports*, London: HMSO.
Farmer, E. (1993) 'The impact of child protection interventions: the experiences of parents and children' in L. Waterhouse (ed.), *Child Abuse and Child Abusers: Protection and Prevention*, London: Jessica Kingsley.
Fisher, T., Bingley-Miller, L. and Sinclair, I. (1995) 'Which children are registered at case conferences?', *British Journal of Social Work*, 25, 191–207.
Gelles, R. J. (1987a) *Family Violence* (2nd edn), Sage Library of Social Research, no. 84, Beverly Hills, CA: Sage.
Gibbons, J., Conroy, S. and Bell, C. (1995) *Studies in Child Protection: Development After Physical Abuse In Early Childhood*, London: HMSO.
Gil, D. (1970) *Violence Against Children*, Massachussets: Harvard University Press.
Gough, D. (1993) *Child Abuse Interventions: A Review of the Literature*, London: HMSO.
Hills, J. (1995) *Joseph Rowntree Foundation Inquiry into Income and Wealth Volume 2: A Summary of the Evidence*, York: Joseph Rowntree Foundation.

Home Office, Department of Health, Department of Transport, Department of Education and Science, and Welsh Office (1991) *Working Together Under The Children Act 1989: A Guide to the Arrangements for Inter-agency Co-operation for the Protection of Children from Abuse*, London: HMSO.

House of Commons (1977) *Violence to Children: First Report for the Select Committee on Violence in the Family, Session 1976–7*, London: HMSO.

Magura, S. and Moses, B. S. (1984) 'Clients as evaluators in child protective services', *Child Welfare*, 53(2), 99–112.

Parton, N. (1985) *The Politics of Child Abuse*, London: Macmillan.

Pitcairn, T. and Waterhouse, L. (1993) 'Evaluating parenting in child physical abuse', in L. Waterhouse (ed.), *Child Abuse and Child Abusers: Protection and Prevention*, London: Jessica Kingsley.

Richman, N., Stevenson, J. and Graham, P. J. (1984) 'Pre-school to school: a behavioural study', in R. Schaffer (ed.), *Behavioural Development: A Series of Monographs*, London and New York: Academic Press.

Roberts, J. and Taylor, C. (1993) 'Sexually abused children and young people speak out', in L. Waterhouse (ed.), *Child Abuse and Child Abusers: Protection and Prevention*, London: Jessica Kingsley.

Rutter, M. (1967) 'A child behaviour questionnaire for completion by teachers: preliminary findings', *Journal of Child Psychology and Psychiatry*, 8, 1–11.

Sears, R., Maccoby, E. and Levin, H. (1957) *Patterns of Child Rearing*, New York: Harper & Row.

Taylor, S. (1992) 'How prevalent is it?' in W. Stainton Rogers, D. Hevey, J. Roche and E. Ash (eds), *Child Abuse and Neglect: Facing the Challenge*, London: B.T. Batsford in Association with the Open University.

Vernon, J. and Fruin, D. (1986) *In Care: A Study of Social Work Decision Making*, London: National Children's Bureau.

Waterhouse, L., Dobash, R. and Carnie, J. (1994) *Child Sexual Abusers*, Edinburgh: The Scottish Office.

Learning Difficulties

Tim Booth

The Third International Conference of the world-wide self-advocacy movement for people with learning difficulties was held in Toronto, Canada in 1993. Almost 1,400 delegates and their supporters from 32 countries gathered together to renew their commitment to improving the lives of people with learning difficulties by doing it for themselves.

Delegates from all parts of the world voiced the same demands for *integration* (in ordinary homes in the community); *productivity* (in proper jobs paying real wages); and *inclusion* (as full citizens in mainstream services and facilities). Six major issues dominated the conference: real homes, worthwhile jobs, relationships, power and decision making, gender issues, and language and history (Booth and Booth, 1993). These issues and demands represent a set of goals, grounded in the lives and experience of people with learning difficulties, that can be used for assessing what progress has been made in meeting their aspirations and how much remains to be done. The gap between these aims and achievements amounts to an agenda for change defining the challenge facing social work into the new millennium.

Real Homes

Meeting people's demands to live like others in a home of their own means enabling them to choose where they live, who they live with (if anyone), who supports them and how (Kinsella, 1993a). The programme of hospital closure and

relocation that has seen the hospital population decline by 37 per cent from 51,500 in 1980 to 32,700 in 1990 was an essential step in moving towards this objective. However, experience has shown that merely shifting resources from institutional to community care succeeds only in relocating the old practices. Simply providing ordinary houses in ordinary neighbourhoods is not enough. Very few adults with learning difficulties have their own homes or even the tenancy rights of other citizens. A shift in thinking and attitudes is called for as well. Among other things, this means abandoning the idea that people must earn the right to live independently. This idea is embodied in the widespread notion that there exists a 'continuum of care' ranging from more restrictive types of accommodation providing intensive support for people with multiple disabilities at one end to more independent living arrangements for more able people at the other (Kinsella, 1993b).

The image of a care continuum has exerted a significant influence on thinking about the planning and design of services. It has placed the emphasis on fitting people into facilities rather than tailoring services and supports to the needs of individuals wherever they live. People have been required to move home as their needs change. They have been obliged to prove their fitness before graduating to some more independent accommodation. It has also meant that people have often been prevented from moving on because of blockages in the system. Acting on the demand for 'real homes' voiced by the self-advocacy movement involves ditching the thinking and assumptions built into the continuum model. An alternative paradigm is available in the set of beliefs and principles known as Supported Living (National Development Team, 1993). The core idea of Supported Living is that services should be developed and adapted to sustain the choices people make instead of them having to take whatever is available. Such an approach requires that practitioners take the lead from people with learning difficulties and learn to work in alliance with them. This represents a fundamental challenge to traditional forms of agency accountability and professional practice. From this point of view, securing real homes for people will entail creating a new service culture (Dowson, 1991).

Worthwhile Jobs

The issue of real homes is linked with the demand of self-advocates for worthwhile jobs in a perverse way: very often the one can only be obtained at the expense of the other. Under community care arrangements, the costs of people's housing and support are generally met from social security benefits that are only available in full to those who are classified as incapable of work. There are strict limits on what can be earned while on benefit. Part-time working too has implications for people's benefit entitlement. Any move into employment – even on a temporary or trial basis – can lead to an immediate loss of benefit income and put in jeopardy a person's package of care. People are effectively rendered incapable of work by the system rather than their own lack of skills.

The benefit trap, like the continuum trap referred to above, puts barriers in the way of independence. People are forced into dependent roles by policies that prevent them from exercising greater

Five Key Points

1 It is estimated that between 2 and 3 per cent of the population have a learning difficulty ranging from mild or moderate to severe or profound.

2 There are between 120,000 and 160,000 adults in England with severe or profound learning difficulties.

3 There are about 30,000 children under 16 with severe or profound learning difficulties.

4 The great majority of children and at least half of all adults live with their parents or other carers.

5 Around one-fifth of adults live in hospital and NHS community units and just over a quarter live in residential accommodation provided by local authorities or the independent sector.

control over their lives. This throws a different light on the nature of the disadvantages and restrictions faced by people with learning difficulties in meeting the demands of ordinary living. The clinical or developmental model sees the problems in living experienced by people with learning difficulties as a function of their intellectual impairment. In this model, intervention – in the form of treatment, therapy, rehabilitation or training – is focused on the person and under the control of a professional. Yet the example of the benefit trap demonstrates how people with learning difficulties are additionally disadvantaged by socially created barriers to competence and the effects of direct and indirect discrimination. This recognition gives rise to an alternative, social model of disability as 'the loss or limitation of opportunities to take part in the normal life of the community on an equal level with others due to physical and social barriers' (Disabled People's International, 1986). From this point of view, the locus of the problem shifts from the individual to the workings of the wider society, and professional intervention as a response gives way to the need for social action and social change.

Few people with learning difficulties have jobs. The benefit rules that effectively exclude them from the world of work also act as a disincentive to the creation of supported employment programmes designed to facilitate access to the labour market. Consequently, many people become locked into a merry-go-round of training. There has been an expansion of opportunities in further education for students with learning difficulties (Sutcliffe, 1990), who also have priority access to the training programmes delivered by local Training and Enterprise Councils. But too often students complete their courses only to find there is nowhere to go except back to their local Adult Training Centre (ATC) or Social Education Centre (SEC).

ATCs and SECs remain the main source of day-time occupation for adults with learning difficulties. Local authorities currently provide about 56,000 day centre places. This figure falls well short of the 1991 planning target of 74,900 places. Although some of the slack has been taken up by further education, there remains a hole in the week for large numbers of people with learning difficulties and, as self-advocates have argued, 'leisure is not an acceptable alternative to work'.

There has long been confusion about the purpose of segregated, building-based day services. In 1977, Whelan and Speake reported that staff identified 21 aims of ATCs. There is no sign of any greater coherence of purpose today. The fact that their primary contract is not with the users is evidenced by the latter's criticisms of the congregate settings and activities ('I call it the doghouse'), the lack of things to do ('No one should be expected to sit around and do leisure all day') and the way attendance is regarded

as a poor substitute for work ('It's not a proper job'). Their main social functions are containment and the provision of respite for carers – against which must be set their failure to enlarge the opportunities available to people with learning difficulties and to help them achieve the important transition into the adult world.

Relationships

Growing up is about breaks and new beginnings – from home to school, school to school, school to work, parental home to own home, job to job, etc. Each step brings opportunities for meeting new people and making new relationships. Many of these transitions are closed to people with learning difficulties and the possibility of them developing relationships that satisfy their needs for company, practical help and intimacy is diminished as a result.

• Far too many people with learning difficulties lead lives starved of friendship (Richardson and Ritchie, 1989a). For those living with parents, there is often a lack of companionship with others of the same age, loneliness during their leisure hours and isolation from activities outside the family. Those living outside the parental home can find themselves locked into a very small social network comprising mainly paid staff and other people with learning difficulties which fails to provide the kind of emotional sustenance gained from close family relationships.
• The experience of caring for a person with learning difficulties over many years frequently leads to a strong sense of protectiveness on the part of parents that can, in turn, hamper the development of independence. This can make for problems in 'letting go', especially where their son or

daughter shows little initiative in making the break. Equally, it can mean they fail to acknowledge or even dismiss their adult child's choices about, for example, having a boyfriend or girlfriend or a 'place of my own' (Richardson and Ritchie, 1989b).

- Too many people are moved around without their consent. Relocation is often driven by resource considerations with too little thought given to the importance of keeping friends together or to the compatibility of those who are expected to live under the same roof. Research has shown that such upheaval in people's lives and relationships can induce a sort of 'transition shock' characterized by a range of short-term deficits in behavioural and emotional functioning (Booth, Simons and Booth, 1990). The impact on people of the loss of long-standing friends is frequently overlooked, as too are the difficulties they face in trying to make new relationships in the community (Flynn, 1989). More attention needs to be given to helping people maintain existing friendships through the trauma of a move.

- Discontinuities in front-line service provision frequently disrupt individual programmes and the personal relationships between staff and users. Staff assume a big role in the lives of people with few close bonds, and are widely named by them as best friends. High rates of staff turnover bring frequent partings and the loss of those who are liked and trusted. They also entail people accepting relationships with others not of their own choosing and with whom they may not get on. Part of the vulnerability of people with learning difficulties is that these service relationships are invariably more important to them than to the paid worker.

- The sexuality of people with learning difficulties continues to pose a challenge to the affirmation of their rights as citizens. They are still widely viewed as being either asexual ('permanent children') or over-sexed. These two pervasive myths have contributed to keeping people with learning difficulties ignorant of sex and to the repression of their sexuality. They have also played a part in concealing their position as victims of sexual abuse by others (Brown and Craft, 1989). The law in these matters is generally held to be fragmented, confused and out of date (The Law Commission, 1991): it has

---

Three Questions
1 Consider the ways in which people with learning difficulties are forced into dependent roles in society.
2 What practical steps might be taken to promote the integration of people with learning difficulties in the community?
3 What implications does user empowerment have for professional practice?

---

failed to strike a proper balance between protecting people from exploitation and securing their freedom to take risks. One consequence has been to hinder the development of policies and practices that allow individuals the scope and opportunity to fulfil their need to love and be loved.

Service development entails more than just improving activities and facilities for people with learning difficulties. It also means investing in their relationships. More attention must be paid to ways of supporting personal relationships of all kinds from friendships through marriage to parenthood (Booth and Booth, 1994). Ordinary living depends on them.

Power and Decision Making

One of the main objectives of the raft of reforms introduced by the NHS and Community Care Act 1990 is 'to give people a greater say in how they live their lives and the services they need to help them to do so' (Department of Health, 1989). Such changes will not be achieved with old attitudes and old practices. People with learning difficulties enjoy little more than 'titbits of autonomy' (Flynn and Ward, 1991). Their powerlessness leaves them ill-placed to resist those who would take over their lives. Against these odds, compliance to the dictates of others becomes a strategy for survival and at the same time reinforces their dependent status. Enabling people with learning difficulties to realize their aspirations for greater self-determination means tackling the fundamental imbalance of power in their relations with their families and the services.

The self-advocacy movement provides a touchstone against which progress in this direction may be assessed. Self-advocacy is about people with learning difficulties speaking up for themselves, defending their rights and organizing to advance their own interests (Simons, 1993). It defines an arena of political struggle over whose voice and whose choices and wishes should prevail (Crawley, 1988). There are many barriers to the development of self-advocacy, not least the danger of professionals taking over (Dowson, 1990), but it is inconceivable that the goal of greater user participation in services can be accomplished without a vigorous self-advocacy movement. Other projects that similarly serve to challenge a system dominated by the views of professionals are citizen advocacy (Butler et al., 1988),

quality action groups (Ritchie and Ash, 1990) and service brokerage. The empowerment of users rests on the continued growth of schemes such as these which set out to increase both their autonomy and the accountability of the services.

Gender Issues

Gender shapes how men and women with learning difficulties experience their disempowerment. Many of the obstacles to sexual and reproductive freedom encountered by women with learning difficulties are merely extreme examples of ones that affect large numbers of women in society: inadequate control over their own fertility, lack of knowledge and education, medical dominance, poverty, communal living and lack of privacy, sexual victimization and abuse (Petchesky, 1979). Sexism is rife within the services where gender relations within the wider society are reproduced in sharper form because people lack the personal freedom to establish an identity of their own. Greater responsiveness to gender issues (as well as to the impact of other social divisions such as class and race on people's lives) entails looking beyond the label and seeing men and women with learning difficulties as people first.

Language and History

Labels are part of the language of oppression. People with learning difficulties know at first hand the power of language to imprison and exclude. Big words (and big meetings) shut them out. Participation by users involves more than just their presence at the table. It demands a different way of working adapted to their abilities rather than the customs and practices of the organization. At the same time, language can also liberate. The use of simple words increases people's access to information. Learning to read and write improves people's mastery of their environment. Finding a voice enables people to articulate their demands, protest against abuse, tell their stories and gain strength from their own history.

The agenda for change mapped out by the self-advocates in Toronto offers social workers an opportunity to contribute to the making of a new stage in their history by siding with them to transform their place in society. It remains to be seen if they are up to the job.

Further Reading

1 Atkinson, D. and Williams, F. (eds) (1990) *'Know Me As I Am': an Anthology of Prose, Poetry and Art by People with Learning Difficulties*, London: Hodder and Stoughton.

2 Philpot, T. and Ward, L. (eds) (1995) *Values and Visions: Changing Ideas in Services for People with Learning Difficulties*, London: Butterworth-Heinemann.

3 Simons, K. (1992) *'Sticking Up For Yourself': Self-Advocacy and People with Learning Difficulties*, York: Joseph Rowntree Foundation in association with Community Care.

References

Booth, T. and Booth, W. (1993) 'People First celebrate their success stories', *Community Living*, 7(2), October, 14–15.

Booth, T. and Booth, W. (1994) *Parenting Under Pressure: Mothers and Fathers with Learning Difficulties*, Buckingham: Open University Press.

Booth, T., Simons, K. and Booth, W. (1990) *Outward Bound: Relocation and Community Care for People with Learning Difficulties*, Buckingham: Open University Press.

Brown, H. and Craft, A. (1989) *Thinking the Unthinkable*, London: Family Planning Association.

Butler, K., Carr, S. and Sullivan, F. (1988) *Citizen Advocacy: A Powerful Partnership*, London: National Citizen Advocacy.

Crawley, B. (1988) *The Growing Voice: A Survey of Self-Advocacy Groups*, London: VIA Publications.

Department of Health (1989) *Caring for People: Community Care in the Next Decade and Beyond*, Cm 849, London: HMSO.

Disabled People's International (1986) 'DPI – calling', *European Regional Newsletter No. 1*, March.

Dowson, S. (1990) *Keeping It Safe*, London: VIA Publications.

Dowson, S. (1991) *Moving to the Dance: Service Culture and Community Care*, London: VIA Publications.

Flynn, M. (1989) *Independent Living for Adults with a Mental Handicap – A Place of my Own*, London: Cassell.

Flynn, M. and Ward. L. (1991) ' "We can change the future": self and citizen advocacy', in S. Segal and V. Varma (eds), *Prospects for People with Learning Difficulties*, London: David Fulton Publishers.

Kinsella, P. (1993a) *Supported Living: a New Paradigm*, Manchester: National Development Team.

Kinsella, P. (1993b) *Group Homes: An Ordinary Life?*, Manchester: National Development Team.

Law Commission, The (1991) *Mentally Incapacitated Adults and Decision-Making: An Overview*, Consultation Paper No. 119, London: HMSO.

National Development Team (1993) *Supported Living Initiative: A Home of my Own*, Manchester: NDT.

Petchesky, R. (1979) 'Reproduction, ethics and public policy: the Federal sterilization regulations', *Hastings Center Report*, October, 29–41.

Richardson, A. and Ritchie, J. (1989a) *Developing Friendships: Enabling People with Learning Difficulties to Make and Maintain Friends*, London: Policy Studies Institute.

Richardson, A. and Ritchie, J. (1989b) *Letting Go*, Buckingham: Open University Press.

Ritchie, P. and Ash, A. (1990) 'Quality in action: improving services through quality action groups', in T. Booth (ed.), *Better Lives: Changing Services for People with Learning Difficulties*, Social Services Monographs: Research in Practice, Sheffield: Community Care and Sheffield University.

Simons, K. (1993) *Sticking Up For Yourself: Self-Advocacy and People with Learning Difficulties*, York: Joseph Rowntree Foundation/Community Care Magazine.

Sutcliffe, J. (1990) *Adults with Learning Difficulties: Education for Choice and Empowerment*, Buckingham: Open University Press.

Whelan, E. and Speake, B. (1977) *Adult Training Centres in England and Wales: Report of the First National Survey*, Manchester: NATMH.

The Frailty of Old Age

Chris Phillipson

Older people present a significant challenge and opportunity for social work. As a group they have moved from being a marginal concern (in the period of the 1950s and 1960s), to one of central importance to the profession. A combination of forces associated with demography, social attitudes and legislative change, have assisted this development (Fennell, Evers and Phillipson, 1988; Bond, Coleman and Peace, 1993). The first of these – demographic change – represents a crucial factor in terms of the rationale for social work with older people. The number of people in Britain over age 65 increased from 1.7 million to 8.8 million between 1901 and 1991, or from 4.7 per cent to 15.8 per cent of the population. By the year 2021, the respective figures will be 10 million or 17.2 per cent.

This ageing of the population reflects the convergence of two main factors: first, the downward trend in the birth rate, so that the proportion of older people is increasingly larger than the proportion of children in the population. Second, improvements in life expectancy (an increase of 20 years over the course of the twentieth century in the case of Britain). For social workers, the absolute rise in the numbers of older people is probably less important than the growth in particular groups such as the very elderly (those aged 75 and over). In 1991, 44 per cent of the elderly population were aged at least 75, compared to one-third in 1951. By 2041 it is expected that for the first time the proportion of elderly people aged at least 75 will have exceeded 50 per cent (Henwood, 1992).

The growth in the numbers of people aged 75 and over has important implications for the practice of social work. On the positive side, this is a group where there are significant numbers without major health and social problems: even amongst those aged 85 and over, around one-third of men and women do not have a long-standing illness or disability (Sidell, 1995). Conversely, the impact of ill-health does become a significant issue for most older people. For example, it is estimated that among those people aged 85 and over, one in five will have dementia (Jorm, 1990) and three in five a limiting long-standing illness such as osteoporosis or arthritis.

In terms of social relationships, it is the loss of close friends and relations which is such a striking feature of later life (for women especially). Unlike earlier generations, death is now clustered towards the end of the life course. Invariably, also, people experience death when their own personal resources of health and income may be diminished. Social work with older people, in these circumstances, is often inseparable from help in the context of bereavement and assisting people through the process of rebuilding their lives and social networks (Machin, 1993; Jerrome, 1993).

Family Support

Despite significant changes, the social world of older people is still closely associated with their immediate family

(Finch, 1989). Clare Wenger's (1984, 1992) research showed that among those older people with children, residential proximity tended to increase with age, with widowhood resulting in a move closer to children. More than half of the parents in her study saw a child at least once a week, and this rose to three-quarters in the case of parents over 80.

Surveys in Britain based on nationally representative samples, have confirmed the existence of high levels of contact between older people and relatives and friends (Allen and Perkins, 1995). At the same time, there is also strong evidence that this is translated into extensive care and support. The 1986 General Household Survey (OPCS, 1989) confirmed that for those older people unable to carry out domestic tasks unaided, relatives were the usual source of help. For example, 11 of the 15 per cent of all elderly people unable to do their own shopping received help from relatives and another 2 per cent from friends, while 7 per cent of the 11 per cent who could not clean or sweep floors, and 6 of the 7 per cent who could not cook a main meal had help from family members (OPCS, 1989).

Research has also highlighted the range of physical, social and financial costs associated with the type of care provided by partners, relatives and friends. The physical stresses of care may include the daily pressures associated with dealing with incontinence, lifting someone in and out of bed, manoeuvring a wheelchair; all of this carried out with limited help and alongside a range of other domestic and non-domestic tasks. Again, these activities have to be seen within the context of many carers themselves being in their sixties and seventies, with the likelihood of them also having a chronic illness or disability (OPCS, 1989). The social costs attached to caring will include the isolation and possible loneliness associated with intensive care work, loss of friends and limited opportunities for

---

Five Key Points

1 Demography, changing social attitudes and legislation have all made older people a target group of critical significance for social work.

2 Social work with older people often involves helping them to rebuild their lives following bereavement.

3 Work with carers – many of whom are themselves no longer young – is a major task for social work.

4 Social class, gender and ethnicity are all factors which need to be taken into account when considering the nature of social work with old people.

5 Social work with older people must be anti-ageist; it must be supportive; it must recognize client strengths; and it must use advocacy.

---

holidays and regular breaks.

Levin et al.'s (1989) study of carers of older people with dementia identified a range of social costs arising from this kind of care. For example, only two-fifths of the supporters had taken holidays in the previous year and over half the others had gone without them for at least five years. Supporters who did most for their relatives, those who coped with incontinence and other major problems, were no more likely to have had a holiday in the previous year. Similarly, many carers experienced difficulties in getting to see friends on a regular basis and felt less free to initiate meetings with friends and relatives (Lewis and Meredith, 1988).

There is growing evidence that some of the stresses associated with informal care may lead to the abuse and/or neglect of the older person. One British researcher has suggested that around 500,000 older people in Britain (around one in ten) are at risk of abuse (Eastman, 1984; see also, Biggs, Kingston and Phillipson, 1995). A study of caregivers of people with dementia found one-fifth reporting that they had, on occasions, recourse to shaking or hitting their elderly relative (Levin et al., 1989).

The social pressures facing carers may be reinforced by financial problems associated with the loss of earnings and promotion (Philips, 1995). Amongst sole carers (spouses or parents), Evandrou et al. (1990) note that a higher proportion are likely to be in poverty (as measured by those with an income on or below 140 per cent of the poverty line) in comparison with other groups of carers. Evandrou et al. (1990) found that nearly one-third of sole carers were 'in' or 'on' the margins of poverty. In the case of carers with the dependant in the same household, 35 per cent had incomes 'in' or 'on' the margins of poverty.

The significance of the 'informal sector of care' (or the second welfare state), indicates the importance of recognizing the kind of social networks within which older people are located. These may vary considerably in terms of the kind of help provided and their ability to respond to particular crises in old age (Wenger, 1992). Moreover, there is also the issue of effective co-ordination between formal and informal sources of care, with the need for effective advocacy where appropriate both for the older person and the carer. Both these issues suggest an important role for the social worker, one which is likely to become of increased importance as community care evolves (Hughes, 1995).

Divisions in Later Life

So far this chapter has discussed old age without reference to some of the key social, cultural and economic distinctions affecting older people. Bond and Coleman (1993), for example, suggest that social class is a much stronger predictor of life-style than age and argue that older people have much more in common with younger people of their own class than they do with older people from other classes. The importance of social class in influencing opportunities in old age is likely to increase, as the sources of income in old age become more dependent upon benefits such as private and occupational pensions.

Gender is another major social division (Arber and Ginn, 1995; Bernard and Meade, 1993). The gender imbalances of later life are now well-established. Because women outlive men by an average of six years, there are 50 per cent more women than men amongst those 65 and over. The gender imbalance is even more marked in late old age: amongst those aged 85 and over, women outnumber men by three to one. As Arber and Ginn (1995, p. 11) comment: 'The fact that over half of older women are widowed, whereas three-quarters of older men are married, has consequences for gender, identity, relationships and roles in later life.'

Race and ethnicity is another important division. Over the next two decades there will be a significant ageing of the black community as the cohorts of migrants of the late 1950s and 1960s reach retirement age (Blakemore and Boneham, 1994). Research suggests a significant role for social work in relation to older people from minority ethnic groups. Some key factors here are: first, the increased susceptibility to physical ill-health of this group because of past experiences such as heavy manual work and poor housing; second, greater vulnerability to mental health problems, a product of racism and cultural pressures; third, low uptake of health and social services; fourth, acute financial problems, with evidence of elderly Asians being at a particular disadvantage. The problems faced by ethnic elders have been defined as representing a form of 'triple jeopardy' (Norman, 1985). This refers to the fact that ethnic elders not only face discrimination because they are old; in addition, many of them live in disadvantaged physical and economic circumstances; finally, they are likely to face discrimination because of their culture, language, skin colour or religious affiliation. All this suggests a key role for social work over the next 20 years, as the size of this group is substantially increased.

Reasons for Social Work with Older People

The context of ageing reviewed above provides a number of suggestions about the purpose of social work with older people, and especially those in late old age. First, social work has a major contribution to make in the area of 'anti-ageist practice' (Biggs, 1993; Bytheway, 1994). Ageism may be defined as discrimination against older people merely by virtue of their age. Ageism affects many institutions in society and has a number of dimensions – job discrimination, loss of status, stereotyping and dehumanization. Ageism is about assuming that all older people are the same, despite different life histories, needs and expectations. Ageism not only affects the lives of older people, but like ageing itself, it affects every individual from birth onwards, putting limits and constraints on experiences, expectations, relationships and opportunities. These points underscore the importance of social work adopting a clear anti-ageist framework, recognizing principles such as the following:

- ageing as a period of normal development;
- the positive social and economic functions performed by older people;
- the importance of using the term older people not 'the elderly';
- the importance of talking about the rights and responsibilities of older people;
- the importance of listening to what older people have to say about their experiences and emotions; and

- the necessity of standing alongside older people, in some cases where there is conflict with carers – informal as well as formal.

Social work has a significant part to play in fostering greater awareness of the impact of ageism in society (and on the professions working with and for older people). The goal of working towards a society free of ageism should be as important as that of achieving a society devoid of racism and sexism.

A second important reason for social work relates to the provision and management of different kinds of social support to elderly people. This reflects

---

Three Questions

1 How might an anti-ageist practice be developed in work with older people?
2 What sort of conflicts are likely to arise in the relationship between older people and informal carers?
3 What are the issues that might be faced by particular minority ethnic groups as increased numbers move into late old age?

---

the vulnerability of the old not just to losses which are inevitable (such as the death of a partner or friend), but also to events which reflect particular types of tensions and divisions in society (such as domestic violence or racist attacks). Elderly people experience problems which would be distressing at any point of the life course (and of course problems such as poor health or poverty affect the young as well as the old). But to repeat an earlier point: people experience these changes when their own resources are invariably depleted. The resources social work has to offer may, therefore, be crucial in terms of helping people forward to the next phase in their lives.

Third, within this process of support,

recognition of the strengths of older people is vital. It is relatively easy to highlight the problems of the old; and, indeed, this is important in terms of constructing different forms of social work intervention. Equally, though, social work has a major role in reaffirming the resilience and power of older people. Of course, elderly people have achieved this themselves through their writings and their political organizations (Sarton, 1988; Curtis, 1993). Social work interventions can, however, be used positively (through forms of practice such as personal biography work and life review therapy), to enhance the process of individuals rediscovering a sense of purpose and identity in later life (Bornat, 1994; Hughes, 1995).

Fourth, social work in the twenty-first century will be closely concerned with advocacy for groups such as older people. The case for this reflects both social changes and the impact of social legislation. Dunning (1995) observes that changes in family structures, living arrangements and patterns of employment, mean that some older people might not have a partner or close relative who can provide support or speak out on their behalf. For others, family relationships may be poor and conflicts of interest are likely to arise. At the same time, greater emphasis is being given to the idea of consumer choice and user empowerment in the provision of services.

More specifically, social work and advocacy is important because of the likelihood of older people entering situations where their frailties may be exposed or enhanced. This may happen as people move into residential care, or are discharged from hospital, or embark on long-term domiciliary support. As events, these *may* lead to greater independence for an older person; equally, though, the elderly person may feel their autonomy undermined by professional carers taking key decisions on their behalf. This possibility underlines the importance of advocacy as a central social role in work with older people.

Conclusion

This chapter has reviewed some of the key reasons for undertaking social work with people entering late old age. The chapter has noted, first, the increased importance of older people for the practice of social work; second, the pressures which they face through the loss of key relationships, this coming at a time when their own resources may be reduced; third, the possibility of frailty being enhanced within the context of developments such as a move into residential care.

Further Reading

1 Blakemore, K. and Boneham, B. (1994) *Age, Race and Ethnicity: a Comparative Approach*, Buckingham: Open University Press.
2 Bond, J., Coleman, P. and Peace, S. (eds) (1993) *Ageing in Society: an Introduction to Social Gerontology*, London: Sage.
3 Hughes, B. (1995) *Older People and Community Care*, Buckingham: Open University Press.

The implications of the approach taken in this chapter is that social work with older people needs to recognize both the ac8tual and potential disabilities of later life, *and* the possibilities for further growth and development even in very late old age. This points to the importance of the social worker adopting a clear anti-ageist framework, using this to guide the complex decisions which have to be made in the 'triangle' of user, carer and service provider. In the twenty-first century, social work with older people will become fundamental to the profession and will be a central reason for wanting to assume the identity and practice of being a social worker.

References

Allen, I. and Perkins, E. (1995) *Family Care in Great Britain*, London: HMSO.

Arber, S. and Ginn, J. (1995) *Connecting Gender and Ageing*, Buckingham: Open University Press.

Bernard, M. and Meade, K. (1993) *Women Come of Age: Perspectives on the Lives of Older Women*, London: Edward Arnold.

Biggs, S. (1993) *Understanding Ageing*, Buckingham: Open University Press.

Biggs, S., Kingston, P. and Phillipson, C. (1995) *Elder Abuse in Perspective*, Buckingham: Open University Press.

Blakemore, K. and Boneham, B. (1994) *Age, Race and Ethnicity: a Comparative Approach*, Buckingham: Open University Press.

Bond, J. and Coleman, P. (1993) 'Ageing into the twenty-first century', in J. Bond, P. Coleman and S. Peace (eds) (1993), pp. 333–50.

Bond, J., Coleman, P. and Peace, S. (eds) (1993) *Ageing in Society: an Introduction to Social Gerontology*, London: Sage.

Bornat, J. (ed.) *Reminiscence Reviewed*, Buckingham: Open University Press.

Bytheway, B. (1994) *Ageism*, Buckingham: Open University Press.

Curtis, Z. (1993) 'On being a woman in the pensioners movement', in J. Johnson and R. Slater, *Ageing and Later Life*, London: Sage.

Dunning, A. (1995) *Citizen Advocacy with Older People*, London: Centre for Policy on Ageing.

Eastman, M. (1984) *Old Age Abuse*, London: Age Concern England.

Evandrou, M. (1986) 'Who cares for the elderly: family care provision and receipt of statutory services', in C. Phillipson, M. Bernard and P. Strang (eds), *Dependency and Interdependency in Old Age*, London: Croom Helm, pp. 150–66.

Fennell, G., Evers, H. and Phillipson, C. (1988) *The Sociology of Old Age*, Buckingham: Open University Press.

Finch, J. (1989) *Family Obligations and Social Change*, Oxford: Basil Blackwell.

Henwood, M. (1992) *Through a Glass Darkly: Community Care and Elderly People*, Kings Fund Centre Project Paper No. 14, London: Kings Fund Centre.

Hughes, B. (1995) *Older People and Community Care*, Buckingham: Open University Press.

Jerrome, D. (1993) 'Intimate relationships', in J. Bond, P. Coleman and S. Peace (eds), *Ageing in Society*, London: Sage Books, pp. 226–54.

Jorm, A. (1990) *The Epidemiology of Alzheimer's Disease and Related Disorders*, London: Chapman and Hall.

Levin, E., Sinclair, I. and Gorbach, P. (1989) *Families, Services and Confusion in Old Age*, Aldershot: Avebury.

Lewis, J. and Meredith, B. (1988) *Daughters Who Care: Daughters Caring for Mothers at Home*, London: Routledge.

Machin, L. (1993) 'Rage, rage against the dying of the light', in K. Tout (ed.), *Elderly Care*, London: Chapman and Hall, pp. 226–34.

Norman, A. (1985) *Triple Jeopardy: Growing Old in a Second Homeland*, London: Centre for Policy on Ageing.

Office of Population Censuses and Surveys (1989) *General Household Survey 1986*, London: HMSO.

Phillips, J. (1995) *Working Carers*, Aldershot: Avebury.

Sarton, M. (1988) *After a Stroke*, London: The Women's Press.

Siddell, M. (1995) *Health in Old Age*, Buckingham: Open University Press.

Wenger, C. (1984) *The Supportive Network*, London: George Allen and Unwin.

Wenger, C. (1992) *Help in Old Age*, Liverpool: Liverpool University Press.

Part V
Theory and Method

Introduction to Part V

Our authors provide a succinct introduction to nine theoretical approaches, each one of which has had and continues to have an important part to play in social work. David Howe reflects upon the interaction between practice and theory, and readers will doubtless find their sympathies tilting towards one model rather than others. The fascination of this section, however, can best be engendered by a straight reading of the ten chapters, which together prompt in the reader the crucial question of how the various theoretical perspectives relate to each other, to what extent they are mutually compatible and why it is that a still growing field of professional activity can accommodate such different methods. Do they relate to the different frameworks outlined in part IV or to the different work settings described in part VII? Do they reflect personal or political differences among practitioners and those who train them? And is there a logical connection between the theoretical perspective employed and the identified needs of different service users?

V.1
Relating Theory to Practice
David Howe

In their day-to-day practice, social workers face a busy and complex world of human behaviour in a social context. It is a world in which relationships break down, emotions run high, and personal needs go unmet. It is a world in which some people have problems and some people are problems.

If they are to function in this confused mix of psychological upset and social concern, practitioners must begin to see pattern and order behind the tumult (Coulshed, 1991). They must try to understand and *make sense* of people and the situations in which they find themselves. Striving to make sense of experience is a fundamental characteristic of being human. If we are to cope with and be competent in social situations, we need to have ideas about what might be going on. This need becomes pressing in situations where need, stress and upset are present in large measure. Professionals who work in such situations develop more deliberate, systematic and formalized ways of making sense. It is these more self-conscious attempts to 'make sense' which we call 'theory'.

If social workers are to act clearly, competently and usefully in practical situations, they need to make sense of what is going on, which is to say they need to think theoretically. If we did not theorize, social life would remain a cauldron of unorganized experience and to all intents and purposes all practical action would be impossible. The join between theory and practice is a seamless one. And, it has often been said, there is nothing so practical as a good theory.

If practice is to be compassionate as well as appropriate, it is important that social workers retain a deep interest in people. The struggle to understand behaviour and relationships, actions and decisions, attitudes and motivations needs to be maintained at all times if practice is to be sensitive and effective. The more social workers think about, puzzle over and engage with people and the situations in which they find themselves, the more sense they will be able to make. The challenge is to remain curious about and thoroughly interested in people. The social worker needs constantly to ask herself the 'reason why' of things, to develop an active and enquiring mind. Why does this woman stay with her violent husband? Why is this four-year-old child so subdued and withdrawn? Why does this daughter feel so hostile towards her increasingly dependent 81-year-old mother? So, although there is no consensus about which theories best explain particular situations, there is agreement that practitioners who develop and offer coherent understandings of what might be going on are those best able to keep their professional bearings and sustain personal commitment. Both abilities are highly prized by the users of social work services.

The argument is that by analysing practice and reflecting on people's needs and relationships, social workers become clearer about their theoretical assumptions. However, it is also possible to turn this process around. As well as *induce* theory from practice and observation, it is also possible to *deduce* from theory what to do and what to see. The social worker in possession of a clear theoretical outlook finds that it guides and influences her practice in five key areas:

1   Observation: it tells her what to see and what to look out for.

2   Description: it provides a conceptual vocabulary and framework within which observations can be arranged and organized.

3   Explanation: it suggests how different observations might be linked and connected; it offers possible causal relationships between one event and another.

4   Prediction: it indicates what might happen next.

5   Intervention: it suggests things to do to bring about change.

Different theories, of course, lead to different observations and explanations. For example, in the case of a difficult toddler, the behaviourist notes that the young mother reinforces her child's poor behaviour by only giving him attention when he is naughty; the feminist practitioner is struck by the mother's stress, low self-worth and lack of support from her oppressive partner; and the social worker using a developmental perspective observes that the mother, who was neglected herself as a child, grows anxious and agitated when her son becomes too demanding and dependent. This is not to argue that these three observations are mutually exclusive. However, in practice it is often the case that a practitioner with a strong theoretical preference is inclined to observe, describe, explain, predict and intervene in a style and a language that is noticeably different from a social worker holding a contrasting theoretical outlook.

Five Key Points

1   Social work theories help practitioners make sense of complex and difficult human situations.
2   Different social work theories generate different understandings of human behaviour and social situations.
3   The social work process of 'defining problems and needs – making an assessment – setting goals – carrying out methods to achieve those goals' describes a sequence and a structure which helps social workers practise in a systematic way.
4   Social workers who use theory to inform their use of the social work process are more likely to practise in a thoughtful and professional manner.
5   The purposes of social work and the theories which support them vary depending on the cultural context in which social work finds itself.

The Social Work Process

A simple but effective way of exploring the relationship between theory and practice is to ask a series of seemingly innocuous questions about a case or a piece of practice. By insisting on clear answers to these questions, the practitioner finds that she is able to reflect on matters at a surprisingly deep level. It is during this reflection process and the answer-giving stage that the relationship between theory and practice becomes explicit and available for discussion. Five questions can be asked of a case or piece of work:

1   *What is the matter?* This question helps the social worker define problems and identify needs. Supplementary questions might include: For whom is it a problem? Who benefits if the need is met? (Pincus and Minahan, 1973)

2   *What is going on?* This is perhaps the most important question. It demands that the situation is assessed, analysed, diagnosed, interpreted or explained. The social worker makes sense of what is going on.

3   *What is to be done?* In the light of the assessment, goals are set, objectives identified, plans made and intentions declared.

4   *How is it to be done?* The methods, techniques, skills, services and resources needed to achieve the goals are chosen and deployed.

5   *Has it been done?* The outcome is reviewed and evaluated.

It will be apparent from what has been said so far that different theories sponsor different answers to these five questions. But whatever the response, the answers and activities map out the basic features of *the social work process* with its five-stage sequence of: (i) the formulation of problems and the identification of needs, (ii) the analysis of cases and the making of an assessment, (iii) the setting of goals and objectives, (iv) the design of methods of work and intervention, and (v) the review and evaluation of the involvement. This process describes a sequence and a structure to help social workers practise in a thoughtful and systematic way. It provides the basis of a disciplined and professional social work practice. It is also designed to overcome the tendency of social workers and their agencies to jump from problem to solution in one bound. Within the social work process, considerable importance is given to the stage of assessment. This is a time for reflection, enquiry and vigorous analysis. Assessments encourage practitioners to stop and think about what is going on. They provoke thought and liberate practice from the routine and humdrum.

Theories for Social Work

Things might be relatively simple and straightforward if social work was underpinned by one or two generally agreed theories for practice. In any one case the five questions of the social work process would receive a limited range of acceptable answers. Unfortunately, the theoretical world underpinning social work practice is a far from stable place. Because social workers deal with people in social situations, most of their theories, albeit adapted to the social work context, derive ultimately from psychology, sociology and social psychology.

However, these primary disciplines have not established a consensus about the true character of human nature, individual development and social interaction. Although they strive to 'make sense' of people and society, the range of theories and understandings on offer are numerous and diverse. Sociology and psychology provide intellectual arenas in which fierce debates rage about the individual and society, the personal and the political, order and conflict, biology and culture, free will and determinism, causal explanation and subjective understanding. To the extent that social work's theories are based on psychological and sociological theories, they, too, will reflect the range, diversity and disagreements present in the parent disciplines.

So long as these epistemological disputes exist, there can be no universally agreed criteria by which to judge social work's theories and practices. This is not to say that some theories will be preferred at certain times and in particular places. Political and cultural factors also come into play and influence what is thought and what is done in the name of good social work. Nevertheless, social work theory remains a highly varied and contested activity. If the argument holds good that in practice there is no escape from theory, the social worker, denied an

Archimedean point, needs to understand how and why different psychological and sociological theories vary as they do. Rather than bemoan the number and range of theories, the practitioner needs to acknowledge that the diversity reflects the subtlety and complexity of the human condition. Appreciation of the elegance and multi-dimensionality of these conceptual landscapes can be highly stimulating.

Types of Theory

Many frameworks and taxonomies have been developed to help practitioners find their way around the confusion of social work's many theories. The attempts to classify the theories rely on recognizing a limited range of key conceptual dimensions, various combinations of which help define particular sets of related theories. At root, most of the classifications draw on discussions about (a) human nature; (b) the relative importance of biology, culture and experience in human development; and (c) the social movements and ideological climates that define and shape human society (for example see Turner, 1986; Howe, 1987; Payne, 1991). Mapping out social work's theoretical terrain helps practitioners locate themselves intellectually and invites them to explore new areas of thought and practice.

Although in some circles there is a coming together of psychology and sociology, these two disciplines still create one of the main divisions in social work theory between structural and psychological explanations of personal difficulty. Within the structural perspective, the focus is on the political, economic and material environment in which people find themselves. The approach includes anti-oppressive and anti-discriminatory perspectives. Poverty and inequality, the lack of opportunity and social injustice

seriously disadvantage some people. The disadvantages induce stress, anxiety and 'poor social functioning'. Such problems bring them to the attention of society and its agents. However, structural theorists maintain that for these groups, the individual should not be seen as a problem for society, rather society should be seen as a problem for the individual. This outlook influences the way problems are defined, the type of assessment made, the goals planned and the social methods employed (for example, see Mullaly, 1993).

In practice, though, most social work

Three Questions

1 How might different social work theories explain or make sense of the same case or social situation?
2 What assumptions does a particular social work theory make about (a) human nature; (b) the influence of human biology, culture and social experience on personal development; and (c) appropriate political and personal values?
3 In particular cases and situations, how do different social work theories influence the content of the social work process?

---

theories remain heavily influenced by the more psychological approaches to human behaviour. There are many ways in which these psychological theories can be categorized. Most rely on making particular assumptions about human nature and the ways in which we learn, develop and respond. One simple division which works in social work is to see whether a particular theory emphasizes either the client's emotional condition or his or her capacity for rational action.

Theories which pay most attention to the emotional side of people's lives and the quality of their relationships seek to understand present behaviour in terms of past experiences. The character of our relationship history influences our personality and social competence. As most social work clients experience or express difficulty in one or more of their key relationships (say with partners, parents or children), it seems appropriate to try and understand the quality of their social and interpersonal development and how it might be affecting current behaviour. Understanding, support, nurturing, the meeting of emotional and developmental needs, containment and insight are present in many of the practices associated with these theories. By understanding past events, the client and the worker might be able to contain or make sense of current experiences. Making sense allows people to gain control of the meaning of their own experience and move into the future with a more robust, mature, independent and strengthened personality. Such a personality is likely to be more socially competent, and socially competent people handle relationships more effectively. Altering the meaning of experience brings about changes in behaviour.

Theories of this persuasion include all those which take a developmental perspective. They are person-focused. They consider people from the psychological inside. Psychoanalytic theory, attachment theory, theories of loss and separation, many forms of feminist theory and elements of the person-centred approach can all be placed within this broad category of developmentally-orientated and relationship-sensitive approaches to social work practice.

Theories which appeal to clients' rational capacities and cognitive strengths tend to adopt a problem-solving approach. These approaches are based on the belief that people with problems can resolve them by the use of rational thought, cognitive understanding and behavioural advice. Practitioners work with clients in problem-solving

partnerships. Typically, the approach involves (a) the identification, description and quantification of the problem, (b) analysis of the factors, including the behaviour of other people, which maintain the problem, (c) the selection of goals and (d) the identification and implementation of those actions which will achieve the goals and resolve the problem. Based on an analysis of present conditions, problem-solving approaches encourage clients to identify what steps they will need to take if they wish to move themselves into a problem-free future. Practice is often pragmatic, time limited and task-centred. People are viewed from the behavioural outside. The belief is that by changing behaviour, personal experience is improved.

Social work theories that fall into this category include task-centred approaches, cognitive-behavioural theories, many forms of family therapy, brief solution-focused therapy and some aspects of systems theory.

Theory and Practice in Social Context

One further layer of analysis has to be added if we are to gain a full understanding of the relationship between social work theory and practice. Social work takes place and is formed within a social and political context. It occupies and is defined by the space between the personal and the political in which the state relates to the individual and the individual relates to the state. So, although social work practices need the help of the psychological and sociological sciences if they are to make sense of people in social difficulty, the *purposes* of social work and its practices are defined by a different set of intellectual traditions.

In the broadest sense, the purposes of social work are determined by the prevailing political values. These values influence welfare legislation, political policy, government guidelines, and the distribution and definition of resources. The politically defined purposes of social work also influence the psychological and sociological theories chosen by practitioners to help them 'make sense' and practise.

Political philosophies which emphasize collective responsibility and action also value harmony and co-operation, equality and interdependence. They support theories and practices which are more structural, developmental and therapeutic in their outlook. Psychologically healthy development occurs only if the individual is embedded in a good quality social environment. A sense of belonging and being wanted in a community of close personal relationships is essential if a secure and coherent personality is to form.

When the political pendulum shifts away from welfare collectivism towards neo-liberal concepts of freedom, choice and personal responsibility in the context of a market economy, theories and practices tend towards the brief and the behavioural (Howe, 1996). The individual is seen as independent and free, disembedded from and unconstrained (and not limited) by his or her social environment. Such freedom and autonomy allows full scope for creative endeavour and the rational pursuit of what is in one's own best interests. Morally and psychologically, the individual must stand alone. Individuals are personally responsible for who they are and what they become, for what they do and how they do it. This represents a shift away from explaining people's psychological insides to measuring their behavioural outsides. The external performance, of both worker and client, becomes the unit of audit. *What* people do is more important than *why* they do it. Economic and political partnerships replace therapeutic relationships. The theories which come to the fore in this

political climate are those which encourage brief, task-centred and behaviourally measurable practices in which the act rather than the actor becomes the focus of interest.

Summary

Practice, as defined by the social work process, varies as practitioners make use of different theories. Theories vary as they appeal to different understandings of human nature, personal development and society. And different theories come in and out of fashion as political values and social philosophies change with the flow of large social movements through history. Just as theory relates to practice, so practice relates to theory. Only the faint-hearted despair at the inordinate subtlety of personal experience and social life. So long as social workers retain a passionate interest in and concern for the quality of human experience, and so long as they strive to 'make sense', the relationship between theory and practice will continue to invigorate, fascinate and professionally uplift.

References

Coulshed, Veronica (1991) *Social Work Practice: an Introduction* (2nd edn), Basingstoke: Macmillan.
Howe, David (1987) *An Introduction to Social Work Theory*, Aldershot: Gower.
Howe, David (1996) 'Surface and depth in social work practice', in N. Parton (ed.), *Social Theory, Social Change and Social Work*, London: Routledge.
Mullaly, Robert (1993) *Structural Social Work: Ideology,*

Further Reading

1   Coulshed, Veronica (1991) *Social Work Practice: an Introduction* (2nd edn), Basingstoke: Macmillan.
2   Howe, David (1987) *An Introduction to Social Work Theory*, Aldershot: Gower.
3   Payne, Malcolm (1991) *Modern Social Work Theory*, Basingstoke: Macmillan.

Theory and Practice, Canada: McLelland.

Payne, Malcolm (1991) *Modern Social Work Theory: a Critical Introduction*, Basingstoke: Macmillan.

Pincus, Allen and Minahan, Anne (1973) *Social Work Practice*, Itasca, Ill.: Peacock.

Turner, Francis J. (ed.) (1986) *Differential Diagnosis and Treatment in Social Work* (3rd edn), New York: Free Press.

Person-centred Counselling

Brian Thorne

There are widespread and hostile misunderstandings about the person-centred approach to counselling which imply in accusatory fashion that its theoretical base is flawed at best and naïve at worst. Furthermore, the name of Carl Rogers (1902–87), its originator, is often associated with the permissiveness of the 1960s and the approach is discredited as being totally at variance with the current age which seemingly values efficiency, speed and the slick interventions of experts. The more social work as a profession is seen by government and public alike as an essentially 'containing' or 'monitoring' activity, the more person-centred counselling runs the risk of being judged as a sentimental throw-back to a former era when people fondly imagined that the world could be made a better place. Person-centred counselling, by this kind of reckoning, has no role in the robust environment of the approaching millennium where what counts is the line-up of market forces and the dominant language is that of the provider–consumer relationship. In such a climate, therapy, where it is admissible at all, needs to be task-oriented, interventionist and concerned with behaviour modification and the achievement of manifestly observable goals which can provide conclusive evidence of value for money.

Carl Rogers often described himself as a quiet revolutionary and he had scant respect for power-hungry institutions or for those who believed that the relief of human suffering depended on the application of sophisticated techniques or on the deployment of recondite knowledge of the human psyche. Both, he believed, could lead therapists to the fond illusion that they knew more about their clients than the clients themselves. For Rogers, the origins of psychological disturbance lay in the essentially judgemental and invalidating relationships which many people experience not only in their early years but throughout their lives. The healing of such disturbance, he believed, could best be achieved through the provision of a therapeutic relationship characterized by the elements which were so evidently absent in previous relationships. We shall see later how Rogers came to conceptualize these elements and the implications of their application in practice. At this point, however, it is worth a further digression on the prevailing culture which forms the context for social work practice at the end of the twentieth century. That person-centred counselling remains quietly revolutionary will then become the more apparent.

The Competitive Society

The encouragement of competitiveness as a social good has about it a chilling undertone. Competition means by definition that there are winners and losers. It also suggests a preoccupation with proving superiority and gaining advantage. In commercial circles it inevitably means achieving more for less.

Increasing profits and cutting costs, if not inseparably linked, are likely to form an incestuous relationship. This is the context in which such concepts as cost-effectiveness, accountability, performance related pay, strategic objectives, service delivery, customer power and the like flourish and proliferate. It is a climate, too, where it becomes dangerous to fail because once a loser it is difficult if not impossible to climb back on to the winning bandwagon. Critical judgement is rife in such a culture. Big Brother is always watching and often becomes internalized so that there can be no respite from the push towards ever greater performance. The cultivation of such a climate has brought with it in Britain a pressure in the work place which has resulted in stress levels of unprecedented severity for probably millions of workers. Throughout the helping professions, for example, previously competent and well-motivated doctors, nurses, teachers, lawyers, even clergy, have succumbed to depression, ill-health and in some tragic cases to self-destruction, as they have battled unsuccessfully against the rising tide of clientele amidst the escalation of bureaucratic procedures devised to ensure quality control, accountability and cost effectiveness. Early retirement on the grounds of ill-health is increasingly common and the resulting loss to the professions of some of their most conscientious and talented members is a cause for grave concern. In the commercial and industrial sectors the picture is scarcely more reassuring. The need to cut costs and maximize profits has resulted in the 'down-sizing' of many work forces and the introduction of increasingly sophisticated information technology which serves to create an environment of perpetual freneticism for the employees who remain. The fax machine, the portable telephone, the lap-top are the symbols of a culture where today is all and tomorrow too late.

Alongside the increasing number of exhausted and demoralized workers there is the accompanying spectre of the permanently unemployed. Young men in particular who might previously have found manual or unskilled work in the manufacturing industries have nowhere to go. The jobs have disappeared and those which remain require skills and attributes which they do not possess and despair of attaining. The resulting build-up of a substantial population of marginalized people who have no effective role in society and who are perceived both by themselves and others as failures is one of the most threatening aspects of life in contemporary Britain. What is more there seems little prospect of this trend being reversed in the years ahead. The competitive, judgemental and essentially contemptuous culture of the 1980s and 1990s has produced an environment of fear where loss of esteem, loss of employment or loss of meaning are not just recurrent nightmares but the harsh reality for large segments of the working population.

Social Work and the Person-centred Approach

Social workers and their clients are clearly not immune to these societal trends. On the contrary, they are likely to be among the principal victims of the prevailing ethos. It is no coincidence that the first substantial (and successful) claim against an employer for causing stress-induced illness was made in 1994 by a senior social worker against his employing authority (John Walker vs. Northumberland County Council). Fear of accusations of incompetence and negligence permeates almost every social work agency while the administrative burden imposed by accountability procedures adds to the exhaustion which is likely to lead to the very errors of judgement or impulsive actions which they seek to eliminate. For social work clients themselves, the often intractable practical difficulties which they are experiencing are compounded by a permeating sense of worthlessness, of having been rejected and demeaned by a society which values success on its chosen terms and prefers not to know about those who have failed to come up to the mark.

It is against this background that the person-centred approach to counselling needs to be viewed for, perhaps of all the major therapeutic orientations, it offers to practitioners and clients alike the most powerful antidote to what has been aptly dubbed the 'culture of contempt'. In no sense is person-centred counselling merely a therapeutic technique which can be applied as a form of 'treatment'. It is, rather, a functional philosophy and its practice is the living out of a set of beliefs about the nature of human beings and the relationships which they have with each other. More specifically it is the application of an empirically tested way of being within a helping relationship which draws its inspiration from a belief in the value and wisdom of each unique person no matter what their current predicament may be or the adverse judgements which may have been passed upon them or, as is frequently the case, which they may habitually pass upon .themselves. It is, in brief, an approach to persons which is deeply validating, restorative and, to use a word drawn from another field of discourse, redemptive.

Person-centred Counselling: Theoretical Assumptions

Person-centred counsellors begin from an assumption which may immediately prompt the raising of cynical eyebrows. They assume that both they and their clients are essentially trustworthy. This trust springs from a belief that human beings, along with all other created

Five Key Points

1 Every individual has the internal resources for growth.
2 The actualizing tendency is trustworthy.
3 The need for positive regard is paramount.
4 Conditions of worth lead to the creation of a negative self-concept.
5 When a counsellor provides a relationship characterized by the qualities of acceptance, empathy and congruence, therapeutic movement will take place.

organisms, have an underlying and instinctive movement towards the constructive accomplishment of their inherent potential. Carl Rogers called this movement the *actualizing tendency* and saw it as the sole motive for human development. For him actualization included such motivational drives as need-reduction or tension-reduction and incorporated, too, what are often termed growth motivations such as the desire to learn or the need to seek creative challenges. While the actualizing tendency is itself trustworthy the tragedy of human life as Rogers saw it resided in the many constraints which are frequently placed upon it by the environment in which the person finds himself or herself. Drawing on agricultural metaphors it is possible to think in terms of, for example, poor soil or bad weather conditions which will adversely affect the organism. Extending this metaphor, many clients can be seen as having experienced the most unpropitious environment and climate for growth. The person-centred counsellor, sometimes against the apparent evidence, will nonetheless continue to have faith in the inherent actualizing tendency of the human organism and will see his or her task as helping to create the best possible conditions for its fulfilment.

In the face of such a hopeful view of both the essential human organism and of its capacity for survival and recovery, it may well be asked why so many individuals seem to display such warped or stunted development. It is the person-centred counsellor's belief that this sad state of affairs comes about because there occurs for many, if not most, of us a conflict between the actualizing tendency and its trustworthiness and the way we come to experience ourselves. Before the arrival of self-consciousness (and there is endless debate about when that moment occurs), we are at unity with ourselves. Once self-awareness has dawned, however, this unity is threatened. It was Rogers' belief that self-awareness heralded the birth of the *self-concept* which, in its turn, required nurturing and protecting. Put more simply, once I am conscious of me it becomes imperative that I can think and feel well of myself. Rogers believed that for this reason the potency of the need for what he termed *positive regard* could not be exaggerated for on its satisfaction depended the emergence of at least a modicum of *self-regard* without which it becomes impossibly difficult to function satisfactorily in the world.

It is clear that this overriding need for positive regard puts the growing infant almost entirely at the mercy of those who constitute his or her social environment and this is precisely where the trouble for many of us begins. If we are fortunate, our need for positive regard will be readily and consistently satisfied by those close to us and we shall be enabled to remain healthily in contact with the actualizing tendency and to have its trustworthiness confirmed in experience. If we are unfortunate, however, and are brought up amongst a number of significant others who are constantly critical of us, judge us adversely and show no confidence in our capacity for self-direction, then we become desperate in our search for positive regard. In the worst case, we lose touch altogether with the actualizing tendency for we can no longer find there any confirmation of our essential worth as persons. Instead we are condemned to a self-concept which is heavily dependent on the attitudes of those who surround us. Whatever sense of self-worth we manage to cultivate will result from our ability to conform to the value system and expectations of others and to behave in ways of which they approve. In the terminology of the person-centred tradition, the individual whose self-concept is constructed on such shaky foundations is said to have introjected and internalized *conditions of worth* imposed from outside, to have lost touch with his or her own actualizing tendency and to have no internal *locus of evaluation*. This last somewhat cumbersome term describes the faculty which determines an individual's ability to trust his or her own thoughts and feelings when making decisions or choosing courses of action.

It will perhaps now be apparent why the person-centred approach to psychological distress is particularly relevant to the contemporary situation. The competitive society and the accountability culture encourage precisely the critical and comparative judgements which undermine the individual's trust in his or her innate resourcefulness for determining self-direction. It is as if the prevailing ethos reinforces the notion that an individual's worth depends on his or her accomplishments as determined by the externally imposed criteria of an achievement-oriented society. In brief, the task for the individual of maintaining a sense of self-worth based on a connectedness with the actualizing tendency is rendered supremely difficult in a society which has embraced an essentially negative view of human nature and enshrined this in a complex system of thinly disguised rewards and penalties.

The Practice of Person-centred Counselling

The person-centred counsellor will typically be faced by a client who has little self-respect and whose self-concept is predominantly negative. What is more, there is likely to be little confidence on the client's part in the validity of his or her own thoughts and feelings: in many cases, indeed, there may be only intermittent contact with such internal promptings anyway. It is not uncommon for a person who has been consistently denigrated or who has been overtaken by catastrophe to experience a numbness which makes almost all thoughts and feelings well nigh inaccessible.

In the face of someone who may appear utterly self-rejecting or divorced from themselves it may be difficult for the counsellor to retain a belief in their essential trustworthiness and resourcefulness. There will almost inevitably be a desire to take over and to rescue the client from their seemingly desperate predicament. For the social worker this temptation may be particularly strong and the need to 'do something' almost overwhelming. For the person-centred counsellor, however, the task is easy to state and immensely difficult to accomplish. It may be summarized as the challenge to offer a relationship of a particular quality in the belief that to do so will be to give the client the opportunity to discover or rediscover his or her own strength or wisdom. The counsellor will find such a challenge impossible, however, if he or she is motivated by a need to effect rapid change or to direct the course of events. Instead, there must be a deep commitment to the belief in the client's capacity to grow in constructive ways if the appropriate conditions can be provided. The counsellor's task is not to guide or to direct but patiently to accompany in a way which ensures that clients can breathe a new air which makes

it possible for them to face themselves and their situation without fear. Once this begins to happen the way is open to a radical reordering of the self-concept with all that this may entail both for the sense of self-worth and for behaviour.

The Facilitative Relationship

It was perhaps Carl Rogers' greatest achievement to arrive, after much clinical experience and considerable empirical research, at precise conclusions about the nature of the companionship which is both necessary and sufficient to effect therapeutic change in the client. Rogers'

Three Questions

1 How can the person-centred approach to counselling become a possible option for social workers in a cost-effective climate?
2 Can social workers risk the level of commitment and involvement required by person-centred counselling?
3 Can the spiritual dimension be a legitimate domain for the social worker's activity?

---

discovery is as radical today as it was when he first formally presented it (Rogers, 1959). He concluded that the truly facilitative relationship is characterized by the counsellor's ability to be acceptant, emphathic and congruent, and by the client's perception, to some minimal degree, of these qualities in the counsellor. The contrast between the facilitative and the damaging relationship is striking: acceptance replaces adverse judgement and condemnation, emphathic understanding replaces indifference and misunderstanding, congruence or genuineness replaces pretence and deceit.

The person-centred counsellor cannot assume the attitudes of acceptance, empathy and congruence at whim. They are not techniques to be employed or even skills to be learned. They are rather qualities of being which demand a level of maturity which is not easily or painlessly acquired. Congruence, for example, means that the counsellor is what he or she is in the relationship without façade and without any attempt to assume or hide behind a professional role. Such genuineness cannot be achieved without the counsellor's capacity to maintain a high level of self-awareness which involves a continuing openness to inner experience even if what is experienced poses a threat to the counsellor's own self-concept. This is no easy task for a harassed social worker who may have been told not to get too close to clients or even to remain *uninvolved* and *objective*. Acceptance, too, or what Rogers called 'unconditional positive regard' implies a caring by the counsellor which is totally free of judgements or evaluation of the thoughts, feelings or behaviour of the client. The counsellor does not accept some aspects of the client and reject others. He or she experiences an outgoing, positive, non-possessive warmth for the client and there is no way in which such an attitude can be simulated. In his final statement about person-centred therapy published after his death (Rogers and Sanford, 1989) Rogers went so far as to say that what the person-centred counsellor aspires to achieve is a *gullible* caring. Clients are to be accepted as they present themselves to be and the counsellor is to avoid the lurking suspicion that they may be otherwise. Such ideas will not be readily assimilated by social workers who may have been constantly cautioned to watch out for *manipulative* clients to make sure that they are not taken for a ride. What is more, acceptance of this kind can only be offered by those who are themselves deeply self-acceptant. Rogers' overriding concern with the client's subjective perceptual world made it imperative that the counsellor should achieve as full an understanding as possible of the way in which clients viewed themselves and the world. Such empathy, however, with all its power to facilitate changes in the client's self-concept, requires of the counsellor a willingness to enter the perceptual world of another without fear. No counsellor can undertake this kind of companionship who is not thoroughly secure in his or her own identity for to do so without such security is to risk becoming lost in what may turn out to be the bizarre or even frightening landscape of the other's inner world. Empathy of this order is no task for the faint-hearted and cannot be responsibly undertaken by a counsellor who is fearful of deep involvement.

A Further Dimension

Rogers believed – and he held to the belief for over 40 years – that if the counsellor is able to offer a relationship where congruence, acceptance and empathy are all present, then therapeutic movement will almost invariably occur – as long as the client is to some degree aware of these qualities in the counsellor. Towards the end of his life, however, Rogers points to another dimension of the relationship which he saw not as additional to the core conditions but as sometimes resulting from their consistent application. He names this 'presence' and, having first written about it in *A Way of Being* (Rogers, 1980), he came back to it in an article published shortly before his death (Rogers, 1986). He writes in terms which seem markedly at variance with the somewhat hard-headed tone of the scientist of earlier years but what he has to say captures an aspect of the therapeutic relationship which is strikingly relevant to those who have lost all hope of sharing in the fruits of materialistic affluence. Rogers wrote: 'When I am at my best, as a group facilitator or a therapist, I discover another characteristic. I find that when I am closest to my inner intuitive self, when I am somehow in touch with the unknown in me, when perhaps I am in a slightly altered state of consciousness in the relationship, then whatever I do seems to be full of healing. Then simply my *presence* is releasing and helpful. There is nothing I can do to force this experience, but when I can relax and be close to the transcendental core of me, then I may behave in strange and impulsive ways in the relationship and ways which I cannot justify rationally, which have nothing to do with my thought processes. But these strange behaviours turn out to be *right* in some odd way. At those moments it seems that my inner spirit has reached out and touched the inner spirit of the other' (Rogers, 1986, p. 199).

There is no escaping the fact that in this passage Rogers claims for person-centred counselling the capability of becoming a gateway for clients into the realm of spiritual experience. In the same article he admits that his account *partakes of the mystical* and goes on to speak of *this mystical, spiritual dimension* and of the relationship transcending itself and becoming *part of something larger* (Rogers, 1986, p. 199). At a time when for many people the prevailing culture offers no spiritual nourishment and the power of institutional religion has waned, this possibility that human relating can itself provide access into an infinitely greater world is of compelling significance. The implication is that the counsellor/social worker simply by offering a relationship of a particular kind may induce a spiritual awakening which can prove transformative.

It is my own experience that the counsellor's ability to be *present* in this way is often dependent on his or her ability to be alongside the client's experience even when there is little if any understanding of what is truly occurring

in the client's world. Such an ability is likely to develop in a relationship where mutuality is increasingly possible. The very notion of such equality of relationship will be fear-provoking to the worker who is concerned to maintain rigid boundaries or is unwilling to deviate an inch from the rule book. There is little doubt, however, that person-centred counselling at its best moves through three distinct phases. The first stage, which may last a few minutes or several months, is characterized by the establishing of *trust* on the part of the client. The second stage sees the development of intimacy during which the client moves from talking *about* feelings to the actual *experiencing* of feelings within the counselling process itself. The third stage, which is only seldom reached, sees an increasing *mutuality* between counsellor and client. When this occurs there is not only the possibility of the heightened awareness which can lead to transcendental experience but also the challenge to the counsellor to risk more of himself or herself in the relationship and thus to be changed by the experience. The person-centred counsellor, if he or she remains true to the beliefs and practice of the orientation, will delight in process and endure the frequent agony of only glimpsing provisional staging posts. This may not be good news for those who have to tick boxes demanding information about the therapeutic objectives achieved but it may result in clients who have come to the point where they have internalized the ability (learned

Further Reading

1   Mearns, D. and Thorne, B. (1988) *Person-centred Counselling in Action*, London: Sage.
2   Rogers, C. R. (1961) *On Becoming a Person*, Boston: Houghton Mifflin.
3   Thorne, B. (1992) *Carl Rogers*, London: Sage.

from their counsellor) to treat themselves with the deepest respect and understanding and who can take the risk of listening with the utmost attentiveness and without fear to what they are experiencing. Such persons will be more than a little way along the road to becoming what Rogers hypothesized as a 'fully functioning' human being.

Conclusion

This brief introduction to the theory and practice of person-centred counselling will have dispelled any notion that it is an easy option for the social worker. On the contrary it demands a willingness to take a stand against much that characterizes our culture at the end of the twentieth century and to come alongside clients whose woundedness may well have been caused or exacerbated by the current obsession with competitiveness, efficiency and accountability. At a time when social workers themselves are constantly subjected to the hostile glare of the media and are much preoccupied

with self-protection, the person-centred approach to counselling stands as a reminder of the values which probably motivated many of them to enter the social work profession in the first place. Perhaps too, it will enable them to find the courage to re-engage in the quiet revolution which is yet to be accomplished and which has as its starting point the belief that the human being – mind, heart, body and spirit – is only a little lower than the angels.

References

Rogers, C. R. (1959) 'A theory of therapy, personality and interpersonal relationships as developed in the client-centered framework', in S. Koch (ed.), *Psychology: a Study of Science, Vol. III. Formulations of the Person and the Social Context*, New York: McGraw Hill.

Rogers, C. R. (1980) *A Way of Being*, Boston: Houghton Mifflin.

Rogers, C. R. (1986) 'A client-centered/person-centered approach to therapy', in I. L. Kutash and A. Wolf (eds), *Psychotherapist's Casebook*, San Francisco: Jossey-Bass.

Rogers, C. R. and Sanford, R. C. (1989) 'Client-centered psychotherapy', in H. I. Kaplan and B. J. Sadock (eds), *Comprehensive Textbook of Psychiatry V*, Baltimore: Williams and Wilkins.

V.3
Family Therapy
Jan White

Social work is concerned with the relationship between individuals and their social context. The way that an individual constructs his world and his sense of self is mediated through a variety of large and small social groupings, including family, school, neighbourhood and social agencies. Intertwined with these social realities are the unique meanings that we put upon them, which will be influenced by personal history, religion, culture, race and so on. Family therapists are concerned with the most primary of these social groupings, literally, that which is most 'familiar'. Families are socially constructed units, based upon relationships of kinship, obligation and intimacy which exert a powerful socializing influence on the behaviour and understandings of their members.

It is rare for families to present themselves for therapy. Much more commonly, an individual will be presented as 'having a problem'. The worker using a family therapy approach will view the individual's 'symptom' as part of an interactional pattern, and herself as a facilitator, enabling the family to harness its own strengths and flexibility towards a solution.

The essence of family life is that it is complex and changing and that unique situations and combinations of needs continually arise. Families therefore need to be able to act in creative ways to find solutions to their circumstances
(Dallos, 1991, p. 7)

Family Therapy and Systems Theory

The family is a self-governing system which controls itself according to rules formed over a period of time through a process of trial and error
(Palazzoli et al., 1978)

Family therapy draws upon two traditions; psychoanalytic practice and systems theory: During the 1950s psychoanalytically-orientated psychiatrists such as Bell and Jackson (in Bateson et al., 1956) observed that improvement in schizophrenic patients was often accompanied by a crisis in another family member. In seeking explanation they looked to the anthropological theories of Bateson and Mead. These writers were interested in two ideas; how society and groups within it maintain a state of balance, and how they may escalate towards instability and change.

Jackson related their work to families, which he saw as developing a pattern of predictable relationships, or 'homeostasis', governed by implicit or explicit rules. Rules may open or close options, for example, the Victorian saying 'children should be seen and not heard' served to support the strict rules of social behaviour in upper-class England but limited parents' understanding of children's experience and behaviour.

Bateson also contributed the idea of 'circular causality' according to which, each person's behaviour influences *and* is in turn *influenced by* the other. Thus behaviour becomes self-reinforcing, as indicated in figure V.3.1. The search for a 'cause' (and by implication blame and responsibility) becomes irrelevant. Pattern and process acquire new importance as the worker seeks to tease out habitual patterns of interaction, and, where they contribute to distress, to interrupt the cycle. Patterns may exist intergenerationally, for example, Boszormenyi-Nagy (1965) describes families as keeping an 'unconscious ledger' through the generations which may be balanced to the advantage or disadvantage of the succeeding generation; for example, the parent who felt unloved by her parents, may compensate with devotion to her own children. Alternatively, she may expect unconditional love from them to compensate for her own deprivation.

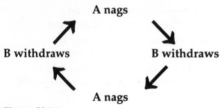

Figure V.3.1

Family styles of problem solving will relate to their habitual patterns. For instance the family which repeatedly solves child care problems by the reception of the child into care will be matched by the social work agency which cites this as evidence of the family's inability to cope. Thus agencies frequently become part of the repetitive, 'more of the same' phenomena.

Ferreira (1963) made a link between family therapy and psychoanalytic ideas in the 'family myth', a collective distortion of events or feelings which serves to protect family members (similar to denial and repression). For example, the myth 'We are a happy/close/loving family' can easily be translated into 'We are all OK, except A is sick, ill, mad or bad.'

The idea of the family as an 'open system' allows us to consider its relationship to other social and belief systems. The family becomes a powerful mediator of internal and external influences (see figure V.3.2). It is continually creative, renegotiating roles and responsibilities and acting upon its environment to find a comfortable enough fit.

Professional help may be sought when a family has been unable to move forward in response to changed circumstances. The adolescent who seeks increased independence and begins dating, may find himself out of fit with parents who continue to respond to him as a dependent child. Further complexity may be introduced if the family have migrated from another culture which accentuates family responsibility above individual needs, and where religious mores do not support 'dating'. Moreover, part of that family's response may be a protective one to shelter their child from the experience of racism.

Key Ideas and Issues

Pioneers in America carried out family therapy in a variety of settings often with poor and ethnic minority families (see *Families of the Slums*, Minuchin et al., 1967). Sadly, in Britain, the ideas fell prey to the power relations of the welfare professions – a 'specialist' approach to be carried out within prestigious clinical settings uncontaminated by the overt issues of social control which are central to social work. Social work agencies often experienced the method as a form of elitism. It was only much later, with the contributions of Treacher and Carpenter (1983), Dimmock and Dungworth (1985, and Dale et al., 1986) that the central relevance to social services settings was recognized.

However, a number of issues arise for social workers wishing to practise family therapy. I shall discuss three key areas; Therapist Style, Power and Empowerment, and Agency Context and Resources.

Therapist style

Up to the mid-1980s a number of models of family therapy were elaborated (see Hoffman, *Foundations of Family Therapy*, 1981).

The three models most commonly practised, Structural, Strategic and Milan, differ in their approach, but are all firmly rooted in the 'modern' philosophical tradition of searching for observable truths. The therapist as 'scientific observer' is expert, carrying in her head a blueprint both of what is and what should be. She is thus able to make powerful judgements about 'pathology', 'dysfunction' and so on.

Within Structural Family Therapy (Minuchin, 1974) the blueprint consists of a healthy 'family structure', that is one which has a clear hierarchy, in which parents are in charge of children, and flexible boundaries exist between individuals which allow for individuation whilst retaining open communication. Problem behaviour relates to faulty structure. The therapist intervenes powerfully to block 'dysfunctional' interactional patterns, and coach the family in new behaviours.

Strategic therapists (e.g., Haley, 1980 and the Palo Alto Group in California) went further, often using their power covertly to force change. Strategies were employed to address the family's 'resistance', the most simple of which was the prescription of 'no change' for the time being. Continued resistance required the family to change. Social workers trained within the more gentle traditions of facilitation and client empowerment often found the combination of expert style and robust technique worrying and unethical.

The Milan Associates (Palazzoli et al.,

Five Key Points

1 'The family is a self-governing system which controls itself according to rules formed over a period of time through a process of trial and error.' (Palazzoli et al., 1978)

2 Each family is unique in structure and beliefs. The first aim of the worker should be to find a therapeutic style which makes sense with this family.

3 Consumer research amongst family therapy users suggests the need for an integrationist approach to theory, clear information about the method of work, and keeping technology and team size to a minimum.

4 Family therapists aim to expand upon strengths and, through the introduction of difference, to increase the range of choices available to families to think and act creatively in relation to their circumstances.

5 A systemic perspective increases the effectiveness of a range of social work practices, management and interprofessional relationships.

1978) proposed a different therapist style, that of 'neutrality'. Unlike the Structural family therapist who is principally interested in changing behaviour in the room, their aim was the discovery of the meanings and beliefs underlying problem behaviour. They carefully elicited each person's position and ideas in relation to the problem giving equal weight to all views. The Milan Associates considered the relevant system to be therapist and family, i.e., the process of therapy itself exerts an influence upon events. A consulting team, which remained 'meta', or outside the therapist/family system was responsible for devising interventions, sending powerful 'expert' messages to the family. The use of one-way screens and video became commonplace posing a further disincentive to social work agencies which lacked a collective model of

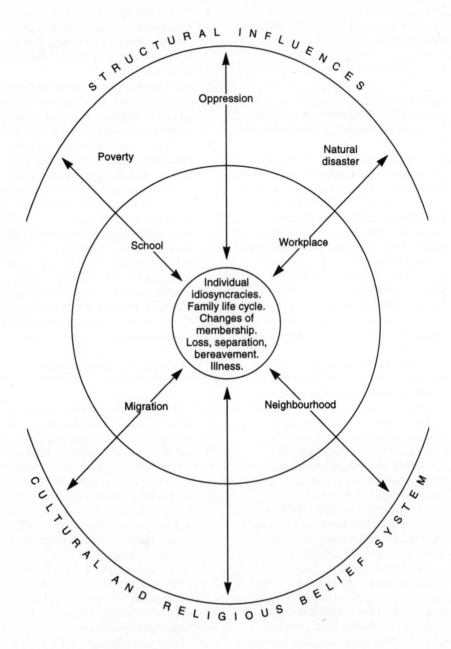

Figure V.3.2   The family as an open system:
influences promoting change at different levels.

working, and where facilities for workplace interviews were often basic.

Power and empowerment

Early family therapy literature has been justly criticized for its failure to understand the nature of power relationships, both within the family, and between family and social agencies. The blueprint of the 'healthy' family which emerges is firmly rooted in white western culture, and fails to consider gender relationships or differences of power within and between diverse races, cultures and classes.

For social workers, a central discourse is the relationship between therapy and social control. Dale et al. (1986) were influential in addressing this in the context of child protection work. Where statutory authority had hitherto been seen as a drawback to therapeutic work, these writers turned it to advantage. Typically they worked with families where the child was the subject of care proceedings, making explicit use of their authority to negotiate change in family structures and behaviour. Their approach fitted with prevailing government guidelines which encouraged powerful statutory intervention. However, it requires adaptation in the light of more recent moves enshrined in the Children Act 1989, towards partnership, and the least possible intervention to protect the child. Burnham (1986) contributes the idea of 'domains' within family therapy. Some 'domains', for example statutory responsibilities, will be given, others will be open to negotiation.

Agency context and resources

Many social service agencies are unused to the concept of team working, and resources do not run to elaborate arrangements for workplace interviews. Moreover, decisions about resource allocation tend to favour statutory and crisis intervention over preventive or therapeutic services. Recent developments towards contracting out non-statutory services to providers from within the voluntary sector are also significant. There is a lively discourse on the question of professional identity. Should family therapy move towards a specialist profession in its own right, or remain integrated within existing welfare professions?

In approaching these important questions, I shall consider the contributions of co-constructionism, feminist theory and user friendly approaches to the debate, before considering the social work context in more detail.

Three Questions

1 How can we usefully decide who to invite to a 'family therapy' session?
2 What approaches best enable a social worker to join with families different to him/herself in race, gender, class, culture, ability or sexuality?
3 What aspects of social work training, and work context enable family therapy, and what might be the obstacles to working in this way?

Co-constructionism and Second Order Approaches

The Co-constructionist approach, also described as 'post-Milan', or 'second order cybernetics' signals a move from the 'modern' philosophical position described. A 'postmodern' approach recognizes the importance of joint exploration of problems, and therapy as a 'narrative', which is co-created by therapist and family and which develops according to its own evolving 'rules'.

Central to this is the attribution of meaning and belief. It is impossible for a family to hear what I say in exactly the same way as I intended it, because their understanding will be mediated by the unique meanings and beliefs which they put upon it. The worker must find ways to understand the 'sense' that the family make of their own situation. This is particularly crucial in the context of differences of gender, race, culture and belief between therapist and family.

Anderson (1987) proposed a 'reflecting team' approach, whereby the team of workers meet with the family after the initial part of the interview, not to deliver 'expert' messages, but to offer tentative observations upon what they have heard. The family is then invited to comment on the sense that they make of what is offered.

The most important contribution of co-constructionism, is the removal of the 'therapist as expert' and the central idea of joint exploration and developing choice. This fits with philosophies within social welfare of client empowerment and partnership. However, it also carries with it a problem for social workers. Carried to its logical extreme, it assumes that 'anything goes', that the family's story is the only important thing. As such it has little to say about justice, morality or collective ideas of right and wrong. Social workers dealing with such issues as domestic violence, and child abuse are left with no yardsticks against which they can judge behaviour. Feminist inspired writers (Walters et al., 1988; Goldner et al., 1990; Jones, 1993) have made significant contributions in this area.

The Question of Power and Injustice

Jones (1993) points out that Bateson, like Freud, was a patriarch of his time, and had little to say about power. Traditionally power in family therapy has been thought of in relation to 'complementary' roles, for example, abuser/abused with a focus on the way in

which the roles reinforce one another. The notion of 'no blame' can come dangerously close to denying injustice. However, as she points out (p. 144):

There are differences between individuals and their ability, within a particular systemic pattern to influence the outcomes of actions and interactions in that pattern.

She cites the example of the incestuous abuse of a young girl by her father. The worker needs to be clear about the differences of choice, responsibility, influence and independence of father and daughter. Each will be influenced by social attitudes (obedience to parents, the myth of male uncontrolled sexual drive, etc.) as well as family and personal events and beliefs, but to assume equal responsibility in the therapeutic work is to guarantee further abuse of the child. To be 'neutral' is to be partial. Boyd-Franklin (1989) makes a similar point in referring to the family worker, who in working with a black family, does not consider the possibility of racism as an important organizing principle in the family's thinking and behaviour. This could be construed by the family as condoning their experiences of persecution.

Walters et al. (1988) demonstrates the importance of the 'gender lens' in reconstructing some important ideas from Structural Family Therapy. For instance, in considering 'enmeshment' (a pathological state of over-closeness), she points out that women more frequently seek greater intimacy, seeing this as a valued experience of connectedness. Women tend to see relationships as more consensual, less hierarchical than men. Goldner et al. (1990) noted that women often seek 'second order' change (at the level of meaning and belief): for example, I want my relationship to my husband to be closer; where men seek first order, (behavioural) instructions, for example, what exactly do you want me to do differently?

Walters lists a number of issues which should be incorporated into therapists' thinking, including the valuing of attitudes and beliefs such as connectedness, nurturing, emotionality and support and the recognition of the different choices and access to resources of women and men.

Family therapists need to consider ways in which gender-patterning may contribute to difficulties, and be prepared to encourage both women and men to increase their range of behavioural choices. They must be prepared, where necessary, to *selectively empower* members of the family, to enhance their safety and well-being, whilst encouraging powerful members to try out different behaviour.

Putting the Family Back in the Centre

A central discourse within family therapy, is how best to share power with families in a way which allows them to take responsibility for their own choices, but retains safety for all members. Power should be reframed as the responsibility to create a safe environment within which the family can find its own solutions. The worker should use her expertise in systems theory and family relationships to get alongside the family, help them to make sense of their world, and explore differences and alternatives available to them.

Reimers and Treacher (1995) make a number of proposals for 'user friendly' family therapy, based upon consumer research. They advocate the provision of clear information in written and verbal form prior to the commencement of work. The first interview should be used to discuss the method of work rather than to begin an assessment. The use of technology, and the size of the team, should be kept to a minimum, video being used only for specified and explained purposes, for example,

training, or for the family to review their progress. Where supervising teams are used members should be introduced to the family, their composition should reflect a gender balance, and their workings should be explicit to the family. My own experience is that working in this way enables the family to make a relationship with, and feel contained by, the whole team.

Reimers and Treacher place the 'therapeutic alliance' back in centre stage. They point out that authenticity is an important component of style, as are openness and transparency in their own and the team's workings. The most important consideration is to find a 'fit' with the family. Some families will seek understanding, others, particularly in the early stages will seek advice and clarity. Some cultures and individuals will prize hierarchy and instruction, others will value equality and exploration. They point, above all else, to the importance of acting ethically. To do so means to be client, rather than technique-centred. Thus an *integrationist* approach to theory, accentuating 'family fit' and choice is offered.

The Social Work Context: Family Therapy or Systemic Practice?

Family therapists are fond of posing the question 'Are you part of the problem or part of the solution?' An example was given earlier of a social service agency

---

Further Reading

1 Burnham, J. (1986) *Family Therapy: First Steps Towards a Systemic Approach*, London: Tavistock.
2 Dallos, R. (1991) *Family Belief Systems: Therapy and Change*, Milton Keynes: Open University.
3 Reimers, S. and Treacher, A. (1995) *Introducing User Friendly Family Therapy*, London: Routledge.

becoming part of the problem. Farmer and Owen (1995) and Gibbons et al. (1995) pointed to an over-emphasis in child protection work on investigation and registration, to the detriment of prevention and longer term work towards protection. Children often remained at risk, and families who might otherwise have used services to enhance the welfare of their children were alienated. A systemic approach to practice enables the social worker to view the 'whole' of the context in which they are working, including their own and their agency's contribution to it. Systemic thinking may be used to underscore a number of routine social work activities.

Initial assessments

The focus here would be on the whole context of the referred person, and how the identified problem is embedded in a set of behaviours which may reinforce it. The strengths and resources of the family and choices available to them must be taken into account at an early stage.

Supervision

Wheeler (1984) has described the impact of systemic thinking upon first-line management in social service departments. For example in the management of the duty desk, where such questions as 'who else is affected by this problem?' and 'who is most concerned?' enable the worker to map the relevant 'problem organized system' and begin to create a context for the referral. Within supervision the manager would consider the full context of the work, including the impact of agency and worker. Wheeler describes reviews with social worker and family at key stages of the work. The manager interviews the family and social worker together to tease out their different perspectives about the progress of the work. Each person is asked to comment on how they see 'the

problem' currently, which ideas they have found useful, and what they would like to use/offer in the future.

Interprofessional workgroups

White, Essex and O'Reilly (1993) describe the application of systemic ideas to interprofessional groups in child protection work. Any interprofessional group will come together with a number of strengths and resources as well as possibilities for conflict and difference. Power relationships, differences of training and approach, different agency structures and priorities will all contribute to the group taking on a pattern of its own which may undermine the aim of individual and family welfare. An examination of the whole professional context may show up how agencies contribute to unhelpful outcomes, the group sometimes mirroring the family's own conflicts.

Working between systems

Social workers habitually work with the relationships between families and other agency systems, for example, school, housing organizations and social security. Ahmed was referred to a child guidance clinic by his school who were concerned about academic under-functioning and withdrawn behaviour. When the family attended the clinic, they were confused about the referral. They saw him as a bright, outgoing and intelligent boy. However, this description belied the behaviour of the whole family during the interview which was quiet and passive. Since the family were from Bengal and the (white) worker identified her need to understand more of their way of life, she arranged to visit them at home. She found that Ahmed was indeed bright and cheerful, playing happily with his brothers. She hypothesized that the family's behaviour in the (predominantly white middle class) context of the clinic may mirror Ahmed's behaviour in school. She discovered that Ahmed was in a predominantly white school where the family felt that their cultural needs were not understood. Her focus of work recentred on facilitating communication between family, school and Education Authority to promote a better understanding of Ahmed's needs.

Whilst all social workers and their managers can benefit from a knowledge of systems theory, those wishing to do family therapy will benefit from organization and support. In my experience of consulting to social work agencies, we have found it helpful to establish a small group of interested people with a sympathetic line manager. The group provides training for its members, and a service for their teams of origin. A number of strategies have contributed to success:

1 Recruiting members from across a spread of teams and identifying those members as a team resource. This serves the dual purpose of spreading influence and reassuring hard-pressed managers.

2 Negotiating a protected period of time, perhaps one afternoon a week, when the team works together.

3 Linking priorities with the perceived needs of colleagues, for example, child protection assessments, community care plans, etc. Careful monitoring of referrals and outcomes and regular feedback to local management groups.

4 Retaining open boundaries with colleagues, for example, inviting referrers to watch/review the work, inviting feedback from managers.

5 Including within the team resources of alternative expertise such as health visitors, community nurses, psychiatrists and psychologists. This enriches the service and meets other political needs of access to local services as well as 'spreading the burden'.

Conclusion

Taken together, family therapy and systemic practice form important social work tools. Family therapy has developed from an obsession with models and technology, to a more gentle, power-sharing approach focusing on the family's own style and choices. In so doing it has come into line with social welfare principles of partnership and empowerment and has acquired the flexibility to survive contemporary changes in the nature of families and kinship systems.

References

Anderson, T. (1987) *Reflecting Teams: Dialogues and Dialogues about the Dialogues*, Broadstairs, Kent: Borgmann.
Bateson, G., Jackson, D. and Haley, J. (1956) 'Towards a theory of schizophrenia', *Behavioural Science*, 1, 251–64.
Boszormenyi-Nagy, I. and Framo, J. (eds) (1965) *Intensive Family Therapy: Theoretical and Practical Aspects*, New York: Harper and Row.
Boyd-Franklin, N. (1989) *Black Families in Therapy*, New York: Guilford.
Burnham, J. (1986) *Family Therapy: First Steps Towards a Systemic Approach*, London: Tavistock.
Carpenter, J. and Treacher, A. (eds) (1995) *Using Family Therapy in the 90's*, Blackwell: Oxford.
Dale, P., Davies, M., Morrisson, T. and Waters, J. (1986) *Dangerous Families; Assessment and Treatment of Child Abuse*, London: Tavistock.
Dallos, R. (1991) *Family Belief Systems; Therapy and Change*, Milton Keynes: Open University.
Department of Health (1995) *Child Protection; Messages from Research*, London: HMSO.
Dimmock, B. and Dungworth, D. (1985) 'Beyond the family; using network meetings with statutory child care cases', *Journal of Family Therapy*, 7, 45–68.

Farmer, E. and Owen, M. (1995) *Child Protection Practice: Private Risks and Public Remedies*, London: HMSO.

Ferreira, A. J. (1963) 'Family myths and homeostasis', *Archives of General Psychiatry*, 9, 457–63.

Gibbons, J., Conroy, S. and Bell, C. (1995) *Operating the Child Protection System*, London: HMSO.

Goldner, V. (1985) 'Feminism and family therapy', *Family Process*, 24, 31–47.

Goldner, V., Penn, P. and Steinberg, M. (1990) 'Love and violence; gender paradoxes in volatile attachments', *Family Process*, 29, 343–64.

Haley, J. (1980) *Leaving Home*, New York, McGraw-Hill.

Hoffman, L. (1981) *Foundations of Family Therapy: a Conceptual Framework for Systems Change*, New York: Basic Books.

Jones, E. (1993) *Family Systems Therapy*, Chichester: Wiley.

Minuchin, S. (1974) *Families and Family Therapy*, London: Tavistock.

Minuchin, S., Montalvo, B., Gurney, B. and Schumer, H. (1967) *Families of the Slums: an Exploration of their Structure and Treatment*, New York: Basic Books.

Palazzoli, M., Boscolo, L., Cecchin, E. and Prata, G.

(1978) *Paradox and Counter-Paradox*, New York: Jason Aronson.

Perelberg, R. and Miller, A. (1990) *Gender and Power in Families*, London: Routledge.

Reimers, S. and Treacher, A. (1995) *Introducing User-Friendly Family Therapy*, London: Routledge.

Selvini Palazzoli, M., Boscolo, L., Cecchin, G. and Prata, G. (1980) *Hypothesizing, Circularity and Neutrality; Three Guidelines for the Conductor of the Session*,

Treacher, A. and Carpenter, J. (1983) *Using Family Therapy*, Oxford: Blackwell.

Walters, M. et al. (1988) *The Invisible Web; Gender Patterns in Family Relationships*, New York: Guilford.

Watzlawick, P. et al. (1974) *Change: Principles of Problem Formation and Problem Resolution*, New York: Norton.

Wheeler, R. (1984) *Family Therapy and Management in the Social Services Department*, Personal Social Services Fellowship, University of Bristol.

White, J., Essex, S. and O'Reilly, P. (1993) 'Family therapy systemic thinking and child protection', in J. Carpenter and A. Treacher, *Using Family Therapy in the 90's*, Oxford: Blackwell.

Task-centred Work

Peter Marsh

Task-centred practice has a high profile as a social work theory. It is reported by social work students as one of the most influential theories for their practice (Marsh and Triseliotis, 1996), and it is one of the very few approaches that will be mentioned if practitioners are asked about the theoretical basis of their work. It has survived through many decades of changing structures, developing practices and fashionable trends, in both social services and probation.

However, whether or not it is widely used in day-to-day practice is quite another matter. One of the social work students interviewed in the study mentioned above said, describing her many years of experience before going on qualifying training – 'before I went on the course, I thought I did task-centred work. Now I know more about task-centred, I don't think I do.'

Because task-centred work does have a clearly articulated model of practice, it may be that the approach is well-known as a set of activities – rather than as a theoretically-based approach from which a set of activities flows. If tasks are undertaken then you are doing task-centred work. But going through the motions of task-centred work does not necessarily mean a task-centred approach.

Task-centred work is more than a set of activities. It is more than 'doing tasks'. It is an approach which is founded on a set of key elements and which needs, in its practitioners, a commitment to those elements.

The elements, for example, clarity about the voluntary and compulsory nature of work, a multi-service approach and a development of work by evaluation and research, have often been seen as lacking in social work practice (see, for example, a series of studies on child protection; Department of Health, 1995). Many social workers and probation officers, before or after their course, probably think that they 'do task-centred social work' but actually they are carrying out a number of activities which do not hold together, and which will not necessarily lead to the successful outcomes that research has found in task-centred work. The emphasis in the discussion below is on the main elements of the approach, and not on the detailed activities carried out within the model.

Task-centred Practice

The main elements of task-centred practice, are perhaps best described as the building blocks of the approach. Each one is needed. Therefore each one needs to be understood, and to be integral to the worker's approach.

The overall approach

Task-centred practice is based upon a clear mandate for action from either the user, or the courts, or both. It may accommodate within it other approaches, for example, counselling or behavioural work. The agreement for work may be with individuals, groups or communities.

The purpose of practice is to move from

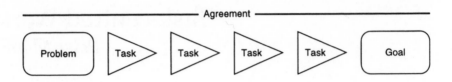

Figure V.4.1

agreed problems ('what is wrong') to agreed goals ('what is needed') in a set period of time. Goals are rarely complete solutions to problems.

Motivation is a key issue, hence the need to be clear about the mandate for the work: users must be concerned about the problems, and want to achieve the goals. This still applies when the mandate is set in the context of legal processes that specify a number of concerns that users must address.

The movement from problem to goal takes place via tasks. These are undertaken by the users, by the social worker or by others. Tasks are at the core of the model. It is 'task-centred' social work. Tasks are the method of exploring motivation in more detail, of building on users' strengths, of holding workers to account, of generating change and of working in collaboration across services.

Negotiation (Fisher and Ury, 1983) is needed to establish the agreement, to specify goals, and to develop tasks. If there is one key *activity* of a task-centred worker then negotiation is it. There is clear respect for users' cultures and views in this approach (Ahmad, 1990), and negotiation will help to make the mandate for work clear, and make the tasks as effective as possible.

Finally, a major requirement of a task-centred worker is to have a good knowledge of research, as both a basis of practice and as part of the development of practice that is inherent in task-centred work. Task-centred workers use research and make a direct contribution to research.

Overall, task-centred practice is a highly structured model of practice, requiring substantial knowledge and good training. It is based on a number of building blocks which lead to a set of activities within the overall model. Workers negotiate with users, and may agree that problems should be tackled, with success being indicated by a set of agreed goals. The movement from problem to goal is by tasks, which are as diverse and varied as the problems, goals, users and services which generate them.

A simple diagram (figure V.4.1) may help to show the overall process of the work and emphasize the key role of both the agreement that specifies problem and goals, and the tasks that link the two. The model is well described elsewhere (Doel and Marsh, 1992; Tolson, Reid and Garvin, 1994; and in summary in Marsh, 1991). The outline below covers the building blocks that underpin it.

Recognizing the voluntary and compulsory basis of social work

The users of social work often see themselves as subject to some form of compulsion. At its most obvious social workers and probation officers have, from court orders, and legal processes, considerable power to intervene in people's lives. Perhaps less obviously many users feel they have little alternative but to turn to social workers for help because they have few, if any, other options.

Task-centred practice is based upon a clear understanding of the basis of the work. To put it at its starkest, each time a task-centred practitioner enters into negotiation about service they should ask 'what right do I have to be engaging in this person's life?'. On many occasions intimate details of families are discussed, on other occasions actions are taken by social workers with far-reaching implications for relationships and the well-being of the users. These facts should lead to humility when beginning, continuing or ending work – it is often intrusive and it may be disruptive. Clarifying *what right a practitioner has to undertake the work at all* emphasizes the involvement and respect for the user.

The basis of task-centred work should, at the end of the day, be either the desire of the user to work on the problems outlined, or the clear mandate of the law to deal with the problems. On the other hand the pressure of neighbours, or the concerns of other professionals do not, in this approach, form a mandate for the work. They might, of course, strongly influence the user, and the skilled worker will, via negotiation, help the user to judge how they should respond to such influence (Rooney, 1992).

It is also important to note that the two bases of work, the wishes of the user, and/or legal powers, may co-exist. There might be full agreement to the legal order. There might be an order, and alongside this legally mandated voluntary problem, there might be some additional voluntary work. But if there is no agreement at all, then task-centred work cannot take place and the worker will need to proceed by some form of surveillance or monitoring.

The real world of social work and probation practice will often make these definitions difficult to clarify, and there will be blurred edges. Indeed, social work has sometimes institutionalized a confused mandate, for example that deriving from the child protection conference, where the legal power of any agreed plan is negligible, but the plan could hardly be said to be voluntary (see,

Five Key Points

1 Task-centred practice is based on user agreement, or user acceptance of a legal justification for action.
2 Task-centred practice aims to move from problem to goal, from what is wrong to what is needed.
3 Task-centred practice is based around tasks, which are central to the process of change and which build on user strengths as far as possible.
4 Task-centred practice is open to other approaches and services, and can link with them via tasks.
5 Task-centred practice develops and changes by continuing evaluation.

for example, the discussion of this 'third mandate' in Marsh and Fisher, 1992, pp. 21–9).

However the fact that mandates are tricky to clarify does not make them less important, nor does it make the need to establish them as clearly as possible less important.

Working hard to establish with the user why the work is taking place, and what is available for them to disagree with or establish, is central to task-centred work, and an important contribution to anti-oppressive practice (Ahmad, 1990).

Combining different services

Social workers may offer direct services themselves. For community-based staff this may, for example, be counselling, or behavioural programmes, and for residential and day care staff this may also be different forms of service within their centre. On many occasions others will offer services, of education, health, justice or perhaps social care. It is fundamental to task-centred work that this range of services are considered and when needed offered, at both the initial stages and as work progresses.

Negotiation regarding problems and

goals will often establish this need, as in other approaches to social work. The particular contribution of task-centred work is that tasks will allow the need for other services to be kept under review, and demonstrated through actions rather than solely through discussions. Tasks act as a mechanism to allow workers to assess the need for other services, for example discussing which tasks might work best, or how a new service may help with a task which so far has been difficult to complete.

Other services and approaches are integral to the task-centred approach. The tasks themselves mean that there is regular review, and they allow a clear demonstration of the need, or the lack of need, for a particular service.

Work with individuals, families, groups and communities

Although some work will be solely with individuals, it is most likely that more than one person is involved in defining problems, and in undertaking tasks. When considering relevant tasks, the willingness of the people concerned to undertake them will be important. When considering problems, and the mandate/agreement basis of work, the willingness of people to start off the work will be important. This is considered further below, but the question here is 'which people do social workers need to contract with?'.

Is it the teenager in the family, or the parents as well? Is it the family with a child with disability, or the relevant support group as well? It must be clear which system is contracted with (Fortune, 1985). The source of mandate is the key issue. The focus of the legal order, and/or the willingness to take part will be the bottom line for the decision about the primary system that is to be engaged with (Tolson, Reid and Garvin, 1994, pp. 8–11).

This will not necessarily be the same as the focus of the tasks that are undertaken.

For example, the work with the teenager may include the school staff in the tasks, but the teacher may not have been a partner to the agreement. Here again tasks will act as an indicator, this time of the way that the agreement for work may need to change to be based on a wider system (Reid, 1985). The work with the school may grow to the point where including them in the discussion of problems and goals is necessary.

Task-centred practice does not take as given the 'size' of system that should be engaged with at the start. It may be individuals or complete communities (for examples of the latter see Tolson, Reid and Garvin, 1994, pp. 339–90). Negotiation needs to establish which system is contracted with, and tasks will clarify whether that decision should be reviewed.

Building on user strengths

Most, perhaps all, social workers will have thought that they personally could not deal very well with the difficulties and pressures that face many of the users of their services. Providing care for children, for example, while struggling with poverty and discrimination requires feats of ingenuity, and of sheer effort, that will often be remarkable. The feats may be skilful, and they will certainly be varied. It is inevitable that they will often be unknown to the practitioner.

Task-centred practice takes very seriously at least two consequences from these facts. The first is that users have a great deal of expertise in coping with their own circumstances. The second is that users understand their own circumstances in ways that workers, ultimately, cannot. Users would not be seeing social workers if there were no problems, but users are, at least in regard to the other areas of their lives, usually the 'primary experts' (Bricker-Jenkins, 1990).

Task-centred practice is based on users'

strengths. It is those strengths which will provide change, sometimes in directions that users clearly wanted, sometimes in directions that they have agreed to, however reluctantly, as a result of legal processes. Tasks use those strengths, and fill any gaps in strengths.

Task-centred practice should also acknowledge the reality of the users' day-to-day relationships. Attempts to involve family members, for example, will often founder on the lengthy history that has shaped their relationships. This complex reality is known best by the user, although of course it may not be clearly articulated in words. It may also change with the impact of social work practice. The grandmother who was previously a great support may become less so because of what she has learnt from the child protection enquiry.

Tasks will need to reflect the reality of users' relationships. Users will need to develop them in ways that are most likely to function in the circumstances of their own lives. Tasks may also provide a way to articulate social relationships, and can therefore add to discussion as a means of assessment or of change. Attempting to work with a grandmother on a task, will demonstrate the nature of family relationships in a way that debating them in the office will not.

Change occurs in task-centred practice as a result of tasks. Tasks are founded on the idea of searching for strengths, recognizing lack of them and developing ideas that reflect the actual reality of the users' relationships and lives.

Developing partnerships

Partnership between users and workers is an important element of social work practice (Lindow and Morris, 1995; Marsh and Fisher, 1992; Smale et al., 1993; Social Services Inspectorate, 1995). This does not imply an equality of power, nor an equality of work, and partnerships will come in all shapes and sizes. Users

themselves have defined partnership, in one action research project, as 'a group of people who have agreed a common aim and who will pool resources in order to achieve it' (From Margin to Mainstream, 1995) and this working definition would form a very suitable foundation for task-centred practice.

Finding a common aim by negotiation (with due respect for mandates), and then

---

Three Questions

1 Ethical, effectiveness, efficiency and user-satisfaction arguments all suggest that practice should respect and involve the user's own views as far as possible. Is task-centred work's concern with this area a good reason to adopt the approach?

2 How important is it to accommodate multiple users (individuals, families, etc.), and multiple services in social work practice? Does task-centred work do this particularly well?

3 Task-centred work is dynamic, capable of responding to research and to changing social values and policies – are other approaches? How important is this to the future of social work?

---

pooling the resources, of users, workers and others, via tasks: this is partnership in action in task-centred work.

Evidence-based practice

Task-centred work has been a pioneer of the linking of research, practice and policy. The importance of these links has been supported in major recommendations to the Department of Health (Department of Health, 1994a and 1994b; Richardson, Jackson and Sykes, 1990). Task-centred practice developed from research (Reid, 1963) and this has been central to its continuing development (Marsh, 1991). For example, early research suggested that goals without deadlines to meet them are much less effective, and therefore that time limits for the work are important (Reid, 1963; Reid and Shyne, 1969), and that longer term work should be divided up into a series of shorter periods. Research has shown that there is a particularly effective approach to task development (Reid, 1975), that the use of tasks within sessions, as well as between sessions, is valuable (Reid and Helmer, 1985), and that there is an interrelationship of different task strategies with different problem areas (Reid, 1992).

But task-centred work's link with research does not depend solely on the work of researchers. It also depends on the work of practitioners and managers. It is developed through a research-like stance from those who practise it. They look for evidence of the links between their work and successful outcome. They ask users directly for their views about progress and their satisfaction about the work at each and every meeting. Tasks themselves are a miniature form of action research, trying different ways to achieve goals and learning from successes and failures.

A structured approach

Task-centred practice is a structured approach to social work. There is a clear model and a set of techniques within this. Development occurs within this structure. As such it can be replicated, improved and learnt. The evidence is that learning to *apply* the model, as distinct from learning *about* the model, is far from easy (Newton and Marsh, 1993; Reid and Beard, 1980; Rooney, 1985 and 1988; Tolson, 1985). All of the building blocks, including this one of structure, must be in place in order to carry out task-centred practice. 'Tasks' are not just activities carried out by the worker or user, they have meaning because of the overall structure within which they take place.

Discussion, action and change

Task-centred practice needs a firm base, a mandate for action, from users or from legal process. On this base the notion of 'task' is central to the work, providing the means to link services, build on user strengths, develop partnerships, and develop the task-centred approach itself. It also provides an excellent example of the way that the approach moves beyond the use of discussion as the main basis of assessment and change. The idea that demonstration and personal experience are influential aspects of understanding is important to task-centred work.

Doing something adds to discussing something. Acting your way into a new way of thinking, may be easier than thinking your way into a new way of acting. This does not mean that major action is required for all tasks, simple activities can be powerful indicators of ability or the lack of it. Task-centred work is designed to provide indicators by both discussion and demonstration: indicators of need, of motivation, of lack of progress and of progress. It enables users to develop ideas about what they need and to call services to account, it enables workers to estimate their success. These seem highly relevant developments for social services to adopt.

Conclusion

Task-centred practice requires intellectual rigour, skilled practical application, serious commitment to respecting users and combating discrimination, and courage in specifying what social work is trying to achieve.

High quality professional practice needs a cogent and coherent theoretical base, accompanied by a relevant model and techniques. The degree of genuine task-centred use and development may be one indicator of the state of health of social work as a professional activity.

Further Reading

1   Bricker-Jenkins, M. (1990) 'Another approach to practice and training – clients must be considered the primary experts', *Public Welfare*, Spring, 11–16.

2   Doel, M. and Marsh, P. (1992) *Task-centred Social Work*, Aldershot: Ashgate.

3   Reid, W. J. (1992) *Task Strategies*, New York: Columbia University Press.

References

Ahmad, B. (1990) *Black Perspectives in Social Work*, Birmingham: Venture Press.

Bricker-Jenkins, M. (1990) 'Another approach to practice and training – clients must be considered the primary experts', *Public Welfare*, Spring, 11–16.

Department of Health (1994a) *Supporting Research and Development in the N.H.S. – A Report to the Minister for Health by a Research and Development Task Force Chaired by Professor Anthony Culyer*, London: HMSO.

Department of Health (1994b) *A Wider Strategy for Research and Development Relating to Personal Social Services – A Report to the Director of Research and Development, Department of Health, by an Independent Review Group*, London: HMSO.

Department of Health (1995) *Child Protection – Messages from Research*, London: HMSO.

Doel, M. and Marsh, P. (1992) *Task-centred Social Work*, Aldershot: Ashgate.

Fisher, R. and Ury, W. (1983) *Getting to Yes*, London: Hutchinson.

Fortune, A. E. (ed.) (1985) *Task-centred Practice with Families and Groups*, New York: Springer Publishing Company.

From Margin to Mainstream (1995) *Social Care Summary Three*, York: Joseph Rowntree Foundation.

Lindow, V. and Morris, J. (1995) *Service User Involvement – Synthesis of Findings and Experience in the Field of Community Care*, York: Joseph Rowntree Foundation.

Marsh, P. (1991) 'Task-centred Practice', in J. Lishman (ed.), *Handbook of Theory for Practice Teachers in Social Work*, London: Jessica Kingsley, pp. 157–72.

Marsh, P. and Fisher, M. (1992) *Good Intentions: Developing Partnership in Social Services,*

Community Care into Practice Series, York: Joseph Rowntree Foundation.

Marsh, P. and Triseliotis, J. (1996) *Readiness to Practise*, Aldershot: Avebury.

Newton, C. and Marsh, P. (1993) *Training in Partnership – Translating Intentions into Practice in Social Services*, York: Joseph Rowntree Foundation.

Reid, W. J. (1963) *An Experimental Study of Methods Used in Casework Treatment*, DSW, Columbia University, New York, USA.

Reid, W. J. (1975) 'A test of task-centred approach', *Social Work*, 20 (January), 3–9.

Reid, W. J. (1985) *Family Problem Solving*, New York: Columbia University Press.

Reid, W. J. (1992) *Task Strategies*, New York: Columbia University Press.

Reid, W. J. and Beard, C. (1980) 'An evaluation of in-service training in a public welfare setting', *Administration in Social Work*, 4 (Spring), 71–85.

Reid, W. J. and Helmer, K. (1985) *Session Tasks in Family Treatment*, State University of New York at Albany, School of Social Welfare.

Reid, W. J. and Shyne, A. W. (1969) *Brief and Extended Casework*, New York: Columbia University Press.

Richardson, A., Jackson, C. and Sykes, W. (1990) *Taking Research Seriously – Means of Improving and Assessing the Use and Dissemination of Research*, London: HMSO.

Rooney, R. H. (1985) 'Does in-service training make a difference? Results of a pilot study of task-centred dissemination in a public social service setting', *Journal of Social Service Research*, 8(3), 33–50.

Rooney, R. H. (1988) 'Measuring task-centred training effects on practice: results of an audiotape study in a public agency', *Journal of Continuing Social Work Education*, 4(4), 2–7.

Rooney, R. H. (1992) *Strategies for Work with Involuntary Clients*, New York: Columbia University Press.

Smale, G., Tuson, G. with Biehal, N. and Marsh, P. (1993) *Empowerment, Assessment, Care Management and the Skilled Worker*, London: HMSO.

Social Services Inspectorate (1995) *The Challenge of Partnership in Child Protection: Practice Guide*, London: HMSO.

Tolson, E. R. (1985) 'Teaching and measuring task-centred skills: the skill assessment teaching model', in A. E. Fortune (ed.), *Task-centred Practice with Families and Groups*, New York: Springer Publishing Company.

Tolson, E., Reid, W. J. and Garvin, C. (eds) (1994) *Generalist Practice: A Task-centered Approach*, New York: Columbia University Press.

V.5
Cognitive–Behavioural Therapy
Tammie Ronen

Cognitive–behavioural therapy (CBT) is a dynamic mode of intervention – both subjecting itself to a constant process of change incited by our rapidly developing society as well as guiding therapists to modify their thinking and adapt their methods to the vastly changing needs of their individual clients. CBT's main role – of helping people change – can be realized only by combining new theoretical knowledge with empirically-tested interventional approaches that account for the cultural, social, economic and political transformations typifying modern life. Unlike the common view of CBT as a technical intervention mode, it is neither a strict implementation of learning theory, nor is it merely a collection of effectual techniques. Rather, CBT constitutes a holistic way of life, a way of thinking and perceiving human functioning and needs, and a way of operating within the environment in order to achieve the most effective means for accomplishing one's aims. Being a cognitive–behavioural therapist necessitates dynamic thinking, considering that no one correct approach or intervention or main technique exists for treating the variety of clients encountered in social work. The therapist always needs to make decisions adapting available techniques to specific client-related factors (i.e., the individual client and problem) and to therapist-related factors (i.e., the service setting, the therapist's abilities, knowledge and skills).

The Dynamic Nature of CBT Theory

The beginning of behaviourist approaches in psychology emerged in the 1920s when Watson brought together concepts and methods of conditioning research developed in Russia. Psychologists attempted to contest psychiatrists' medical intervention model by proposing a scientific theoretical foundation for human disorders rooted in behavioural principles. The theoretical base for Behavioural Theory (BT) has since undergone a continuous process of change, as new knowledge arose enabling new explanations of human behaviour and later as behavioural theory was integrated into cognitive theory. Behaviour therapy thus saw a dynamic evolution from its original conceptualizations: these were based on laboratory study and the theory of learning, branching in three directions: classical, operant and social learning (modelling; see figure V.5.1).

Classical conditioning as demonstrated by Pavlov's study of dogs' digestion depicted the connection between stimulus (food) and response (salivating). Classical learning principles soon became the basis for explaining human habits, behaviours and disorders and the source from which relaxation training and desensitization techniques were developed (Wolpe, 1982). The latter are still considered an important contribution to the treatment of anxiety disorders. Yet these main concepts (i.e., stimuli, response, conditioning) analysed behaviour

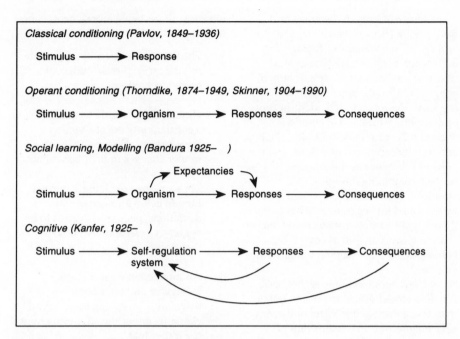

Figure V.5.1   Patterns of behavioural intervention.

without relating to the person as a human being.

Skinner's contribution of the notion of consequences triggered the development of operant conditioning, giving a specific role to the organism and focusing on the ability to modify a behaviour by changing its consequence. Behaviour eliciting positive outcomes would continue, whereas behaviour eliciting negative outcomes would be eliminated, decreased or made extinct. Operant conditioning pin-pointed the need for environmental change, emphasizing techniques such as positive and negative reinforcement (Skinner, 1938), extinction and punishment (Hughes, 1993), and more complex programmes such as contingency contracts, token economies and exposure techniques.

The inability of classical and operant conditioning to yield explanations for all kinds of learning (e.g., for gender roles or social skills) led to a third learning theory: social learning, or modelling (Bandura, 1969, 1977). Bandura demonstrated that

learning can occur as a result of observation and in the absence of reinforcement either to the model or to the learner. His social learning theory in general and his notion of vicarious (observational) learning provided the basis for conceptualizing the person–environment relationship as a reciprocal process of influence. People are hereby perceived as active participants in their own learning.

Through the 1970s, psychologists' interest in cognition, memory, perception and motivation was reflected in behavioural theory by extending it towards cognitive learning. Bandura's (1977) identification of the role of expectancies and self-regulation in the control of behaviour as key concepts in vicarious learning provided new information serving as an incentive for an increase in cognitive therapy. Research began to focus directly on the alteration of covert behaviour and the role of cognitive processes in different populations. Ellis's (1973) idea of irrational thinking as the main source of human disorders and Beck's work (Beck, Rush, Shaw and Emery, 1979) on cognitive therapy for depression demonstrated the clinical utility of mediational models of human behaviour. Clinical implications of cognitive theory included: identification of thoughts, awareness of emotions elicited following those thoughts, the link between thoughts and emotions, and the view of behaviour as the outcome of a process combining thoughts and emotions. Behaviour therapy had transformed into cognitive–behavioural theory, with a multi-dimensional focus on changing overt as well as covert behaviour such as imagery, thoughts and emotions.

Adding cognition to the earlier basic learning model placed the *person* rather than the *problem* at the centre of therapy. CBT now moved in the direction of helping people to help themselves and control their own lives. Theories of self-control were developed to explain human functioning, noting the role of language as an important mediating feature in the natural acquisition of self-control (Luria, 1961; Ronen, 1994a). Self-control was described as a shift from being directed by others' talk to the development of self-talk aloud, and finally to the capacity for silent self-talk (thoughts). Being in control of oneself was seen as facilitating: coping with stress, pain or disturbing emotions; delaying temptation and establishing criteria and targets for conducting one's own life (Thoresen and Mahoney, 1974). Self-control was conceived as the way new behaviours need to be learned and as necessary when choices need to be made or when habitual response sequences are interrupted or prove ineffective (Rosenbaum, 1990). Kanfer and Schefft (1988, p. 49) drew the self-control model as a change from the basic linear model to a non-linear, open-loop model with non-stop feedback and feedforward processes (see figure V.5.1).

Several assumptions have characterized

basic cognitive–behavioural theory since its inception:

1   The theory is a scientific approach relying on empirical studies of human behaviour.

2   Human behaviour is seen as being in a constant process of change; therefore, people are always able to render changes in their behaviour.

3   The same rule explaining normal human behaviour can explain deviations; people who learn to be aggressive can learn to behave themselves.

4   An interaction exists between behaviour and environment; therefore, change can be achieved by changing either the environment or the individual.

In the most recent development, CBT, which shifted from traditional behaviour theory to more cognitive theory, has now moved towards constructivist theory. Constructivism emphasizes people's role in making their own realities by the way they reconstruct and construe their life events and how they attribute meaning to their personal experiences (Mahoney, 1993).

Replacing Diagnosis with Assessment

CBT has replaced the traditional meaning of *diagnosis* (i.e., a rigid concept emphasizing the medical model where common pathological characteristics of disorders are identified before treatment) with the dynamic notion of *assessment* that continues throughout the entire therapeutic process. Continuous assessment is conducted regarding the client, the problem and specific objectives and their meaning, with the therapist constantly re-examining his or her decisions and approach. The therapist is interested not in rigid definitions (e.g., depression) but rather in how the problem manifests itself (e.g., the person does not leave home, is not involved in social activities, does not eat or smile, cries often).

Assessment is based on the role of contemporaneous determinants of behaviour, rather than early life events or the client's past (Hughes, 1993). Objectives, target behaviours and appropriate methods of measurement are carefully identified, determining the variables controlling both environment and organism, and discerning the individual thinking style and emotions controlling behaviour. Assessment throughout the therapeutic process focuses on the *'what'* and *'how'* and not the *'why'*: *how* one learns to act this way and *what* maintains the behaviour. The therapist aims to construct a behaviour profile of the client based on the following questions:

- How do you behave today? What disturbs you regarding this behaviour?
- What happens when you face your difficulties – how do you behave?
- What (actual experiences) do you think influenced your behaviour in the past?
- What interferes with you trying to overcome your problem?
- What would be better if your problem was solved?
- How should the therapist know that the problem is over?

Five Key Points

1 Cognitive–behavioural therapy is a direct application of empirical behavioural and cognitive theories.
2 Cognitive–behavioural therapy is a dynamic model for helping people change and acquire self-help skills.
3 The process of change is an active process aiming to impart clients with knowledge and skills and to facilitate practice and application of the newly acquired skills.
4 Cognitive–behavioural therapy involves changing people's way of thinking, feeling and behaving.
5 Cognitive–behavioural therapy aims to help people identify their automatic thoughts, become aware of their emotions, link their thoughts and emotions to behaviour and change their automatic thoughts to more adequate ones.

Table V.5.1 Development and treatment of social phobia (fear of participating in social events) according to different CBT theories.

Learning theory	Phobia aetiology	Suggested treatment
Classical	Repeated experiencing of fears while attending social events caused a contingency between the event and the response	Disconnect the fear from the event by desensitization and relaxation
Operant	Repeated positive reinforcement of the avoidance behaviour; punishment while exposed to the feared event	Gradual exposure to the feared event and positive reinforcement for successful exposure
Modelling	Repeated exposure to an admired model who fears social events caused vicarious learning of avoidance	Presenting a new model who is not afraid of social events and is reinforced for attendance
Cognitive	Negative expectancies and automatic negative thoughts on the result of attending social events elicit stressful emotions and avoidant behaviour	Changing negative thoughts, developing positive expectancies, and teaching coping skills

Table V.5.2   Types of self-control.

	Redressive	Reformative	Experiential
Aim	To solve existing problems, decrease disruptions	To change life-style, improve coping	Opening up to experiences
Target	Homeostasis	Heterostasis	Heterostasis
Time	Present	Future	Present, future
Problem's setting	Environment	Person	Person
Targeted behavioural classification	Under-controlled, externalizing	Over-controlled, internalizing	Over-controlled, internalizing
Client behaviour problems	Aggression Anger Conduct disorders Delinquency Disruptiveness Fears Hostility Hyperactivity Phobias Sociopathy Stress	Anxiety Apathy Depression Impulsivity Inhibitions Sensitivity Shyness Submissiveness Withdrawal	Anxiety Avoidance Depression Mental retardation Shyness Special education Withdrawal
Treatment setting	Therapy, educational	Therapy, educational, practice in natural environment	Primarily natural environment
Techniques	Self-instruction Imagination Relaxation	Criteria establishment Relaxation Problem solving Resisting temptation	Exposure to new experiences Relaxation Exposure to music, etc.
Methods	Modelling Role playing Rehearsal Record taking Discussions Written manuals	Homework assignments Practice exercises	Exposure to hobbies, youth groups, art, music, etc.

- Why do you wish to solve this problem?
- Imagine your life without the problem: how would you liké it to look?
- Who are the people who can help you fight the problem?

Therapy: Trick or Treatment?

There is a misconceived tendency to look at CBT as a collection of magic tricks that the therapist pulls out to solve human disorders and maladaptive behaviours. Instead, CBT comprises a very careful, continuous assessment process that attempts to analyse the client's needs, our knowledge about the specific problem and the client's skills and abilities, to determine the treatment of choice. The same problem could be treated differently as a result of decision making related to personal, environmental and behavioural considerations.

To illustrate the link between theory and therapy, table V.5.1 describes the explanation and treatment of social phobia.

While in the past therapists were either behavioural or cognitive oriented, most therapists today are cognitive–behaviourally oriented, meaning that they apply principles derived from research, experimental and social psychology for the alleviation of human suffering and the enhancement of human functioning, with systematic evaluation of the effectiveness of these applications and a commitment to an applied science of clinical treatment (Franks and Wilson, 1975; O'Leary and Wilson, 1987). The field of CBT espouses direct links between theory, assessment, intervention and evaluation (Ronen, 1994a, 1994b, 1995a). CBT interventions are devised empirically, based on the results of behavioural assessment, and constantly evaluated (Hersen and Bellack, 1981). The targeted change of CBT is overt as well as covert behaviour, and thinking

is considered by today's therapists to play an important role in the aetiology and maintenance of disorders (Hollon and Beck, 1994).

CBT advocates the selection of intervention strategies with: a high probability of success; sequential steps that match available skill levels; clear, relevant means of monitoring progress; practice opportunities and maintenance and follow-up periods (Gambrill, 1990). Homework assignments are considered an integral part of most CBT interventions due to the strong need to exercise and apply knowledge from the intervention setting to the natural

---

Three Questions

1 With so many similarities between social work as a profession and cognitive–behavioural therapy, why has CBT not become the treatment of choice for social workers?

2 How does CBT's development towards the future affect social work interventions?

3 What modifications need to be undertaken in order to adapt CBT to social work's specific clients and targets?

---

environment (Ronen, 1995a). The therapeutic setting is not limited to time sequences (once a week) but rather is linked to role accomplishment ('We will meet again when you complete your homework assignment'). Therapy is terminated not when the problem decreases but only when clients prove their ability to maintain their achievements and generalize them to other settings and problem areas.

As CBT theory develops, new intervention modes and therefore new strategies and techniques are supplied to aid the therapist. From Wolpe's (1982) desensitization methods in the early days of CBT theory to the modern treatment of anxiety disorders through exposure, primarily self-exposure: instead of the therapist conditioning clients to relax, clients are instructed in the importance of exposing themselves to unpleasant feelings and are encouraged to select their own assignments and exposure targets (Marks, 1987).

As an example of the cognitive self-help evolution, I will present self-control theory. Rosenbaum (1993) described three types of self-control to elucidate different behavioural problem areas. *Redressive* self-control is required when one's behaviour is disturbed and one needs to overcome existing concrete difficulties (e.g., a woman wants specific techniques to lose five kilos before her anniversary in a month's time; she needs to learn self-talk, imagination and relaxation to overcome her wish to eat). *Reformative* self-control is needed to change one's whole way of life, eliminate poor habits, and set up new targets and expectancies (e.g., the problem is not an immediate weight loss but rather the poor eating habits that caused her to eat when she was tired, frustrated, angry or bored; she needs to learn how to change her eating patterns and entire way of life). *Experiential* self-control targets one's ability to let go of control and expose oneself to new experiences (e.g., the eating stems from avoiding social activities, low self-image, and poor self-esteem; she needs to learn to accept herself and her body and stop avoiding social activities, in order to change her appearance). Ronen (1995a, 1995b) applied these three self-control types to the understanding and treatment of different behaviour disorders. In general, the redressive type denotes therapy, reformative implies a preventive model, and experiential suggests the development of self-fulfilment and personal potential. Table V.5.2 presents the adaptation of Rosenbaum's three types of self-control to intervention with children.

Learning to Think Like a Cognitive–Behavioural Therapist

The therapist's role has changed over the years in the field of CBT. Therapists in the past were conceived as being in charge of the entire intervention process, from planning to method selection and pace. Whereas most of the literature in the 1960s and 1970s suggested effective procedures for therapists' intervention, the 1980s saw more attention given to the therapist's role as an educational, therapeutic trainer and an increased focus on the process of therapy. In the 1990s therapists have been conceived as enabling experiences and providing a safe setting for practising skills. Safran and Segal (1990), for example, presented most of their therapy in the context of the client–therapist relationship. The CBT intervention process has become an educational, therapeutic process aimed at teaching, practising and applying new skills, knowledge and coping strategies as well as offering an experiential setting.

Kanfer and Schefft (1988) have suggested six rules summarizing the cognitive–behavioural therapist's way of thinking:

1. *Think behaviour*: Often, therapists think problems. They concentrate on the client's problem, making assumptions and interpretations regarding its causes. The cognitive–behavioural therapist defines the problem in terms of consequences, by-products of actions, and personal traits. The action is the main dimension on which interchanges in therapy are focused.

2. *Think solution*: Most often therapists devote more time to thinking of difficulties and problems than to finding solutions. A full problem description requires knowledge not only of the current situation or state but also of a more desirable future end-state and some indication of how to achieve it.

3. *Think positive*: Just as therapists help the client to think positively and to focus on small changes and positive forces rather than on difficulties, they must themselves also aspire to positive thinking. CBT reinforces positive outcomes and strengthens any strategies, plans or actions that make these outcomes more likely.

4. *Think small steps*: Although clients are usually interested in the major, significant changes in their lives, extreme changes are difficult to obtain. Targeting small gradual changes reduces fears, motivates clients and helps therapists observe and pin-point difficulties. An accumulation of many small changes constitutes one final, large and significant change.

5. *Think flexible*: Sheldon (1987) emphasized the need for therapists to think and to change themselves throughout the whole process of change. He accused therapists of falling in love with the methods they use, which precludes them from asking questions about effectiveness or from negotiating the best method for particular clients. 'Think flexible' challenges therapists to be creative, modify their traditional interventions, and try to adapt themselves to the clients' needs. Gambrill (1990) suggested that therapists look for disconfirming evidence (which points to alternatives), try to understand other people's point of view (instead of being convinced by your own point of view), use language carefully, watch out for vivid data, move beyond the illusion of understanding, complement clear thinking skills with knowledge and ask about accuracy.

6. *Think future*: Many therapeutic approaches focus on the past and its role on the client's present. CBT challenges therapists to think towards the future, predicting how their client will cope and how they themselves would like to be different or better in the future.

As therapy is a planned, designed process, much attention has been given to the construction of the intervention process. The most familiar procedure for intervention, Gambrill's 12 steps (Gambrill et al., 1971), has provided guidelines for social workers and other therapists as well as for students learning to conduct the process of intervention. Each step comprises three components – its objective, rationale and means of operation (table V.5.3).

Kanfer and Schefft (1988) added client-related components and phases to this 12-step procedure, such as creating an alliance and developing a commitment for change. The difficulties lie in pin-pointing each client's personal motivations and how to help increase the motivation for behaviour change. Motivating the client to continue therapy is inseparable from strategies of role definition. In preparing clients to respond to later strategies that increase readiness for change, therapists help them in early sessions to take small steps to reduce their current misery or ineffectiveness (Kanfer and Schefft, 1988).

Further Reading

1 Bandura, A. (1986) *Social Foundations of Thought and Action: a Social Cognitive Perspective*, Englewood Cliffs, NJ: Prentice Hall.
2 Kanfer, F. H. and Schefft, B. K. (1988) *Guiding the Process of Therapeutic Change*, Champaign, Il: Research Press.
3 Kazdin, A. E. (1994) *Behavior Modification in Applied Settings*, Pacific Grove, CA: Brooks/Cole.

Table V.5.3 Gambrill's 12 steps in the intervention process.

STEP	Objective	Rationale	Means of operation
1 Inventory of problem areas.	Obtain the whole spectrum of problems.	Helps draw the problem area profile.	Accumulating full descriptions of presenting problems.
2 Problem selection and contract.	Reach client/therapist agreement on problem areas selected for change.	Stimulates client co-operation and involvement.	Conversing about the problem list and negot- iating the selection.
3 Commitment to co-operate.	Obtain client agreement to co-operate with the process.	Facilitates compliance.	Providing explanations, reading of the agreement, and asking for agreement.
4 Specification of target behaviours.	Specify details about the selected problem.	Demonstrates what maintains and re- inforces the problem.	Using samples of problem behaviours and desirable alternatives and examples.
5 Baseline of target behaviour.	Obtain pre-intervention frequency and duration of the problem.	Provides a concrete basis for judging change.	Charting, estimating.
6 Identification of problem- controlling conditions.	Learn the conditions preceding and following the problem's occurrence.	Demonstrates the importance of discriminatory stimuli affecting the problem.	Charting incidents before, during and after the problem's occurrence.
7 Assessment of environmental resources.	Identify possible resources in the client's environment.	Enlists environ- ment's help, without which change is difficult to induce.	Asking the client or interviewing significant others in the environ- ment or mediators.
8 Specification of behavioural objectives.	Specify the behavioural objectives of the modification plan.	Elicits the client's terminal behavi- oural repertoire.	Using baseline repertoire.
9 Formulation of a modification plan.	Select an appropriate technique.	Enables selection of most efficient prog- ramme for change.	Reviewing information in previous steps, and exam- ining available interventions
10 Implementation of modification plan.	Modify behaviour.	Focuses effort on change.	Conducting specific intervention techniques.
11 Monitoring outcomes.	Obtain information about the effectiveness of intervention.	Gives feedback on effectiveness.	Data-gathering techniques.
12 Maintenance of change.	Achieve maintenance and stabilization.	Helps prevent relapses.	Using the environment for maintenance or specific plan.

Clients, Problem Areas and Important Concepts in CBT

The development of CBT can also be traced by examining the main concepts of the therapy, the client population and the type of problems being treated.

A major change in concepts has occurred, where CBT moved from *doing something to* people towards *working with* them, and from teaching how to *overcome* problems towards teaching to *live with and cope with* them. In the early days of behaviour therapy, the focus was mainly on psychiatric disorders (Eysenck, 1959), children with severe handicaps in institutional settings, mental retardation and autism (Bijou, 1970; Lovaas, 1967). Over the years, health attitudes and modern science have highlighted the importance of helping people remain in their natural environments. As a result, CBT began to focus its attention on open clinics and day care centres and started treating less severe problems such as anxiety and depression. Another change was extending interventions to non-clinical populations and environments (Ullman and Krasner, 1965). CBT nowadays tries to work with large ranges of the whole population: different cultural influences, children, adults, families and organizations.

During the 1970s and the 1980s much attention was given to the treatment of social anxiety, fears, phobias and depression (Beck et al., 1979; Marks, 1987), whereas the late 1980s saw a move towards hysterical disorders, post-traumatic stress disorders, obsessive-compulsive disorders and social skills training. Social changes raised new social problems, focusing attention on abused and neglected children, abused women, drugs and alcohol, homosexuality and the treatment of AIDS. New medical developments expose people to new problems: the ability to live longer necessitates helping geriatric people get the most out of their lives; surgical techniques such as transplants necessitate helping people live with their changing bodies; and coping with new treatments for illnesses such as cancer, diabetes and anorexia facilitates the generation of new intervention techniques. One focus of modern life is the urge to improve life quality, as reflected by the development of interventions in institutions, work organizations and individual therapy.

A few decades ago the focus of CBT was on studying human disorders – anxiety, stress, depression – and teaching effective ways to overcome (i.e., decrease, eliminate) them. It seems that towards the year 2000, CBT has introduced new concepts into its vocabulary – not only depression and fear but also happiness, joy, satisfaction and love. Therefore, the 1950s and 1960s emphasized overt behaviour, responses and stimuli; the 1970s focused on vicarious learning, modelling and expectancies; and the early 1990s accentuated emotions and opening up to new experiences as the most studied concepts.

The Adaptation of CBT to Social Work

Cognitive–behavioural therapy has gained a prominent position in clinical social work probably because of its relevance to social work concepts, purposes, ethics and intervention modes. Social work as a profession is built on the notion that theoretical knowledge can be translated into skills and practical know-how in order to achieve change (Kondrat, 1992), with clearly defined objects for change and clear, concrete and well-defined targets (Gambrill, 1983, 1990; Loewenberg, 1984; Perlman, 1953; Schinken, 1981). CBT puts the client centre stage by focusing on action and change, examining a person's behaviour, emotions and thinking style, in light of her/his strengths, weaknesses and goals (Ronen, 1995b).

As social work involves weak populations, empowerment constitutes an important interventional goal. Instead of instituting long-term dependent relationships between therapists and clients, social workers aim to assist clients to become independent and help themselves. The purpose of CBT is to help individuals find their own resources, learn to recognize and use their own wisdom, and discover personal methods for self-help. These are expected to lead them towards greater independence, self-trust and capability for self-change.

References

Achenbach, T. M. (1985) *Assessment and Taxonomy of Child and Adolescent Psychopathology*, Beverly Hills, CA: Sage.

Bandura, A. (1969) *Principles of Behavior Modification*, New York: Holt, Rinehart and Winston.

Bandura, A. (1977) 'Self-efficacy: toward a unifying theory of behavioral change', *Psychological Review*, 84, 191–215.

Beck, A. T., Rush, A. J., Shaw, B. F. and Emery, G. (1979) *Cognitive Therapy of Depression*, New York: Guilford.

Bijou, S. W. (1970) 'What psychology has to offer education – now', *Journal of Applied Behavior Analysis*, 3, 65–71.

Ellis, A. (1973) *Humanistic Psychotherapy: The Rational–Emotive Approach*, New York: McGraw-Hill.

Eysenck, H. J. (1959) 'Learning theory and behavior therapy', *Journal of Mental Science*, 105, 61–75.

Franks, C. M. and Wilson, G. T. (1975) 'Ethical and related issues in behavior therapy', in C. M. Franks and G. T. Wilson (eds), *Annual Review of Behavior Therapy: Theory and Practice*, vol. 3, New York: Brunner/Mazel, pp. 1–11.

Gambrill, E. (1983) *Casework: a Competency Based Approach*, Englewood Cliffs, NJ: Prentice Hall.

Gambrill, E. (1990) *Critical Thinking in Clinical Approach*, San Francisco: Jossey-Bass.

Gambrill, E. D., Thomas, E. J. and Carter, R. D. (1971) 'Procedure for sociobehavioral practice in open settings', *Social Work*, 16, 51–62.

Hersen, M. and Bellack, A. S. (1981) *Behavioral Assessment*, New York: Pergamon.

Hollon, S. D. and Beck, A. T. (1994) 'Cognitive and cognitive–behavioral therapies', in A. E. Bergin and S. L. Garfield (ed.), *Handbook of Psychotherapy and Behavior Change* (4th edn), New York: Wiley, pp. 428–66.

Hughes, J. (1993) 'Behavior therapy', in T. R. Kratochwill and R. J. Morris (eds), *Handbook of Psychotherapy with Children and Adolescents*, Boston: Allyn & Bacon, pp. 181–220.

Kanfer, F. H. and Schefft, B. K. (1988) *Guiding the Process of Therapeutic Change*, Champaign, Il: Research Press.

Kondrat, M. E. (1992) 'Reclaiming the practical: formal and substantive rationality in social work practice', *Social Service Review*, 66, 237–55.

Loewenberg, L. F. (1984) 'Professional ideology, middle range theories and knowledge building for social work practice', *British Journal of Social Work*, 14, 309–22.

Lovaas, O. I. (1967) 'A behavior therapy approach to the treatment of childhood schizophrenia', in J. P. Hill (ed.), *Minnesota Symposium on Child Psychology*, Minneapolis: University of Minnesota Press.

Luria, A. R. (1961) *The Role of Speech in the Regulation of Normal Behaviors*, New York: Liverwright.

Mahoney, M. J. (1993) 'Introduction to special section: theoretical developments in the cognitive psychotherapies', *Journal of Consulting and Clinical Psychology*, 61, 187–93.

Marks, I. (1987) *Fears, Phobias, and Rituals*, New York: Oxford.

O'Leary, K. D. and Wilson, G. T. (1987) *Behavior Therapy: Applications and Outcomes* (2nd edn), Englewood Cliffs, NJ: Prentice Hall.

Pavlov, I. P. (1927) *Conditioning Reflexes*, G. V. Anrep (Trans), New York: Liveright.

Perlman, H. (1953) 'The basic structure of the casework process', *Social Service Review*, 27, 308–15.

Ronen, T. (1994a) 'Clinical intervention with children: challenge for the Social Workers', *Asia Pacific Journal of Social Work*, 4, 7–19.

Ronen, T. (1994b) 'Cognitive–behavioural social work with children', *The British Journal of Social Work*, 24, 273–85.

Ronen, T. (1995a) 'From what kind of self-control can children benefit?', *The Journal of Cognitive Psychotherapy: An International Quarterly*.

Ronen, T. (1995b) 'The social worker as an educator for self-control', *International Social Work*.

Rosenbaum, M. (1990) 'The role of learned resourcefulness in self-control of health behavior', in M. Rosenbaum (ed.), *Learned Resourcefulness: On Coping Skills, Self-Control and Adaptive Behavior*, New York: Springer, pp. 3–30.

Rosenbaum, M. (1993) 'The three functions of self-control behavior: redressive, reformative and experiential', *Journal of Work and Stress*, 7, 33–46.

Safran, J. D. and Segal, Z. V. (1990) *Interpersonal Process in Cognitive Therapy*, New York: Basic Books.

Schinken, S. P. (1981) *Behavioral Methods in Social Welfare*, New York: Adline.

Sheldon, B. (1987) 'Implementing findings from social work effectiveness research', *The British Journal of Social Work*, 17, 573–86.

Skinner, B. F. (1938) *The Behavior of Organism*, New York: Appleton-Century-Crofts.

Thoresen, C. E. and Mahoney, M. J. (1974) *Behavioral Self-Control*, New York: Holt, Rinehart and Winston.

Thorndike, E. L. (1989) Animal intelligence: An experimental study of the associative processes in animal. *Psychological Review, Monograph Supplements, 2.*

Ullman, L. P. and Krasner, L. (ed.) (1965) *Case Studies in Behavior Modification*, New York: Holt, Rinehart and Winston.

Watson, J. B. (1970) *Behaviorism*, New York: Norton.

Wolpe, J. (1982) *The Practice of Behavior Therapy* (3rd edn), New York: Pergamon.

V.6
Networking
Nigel Reigate

The analysis of networking in social support systems has developed, in large part, from systems theory which has gained some significance in writing on social work. In the field of social research and the development of social work theory and practice, a systems approach may be applied to the analysis of 'the complexity of biological, psychological, social and cultural forces at work in the relations between formal social work and informal social support networks' (Garbarino, 1986, p. 24). Network analysis is of significance to social work because it offers a means of examining how people's social networks may act to facilitate coping within communities.

This chapter is concerned with the application of network analysis and networking to social work practice. Before discussing the nature and method of work in this area, a definitive and theoretical background to the issue is called for. Subsequently, methods of network analysis and social work intervention will be outlined.

Background

From an anthropological perspective, a network may be defined as 'a specific set of linkages among a defined set of persons with the additional property that the characteristics of these linkages as a whole may be used to interpret the social behaviour of the persons involved' (Mitchell, 1969, p. 2). In more concrete terms, Seed has defined a network as 'a system or pattern of links between points,

usually shown in a diagram, which have particular meanings . . . In social networks, the points are people, places where people meet or activities that people pursue. The links . . . represent the journeys that people undertake to meet other people, to visit places or engage in activities' (1990, p. 19).

Thus, interpreting social behaviour through attention to social networks has implications for social work practice in that it offers a tool for understanding the social experience of clients from their point of view plus an opportunity to compose a picture of the informal support systems that may or may not be available. Consequently, in terms of social work practice, network analysis may provide frameworks for assessments and reviews including needs-led assessments of clients and carers.

In the context of developing community care policies, which are explicitly concerned with utilizing non-formal resources, network analysis may be seen to offer a means of understanding people's relationships at the local level. Thus, the use of the concept of the social network has significance in the analysis of local links which are 'at the heart of informal care but . . . are also a mainstay of local social relationships. The value of the term "network" lies in avoiding the reification involved in talking about "community" yet enabling one to talk about a wider set of informal relationships than just the family or the extended kin group' (Bulmer, 1987, p. 108).

Much of the recent writing on the

possibilities of social networks in promoting social care originated in the USA. An influential work was *Natural Helping Networks* by Collins and Pancoast (1976) who argued that 'natural networks' could be successfully utilized to complement and support formal caring provision. A key technique in this process is the identification and recruitment, by social workers, of so-called 'central figures' or 'natural neighbours' from local communities. These people are seen as commanding sufficient psychic and emotional resources to enable them to offer support to those who are in need. Central figures may be, for example (albeit stereotypically), home-based women who play significant roles in the lives of their peers. Alternatively, they may be employed in an occupation, for instance of shopkeeper or utility worker, that brings them into regular contact with needy people. Central figures can help the social worker to understand a network of relationships through this process of liaison by the professional with a single individual, and may also be encouraged to widen their social networks to increase their caring capacity. They would bring others into contact, as appropriate, with the helping services or may fulfil the helping role themselves. A key role for the social worker here is to support the central figure in continuing to operate without the fear or danger of depleting her own emotional or physical resources, to remain 'free from drain'.

A key statement on the development of social work in the UK was the Barclay Report which propounded the necessity of recognizing the role played by informal carers, mutual aid groups and volunteers in the provision of social welfare to local communities. Besides the 'traditional' social work tasks of counselling and casework with individuals and families, the report proposed that social workers should engage in ameliorative and preventive work in communities which are defined as 'local networks of formal

Five Key Points

1 Network analysis offers a way of exploring how people's social networks operate in ways that help or hamper their ability to cope in the community.

2 Natural networks can be used to complement and support formal caring provision.

3 A client's network might include close relatives, neighbours and friends, voluntary helpers, people with similar problems (as might be found in self-help groups) and members of formal organizations like churches or trade associations.

4 Helping clients keep a structured diary of their daily contacts is a useful way of carrying out a network analysis. This can be used to make a needs-led assessment that will, in turn, inform the social worker's practice.

5 Network analysis can be of particular value for the social worker charged with the task of helping people with learning disabilities (or other clients) move into community living after a long period in hospital or institutional care.

and informal relationships, together with their capacity to mobilise individual and collective responses to adversity' (Barclay/NISW, 1982, p. xiii). Social workers and their agencies are thus exhorted to create, stimulate and support networks in the community. Correspondingly, social networks are to have 'ready access to statutory and voluntary services and to contribute their experience to decisions on how the resources contributed by these services are used within their community' (ibid., p. 202). Thus, in partnership with informal caring resources, social workers are advised to turn their attention to individuals and families within the context of all the networks of which they are part. The report suggests three ways in which social workers may approach a variety of networks. Firstly, they should identify those contacts who comprise the most important people in a client's experience 'whether they consist of five people or a hundred, whether they are local or more distant, based on relationships in leisure time or at work' (ibid., p. 206). Secondly, a focus on actual or potential links between people who live in the same geographical area, residential home or hospital or who attend the same day centre could be used by social workers to understand and promote relationships between people who have spent time together and between them and people in the locality. Thirdly, social workers should consider developing networks amongst those who share similar interests and concerns, for example, parents of disabled children. The report goes on to suggest that comparing 'the first with the other two viewpoints may suggest possibilities for enriching individual networks' (ibid.).

The mantle of utilizing informal caring resources was taken up by Griffiths and subsequently reflected in the rhetoric of government pronouncements on community care. It was proposed that local authorities should 'arrange the delivery of packages of care, building first on the available contribution of informal carers and neighbourhood support' (Griffiths, 1988, p. 1). Such proposals were incorporated into the NHS and Community Care Act, 1990. Thus, community care principles, by definition including a concern with informal social networks, were appropriated by a government that had a market-orientated and *laisser-faire* agenda for welfare provision.

Despite the claims made for the constructive application of network analysis to social work and the subsequent utilization of social networks in practice, a number of reservations emerge. Social workers should respond very cautiously to pressures to use alternatives to formal provision especially at a time when financial and other resources are being curtailed and agencies may be looking for cheaper options for the provision of care and support for vulnerable people in the community. The absolute obligation of the state and local authorities to provide a welfare system that aims to increase equality and improve the social functioning and freedom of vulnerable people remains. However, a service that operates to complement rather than replace statutory provision by invoking community-based support systems would seem to be appropriate (see, for example, Olsen, 1986; Timms, 1983).

Networking has a number of implications for social work management and policy especially in the area of developing organizational structures (see, for example, Olsen, 1986). However, the concern here is with networking as a method in social work and, at this stage, a brief examination of some types of social networks is called for.

Types of Social Networks

For helping professionals to work with social networks, they should develop an awareness of the types of networks that exist as well as of the role that they play in the experience of their participants. Additionally, an awareness of the communities (geographical or otherwise) in which clients live is called for, especially when considering existing needs and assessing the opportunities for the development of new forms of community support. As Froland and others (1981) have argued (cited in Bulmer, 1987), employing the concept of networking in analysing social relationships highlights the structure of participants' relationships plus the exchanges between them and the roles that they play. A number of strategies are thus suggested that may be useful in building upon social networks:

(1)   Social workers may build upon the personal links of clients, for instance with kin or neighbours, involving them in solving clients' problems and, where appropriate, may work to expand their supportive social circle.

(2)   Where there is limited personal support for clients, workers may aim to link them up with volunteers who have requisite skills and/or experience of the problems faced. For instance, such a strategy may be invoked to provide one-to-one support for clients who are leaving long-term residential care or who could gain from having an advocate when applying for benefits or in addressing housing issues.

(3)   Professionals may work to bring together those who have similar experiences or problems. Informal mutual aid networks may thus be formed, aimed at developing further sources of support and at the sharing of knowledge. They may also be invoked to build upon existing community-based support systems. Mutual aid networks may be used, for example, to promote social integration amongst people leaving psychiatric care, offering mutual support whilst avoiding feelings of stigma or dependency (Bulmer, 1987). Additionally, such 'artificial networks' (Collins and Pancoast, 1976) may, for example, serve to link up and promote mutual support amongst the carers of physically or learning disabled adults or children. As Collins and Pancoast argue, the aim is to 'create artificial systems that will go on to function as natural systems' (Collins and Pancoast, p. 65). Moreover, they may develop to operate at a local neighbourhood level or may be regional or national, examples being the Carers' National Association and local Carers Forums, being established and run by and

for those whom they aim to support. Professionals in formal caring agencies may use such networks as a resource on behalf of their clients, may refer clients directly to them, may act as consultants to them or may consult them as appropriate for feedback on service provision and development.

(4)   Reflecting the focus upon mutual aid within geographically based helping networks in the work of Collins and Pancoast, professionals can aim to identify and build upon existing local networks, for example of neighbours or communities of concern to promote social functioning and organization. This may be seen to be especially appropriate for

---

Three Questions

1   In what way might social work intervention damage a client's social networks?
2   What kind of social work skills are necessary for good networking?
3   Is the social worker outside the client's network, or is she a part of it? What are the implications of this?

---

promoting the welfare of certain client groups, such as disabled people living in the community. Thus workers may, through identification of and interaction with a number of central figures within a neighbourhood, facilitate engagement with needy members of the wider community.

(5)   Leaning towards the area of community work, groups may be formed that are aimed at addressing local needs through the articulation of the requirements and wishes of those members of a community who share related problems or concerns. Obviously, the focus of this kind of work is more explicitly political and would involve members of the community working with

a range of formal and informal groupings such as voluntary organizations, trade unions and church groups as well as formal agencies. Examples of this type of networking may be found in locally based initiatives aiming to secure improved child care or play facilities. The thrust of such moves is to campaign for improved formal provision and to demonstrate how it may be interwoven with the activities of community-based networks.

Thus, the concept of social network provides a means for understanding the complex informal links within a given geographical community or community of concern. It also offers the social worker a set of tools for planning the interweaving of formal and informal welfare provision. The following section will be aimed towards outlining some possible models of network analysis.

Network Analysis and Social Work

A key component of the social worker's task is to become aware of the perceptions of clients and to consider how social networks may act to facilitate (or obstruct) coping. Additionally, assessment of the consequences for informal networks of formal intervention is called for. Indeed, a further concern of social work is with people's interactions with their social environment and the way in which this operates to enhance or curtail their opportunities and functioning, 'it behoves social workers not only to attend to those personal characteristics of clients which affect coping, but also to the social contexts which will have a bearing . . . on the outcome of tackling life tasks' (Timms, 1983, p. 409). Thus, network analysis may offer a number of insights. Timms (1983) suggests three levels of analysing the relationship between individuals and their environments and the following part

of the discussion is guided by her analysis.

Firstly, at the *micro* level, which comprises people's more personal peer relationships, research demonstrates that 'maladaptive responses to stress are significantly inhibited by the existence of social support' (ibid.). Appropriate strategies for intervention will be based upon rigorous assessment of clients within the context of their social networks. Application of network analysis at this level of social interaction may offer additional insights into the social forces that bear upon a person's functioning whilst not necessarily challenging the more 'traditional' casework relationship between social workers and individual clients.

Secondly, at the *mezzo* level, networks are examined in terms of issues of access to resources and social functioning. Where there is a high level of interconnectedness, there is a reduced need for members to seek external support, with the network acting as a 'forceful reference group' (ibid.), serving to inhibit behaviour that does not conform to network norms whilst also providing a high level of internal support. Consequently, members of close-knit networks may be reluctant to invoke external resources, even when they may improve things for them. Collins and Pancoast's concept of central figures would seem to be of some relevance here. Such people, if identified, may serve as links between members of close-knit networks and external sources of support and aid. In this way, by reference to one or more identified individuals, the social worker could work to build such links as are appropriate.

Thirdly, at the *macro* level, the focus is upon the relationship between people and more formal community organizations such as voluntary and political groupings, clubs and societies etc. Whilst it is important to understand that information regarding such resources is no substitute for gaining an insight into the complexity of relationships within the community, a grasp of the provisions available at this level of community functioning (plus means of access to them) is an essential part of the social worker's repertoire.

In more concrete terms, Seed (1990) proposes a set of methods of social network analysis and considers a number of specific applications. The networks with which social workers are concerned will be focused on the relationships between clients and helping agencies in the context of their day-to-day social and individual lives. The networking social worker should strive to understand the communities in which clients live in the context of the changes that they have undergone or are currently experiencing. An understanding of the specific social realities faced by different groups of clients, for instance physically disabled people and their families, is also called for. A further way of using social networks in the course of social work intervention is to work to develop the client's own network potential, that is her ability to make new contacts. To understand how people leaving long-term hospital care, for example, make new friends it is necessary to understand the nature of the social networks they were part of in hospital. Networking should be aimed towards understanding clients' previous experiences of networks as well as their present patterns of living in order to assess how they may be able to extend and build upon existing networks and how they may be best supported in linking up with resources in their neighbourhoods.

In terms of networking method, Seed suggests that clients should be encouraged to record their daily lives using structured diaries. It is recommended that a standardized format is designed for this purpose, incorporating a structure that is informed by what is already known about the general patterns of a specific client group's day: for instance, of the experience of people in hospital or of people with a specified disability living in the community. It is suggested that diaries for adults are kept for a fortnight; for children, for a week. Sometimes clients will require support from others in keeping their diaries and when this is the case, it is important to understand the extent of the support required to ensure that it is the client who is the focus of the diary. A key role of the social worker in facilitating the keeping of such a diary is to help the client to clarify uncertainties and ambiguities and to pick up on likely omissions.

The social worker then embarks upon a follow-up procedure with the client. This, again, may be done using a standardized format or schedule. After examining the diaries, the social worker asks the client about the three most important activities engaged in and/or places visited during the diary period and the reasons for their salience. Similar questions are asked regarding the three most important people in the client's life. The follow-up schedule is usually completed by the social worker, in consultation with the client, sometimes with the support person present, and, in appropriate circumstances, may be completed solely by the client.

A number of other schedules may be used to collate further information about 'features of performance' regarding self-

Further Reading

1   Bulmer, M. (1987) *The Social Basis of Community Care*, London: Allen and Unwin.
2   Seed, P. (1990) *Introducing Network Analysis in Social Work*, London: Jessica Kingsley.
3   Trevillion, S. (1992) *Caring in the Community: a Networking Approach to Community Partnership*, Harlow: Longman.

management skills, daily living skills and social skills in order to unearth any problems or issues in each area of functioning and to indicate what support may be needed plus any implications for resource planning and provision. Note is taken of any progress made or significant changes that have occurred.

A summary of progress in such areas as home management, social functioning and communication and general confidence is now produced. This is accompanied by an open-ended question to the client regarding what she feels she has learnt over a specified period, for instance, learning to address a particular task or a general increase in confidence. A further open-ended question is asked regarding any lack of progress.

The next step is for the social worker to draw the networks in diagram form using information from the diary and schedules. A standardized layout is recommended for this and figure V.6.1 outlines the main information components of network analysis.

The information thus gleaned about the client and her life may be summarized for use in case recording or may contribute towards the monitoring of resources and their take-up over a period of time. It may also provide a viable tool for use in referral processes to help social workers to reflect on the meaning of the situation

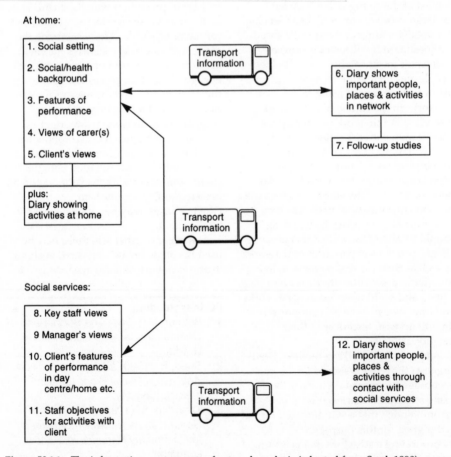

Figure V.6.1 The information components of network analysis (adapted from Seed, 1990)

for the client and also for future reference. Additionally, network analyses will clearly have some significance in field-work assessments and reviews.

Applications

The concluding part of this discussion will be aimed at outlining the application of networking as a social work method. For the sake of illustration, a particular focus will be upon work with clients who are in the process of leaving long-term hospital care.

The maintaining of diaries and the subsequent compilation and use of network diagrams may be seen to be salient in supporting people leaving extended hospital care and entering independent living situations.

Prior to discharge, the use of a form of diary that makes a distinction between activities in hospital is suggested by Seed (1990). This should differentiate between activities on the ward, activities inside the hospital outside the ward setting, and those outside the hospital. Clients should be encouraged to participate in the upkeep of diaries but may need some support in this. If this is the case, and if the relationship with the client is suitably close, the social worker may perform this role, otherwise the diary support worker may be a member of the nursing staff or a friend or relative of the client. Moreover, the client should be encouraged to dictate the diary's contents.

Features of performance schedules will then be compiled. Any social skills or other training that has been undertaken will be discussed with the client and its relevance considered; staff perspectives regarding progress will also be canvassed.

Network analysis may be used to map the patterns and significance of the relationships that have been established by a client whilst in long-term care. It may be of benefit, in certain circumstances, if clients could move towards independence (by means of group patient plans, for example) with friends that they have already made and network analysis would seem to offer a means of addressing this.

Additionally, network analysis may be utilized as a framework for incorporating the feelings and needs, not only of the client, but also of those who are likely to take on the role of carer. It may also serve, alongside suitable advocacy input, to aid the client in asserting her independence and articulating her views through the identification, assessment and encouragement of appropriate sources of support within the community.

Network analysis may serve to facilitate a programme for individual and group development and the articulation of specific and more general goals. It can also be used to assess a client's progress and network potential by examining her interactions with peers and members of wider social networks. Essentially, the method of application should be underpinned by a sound awareness, on the part of the social worker, of the dynamics of the community as well as of the past, present and potential network experiences of clients.

Atkinson (1986) records the findings of a study of a group of learning disabled people moving from long-stay hospital care towards independent living situations, largely in minimum support groups with a small number of peers, and considers their support networks. They coped with life in the community by engaging 'competent others', members of the locality to 'supplement, sometimes to supplant' (p. 83) their formal carers. The study also found that most achieved a stable network which provided support throughout a range of life's ups and downs. The part played by the social worker varied between groups but was significant in each, fulfilling roles of counsellor, mediator in disputes, co-planner, advocate, etc. People with learning disabilities moving into community living after long periods in hospital care need a significant level of support. Their learning disability could itself mean that they have a limited understanding of some necessary living skills. Additionally, the routines and hierarchies of hospital care may leave them unprepared for less structured forms of living and the move into the wider community could itself cut them off from many of their established social networks at a time when they must build new ones. Thus, a primary task for them is to 'begin to forge these new links, to engage those "competent others" into a personalised support network' (Atkinson, 1986, p. 84). 'Competent others' are non-disabled members of the locality such as friends, neighbours and acquaintances such as shopkeepers, postal workers, etc. and may be seen to parallel Collins' and Pancoast's concept of 'central figures'. However, whilst Collins and Pancoast suggested that these people would be recruited by social workers on the strength of their strong internal resources, 'competent others' were recruited by the clients themselves. It is arguable that social workers could work with clients through these people in the way that Collins and Pancoast prescribe, despite the fact that they *may* not possess the qualities that are called for. They will, though, have the trust of the client and, if willing and able, may serve as useful channels for formal caring support.

In conclusion, then, social workers can usefully act to aid clients to build supportive networks through consultation with clients, role modelling and introductions to appropriate people. The social worker can help to maintain networks by means of practical support, resource allocation, advocacy and mediation, etc. However, it is worth repeating that informal community-based networks must never be used to paper over the cracks in grossly under-funded structures of formal welfare provision.

References

Atkinson, D. (1986) 'Engaging competent others: a study of the support networks of people with mental handicap', *British Journal of Social Work*, 16, Supplement, 33–101.

Barclay/NISW (1982) *Social Workers: their Role and Tasks*, London: Bedford Square Press/NCVO/NISW.

Bulmer, M. (1987) *The Social Basis of Community Care*, London: Allen and Unwin.

Collins, A. H. and Pancoast, D. L. (1976) *Natural Helping Networks: a Strategy for Prevention*, Washington: NASW.

Froland, C., Pancoast, D. L., Chapman, N. J. and Kimboko, P. J. (1981) *Helping Networks and Human Services*, Beverly Hill: Sage.

Garbarino, J. (1986) 'Where does social support fit into optimizing human development and preventing dysfunction?' *British Journal of Social Work*, 16, Supplement, 23–37.

The Griffiths Report (1988) *Community Care: Agenda for Action*, London: HMSO.

Mitchell, J. C. (1969) 'The concept and use of social networks' in J. C. Mitchell (ed.) *Social Networks in Urban Situations*, Manchester: University of Manchester Press.

Olsen, M. R. (1986) 'Integrating formal and informal social care', *British Journal of Social Work*, 16, Supplement, 15–22.

Seed, P. (1990) *Introducing Network Analysis in Social Work*, London: Jessica Kingsley.

Timms, E. (1983) 'On the relevance of informal social networks to social work intervention', *British Journal of Social Work*, 13, 405–15.

Groupwork
Allan Brown

Groupwork is recognized as a mainstream method of social work practice because it offers different kinds of opportunities from those available in other approaches, for example in work with individuals, and family work. It also has some problematic aspects which may explain why it is not always used as widely and consistently by agencies and workers as might be expected. We therefore need to understand what groupwork can offer and how the extent and quality of its use is affected by four key variables: the context, small group dynamics, the individual group member and the groupworker's role and skills.

Theoretical understanding about small group behaviour has been strongly influenced by social psychologists (Cartwright and Zander, 1968). Their work has, for example, taught us about the effects of group size and composition, the stages of development in the life of a group, the 'leadership style' of the worker(s), and the powerful ways in which individuals can be influenced by their peers. Sociologists have stressed the importance of the influence of social context and structural factors on behaviour in the small group, and psychodynamic and behavioural theorists contribute understanding of the individual group member in the group (Yalom, 1985; Rose, 1978).

Building on these theoretical foundations, and equally on the grounded experience of groupworkers and group members, social groupwork has developed in the last 30 years towards becoming a discipline in its own right. There is now a considerable groupwork literature on both sides of the Atlantic (e.g., UK: Heap, 1985; Whitaker, 1985; Brown, 1992; USA: Konopka, 1983; Shulman, 1984; Garvin, 1987), which is being supplemented increasingly by contributions from all over the world. The establishment of two groupwork journals (*Social Work with Groups* 1978–; *Groupwork* 1988–) has been a critical factor, not least in model building and the articulation of practice developments.

A continuing issue – especially in the USA – is whether or not groupwork is best regarded as a separate social work discipline requiring specialization both in training and in practice. The current approach in the 1990s in Britain continues to favour a generic methodology with some specialization, but it may be that the trend towards purchasing specialist services for different categories of service user is also creating a demand for method specialists.

Groupwork applies to the whole range of ways in which the small group can be instrumental in the achievement of social work purposes. Thus the aims, agendas and methods of groupwork are as diverse and ubiquitous as those of social work itself. We can, however, identify some of the distinguishing characteristics:

Being with others who in at least one important respect associated with group purpose are similar to oneself

This feature offers myriad opportunities for sharing, learning, supporting, challenging, joint action, role-modelling, relationship building and so on. A common fear in groups is of labelling and shared stigma, and of being 'taken over' by others. This can happen, but the fascinating paradox is that for many the first time they find themselves as an individual with their own identity is when they are in a group with similar others. In the family each person's identity is largely defined by the family group system, as usually there is no one in the same position with whom that individual can make a direct comparison. In the one-to-one relationship of service user and social worker, the inherent role and power differences set limits to self-definition.

The opportunity for individual empowerment, and growth in self-esteem and self-confidence

The opportunity to be a 'helper' as well as a 'helped', and to get positive feedback and support from one's peers – as well as the worker – creates the conditions for personal growth and development. Dependence, whether on family, agencies or drugs, disempowers. In a group an ethos of interdependence can enhance personal empowerment and self-esteem. Many group members have internalized the oppression they have experienced in the wider society; and in a peer group – say of other women, or other disabled people – they can begin to relieve themselves of that burden and put it back where it belongs in the oppressive social structures from which it derives.

The opportunity for change

The power and collectivity of the group creates options for change. These may be for individuals to change their behaviour/feelings/attitudes, for a group to take on a change of direction, or for action to be taken to change things external to the group, perhaps in the neighbourhood or in the way services are being delivered.

A resource for learning

The personal learning opportunities in groups are extensive. Whilst didactic teaching has a limited place in social groupwork, the essence is what emerges from the social interaction between members and between members and workers. Skills can be rehearsed in the safety of the group, and a rich resource of ideas and advice can be offered by other members who face similar life stresses, which may not be in the experience of professional workers or other family members.

What then are the factors which determine whether a group can be established, and if it is, whether it can create optimum conditions for the realization of its potential? To explore this question we return to what we earlier described as 'the four key variables'.

Context

The importance of context cannot be overstated. Overshadowing everything else is the prevailing *socio-economic-political* climate. This impacts in some obvious and many less obvious ways. It determines the allocation of resources to agencies and to individuals; it shapes prevailing values and attitudes and it determines the distribution of wealth and power. The less obvious impact stems from the group itself being a social microcosm of the wider society (Brown and Mistry, 1994). Social attitudes, relative status and the oppression and discrimination experienced by certain populations, will be imported into the group as a major influence on process – unless or until countervailing steps are taken.

The *agency* itself is a powerful influence on both the extent to which groupwork is encouraged and resourced, and in determining the purposes it is expected to achieve – be these control, change, empowerment or learning. Contrast agency influence on a probation group for violent offenders with that on a community group for adult survivors of sexual abuse.

The *setting* of the group can have a profound effect on what happens. This includes its physical location, and whether there is adequate space and comfort. Group living settings in day and residential establishments affect every group and grouping all the time because the participants – particularly in residential care – experience a whole range of organized and informal group contexts, each affecting and being affected by the others (Brown and Clough, 1989).

The *community* from which the group membership is drawn is another contextual factor. This may be a community of interest (as in a group for those with an alcohol problem or a carers group), or a neighbourhood/locality community. In each instance the culture and ethos associated with that particular community will be imported into the group, and the exported impact of the group will be mediated by the environment.

The agency and the workers have to try and create a facilitative environment for groupwork practice. Whether or not they do so may make all the difference between 'success' and 'failure' of a groupwork programme. Some agencies regard groupwork as a peripheral rather than a mainstream method of service delivery. This attitude is sometimes associated with an individualistic orientation, and/or apprehension that group power may become a threat to managerial control. From the group members' perspective, both kinds of communities develop 'received wisdom' about the positive or negative value of local group services.

Five Key Points

1 The small group is a social microcosm, and is likely to replicate patterns of social inequality, unless countervailing steps are taken.

2 The essence of groupwork is how the social interaction between group members is harnessed to the achievement of group purpose.

3 Groupwork is a uniquely empowering method of social work because all are potential 'helpers' as well as 'helped'.

4 Groups are powerful instruments for change, whether of individuals, groups or environments.

5 Four key variables influence what a group can offer: context, group dynamics, the individual members and the worker's role and skills.

The Small Group

There are many ways in which a group forms; it may form spontaneously as some self-help groups do, it may be part of an agency programme of groups, or it may be due to the initiative of an individual worker and/or their team, or to pressure from service users. The members may have joined freely, or there may be a degree of coercion and involuntary membership. There may be a careful, long, drawn-out planning process, or the group may form very quickly with little or no period of preparation. Whatever the history of a group's creation, the subsequent group process will be affected by it.

Research confirms personal experience that the size and composition of a group has a big impact on group process (Bertcher and Maple, 1977; Brown, 1992, pp. 46–55). In larger groups, some individuals will get 'lost' unless the group is structured to ensure participation by all. Redl's 'law of optimum distance' (1951), that groups should be 'homogeneous enough to ensure stability, and heterogeneous to ensure vitality', is still a useful guide to optimum group composition. However in practice this often cannot be achieved, and the group then needs to take steps to compensate for an 'unbalanced membership'. This may mean, for example, ensuring that any individual who is in a minority (perhaps being the only black member) is actively supported and helped to avoid isolation/marginalization, and to get as much benefit from the group as that enjoyed by 'majority' members.

Every group functions at both the task level (what the group aims to achieve) and the process level (the feelings and relationships that develop between the people in the group). Sometimes group process takes over to the detriment of task, as in protracted conflict between two members; sometimes the group is so task-focused that personal feelings of members get ignored. Neither of these is healthy for group development which requires effective group maintenance work to reinforce and sustain the task.

Theorists have identified various models to describe the stages of development of a group (Tuckman, 1965), and some also suggest the corresponding tasks of the worker and the group to navigate successfully the particular stage characteristics through which the group is passing (Henry, 1992). These models reduce to linear, spiral and cyclical in basic format. Groups with open and therefore changing membership are particularly likely to have uneven patterns of development as membership changes and re-forming is needed.

Most groups negotiate 'ground rules' to set the basis on which members agree to work together within the overall contract and purpose. These 'rules' typically refer to such issues as confidentiality, equal treatment and participation for all, opting out and anti-discriminatory practice. In some groups the agency itself sets ground rules which apply to all agency activities, for example, no violence, no racism, no sexism.

The small group is a dynamic system in which whatever happens in any part of it, needs to be understood in the context of the group as a whole (and the external context). A group perspective is therefore essential for the worker and for group members if they are to understand what is happening and to respond positively. Shulman (1984) examines this individual/group relationship, and some of the roles in which members find themselves.

Another dimension is the means by which the group attempts to carry out the task and achieve its aims. This usually includes talking, but may include a whole range of activities like artwork, role-play, games, exercises, going places, telling stories and inviting visitors.

The time-frame of a group needs to relate to the purpose, varying from a block of a few days for an intensive experience, to single meetings once a month perhaps for a support group.

The Individual Member

The first group most of us experience is in the family – or equivalent – group(s) we are part of as a young child. It seems likely that the kind of roles we experience in that formative grouping sets an initial expectation of role-taking in subsequent groups. Thus the family 'scapegoat', 'isolate', 'internal leader' or 'mediator' may find themselves unconsciously taking that kind of role-expectation into peer groups at school and in 'formed groups' at work and leisure activities. Equally if not more influential, will be the structurally determined oppression and marginalization many experience because of their sex, the colour of their skin, their disability or their sexual orientation.

An individual thus enters a group with a whole range of expectations based on these earlier and current experiences, combined with whether they have joined voluntarily and enthusiastically or under some form of duress. It can be a great relief when entering a new group to find someone you already know (unless of course they are someone you would rather not have met again!), or at least someone who seems rather like yourself and with whom you experience a feeling of rapport. On the other hand, some group members prefer 'stranger' groups because this both protects confidentiality about the past, and offers more freedom of choice of behaviour and role-taking in the group.

Groups which develop a caring and collective ethos, offer many opportunities to individuals both psychologically (for example to increase self-confidence and self-esteem), and in practical ways (new ideas and ways of solving practical problems and difficulties). Group support and solidarity can also be a great source of strength. By contrast, groups can be destructive and disempowering for an individual. Someone may leave a group with more difficulties than those they faced on entry. This points out the special responsibility the groupworker has to help create a facilitative environment and group culture.

perspective of worker-as-facilitator. This latter role conceptualizes the worker as the person not who runs the group, but who helps the group to run itself.

Different models of groupwork suggest very different roles for the worker. In group psychotherapy the worker is leader and holds much of the expertise (Yalom, 1985). In social action groupwork, the worker's task is to help the members identify external objectives which they then tackle collectively (Mullender and Ward, 1991). In mainstream social groupwork (Papell and Rothman, 1980) the assumption is that whilst the worker may start the group as 'central person', their task is to move out of that role as the group members gradually take

---

Three Questions

1 What kind of balance needs to be struck between task and process for effective groupwork?
2 What are the prerequisites of empowering anti-oppressive groupwork?
3 What particular demands does groupwork make on the workers' 'use of self'?

The Worker(s)

Working with a group is, by definition, more complicated than working with one other person. There is the need to relate simultaneously to each individual and to the group as a whole, not to mention keeping a firm eye on the task. It is easy to lose sight of task or process or group or individual or some individuals. For this reason, among others, it is commonplace in Britain to have more than one worker (Hodge, 1985) to share all these facets. Co-working has its advantages and disadvantages and is discussed below. However the apparently daunting task of the worker when seen from the perspective of worker-as-leader, looks rather different when seen from the

responsibility for the running of their group. The choice of model obviously depends in part on the type of group and membership, but a core value in social groupwork is that all group members, whatever the extent of any personal difficulty or impairment, have it within them to contribute to group development and goal achievement.

A qualification to a value-base of empowerment applies to groups whose primary function is to work with the perpetrators of harm to others – and/or themselves – where the aim is to try and change behaviour to protect others. For example, it is well established that many sex offenders have no intrinsic motivation to change their behaviour. Left to their own group devices they might simply reinforce each other's offensive and offending behaviour. The worker in this type of group needs a much more controlling challenging role, although ultimately the individual himself still has to develop some personal motivation for change to be effective.

The groupworker needs both process and task skills, and an understanding of how the former can facilitate the latter. She or he also needs to have a clear understanding of the issues of power – including their own – which affect group process and the behaviour of group members. This includes the conscious use of role modelling of group and personal behaviour. For example, if the worker expects members to be frank and open, then he or she needs to role-model this behaviour by being appropriately open and self-disclosing.

Co-working is a highly skilled activity in its own right (Hodge, 1985). Working together effectively with another person first requires checking out for mutual compatability and a shared approach to the forthcoming group. Lack of careful preparation of the co-working relationship can lead to all kinds of confusion in the group, and failure to provide the safe environment which many groups need, and which the members are entitled to expect. Co-working is an opportunity to model an equal relationship, which is particularly important when the social expectation may be of an unequal relationship, say between a man and woman or a white and black person.

Self-help groups do not, by definition, have a designated worker. Leadership may be shared by the group as a collective, or individual members may be given specific roles – for example, chairperson or convenor – by the group, perhaps on a rotation basis. 'Workerless' groups have all the properties of groups generally, which may include dynamics which are disempowering and

marginalizing for some members. Thus people who are not used to being in small groups – whether self-help or worker-led – need help in learning about group dynamics and how to manage themselves as group members. Workers who are experienced in groups can easily underestimate how intimidating being in a group may be to those new to groups and groupwork.

Some Groupwork Issues

Three issues among those common to groups and groupworkers will now be considered.

Package versus process

A fundamental question in any group is how much to plan before it starts, and how much to let the 'programme' evolve as the group develops. The answer obviously depends in part on the type of group and the aims. Groups with a strong educational purpose, for example a social skills or alcohol education group, often have a largely predetermined programme. However, a fundamental of social groupwork is what Papell and Rothman (1980) were referring to when they said 'spontaneous and meaningfully evolving group processes are the instrumental means for realising group purpose' (p. 8). This cannot be achieved if the content and method of the group is largely determined beforehand by the worker(s).

This issue is becoming increasingly important as groupwork 'packages' become very popular. They are popular with agencies because they are tangible and fit the prevailing ethos of competencies and the contract culture. They are popular with stressed practitioners because they provide a ready-made resource for running a group, requiring minimal preparation time and effort. They may even be quite popular with some group members because they take away much of their own membership responsibility.

However, packages put severe limits on the rich resource of social groupwork which is what is generated by the interaction between the members. Furthermore, there is a real danger that the 'package' approach is not responsive to the needs of group members. They are being fitted into the method, rather than the method being responsive to them – a not unfamiliar scenario in social work generally. There is, however, a middle way, which is to use packages as an available resource to be drawn on flexibly and creatively as the needs arise. Group members themselves can express an opinion on what they would prefer and find most helpful.

An anti-oppressive empowering approach to groupwork

As indicated earlier, small groups are a microcosm of the wider society from which the membership is drawn. They will tend to replicate those inequalities of power, status and influence that are prevalent in the external community and social institutions. Thus group members will tend to give higher status to members who are middle class, white, male, heterosexual and without physical or learning disabilities. Those who are working class, black, female, lesbian/gay or with a disability, may experience stereotyping and active discrimination in the group, similar to what they experience outside.

These oppressive phenomena pose a challenge to the groupworker and the group members, raising questions about group composition and group skills. For some purposes, particularly those associated with personal identity, discrimination and the raising of self-esteem, a homogeneous group confined to those who share the same oppression will often be the preferred option. Lee

(1991) has written about an empowerment group for disadvantaged and disempowered black women, which aims both to relieve their internal oppression, and to generate group strength to tackle external disempowering institutions such as housing agencies.

In practice, for all sorts of reasons, groups will often not be homogeneous, and will require the active use of deliberate strategies and skills to counteract inequality and oppression. Brown and Mistry (1994) make some suggestions, including having a clear explicit value-base and ground rules, and being ready to respond actively to any unacceptable behaviour in the group.

The worker's use of self

How a social worker uses herself or himself as a person is probably more significant than any other aspect of their knowledge and skills. Personal and professional selves cannot – and in my view should not – be wholly separated. This applies whatever the setting and method, and particularly in groupwork where workers are in a minority, and often under pressure to be 'one of the group'. For example, in exercises where group members are expected to share something personal, the groupworker has to decide whether or not to join in and do likewise. If they always decline they distance themselves from the members; if they participate in everything as though a

---

Further Reading

1   Brown, A. (1992) *Groupwork* (3rd edn), Aldershot: Ashgate.
2   Mullender, A. and Ward, D. (1991) *Self-Directed Groupwork: Users take Action for Empowerment*, London: Whiting & Birch.
3   *Groupwork* Journal. Published three times a year by Whiting & Birch Ltd (P.O. Box 872, London SE23 3HL).

member they risk moving out of the
worker role. Neither of these options may
be helpful to the group. The skill lies in
being secure enough to disclose personal
matters when this is likely to be helpful,
whilst retaining the distinct worker role
of assisting group members to achieve
their individual and group goals.

Conclusion

Groupwork is the 'natural' social work
method for empowering practice because
it is predicated on the strengths and
active contribution of every individual
group member. It has a firm theoretical
and research base to support it, and has
much to offer to both members and
workers. It is also a potentially radical
approach when group members are given
full reign to determine the nature and
scope of 'their' group.

References

Bertcher, H. and Maple, F. (1977) *Creating Groups*,
London: Sage.

Brown, A. (1992) *Groupwork* (3rd edn), Aldershot:
Ashgate.

Brown, A. and Clough, R. (eds) (1989) *Groups and
Groupings: Life and Work in Day and Residential
Centres*, London and New York:
Tavistock/Routledge.

Brown, A. and Mistry, T. (1994) 'Groupwork with
"mixed" membership groups: issues of race and
gender', *Social Work with Groups*, 17(3), 5–21.

Cartwright, D. and Zander, A. (eds) (1968) *Group
Dynamics: Research and Theory*, New York: Harper
& Row.

Garvin, C. (1987) *Contemporary Groupwork* (2nd edn),
Englewood Cliffs, NJ: Prentice-Hall.

Groupwork Journal, London: Whiting & Birch.

Heap, K. (1985) *The Practice of Social Work with Groups*,
London: Allen and Unwin.

Henry, S. (1992) *Group Skills in Social Work* (2nd edn),
Pacific Grove, CA: Brooks/Cole Publishing.

Hodge, J. (1985) *Planning for Co-Leadership*, Grapevine,
43, Fern Avenue, Newcastle-upon-Tyne.

Konopka, G. (1983) *Social Groupwork: a Helping Process*
(3rd edn), Englewood Cliffs, NJ: Prentice-Hall.

Lee, J. (1991) 'Empowerment through mutual aid
groups: a practice grounded practice framework',
Groupwork, 4(1), 5–21.

Mullender, A. and Ward, D. (1991) *Self-Directed
Groupwork: Users Take Action for Empowerment*,
London: Whiting & Birch.

Papell, C. and Rothman, B. (1980) 'Relating the
mainstream model of social work with groups to
group psychotherapy and the structured group',
Social Work with Groups, 3(2), 5–23.

Redl, F. (1951) 'Art of group composition', in S.
Shulze (ed.), *Creative Living in a Children's
Institution*, New York: Association Press.

Rose, S. (1978) *Group Therapy: a Behavioural Approach*,
Englewood Cliffs, NJ: Prentice-Hall.

Shulman, L. (1984) *The Skills of Helping: Individuals and
Groups* (2nd edn), USA: F. E. Peacock.

Social Work with Groups, New York: Haworth Press.

Tuckman, B. W. (1965) 'Development sequence in
small groups', *Psychological Bulletin*, 63(6), 384–99.

Whitaker, D. (1985) *Using Groups to Help People*,
London: Routledge & Kegan Paul.

Yalom, I. (1985) *The Theory and Practice of Group
Psychotherapy* (2nd edn), New York: Basic Books.

Psychoanalytic Theory
Jack Nathan

Psychoanalysis has declined dramatically as a source of knowledge in social work. It is seen as irrelevant to the dilemmas and conflicts faced by mainstream practitioners in their everyday work. This view needs challenging.

I begin with the assumption that for the insights of psychoanalysis to be of use to social work, a distinction has to be drawn between social work practice informed by psychoanalysis and the practice of psychoanalysis. In the past a psychoanalytic orientation appeared to invite social workers to 'do therapy' which not only failed to meet the key criterion of relevance, it also left workers feeling inadequate to the task. It all seemed too much for the beleaguered social worker in addition to the myriad other legal and administrative requirements of the job.

As a way of coping with these escalating demands, the profession adopted a managerialist approach in the ultimately vain hope that practice issues could be resolved by check-list social work. This is not to decry procedures. They are fundamental to a profession rooted in a bureaucracy that requires that rational, fair and explicit guidelines are evolved.

The danger is that such an approach suggests that the complex, anxiety-provoking problems that confront social workers daily can be solved by 'following procedures'. Howe (1992) has claimed that as a result of the critical reports into child deaths during the 1980s, the social work role has been redefined. There has been a move away from therapeutically-orientated practice towards discourse advanced in terms of judicial and bureaucratic procedures – the check-list approach. This has helped to drive notions of therapy to the margins of social work.

There has been a continuing misconception of what the psychoanalytic project is about. Psychoanalysis is seen as a treatment dealing with the patient's past, and certainly Freud (1937) did refer to the analyst's work of reconstruction as comparable to the archaeologist's excavation of a city. The analyst's task was to unearth the ancient psychic edifice below the surface of the conscious mind.

Yet from the 1950s onwards psychoanalytic therapy has been much less concerned with such reconstruction. Indeed it can be said with some justification, that focusing on the past is one way in which the worker (not just the client) can distance herself from the intensity of the emotional experience in the session. Bion (1967) refers to the work of analysis as being concerned with what is happening here and now and *not* what has happened nor what is going to happen. The past is important because it gives an emotionally meaningful context to the individual's present. Psychoanalysis is concerned with the way that past is actively present and constantly interfering with the realization of a fuller current potential. It is a treatment based on what is going on in the room with the patient. This has been especially so since the concepts of projective identification (Klein, 1946) and counter-transference (Heimann, 1950) have come to be so central in British psychoanalytic practice.

And yet we are left with the question: how does a psychoanalytic knowledge base help the social work practitioner? As already noted, their task involves taking account of a bureaucracy that includes procedures and policies within a legally defined framework.

The practising analyst has a very different agenda. Wilfred Bion (1980), advises the analyst:

Discard your memory; discard the future tense of your desire; forget them both . . . to leave space for a new idea. A thought, an idea unclaimed, may be floating round the room searching for a home. (p. 11)

Bion says the analyst must be able to tolerate 'negative capability'. The state of doubt, the toleration of pain, the anxiety of *not knowing*, transforms what seems like dithering indecision into a potentially creative ignorance. The previously unknown can become known.

Could anything so frightening be further from the practising social worker's mind? Can the worker even begin to indulge in such poetic luxuries? In everyday practice the social worker meets the prospective client(s) with a massive burden – *the need to know*; is this client suicidal? has the child been abused? are the parents lying? What's the history of harm? Is there a chance of injury in the future?

We are faced with two apparently irreconcilable traditions. Within psychoanalysis, the focus of attention is the patient's inner world, where a premium is placed on the analyst's capacity *to be*. By contrast, in social work, attention is focused on the client's external world or life situation, where the worker's competency is derived from being able to investigate, assess and intervene, i.e. *to do*.

Where then is the meeting ground?

The following is a small part of a session in which the worker presented audio-taped material to a social work consultation group.

The case is of an articulate middle-class artist I will refer to as Dawn, who has had a number of schizophrenic breakdowns, two failed marriages and her children adopted.

In the session presented the social worker makes clear just how hard it is for her to make any meaningful interventions. Indeed she feels that to do so is an 'interruption' of the client's beautifully expounded monologue about a book she is currently writing.

The social worker has the insight to recognize that although the client is sounding 'well', at their previous session the woman had been seriously suicidal. Thus towards the end of the session the social worker reminds her of this and asks what has changed?

The client does not answer the question directly but initially gives a moving account of how her suicidal feelings just seem to 'come upon her', that she feels an awful failure and how badly this frightens her. Suddenly the client asks for the phone number of a local agency. The social worker becomes flustered as if she ought to know the number by heart. This soon leads to the client reassuring the worker 'not to worry' and suggesting that she ring Dawn with the number when she gets back to the office.

What is happening in this tiny piece of interaction?

It is perhaps easy to see that Dawn is diverting attention away from the enormity of her distress. Yet what is not clear is why the worker leaves feeling so disoriented. Now she is the failure.

At this stage one psychoanalytic interpretation of this episode is that the worker got entangled in Dawn's attempt to expunge recent memories of being suicidal. Dawn was inviting the worker on a psychological journey in which the client's internal world had been thoroughly transformed. Suicidal desperation had been eliminated. An idealized world, where the only thing on her mind was getting a book ready for publication, had taken its place.

To make sense, psychoanalytically, of how thoughts of suicide had been expunged and this idealized world was formed and maintained, we need to look at a process that Melanie Klein (1946) called, *projective identification*.

Its original form was first described by Freud (1896) when he drew attention to a mechanism of defence which he called projection. He defined this as a defence in which unwanted parts of the subject's experience are expelled from the self and attributed to a 'bad' other or group. Anti-semites project their own unacknowledged greed for money and power onto this now 'justifiably' reviled group. Freud (1925) suggested that in its earliest oral form it is as if the infant says, 'I should like to eat this' [the good], or 'I should like to spit it out' [the bad] (p. 439). In consequence, what is bad and what is external are seen as synonymous.

Klein's (1946) conceptualization of projective identification profoundly deepened our understanding of projection. She agreed with Freud that whatever 'bad' attributes the subject expels, like greed, then that quality is *consciously identified* with the person or group onto whom it has been projected. However, and this is the crucial point, Klein was also claiming that the quality that has been got rid of – 'spat out', is *unconsciously identified* with the unwanted, 'bad' parts of the self. There is no wholesale expulsion of unwanted inclinations. There is no human experience that we do not all share and tolerate, or otherwise, within ourselves.

Since then the concept has been extended by Bion (1955) who demon-strated that projective identification is fundamental to understanding how people affect each other i.e. it is a form of non-verbal, unconscious communication. Indeed, so powerful a form of communi-

Five Key Points

1   The managerialist approach is crucial to the social work task. By itself, however, it is not sufficient to deal with the highly emotionally-charged situations workers find themselves in.

2   Psychoanalytic thinking takes these emotionally-charged situations seriously: as ones worthy of reflection and, ultimately, action. Thus a premium is placed on the worker as a highly valued resource.

3   Psychoanalytic theorizing is about the 'here and now' of interaction, and therefore has much to offer the worker in practice.

4   Whatever the dangers of simplification, social workers can enhance their investigative, assessment and therapeutic skills through careful study of key psychoanalytic concepts such as projective identification and counter-transference.

5   A central place is accorded supervision that includes taking account of worker–client dynamics.

cation, that it *arouses* an affective response in the receiver who experiences emotion-ally that which the subject *unconsciously* wishes to communicate but cannot put into words.

Bion (1955) gives the example of a session in which he felt scared with a psychotic patient. He interpreted that the patient was arousing in him the fear that he would murder Bion. The patient's non-verbal response was to clench his fists so tightly that his knuckles went white. Bion then suggested to the patient that he had now taken the fear of attack back into himself and was having to *consciously* deal with his murderous rage.

Thus projective identification has been extended to include the way in which an 'object' (be it mother, analyst or social worker) can be affected in such a way that they experience that which the subject (infant, patient, client) cannot put into words and can only be communicated non-verbally as an experience aroused in the recipient.

Contemporary analysts have come to recognize the way in which clients can not only arouse feelings in the worker, but they can be 'nudged' (Joseph, 1989) to act on these experiences. For example, a client reports that people in authority often end up being hostile. Without realizing it the worker finds herself also attacking the client in a way that the worker is unfamiliar with in the rest of her practice. Here the projective identification is no longer an intrapersonal matter relating to how the client *perceives* authority, nor can it be said that the client is only *arousing* that critical feeling state in the worker. The worker has been 'lassoed' (Symington, 1983) into *enacting* what began as a perception and has now ended up as being the critical authority in vivo.

This of course is one of the critical reasons why psychoanalytic treatment is fundamentally based on the 'here and now'. The work of analysis is substantially based on interpretation of the way in which fixed, internal, psychic 'ideology' becomes re-invented with the therapist in the consulting room. The analytic task is for that *perception, arousal* and *enactment* to be understood by both parties (see Bott Spillius, 1992).

What then, using the concept of projective identification, can we hypothesize about Dawn's experience? Two things emerge. Firstly, that from the beginning of their meeting Dawn was wishing to eradicate any knowledge of her recent mental state. She had projected, spat out the 'bad'. Dawn was inviting the worker to likewise evacuate the 'badness' so that they could together enjoy a state of peaceful equilibrium. The worker did not go along with this invitation to collude. Thus, it was now only the worker who was carrying the knowledge of Dawn's recent suicidal demeanour.

Secondly, by raising the question of what had happened to her suicidal feelings, the worker was forcing something 'bad' back into Dawn's consciousness that threatened this equilibrium.

Having refused to join in the idealized view of the client's existence, the worker went from being seen as a good, even idealized object into a bad intrusive one. It is significant, I think, that earlier in the session Dawn had referred to how much better it was to talk to the worker than the usual people she had to deal with. But by asking the question the worker was no longer seen as being on the same side projecting badness 'out there'.

The discomfort was manifested by her inability to answer the question directly. She dealt with it by disowning it, by changing the subject, by projecting it back into the worker. In the meantime Dawn had recovered her equilibrium to such an extent that it was she who was reassuring the worker.

If this analysis helps to make sense of what Dawn was doing we are still left with the original question, why did the worker end up flustered, 'feeling a failure'?

The importance of this question arises because a fundamental of psychoanalytic thinking is that the most important resource at the worker's disposal, is the worker herself. This is also true, even if to a lesser extent, in social work. Procedures offer little comfort in the immediacy and intensity of the emotional exchange between client and worker. What psychoanalytic theorizing can provide is a way of making sense of the worker's experience. And more importantly, in the context of the work that needs to be done, highlights the worker-as-resource.

The psychoanalytic hypothesis suggests that taking the worker's affective response as a crucial instrument of study is necessary because it can help to illuminate something about the client's state of mind. For this to be available to the worker, her own difficulties have to be sufficiently known about (not, note, 'resolved') as these might otherwise interfere with the client being able to use the worker more fully.

Indeed, when Freud (1910) first coined the term counter-transference, he was specifically referring to the way in which the analyst's own unconscious reactions and problems limit the capacity to help the patient. 'No psychoanalyst goes further than his own complexes and internal resistances permit' (Freud, 1910, p. 289). In social work practice this might take the dangerous form of colluding with a parent about their child's safety because the worker has difficulty in dealing with the client's potentially angry response, or is unable to use her authority because she wants to be seen as 'helpful'. In our example, the worker could have gratefully colluded with Dawn leaving her vulnerable to relapse and in danger of another suicidal episode. The message would have been clear; like Dawn, the worker could not tolerate dealing with the client's suicidal self.

This view of counter-transference, as simply a manifestation of the worker's own 'neurosis', changed after a seminal paper by Heimann (1950) in which the concept was extended to include all the feelings, conscious and unconscious, the worker has towards the patient. Even more importantly Heimann introduced the notion that the counter-transference could be understood diagnostically as a tool, an 'instrument of research' into the patient's state of mind.

In our example, arousal of powerful emotions, feeling flustered, being a failure were all down to the worker. They were not *created* by Dawn. Dawn appears to have unconsciously tapped into the worker's own problems. Carpy (1989) argues that the client arouses such strong feelings because the worker is 'susceptible' to experiences, like being flustered, on her own account.

However, Heimann's theory is also proposing that Dawn's exploitation of the worker's affective response was a communication of somebody with severe problems. The difference is that Dawn's experience is not communicated by word but by emotional impact. The worker, aroused, acts out (enacts) her own existential 'shadow' (Jung, 1954). Any semblance of professional 'persona' is gone.

It is the worker now who has the experience of feeling flustered, of being a failure 'come upon her', just as Dawn had described. This is known as 'concordant' counter-transference (Racker, 1968) because it

---

Three Questions

1 Why has psychoanalytic thinking been seen as irrelevant to social work practice?

2 What are the advantages of a managerialist approach, especially over psychoanalytic thinking and theorizing.

3 If it is the case that the psychoanalyst focuses on the patient's inner world whilst the social worker focuses on the client's outer world, how can these two worlds, in practice, be reconciled?

---

involves the worker feeling what the client does not want to feel or, as in our example, can only feel momentarily before it is projected. Racker also describes 'complementary' counter-transference in which the worker gets caught up as a figure in the client's inner world. The description of the worker who was perceived as being uncharacteristically critical is an example of the way the client has transformed ('lassoed') the worker into an object that fits the client's view of authority as hostile.

In other words, concordant relates to the patient's disowned experience of *self*, whilst complementary counter-transference relates to the patient's experience of *objects*.

We can now answer the question as to why the worker went away feeling flustered and a failure. Psychoanalytically, there was a fit between Dawn's projective identification and the worker's counter-transference. Dawn has successfully projected her own negative feelings so that the worker is now the flustered, failed one. It is she who enacts the painful experience. Dawn in the meantime recovers her equilibrium to such an extent that she can reassure the worker 'not to worry'.

After this long excursion you might be saying to yourself, 'Well, it's one thing coming to an understanding of what's going on between client and worker, but how does it help me in the heat of the moment with my client?' My proposition is that it is precisely at the 'hot' moment that psychoanalytic thinking is most useful.

This is an example from my own social work practice. I went out with doctors and police to do a community Mental Health assessment on a client who had previously been violent. We were confronted by a woman who was screaming at the top of her voice wanting to know why we were there, telling us to get out of her house, etc. I had already begun to look out of the corner of my eye to see just where the police were as I thought that she would be violent at any moment. Then I tried to reflect upon what I was experiencing and of course the answer was terror. I wondered if this was how she was feeling. After all, strangers, mostly men, had come into her house and were threatening her very existence.

I felt a sense of relief at this insight as I suggested to her that she was terrified by our presence, that she didn't know why we had forced our way into her house. I then added that we were worried about her and therefore needed to talk. I suggested sitting down and continued the interview in a much calmer atmosphere even though this ultimately still ended in her being sectioned.

In the terms of this chapter, again we can see that alongside the conscious fury that the client was expressing, there was also an unconscious communication of terror. She was projecting it to such an extent that terror was experientially aroused in me. In recognizing my (concordant) counter-transference response, I was eventually able to put into words the dread that the client was going through. And making me go through.

There was one difference between us; namely that, on this occasion anyway, I was able to 'sustain' (Heimann, 1950) the feelings as opposed to discharging them ('spitting them out') as the client was doing. In other words, I managed to contain the feelings aroused in me without enacting them by becoming 'violent' myself and handing the situation over to the police. It is also worth noticing that my intervention not only prevented a potentially escalating violence, but the acknowledgement firstly to myself of my experience and then to the client of hers, created a benign environment in which the assessment could be conducted in a non-threatening way.

Conclusion

In this chapter I have tried to reinstate the worker as central to the social work task. The client is constantly communicating information, unconsciously as well as consciously, and that information is vital to getting a greater understanding of what is going on. This can help to guide both the work of assessment and intervention. I have previously suggested ways in which psychoanalytic theory can also be invaluable in making sense of the supervisory relationship and policy formulation (Nathan, 1993, 1994).

In the painful, sometimes turbulent, situations faced by the social worker, the emotional grip of the psychoanalytic paradigm, becomes essential. Procedures alone cannot do this. The worker's affective response and the need for this experience to be accorded an appropriate supervisory space is a prerequisite. As in our example with Dawn, the supervisory task was one of helping the worker re-establish her own boundaries, turning her sense of failure into a containable anxiety so that she could continue to function effectively. For the worker to get a handle on the nature of the issues she was coping with provided an immense relief. The combination of public censure and too many internally critical experiences can leave workers feeling they are not up to the job. The net result is burn-out and even the loss of their expertise to social work.

Further Reading

1   Casement, P. (1985) *On Learning from the Patient*, London: Tavistock.
2   *Journal of Social Work Practice* (Carfax Publishing Company): the house journal for GAPS (Group for the Advancement of Psychodynamics and Psychotherapy in Social Work)
3   Pearson, G., Treseder, J. and Yelloly, M. (eds) (1988) *Social Work and the Legacy of Freud: Psychoanalysis and its Uses*, London: Macmillan.

Psychoanalytic thinking has a crucial role to play in providing a framework where these experiences can be transformed from one of failure to one of learning and growth for both the worker and the client.

References

Bion, W. R. (1955) 'Language and the schizophrenic', in M. Klein, P. Heimann and R. E. Money-Kyrle (eds), *New Directions in Psychoanalysis*, London: Tavistock Publications, pp. 220–39.

Bion, W. R. (1967) 'Notes on memory and desire', *Psychoanalytic Forum*, 2, 272–3; also in *Melanie Klein Today: Volume 2, Mainly Practice*, London: Routledge (1988).

Bion, W. R. (1980) *Bion in New York and Sao Paulo*, (ed. F. Bion), Perthshire: Clunie Press.

Bott Spillius, E. (1992) 'Clinical experiences of projective identification', in R. Anderson (ed.), *Clinical Lectures on Klein and Bion*, London: Routledge, pp. 59–73.

Carpy, D. V. (1989) 'Tolerating the counter-transference: a mutative process', *International Journal of Psychoanalysis*, 70, 287–94.

Freud, S. (1896) 'Further Remarks on the Neuro-Psychoses of Defence', *Standard Edition, Vol. 3*, London: Hogarth Press.

Freud, S. (1910) 'The Future Prospects of Psycho-Analytic Therapy', *Standard Edition, Vol. 11*, London: Hogarth Press.

Freud, S. (1925) 'Negation', *Pelican Freud, Vol. 11*, Middlesex: Penguin Books.

Freud, S. (1937) 'Constructions in Analysis', *Standard Edition, Vol. 23*, London: Hogarth.

Heimann, P. (1950) 'On counter-transference', *International Journal of Psycho-analysis*, 31, 81–4.

Howe, D. (1992) 'Child abuse and the bureaucratisation of social work', *Sociological Review*, 38, 491–508.

Joseph, B. (1989) *Psychic Equilibrium and Psychic Change; Selected Papers of Betty Joseph*, M. Feldman and E. Bott Spillius (eds), London: Routledge.

Jung, C. G. (1954) *The Collected Works*, vol. 16, London: Routledge.

Klein, M. (1946) 'Notes on some Schizoid mechanisms', *The Writings of Melanie Klein Vol. 3*, London: Hogarth Press.

Nathan, J. (1993) 'The battered social worker: a psychodynamic contribution to practice, supervision and policy', *Journal of Social Work Practice*, 7, 73–80.

Nathan, J. (1994) 'The psychic organisation of community care: a kleinian perspective', *Journal of Social Work Practice*, 8, 113–22.

Racker, H. (1968) *Transference and Counter-Transference*, London: Hogarth Press.

Symington, N. (1983) 'The analyst's act of freedom as agent of therapeutic change', *International Review of Psycho-analysis*, vol. 10, 283–91.

V.9
Anti-discriminatory Practice
Neil Thompson

Thomas and Pierson (1995) define anti-discriminatory practice as:

a term used widely in social and probation work, and in social work training, to describe how workers take account of structural disadvantage and seek to reduce individual and institutional DISCRIMINATION particularly on grounds of race, gender, disability, social class and sexual orientation. (p. 16)

Social work theory and practice have changed and developed quite considerably since the mid-1980s when issues of discrimination and oppression started to receive serious attention. We are now much more aware of the need to see the individual in his or her social context. We are also much more aware of the need to see that context in a fuller and richer sense than is traditionally the case in social work literature.

The Need for Anti-discriminatory Practice

The field of anti-discriminatory practice is a broad one that encompasses a number of important issues. I shall address a number of these here, but will inevitably omit discussion of many other important questions.

A basic feature of anti-discriminatory practice is the ability/willingness to see that discrimination and oppression are so often central to the situations social workers encounter. For example, the majority of social work clients are women, and yet the significance of

gender in a male-dominated society is a factor that many practitioners fail to take into consideration. That is, they adopt what is known as a 'gender-blind' approach.

Similarly, it is easy to remain firmly within an ethnocentric frame of reference – that is, to see situations from the perspective of the dominant culture without taking adequate account of the fact that we live in a multi-ethnic society. Social workers operate in a context of diversity, and forms of practice that do not reflect this are likely to undermine the importance of non-dominant cultural patterns, beliefs and expectations.

Consequently, parallel to the 'gender-blind' approach, we also have the 'colour-blind' approach, based on the false premise that 'all people are the same – members of one race with similar problems, needs and objectives' (Dominelli, 1991, p. 167). Such a view denies both the richness of minority cultures and ignores the reality of the experience of racism for very many people.

Other forms of discrimination, most notably ageism and disablism, can also be 'swept under the carpet' by an attitude that fails to recognize the destructive effects of oppression on marginalized social groups. This, then, is a fundamental principle of anti-discriminatory practice – the need to be sensitive to discrimination and oppression, to avoid the pitfall of becoming oblivious to their existence.

For staff schooled in traditional methods, the fact that social work clients are predominantly from disadvantaged groups is unlikely to be seen as a key issue. However, what anti-discriminatory practice teaches us is that discrimination and oppression are vitally important matters and, if we are not attuned to recognizing and challenging discrimination, we run the risk of, at best, condoning it and, at worst exacerbating and amplifying it through our own actions.

There is no middle ground; intervention either adds to the problem (or at least condones it) or goes some small way towards easing or breaking such oppression. In this respect, the political slogan, 'If you're not part of the solution, you must be part of the problem' is particularly accurate.

An awareness of the sociopolitical context is necessary in order to prevent becoming (or remaining) part of the problem.

(Thompson, 1992, pp. 169–70)

In keeping with this line of argument, Giddens (1977) argues that power is intrinsic to all social interaction – we cannot escape the significance of power in our dealings with other people. This means that the potential for transforming structures of oppression is always a possibility for us. The power associated with human action can be used to challenge existing forms and patterns of discrimination. Alternatively, however, such power can be used to reinforce and legitimate structures of inequality. What cannot happen, then, is for our actions to be 'neutral' with regard to existing balances of power.

Of course, some people have more power than others, but we all have some degree of power in terms of being able, as Giddens puts it, to 'make a difference'. Social workers dealing with relatively powerless members of the community are therefore in a pivotal position. Social work interventions can contribute, to some extent at least, to empowerment and emancipation from oppressive circumstances, or can, in themselves, be oppressive. I shall discuss below some of the ways in which workers can seek to

Five Key Points

1 We must develop a sensitivity to the existence all around us of discrimination and oppression.

2 We must recognize that there is no comfortable middle ground – we are either part of the solution or part of the problem.

3 We must address the three key imperatives of justice, equality and participation.

4 We must revisit traditional forms of practice and amend them accordingly.

5 Non-discriminatory and anti-oppressive assessment is a first step towards the achievement of anti-discriminatory practice.

make their actions positive and consistent with anti-discriminatory practice.

A second fundamental principle of anti-discriminatory practice can then be identified as the need to recognize that social work interventions either condone and reinforce discrimination and oppression, or go some way towards countering and undermining them.

Anti-discriminatory practice is part of what Giddens (1991) calls 'emancipatory politics':

I define emancipatory politics as a generic outlook concerned above all with liberating individuals and groups from constraints which adversely affect their life chances. Emancipatory politics involves two main elements: the effort to shed shackles of the past, thereby permitting a transformative attitude towards the future; and the aim of overcoming the illegitimate domination of some individuals or groups by others . . . Emancipatory politics is concerned to reduce or eliminate exploitation, inequality and oppression.

(in Cassell, 1993, pp. 334–5)

From this he goes on to identify three 'imperatives' of emancipatory politics: justice, equality and participation. I shall outline each of these in turn:

• *Justice* The notion of justice implies fairness of treatment, an assurance that we will not be exploited or denied our rights. There is a great deal of evidence to suggest that certain groups do not have the benefit of just treatment. For example, Gordon (1992) discusses the various ways in which black people are treated far less favourably within the British criminal justice system.

• *Equality* An important point to recognize with regard to equality is that it should not be equated with uniformity. To treat everyone the same is not to treat everyone equally, as this fails to take account of significant pre-existing differences and inequalities. For example, many people have specific needs (wheelchair access is a common example), and if these are not addressed, such people will be disadvantaged. That is, where people begin from a position of inequality, a uniform approach will serve only to reinforce such inequalities. In this respect, a failure to take on board different needs, circumstances and backgrounds is actually a barrier to equality, rather than a step towards it. Equality relates to rights and opportunities, and so we need to ensure that the focus is on equal outcomes, rather than uniformity of treatment.

• *Participation* This is an important concept in social work at two levels. On a broader level, the concept of user participation is an important element in the development of anti-discriminatory practice. This refers to the involvement of service users in the planning, co-ordination, evaluation and so on, of services in order to (a) provide opportunities for empowerment and (b) ensure that the services provided are appropriate and responsive (Beresford and Croft, 1993). At a narrower, micro level,

participation is also extremely important in terms of interpersonal interactions within the context of social work interventions. At this level, the term 'partnership' is used to refer to the need to ensure that practice is premised on working *with* clients, towards mutually agreed goals, rather than doing things *to* them (Thompson, 1996). Partnership is a central theme of anti-discriminatory practice, and one to which I shall return below.

A further fundamental principle of anti-discriminatory practice, then, is the need to address the three imperatives of justice, equality and participation.

Countering Discrimination and Oppression

Jordan (1990) argues that the nature of social work tasks makes it necessary for social workers to exercise discretion and professional judgement: 'it is because situations are complex and susceptible to a number of interpretations that the judgement, discretion and skill of a trained person are required' (pp. 3–4). This introduces the need for what he calls 'moral reasoning', a level of analysis above and beyond simple technical reasoning. That is, social work is characterized by 'messy' situations (Schön, 1983) that require more than technical answers. This being the case, the scope for abusing professional power becomes an issue that needs to be addressed. It poses a crucial question for practitioners: How can we ensure that the power inherent in the professional role is used positively, and is not allowed to become a force for coercion?

The remainder of this chapter seeks to answer this question, in part at least, by outlining a number of steps that can be taken to ensure that our moral reasoning is consistent with, and supportive of, equality and emancipation, rather than discrimination and oppression.

There are a number of ways in which traditional approaches to practice need to be changed if practice is to become genuinely emancipatory. Indeed, it can be seen as a basic principle of anti-discriminatory practice that we need to revisit traditional forms of practice and make them compatible with a spirit of countering oppression.

Social work practice has long placed value on the role of enabling as an important means of avoiding the creation of dependency. However, anti-discriminatory practice involves going beyond simply enabling to the point of *empowering* people. The concept of enabling is a very individualistic one. It implies helping people cope with, or adjust to, their circumstances. While this is a valuable notion in some respects, it does not succeed in going far enough. It does not take account of wider cultural and structural issues. This is where empowerment comes in. Empowerment involves helping people gain greater control over their lives and their circumstances. However, it also implies seeking to overcome the effects of discrimination and oppression. Oppression can be seen as an abuse of power, and so empowerment represents a means of using one's own power (and that of other people within a collective effort) to challenge or undermine the disadvantages experienced by being a member of a marginalized social group. This represents the legitimate use of power to challenge the abuse of power inherent in discrimination and oppression.

We can see, then, that enabling is quite a narrow concept that pays little or no attention to the broader social context of clients' lives. Empowerment, by contrast, shares the same emphasis on facilitating personal change, but locates this firmly within a context of structured inequalities (Ward and Mullender, 1993).

Traditional social work has long been criticized for being a form of benign paternalism in which professionals help less fortunate souls to cope with their life demands (see, for example, Bailey and Brake, 1975). There has been considerable movement away from this form of practice over a period of years. However, anti-discriminatory practice has accelerated this movement by emphasizing the significance of partnership.

Three Questions

1 Does the organization where you work (or where you are a student) have policies on equality of opportunity and anti-discrimination? If so, are they actually followed or are they simply rhetorical statements? If there are no policies in existence, are any planned or currently being developed?

2 Have you ever experienced discrimination or oppression? If so, how can you use this experience positively to guide your practice? If you have not, how can you develop an understanding of the experience of oppression?

3 What positive steps can you take to ensure that you make a positive contribution to anti-discriminatory practice?

Working in partnership entails involving clients at every stage in the process:

- defining needs to be met, problems to be solved;
- deciding how best to meet the needs/solve the problems;
- implementing and reviewing such decisions;
- agreeing on termination; and
- evaluating intervention.

This is an essential part of good practice

in so far as any work done outside of a partnership relationship may be experienced as coercive.

Sometimes there is a conflict between a statutory duty and a client's unwillingness to co-operate with planning or intervention. However, although working in partnership may prove very difficult in such circumstances, we should be wary of abandoning our attempts to create a positive partnership. In some cases, it can take a great deal of time to develop the right circumstances for partnership work but, the long-term success can often more than repay the efforts expended.

By working in partnership, we can seek to ensure that inequalities are not reinforced, and that relatively powerless people are given a voice. In this way, professional barriers can be dismantled, in part at least, and the tendency for social workers to be seen as a threat can be undermined.

One of the hallmarks of good practice in traditional approaches to social work has been a sensitivity to feelings. Social work interventions that take no account of feelings can be seen as potentially very dangerous indeed. For practitioners to intervene in people's lives without taking account of the emotional issues involved is clearly an example of bad practice, especially as such insensitive interventions can do considerably more harm than good.

We can now apply the same logic to anti-discriminatory practice. In direct parallel to the emotional dimension of practice, interventions that do not demonstrate a sensitivity to the experience of oppression and the role of discrimination in creating and sustaining inequality and disadvantage are also potentially very dangerous indeed. To intervene in people's lives without taking account of key factors such as race, ethnicity, gender, age, disability, sexual orientation and so on is contrary to anti-discriminatory practice. Such

interventions can do considerably more harm than good.

There is also a direct parallel between learning how to deal with emotional issues and learning how to deal with discrimination and oppression. This applies at two levels. First, in both cases, no simple formulae can be provided for how to deal with specific situations. Both require considerable skill and sensitivity on the part of the worker. Good practice in both depends on building up knowledge and skills over a period of time, and both are likely to involve making a number of mistakes along the line.

Second, the emotional dimension of social work requires us to look critically upon our own responses, our own attitudes and values. Dealing with feelings inevitably involves our own subjective enmeshment, to a certain degree at least. A totally objective approach is neither possible nor desirable. The same is also true of dealing with discrimination:

- We need to look critically upon our own responses to oppression, our own attitudes and values – a certain amount of 'unlearning' is required in order to cast off the destructive stereotypes into which we have been socialized (Thompson et al., 1994).
- There is inevitably a subjective dimension in terms of how we interact with people of a different background from our own, again reflecting the patterns of expectations into which we have been socialized.
- Attempting to be entirely objective is an unrealistic strategy. We need to recognize our own views and possible prejudices so that we are in a position to ensure that they do not stand in the way of good practice.

A further long-established hallmark of good practice is the recognition of the uniqueness of the individual. This is a practice principle that anti-discriminatory practice would not wish to challenge. However, we need to go beyond this to recognize that individuals need to be understood not in the abstract, but within the concrete circumstances of their cultural and social context. For example, consider the case of an older person being assessed for community care services. He or she would need to be recognized as a unique individual with specific needs, qualities and circumstances. However, it would also be important to take account of the person's 'social location' – where the person is situated in terms of class, gender, race, ethnicity and so on. In particular, in working with older people, we would need to address issues of ageism and consider how age discrimination plays a part in the client's life. To work with an older person without taking on board issues of the marginalization and stereotyping of older people as an oppressed group increases the likelihood of poor practice, practice inconsistent with their rights and dignity (Thompson, 1995). As Hughes and Mtezuka (1992) comment:

Social work has not only failed to challenge ageism and its implicit assumptions of assumed homogeneity, it appears to have embraced these values. Furthermore, social work and social service provision have failed to identify the particular needs of the majority of old people – that is, older women – and, within that group, have not recognised the diversity related to social class, race and life history. (p. 233)

In short, then, to deny the uniqueness of the individual can be seen as a form of oppression in its own right, but to see *only* that uniqueness and not recognize common patterns of experience is equally problematic.

The quotation from Hughes and Mtezuka also introduces another important issue in relation to the development of anti-discriminatory practice. Different forms of discrimination – racism, sexism, ageism and so on – do not operate in isolation or independently

of each other. They interact, and therefore act as different but related dimensions of the experience of oppression. We therefore have to be wary of seeing clients in terms of one form of oppression only. In many cases, clients are exposed to multiple forms of oppression, a fact that can produce a complex matrix of interacting factors.

This brings me to the next point I wished to emphasize – the importance of assessment. Assessment is the process whereby information is gathered in order to form a picture of what needs to be done. It is a key part in the social work process, as it forms the basis for intervention, review, termination and evaluation (Thompson, 1996). Consequently, if a worker's assessment is characterized by stereotypical assumptions or, for example, a pathological view of black families (Ahmad, 1990), then the scope for anti-discriminatory practice becomes very limited.

It is important that we are conscious of discrimination at all stages within practice, but the assessment stage can be seen as particularly crucial in terms of how it sets the scene for further involvement with the client. A clear assessment, developed in partnership with the client(s), which takes account of patterns of discrimination and the experience of oppression, is an essential first step in ensuring that subsequent

Further Reading

1 Braye, S. and Preston-Shoot, M. (1995) *Empowering Practice in Social Care*, Buckingham: Open University Press.

2 Dalrymple, J. and Burke, B. (1995) *Anti-oppressive Practice: Social Care and the Law*, Buckingham: Open University Press.

3 Thompson, N. (1993) *Anti-discriminatory Practice*, London: Macmillan.

intervention is not distorted by discriminatory assumptions or oppressive practices. Indeed, this can be seen as a further fundamental principle of anti-discriminatory practice – the need to ensure that assessment is non-discriminatory and anti-oppressive.

Conclusion

Discrimination and oppression are part of the everyday reality of a significant proportion of social work's clientele. Traditional social work practice goes some way towards recognizing the social context of clients' experiences, but the development of anti-discriminatory practice has shown that not enough attention has been paid to certain aspects of that social context, particularly those aspects to do with social divisions, conflict, power, discrimination and oppression.

This chapter has argued the case for making the countering of discrimination and oppression a central feature of good social work practice. One step towards that has been the 'reworking' of some aspects of traditional practice to make them more compatible with an ethos of countering oppression. This I see as a useful stepping stone from some of the strengths of established practice towards an anti-discriminatory practice that does not fall foul of the major weakness of such traditional practice – that is, a tendency to fail to recognize the role of structured inequalities in shaping the experience of social work clients in terms of the problems and deprivations that haunt them.

It is to be hoped that the reworking of traditional strengths can be one positive strand in the development of a truly anti-discriminatory social work practice. Alongside this, we are already seeing the development of new forms of practice (for example, in terms of user participation),

new elements that have an important part to play in making sure that social work makes a positive contribution towards social justice.

References

Ahmad, B. (1990) *Black Perspectives in Social Work*, Birmingham: Ventura.

Bailey, R. and Brake, M. (eds) (1975) *Radical Social Work*, London: Edward Arnold.

Beresford, P. and Croft, S. (1993) *Citizen Involvement*, London: Macmillan.

Braham, P., Rattansi, A. and Skellington, R. (eds) (1992) *Racism and Antiracism: Inequalities, Opportunities and Policies*, London: Sage.

Cassell, P. (ed.) (1993) *The Giddens Reader*, London: Macmillan.

Dominelli, L. (1992) 'An uncaring profession? An examination of racism in social work', in Braham et al. (eds) (1992).

Giddens, A. (1977) *Studies in Social and Political Theory*, London: Hutchinson.

Giddens, A. (1991) *Modernity and Self-Identity: Self and Society in the Late Modern Age*, Cambridge: Polity Press.

Gordon, P. (1992) 'Black people and the criminal law', in Braham et al. (eds) (1992).

Hughes, B. and Mtezuka, M. (1992) 'Social work and older women: where have older women gone?', in M. Langan and L. Day (eds) (1992).

Jordan, B. (1990) *Social Work in an Unjust Society*, London: Harvester Wheatsheaf.

Langan, M. and Day, L. (eds) (1992) *Women, Oppression and Social Work: Issues in Anti-Discriminatory Practice*, London: Routledge.

Schon, D. A. (1983) *The Reflective Practitioner*, New York: Basic Books.

Thomas, M. and Pierson, J. (1995) *Dictionary of Social Work*, London: Collins Educational.

Thompson, N. (1992) *Existentialism and Social Work*, Aldershot: Avebury.

Thompson, N. (1993) *Anti-Discriminatory Practice*, London: Macmillan.

Thompson, N. (1995) *Age and Dignity: Working with Older People*, Aldershot: Arena.

Thompson, N. (1996) *People Skills*, London: Macmillan.

Thompson, N., Osada, M. and Anderson, B. (1994) *Practice Teaching in Social Work* (2nd edn), Birmingham: Pepar.

Walmsley, J., Reynolds, J., Shakespeare, P. and Woolfe, R. (eds) (1993) *Health, Welfare and Practice: Reflecting on Roles and Relationships*, London: Sage.

Ward, A. and Mullender, A. (1993) 'Empowerment and oppression: an indissoluble pairing for contemporary social work', in Walmsley et al. (eds) (1993).

V.10
Feminist Theory
Lena Dominelli

Feminist social work in the academy has developed from its beginnings in the early 1970s when 'women' were added onto the social work curriculum to having a body of theory and practice in its own right by the mid-1990s. This chapter outlines the key characteristics of feminist social work theory and practice, and evaluates its impact on the profession over the last two decades.

What is Feminist Social Work?

Feminist social work has a theory and practice which has drawn on a diversity of developments in feminism and the women's movement more generally (see Tong, 1989; Abbott and Wallace, 1990; Stanley, 1990). Beginning in the voluntary sector and in the field of community action, feminist social work has spread to both the statutory and the commercial sectors. It is perhaps ironic that a movement which looked to publicly funded provisions for the deliverance of women from oppression has been compelled by austerity programmes in the welfare state to engage in the 'dirty' world of profit making for its practitioners to offer a service aimed at empowering women and make a living. Much anguish has gone into the decision some feminists have made to 'go commercial'. Those who have done so have nonetheless sought to uphold feminist principles in the services they make available and the processes through which they engage 'clients'. They have addressed questions of access by having a sliding scale of fees which range from no payment for those who cannot pay to charging the 'market rate' for women holding highly remunerated posts. They have also avoided stigmatizing people through means testing by asking women to self-define their income status. Feminist counsellors and feminists providing women's health services have found 'going private' has also enabled them to practise unencumbered by the bureaucratic constraints stultifying statutory work (Judge, 1993).

Neither feminism nor feminist social work are monolithic entities subscribing to one version of 'the truth'. Rather, there exists a plurality of views: liberal, radical, socialist, anti-racist and postmodernist (see Tong, 1989; Abbott and Wallace, 1990) which can be held by both black and white feminists, for example, white radical feminism, black socialist feminism (Collins, 1990; Dominelli, 1996). Each of the different schools of feminist thought has its own perceptions about the origins of the oppression of women and the task of how this is to be eradicated. Their variety also reflects how feminists have attempted to respond to each other's critiques and given feminism a responsive and non-dogmatic basis. Nonetheless, they share a number of characteristics:

- upholding the right of women to be free from oppression;
- having women speak for ourselves in our own voices;
- listening to what women have to say;

- creating alternative lifestyles in the here and now;
- integrating our theories with our practice;
- seeking compatibility between the ends being sought and the means whereby these are achieved;
- seeking collectivist solutions which respect the individuality and uniqueness of each woman;
- valuing women's contributions; and
- using women's individual experiences to make sense of our social realities (Cook and Kirk, 1983; Collins, 1990; Abbott and Wallace, 1990; Dominelli, 1992a).

I write from a white anti-racist socialist feminist perspective. This position recognizes that alongside other social divisions, 'race', gender and class interact to differentiate one woman's experiences of oppression from another's.[1]

I define feminist social work as a form of social work practice which takes gendered inequality and its elimination as the starting point for working with women whether as individuals, in groups or within organizations and seeks to promote women's well-being as women define it. Rooted in women's experiences of reality and using research which attests to the presence of extensive and systematic discrimination against women, its immediate aim is to use helping relationships predicated on egalitarian values to enable women to develop the resources, skills and confidence necessary for taking control of their own lives.

The fostering of women's self-esteem through a facilitating relationship between the feminist practitioner and the 'client'[2] encourages the woman to make her own decisions by playing an active role in assessing her situation, exploring alternatives, formulating plans of action and implementing them. The assessment process is likely to involve redefining the problem being considered from a feminist perspective. This removes it from the private realm of a personal problem for which the woman is solely responsible and lodges it in the public domain as a social problem which she is experiencing individually along with a number of other women.

Redefining the problem forms an important part of feminist social work intervention (Dominelli and McLeod, 1989). It reduces the 'client's' sense of isolation and feelings of guilt by enabling her to see how her social role, position and status have contributed to her personally feeling powerless. Examining her insight into disempowerment from this perspective is empowering for the woman because:

- her experience is validated;
- she can make links with other women who are similarly situated; and
- she can interpret her questioning of her position as one form of resistance marking the first step in the process of asserting greater control over her life.

A feminist practitioner assists in this development by placing her skills, knowledge and resources at the woman's disposal and sharing her expertise with her. In other words, a feminist practitioner can help the woman unpack the contingent realities in her situation and explore how she has used her knowledge and experience in both reproducing and rejecting her own oppression. Gaining self-knowledge enables the woman to more actively accumulate resources which will give her greater purchase over her circumstances.

In establishing a more egalitarian relationship with a 'client', a feminist social worker helps to unlock the 'client's' capacity for decision making and self validation. The *process* of how they work together becomes as important as their meeting agreed objectives. Implementing a commitment not to disempower women means the feminist practitioner pays attention to how process shapes the quality of the professional relationship between them. Reducing power differentials arising from one's expertise by sharing this with the 'client' rather than seeking to restrict the flow of information and knowledge to maintain a professional superiority constitutes one means of achieving it. Changing the nature of the worker–'client' relationship and questioning the traditional notion of professionals as distanced neutral individuals characterize feminist facilitative working environments.

By challenging traditional professional paradigms in which the expert tells the 'client' what to do, the feminist social worker undermines the idea of the professional as the neutral uninvolved onlooker. Having rejected her own oppression as a woman, the feminist social worker can also use her own self-knowledge and experience of disempowerment as a basis for better understanding the 'client's' responses to her predicament. Thus, the feminist social worker's rejection of injustice helps her to gain the wisdom whereby growth and knowledge can be mutually promoted.

In the longer term, feminist social work practice has a role to play in fulfilling feminism's broader objective: transforming social relations in more egalitarian directions. It makes its contribution towards this by initiating less oppressive social relations within the worker–'client' relationship and reducing the oppressive nature of organizational policies and practices. It can also do so through campaigning activities and networks which tackle social issues that undermine the capacities of individuals to realize their full potential, for example, poverty, violence, sexual abuse.

Feminist social workers' concern with the quality of people's lives and willingness to intervene in ways that promote the welfare of society's most disadvantaged groups make feminist social work a political form of social work and one that adopts a moral position

Five Key Points

1 Feminism covers a number of different schools of thought each of which has its own features, although some general principles are shared.
2 Feminism challenges many taken for granted assumptions in daily life: relationships between men, women and children; the nature and use of power; language.
3 Feminism integrates theory and practice in ways that promote egalitarian relations in the here and now; emphasizes the connections between the content and process in interactions; acknowledges the interlinking of private and public lives; and recognizes people's multiple identities.
4 Feminist social work seeks to promote the empowerment of 'clients' and the realization of their well-being, a feature that puts it in oppositional mode *vis-à-vis* powerful others in the profession, particularly white men.
5 Feminist social work is vulnerable and under attack because it has failed to gain widespread support amongst privileged men and women.

which opposes injustice and oppression, including that perpetrated by women (McLeod and Dominelli, 1982). And, in recognition of women's multiple identities, it condemns the prioritizing of one form of oppression over another (see Dominelli and McLeod, 1989; Collins, 1990). Feminist social work engages both the personal and the social by focusing on the whole person and examining the interconnectedness between people and the structures they live within.

Feminism's main emphasis is on women as the major group whose needs are to be addressed. However, feminist social work practice is also relevant to children and men (Dominelli and McLeod, 1989; Collins, 1990; Thompson, 1993). Though rooted in women's experience of oppression, feminism's principles and methodologies are such that they can also be followed by men. Some authors have called men using feminist theory and practice pro-feminist or feminist sympathizing men.

The Impact of Feminist Social Work

Feminism has placed gender issues on the social work map and transformed its gender-blind nature (Dominelli and McLeod, 1989). But, given that social work is a profession composed primarily of women, its impact has not been as widespread as one would have expected. Indeed, Jill Reynolds (1994) argues that feminism has had minimal influence on the social work curriculum and gives an account of the difficulties that she and her colleagues are currently encountering in getting sexism the same degree of attention that is being given to racism. What she says about the problems which need to be overcome is familiar. Getting feminism on the agenda in the academy is proving to be more difficult than many of us either predicted or would like to see. However, I am not as gloomy about either our current position or future prospects as Reynolds (1994), although I think progress will continue to be an uphill struggle (see Dominelli, 1996). Despite my frustrations with the obstacles to the advancement of feminist social work, there have been a number of significant improvements since the first generation of feminists 'added' women onto the social work curriculum.

Since that time, equal opportunities policies have become commonplace at least on paper, in both agencies and the academy. These now form a backdrop which facilitate the introduction of issues around women's unequal access to the workplace and the inadequacy of services agencies offer women. Feminist social work has become a part of the lexicon on

social work courses and has become increasingly recognized as both a philosophical position and a practice method (see Sibeon, 1991; Dominelli, 1996). There is a literature to which students can be referred covering: practice (see Hale, 1984; Brook and Davis, 1985; Hudson, 1985; Chaplin, 1988; Hanmer and Statham, 1988; Dominelli and McLeod, 1989; Ahmad, 1992; Langan and Day, 1989), policy (Finch and Groves, 1983; Pascall, 1986; Ungerson, 1987; Groves and McLean, 1991; Dominelli, 1991b) and theory (see Dominelli, 1996). Practice placements which follow feminist principles are now options on social work courses although these remain primarily limited to one or two feminist agencies, for example, Women's Aid, Women's Resource Centres. However, both probation and social services now have feminist practice teachers who secure opportunities for students to examine feminist practice in statutory settings.

Some of these practitioners have organized groups for mutual support in their workplaces and unions. Moreover, feminist social workers and scholars have opened up areas others have feared to broach, for example, demonstrating how unsafe the family can be for women, via its work on domestic violence (Hanmer and Saunders, 1984; Gordon, 1986; Mama, 1989); and children through its work on child sexual abuse (Nelson, 1982; Dominelli, 1986, 1989, 1991a; Wilson, 1993); making visible women's contribution to caring services, and raising their status (David and New, 1985; Ungerson, 1987); identifying the neglect of carers (Finch and Groves, 1983; Ungerson, 1987; Walby, 1990); and legitimating the valuing of difference (Lorde, 1984; Collins, 1990).

And of crucial significance, feminists have encouraged men to examine gender oppression not only in their relationships with women, but in their relationships with other men. This has led to the creation of men's groups on social work courses, and to men social workers and probation officers addressing issues of domestic violence (Fagg, 1993) and sexual abuse (see Cowburn, 1993). In taking up this challenge across a range of activities, men have also organized men's groups to address particular types of male behaviour, for example, domestic violence through MOVE, CHANGE, Achilles Heel Collective and Working with Men (see Seidler, 1992). This has meant that considerable movement has occurred since Ric Bowl (1985) exhorted men in social work to take feminism seriously.

In summary, feminism has had a profound effect on social work practice. It has raised gender as an issue and demonstrated how the oppression of women is structured into working relations and service delivery, even in a profession which is staffed largely by women workers and has a preponderance of women 'clients'. Moreover, feminists in social work have raised not only the position of women, but also that of children and men. They have highlighted the importance of child sexual abuse within the family (Nelson, 1982; Dominelli, 1986, 1989; McLeod and Saraga, 1989) and demanded that children's right to non-exploitative caring relations be upheld. They have also highlighted the problematic nature of masculinity, particularly in issues of both physical and sexual violence and demanded that it be redefined more in keeping with nurturing others (Dominelli, 1991, 1992b; Thompson, 1993).

Whilst practice initiatives remain patchy and vulnerable, the impact of feminism on the social work academy has been more fundamental. Drawing on the work of feminist scholars more generally, it has encompassed the content of the curriculum in college and the agencies, the pedagogic processes and working relations on courses whether these be amongst students, between students and

staff or amongst staff (McLeod, 1987; Reynolds, 1994). Feminism has: questioned the epistemological base of knowledge in theory and practice, and highlighted the invisibility of women's experience in traditional approaches to knowledge, including in social work (Marchant and Wearing, 1986); exposed the use of language as a way of putting people down and reinforcing relations of domination, and amended it (Spender, 1980; Abramovitz, 1991); challenged the use of both practice methods and teaching techniques which encourage the passivity of those at the receiving end, and replaced these with more participatory ones (McLeod, 1987);

Three Questions

1 How can the dominant (managerial and policy making) positions white men hold in social work, a profession staffed primarily by white women, be explained?

2 How can feminists relate to 'difference' in ways that are consistent with its egalitarian ethos?

3 What is the nature of feminists' challenge to traditional professionalism?

---

rejected gender-blind research methodologies in favour of ones which acknowledge women's experience and developed a more active set of relations between researchers and the subjects of the research (Stanley and Wise, 1983; Reinharz, 1992; Everitt et al., 1993); and openly sought to use research to improve women's position in society and eliminate gender oppression (Adamson et al., 1988; Kelly, 1988). In short, feminism has demanded a transformation of long-standing and taken-for-granted principles and practices on social work courses.

Gendered Working Relations

Feminists in social work have highlighted how gendered relations are central to social work. These have been shown not to work to the advantage of women, even in a profession in which women form the overwhelming majority (Hanmer and Statham, 1988; Dominelli and McLeod, 1989). Although men are in the minority, they have collared the bulk of posts at the apex of the profession and senior managerial echelons rest predominantly in their hands (Howe, 1986; Hallett, 1990; SSI, 1991; Burgess, 1994). Meanwhile, the majority of front-line workers are women. Men, therefore, shape the parameters in which women carry out their practice through the decisions they make about policies and resource allocation. This situation is not new for social work. It has been a profession dependent on men and the state (dominated by men at higher decision-making levels) since its inception (Walton, 1975; Callahan, 1994; Dominelli, 1996).

Men's career structure in the profession is different from women's. In social services, even if they begin in the residential sector, men tend to leave it quickly for more prestigious child care posts and then move on to management (Howe, 1986). Women who start out in residential work are more likely to stay there, rising at most to head of home. These gendered dynamics are further complicated by racism which makes the progression of black women and black men different from that of their white counterparts. A handful of black men have reached the rank of director of social services. Not one of them has yet attained the post of chief probation officer to date (NACRO, 1992; Burgess, 1994). But no black woman has succeeded in occupying either position. They have been ghettoized in the residential sector, Section 11 posts which have not been mainstreamed, clerical jobs and cleaning posts (Howe, 1986; Bruegal, 1989). More research is needed to pin-point their experiences more specifically, but Durrant (1989) and Ahmad (1992) have written of the impossible demands made of black women managers who wish to implement a different set of priorities to those which dominate social services agendas created by white men.

The situation in the academy reflects this pattern. Although there may be more women professors in social work than in other disciplines (see AUT, 1992), largely because its status in universities is constantly questioned and devalued as 'women's work', there is a preponderance of men at the senior levels. Yet, the majority of students and practice teachers are women. More recently, anecdotal evidence suggests that this trend has been reinforced by the elimination of the binary divide. Although the 'new' universities as a whole are bringing proportionately more women into the professorial ranks, social work seems to be moving in the opposite direction. The 1994 membership list of the Association of University Professors in Social Work showed that the 'old' universities had 13 women professors out of 33. When the 'new' universities joined the organization midway through the year, their numbers rose to 15 and 48 respectively. The percentage of women fell by 8 per cent.

The Backlash against Feminism

Feminist gains in social work have always been vulnerable. To begin with, they have been considered oppositional and appealed to people who were not normally located in high powered positions. Moreover, oppressed people are drawn into (re)producing and (re)creating their own oppression by internalizing the dominant hegemonic group's values, norms and mores, and reproducing oppressive relations through their own interactive processes. In these, women's choices and options as individuals are shaped by the contingent realities of the position(s) in which they are located. Their access to power and resources which provide a foundation for exercising choice, are limited. These constraints can turn resistance to oppression into a reinforcement of it as Willis (1977) has admirably portrayed in the case of class oppression experienced by young working-class men at school. This position should not be seen as 'blaming the victim'. Rather, it indicates the dialectical connection between being at the receiving end of oppression and questioning it.

The persistence of women's commitment and determination to continue resisting gender oppression has succeeded in limiting the damage which has been done to our capacity for independent action. However, opposition to feminist advances has intensified over the past few years as 'angry white men' have taken up cudgels in their own defence (see Lyndon, 1992). In social work, the bulk of this 'backlash' has been carried under the 'politically correct' banner and aimed primarily against anti-racist initiatives, largely because anti-racism has been given a higher profile by CCETSW in Paper 30 – the document setting out the requirements for the Diploma in Social Work (DipSW) (see Phillips,1993; Dunant, 1994). This public attack against anti-racist initiatives in social work has pulled other liberationist philosophies in its wake, and women students, practitioners and academics have been forced into a retreat which makes them fearful of exposing their feminist sympathies and/or credentials.

The shift has been accomplished through a virulent attack on all 'isms' in social work conducted in the press during the summer of 1993, the promise of CCETSW through its Chair to get rid of 'lunatic tendencies' in social work and return it to its more 'proper tasks', and the subtle and sophisticated interventions used to justify a more efficient use of scarce resources. This has included getting rid of policies and practices which have focused on specific 'isms' – primarily racism, sexism and heterosexism, and replacing these with more generalist ones which allegedly cover all forms of discrimination. So, separate Race Equality Units and Women's Units have been replaced with a single 'Equality Unit' with the remit of ensuring equal opportunities for everyone. In some ways, this is similar to the convention that claims 'he' includes 'she' and 'mankind' encompasses all 'humankind' (see Spender, 1980). It becomes a form of unquestioned exclusion which is carried out in the name of inclusion. But, more importantly, feminist and anti-racist solutions which sought to encompass the collective group, have been turned into individualistic ones in which a grievance is associated only with a particular case and divorced from structural inequalities which affect a number of other individuals who are similarly placed.

What has caused this response? White women and black people have questioned privileges which white men have previously taken for granted. Men who have felt threatened by this turn of events have sought to reassert their privileging by blaming white women and black people for their declining influence. However, neither have caused the drop in

Further Reading
1 Burden, D. S. and Gottlieb, N. (eds) (1987) *The Woman Client: Providing Human Services in a Changing World*, London: Tavistock.
2 Collins, P. H. (1991) *Black Feminist Thought: Knowledge, Consciousness and the Politics of Empowerment*, London: Routledge.
3 Dominelli, L. and McLeod, E. (1989) *Feminist Social Work*, London: Macmillan.

men's fortunes. Men's privileges have been tied to their roles in the public domain which they have traditionally accessed through the labour market. The globalization of the economy (Walby, 1990; Hutton, 1995) and recent technological changes have led to substantial losses in men's full-time posts. Widescale redundancies in manufacturing have occurred as jobs have migrated to the 'Tiger' economies of Asia (Arthuis, 1993). There, women work for even lower pay than they do in this country, concerns with health and safety issues are minimal and state funded welfare provisions limited. Full-time manufacturing positions have been replaced with part-time ones in the service industries, including the privatized parts of the welfare state. These are unattractive to white men (Walby, 1990). This keeps capital's reproductive costs low and increases its profit-making potential. Moreover, multinational companies' decisions to restructure and privatize the national economy have seldom involved women.

White women, black women and black men have become convenient scapegoats for the displaced anger of white men who feel they have lost their place in society. Without his role as provider, the key allowing him access to the public sphere, the man becomes an inhabitant of either the streets or private domain of the home. The home as *his* space is not readily available. He now has to share it with women and children who are already ensconced within it in particular ways which do not easily accommodate themselves to his new set of demands. Thus, the home and the street as sites where men can create alternative lifestyles become contested terrains fraught with tensions. In other words, the loss of their role as provider has implications for men's relationships with women and children within the family as well as the workplace. Social workers and probation officers have yet to wrestle

with the consequences of these changes for their practice.

Women have also supported men in opposing the advance of feminism. This reaction has to be recognized as women's rational response to the situations in which they find themselves and understood in terms of the multiple identities and realities in which men and women live. Some women do benefit from the current configuration of social relations. Not only are women privileged *vis-à-vis* children through adultist relations which give both men and women power and authority which does not have to be justified in every interaction over children, some women enjoy privileging over other women. For example, white middle-class women who rely on the availability of cheap labour provided by white and black working-class women to do the domestic chores, child care and elder care for their households enjoy, along with those living with them, a privilege rooted in their position of having greater access to financial and other resources. That these women are oppressed *vis-à-vis* white men in their social grouping does *not* detract from that reality. Whilst it might give them a greater degree of understanding of the mechanisms and impact of oppression, they will not automatically transfer knowledge gained from that area into others. They have to put time, energy and work into achieving this. Thus, white middle-class women social workers cannot assume that they can automatically make connections with white working-class women 'clients' on the basis of a commonly shared gender oppression. Their experiences of it are completely different. The same holds true for white women *vis-à-vis* black women.

Women's multiple realities fracture the potential unity which could exist between us. Differences, therefore, cannot be assumed away. These must be understood and taken hold of as part of the social situations within which we work (Lorde, 1984). Working with differences means that these cannot be taken on board as 'deficits' or 'inadequacies' which are defined as such by those in positions of greater power. They must be valued equally alongside each other. Such valuing suggests that the acceptance of difference requires differentiated initial inputs to reach the same destination. So, discrimination against black women can be taken account of by redistributing power and resources towards black women so that they can have the same starting point as white women, for example. In other words, a level playing field has to be created, not assumed.

Conclusions

Feminist social work as a theory and a method has had a profound impact on both social work practice and the academic curriculum. However, its influence has not permeated statutory social work to the extent that its predominantly woman workforce and clientele would suggest. This is because resistance to the spread of feminist principles and methodologies by those who are privileged by the prevailing social order have been sustained and widespread. The task of safeguarding feminist social work, or as Giddens (1987) suggests achieving continuity over time and space, remains to be adequately addressed by feminists and pro-feminist men. Until this happens, feminist social work in the statutory sector will remain limited and vulnerable.

Notes

1 I use 'race' in quotes to indicate its socially constructed rather than biological nature.

2 I place the term 'client' in quotes to denote its problematic nature and the lack of readily available alternatives. 'User' denotes an asymmetrical passive relationship in which the user is a consumer, not a creator of, services. The

phrase 'the woman the feminist practitioner works with' is too cumbersome.

References

Abbott, P. and Wallace, C. (1990) *An Introduction to Sociology: Feminist Perspectives*, London: Routledge.

Abramovitz, A. (1991) 'Putting an end to doublespeak about race, gender and poverty: an annotated glossary for social workers', in *Social Work*, 36(5), September, 380–4.

Adamson, N., Briskin, L. and McPhail, M. (1988) *Feminist Organising for Change*, Toronto: Oxford University Press.

Ahmad, B. (1992) *A Dictionary of Black Managers in White Organisations*, London: National Institute of Social Work.

Arthuis, J. (1993) *Rapport d'Informations sur les Delocalisations hors des Territoires Nationales des Activités Industrielles et des Services*, Paris: Senate.

AUT (Association of University Teachers) (1992) *Sex Discrimination in Universities*, London: AUT.

Bowl, R. (1985) *Changing the Nature of Masculinity: a Task for Social Work*, Norwich: University of East Anglia Monographs.

Brook, E. and Davis, A. (1985) *Women, the Family and Social Work*, London: Tavistock.

Bruegal, I. (1989) 'Sex and race in the labour market', *Feminist Review*, 32 (Summer), 49–68.

Burgess, R. (1994) *Black Managers in the Probation Service*, unpublished M.Sc. dissertation, the University of Reading.

Callahan, M. (1994) *Women in Social Work*, unpublished Ph.D. Thesis, the University of Bristol.

Chaplin, J. (1988) *Feminist Counselling in Action*, London: Sage.

Collins, P. H. (1990) *Black Feminist Thought: Knowledge, Consciousness and the Politics of Empowerment*, London: Routledge.

Cook, A. and Kirk, G. (1983) *Greenham Women Everywhere: Dreams, Ideas and Action from the Women's Peace Movement*, London: Pluto Press.

Cowburn, M. (1993) 'Groupwork programme for male sex offenders: establishing principles for practice', in A. Brown and B. Caddick (eds), *Groupwork with Offenders*, London: Whiting & Birch.

David, M. and New, C. (1985) *For the Children's Sake: Making Childcare more than Women's Business*, London: Penguin.

Dominelli, L. (1986) 'Father–daughter incest: patriarchy's shameful secret', in *Critical Social Policy*, 16, 8–22.

Dominelli, L. (1989) 'Betrayal of trust: a feminist analysis of power relationships in incest abuse and its relevance for social work practice', in *British Journal of Social Work*, 19, 291–307.

Dominelli, L. (1991a) *Gender, Sex Offenders and Probation Practice*, Norwich: Novata Press.

Dominelli, L. (1991b) *Women Across Continents:*

Feminist Comparative Social Policy, London: Harvester Wheatsheaf.

Dominelli, L. (1992a) 'More than a method: feminist social work', in K. Campbell (ed.), *Critical Feminisms*, Milton Keynes: Open University.

Dominelli, L. (1992b) 'Sex offenders and probation practice', in P. Senior and D. Woodhill (eds), *Gender, Crime and Probation Practice*, Sheffield: PAVIC Publications.

Dominelli, L. (1996) *Contaminating Knowledge: Sociological Social Work*, London: Macmillan.

Dominelli, L. and McLeod, E. (1989) *Feminist Social Work*, London: Macmillan.

Dunant, S. (ed.) (1994) *The War of the Words: the Political Correctness Debate*, London: Virago.

Durrant, J. (1989) 'Continuous agitation', *Community Care*, 13, July, 23–5.

Everitt, A., Hardiker, P., Littlewood, J. and Mullender, A. (1993) *Applied Research for Better Practice*, London: BASW/Macmillan.

Fagg, C. (1993) *Probation Practice and Domestic Violence*, unpublished MA dissertation, The University of Sheffield.

Finch, J. and Groves, D. (eds) (1983) *Labour of Love: Women, Work and Caring*, London: Routledge & Kegan Paul.

Giddens, A. (1987) *Social Theory and Modern Sociology*, Oxford: Blackwell.

Gordon, L. (1986) 'Feminism and social control: the case of child abuse and neglect', in J. Mitchell and A. Oakley (eds), *What is Feminism*, Oxford: Basil Blackwell.

Groves, D. and McLean, M. (1991) *Women and Social Policy*, London: Routledge.

Hale, L. (1984) 'Feminism and social work practice', in W. Jordan and N. Parton (eds), *The Political Dimensions of Social Work*, Oxford: Basil Blackwell.

Hallett, C. (1990) *Women in Social Work*, London: Sage.

Hanmer, J. and Saunders, S. (1984) *Well Founded Fear: a Community Study of Violence on Women*, London: Hutchinson.

Hanmer, J. and Statham, D. (1988) *Women and Social Work: Woman Centered Practice*, London: Macmillan.

Howe, D. (1986) 'The segregation of women and their work in the personal social services', in *Critical Social Policy*, 15, 21–36.

Hudson, A. (1985) 'Feminism and social work: resistance or dialogue', in *British Journal of Social Work*, 15, 635–55.

Hutton, W. (1995) *The State We're In*, London: Jonathan Cape.

Judge, S. (1993) *Feminist Counselling: A Private Practice*, paper given at the Social Work Seminar, Sheffield University, 26 May.

Kelly, L. (1988) *Surviving Sexual Assault*, Cambridge: Polity Press.

Langan, M. and Day, L. (eds) (1989) *Women, Oppression and Social Work*, London: Tavistock.

Lorde, A. (1984) *Sister Outsider*, New York: The Crossing Press.

Lyndon, N. (1992) *No More Sex War: the Failures of Feminism*, London: Sinclair-Stevenson.

Mama, A. (1989) *Hidden Struggle: Statutory and Voluntary Responses to Violence Against Black Women in the Home*, London: London Race and Housing Unit.

Marchant, H. and Wearing, B. (eds) (1986) *Gender Reclaimed*, Sydney, Australia: Hale and Iremonger.

McLeod, E. (1987) 'Some lessons from teaching feminist social work', *Issues in Social Work Education*, 3(2), 131–43.

McLeod, E. and Dominelli, L. (1982) 'The personal and the apolitical: feminism and moving beyond integrated methods approach', in R. Bailey and P. Lee (eds), *Theory and Practice in Social Work*, Oxford: Basil Blackwell, pp. 112–17.

McLeod, M. and Saraga, E. (1989) 'Child sexual abuse', in *Feminist Review*, 28.

NACRO (National Association for the Care and Resettlement of Offenders) (1992) *Black People Working in the Criminal Justice System*, London: NACRO.

Nelson, S. (1982) *Incest: Myths and Facts*, Edinburgh: Stramullion Co-operative.

Pascall, G. (1986) *Social Policy: a Feminist Analysis*, London: Tavistock.

Phillips, M. (1993) 'An oppressive urge to end oppression', in *The Observer*, 1 August.

Reinharz, S. (1992) *Feminist Methods in Social Research*, Oxford: Oxford University Press.

Reynolds, J. (1994) 'Introducing gender issues into social work education: is this just women's work?', *Issues in Social Work Education*, 9, 3–20.

Seidler, V. (1992) *Men, Sex and Relationships: Writings from Achilles Heel*, London: Routledge.

Sibeon, R. (1991) *Towards a Sociology of Social Work*, Aldershott: Avebury.

Social Services Inspectorate (SSI) (1991) *Women in Social Services*, London: SSI.

Spender, D. (1980) *Man Made Language*, London: Routledge & Kegan Paul.

Stanley, L. (ed.) (1990) *Feminist Praxis*, London: Routledge.

Stanley, L. and Wise, S. (1983) *Breaking Out: Feminist Consciousness and Feminist Research*, London: Routledge & Kegan Paul.

Thompson, J. (1993) 'Probation practice with sex offenders', in P. Senior and B. William (eds), *Values, Gender and Offending*, Sheffield: PAVIC Publications.

Tong, R. (1989) *Feminist Thought: a Comprehensive Introduction*, San Francisco: Westview Press.

Ungerson, C. (1987) *Policy is Personal: Sex, Gender and Informal Care*, London: Tavistock.

Walby, S. (1990) *Theorizing Patriarchy*, Oxford: Basil Blackwell.

Walton, R. (1975) *Women in Social Work*, London: Routledge & Kegan Paul.

Willis, P. (1977) *Learning to Labour: How Working Class Kids Get Working Class Jobs*, Farnborough: Saxon House.

Wilson, M. (1993) *Crossing the Boundary: Black Women Survive Incest*, London: Virago.

Part VI
Perspectives on Social Work

Introduction to Part VI

Social work presents itself as a professional activity serving the needs of its service users and reflecting bodies of knowledge interpreted by its practitioners. But the political framework within which social work is practised means that other agents have claimed the right to express a view about social work and, in some degree, to seek to influence its practice. On the one hand, we have the attempt made by academic researchers from a social science base to monitor and evaluate the nature of practice; this dynamic has, furthermore, been taken up by those in positions of administrative responsibility in order to try to measure the quality of social work. On the other hand, the service users themselves have found ways of expressing their own opinions about the service that is available, while at the apex of the political spectrum the agents of central government have evolved systems of law making and inspection which unambiguously reflect the stake which politicians (and the Treasury) have in the publicly funded welfare system.

VI.1
The Research Perspective
Juliet Cheetham

There should be an essential relationship between research and social work. This is essential because research can help develop a solid foundation for understanding the social structures and problems which confront social work, thus clarifying the feasible domain of social services and wider social policies. Research should also illuminate the differences between the ethical, political and technical components of the concerns of social work. Finally, research can identify the impact of social work, for good or ill, and can thus contribute to more effective welfare provision. The functions of research are therefore:

- To illuminate the aetiology of social and personal problems, including the impact of social policies on individual citizens, families and communities. This is the arena of social work.
- To determine the impact of social work. This must include analysis of its explicit and implicit functions, tasks and processes.
- To influence policy and practice.

Experience shows that in these three roles research, taken seriously, can both challenge social work and change it.

This essential relationship is growing but not yet well established, in part because of a narrow perception of research and its functions but also because social work, along with many other human services which face immense pressures to respond and deliver, can still favour – or be forced into – action at the price of critical appraisal. The *Oxford English Dictionary* provides an inclusive definition of research which underlines its relevance to social work:

- the act of searching;
- a search or investigation directed to the discovering of some facts by careful consideration or study of the subject;
- a course of critical and scientific enquiry.

Research, therefore, goes beyond large empirical studies lasting years and costing hundreds of thousands of dollars; with this definition it includes observation, inquisitive and sustained questioning, recording and analysis. These are not simply the tasks of social scientists; they are at the heart of social work practice. The characteristics and qualities of the research enterprise implied by this definition are therefore familiar to social workers and, indeed, to many other practitioners. They are rooted in their mind set in asking questions, in careful observation of complicated behaviour and communication – with service providers and users alike – and in making some sense of partial or conflicting information. These activities are the foundations of research-minded practice, just as they are the cornerstone of fully paid-up researcher skills. This is a good beginning to the relationship between research and social work.

Understanding the Arena of Social Work

Social workers and their teachers, like

other citizens, remain vulnerable to the absorption of ideologies and theories about social and personal problems which may be as appealing as they are untested. Changing fashions in responses to delinquency, to mental illness and to single parenthood provide just a few examples. It is not always easy to distinguish between a passing fad and an important conceptual advance; a research-based analysis is crucial to challenge and to clarify. Research is also a protection against over-simplified understanding or response; it must be a social work priority to press for the incorporation of the full range of research evidence which the complexity of its domain and tasks demands. This intellectual integrity is not easy when research challenges our own and other professions' received wisdom.

For example, schizophrenia and other serious mental health problems continue to plague individuals and families and to challenge social workers and other health professionals. Within the lifetime of many readers institutional care – ranging from drug therapy in locked wards to experimental group living – and a variety of community provision have all been favoured treatments, mostly with a tenuous research base. While research indicates that large questions remain about the origins of schizophrenia (with, perhaps, the fortunate consequence of making illegitimate the blaming of parents for their children's misfortunes) it also now points to better and less good responses which have essential implications for social work (Horobin, 1985; Goldberg and Huxley, 1991). Examples include helping families avoid high levels of expressed emotion and, above all, accepting and acting upon the very ordinary but essential needs of people who want employment, occupation, inclusion and personal contact to promote their quality of life. Here study of the users of mental health services is of major importance; their

Five Key Points

1 The major functions of research are to illuminate the causes and context of social and personal problems, to determine the impact of social work and to influence policy and practice.
2 Research designs and methods should be adapted to the issues to be studied. Researching social work requires a plurality of rigorous methods and disciplined interpretation, and close liaison between those who undertake research and those who use it.
3 The process as well as the outcomes of social work should be studied.
4 In researching the impact of social work the perceptions of experiences of different parties should be taken into account.
5 Research-minded social work practice should be promoted by practitioners, agencies and educational institutions.

voices must be heard loud and clear (Brown, 1987; Rogers et al., 1993).

A second example is provided by research on the aetiology of young teenage pregnancy. This points to the complexity of the questions to be tackled and makes a mockery of claims that 'young girls get pregnant to get public housing' (Miller et al., 1992; Brannen, 1993). It also shows ignorance of contraception and of the outcomes of sexual behaviour to be insufficient explanations of teenage pregnancy and that further illumination comes from an understanding of gender roles, self-esteem and confidence; and of the limitations of the lives and prospects of some women; and of the inadequacies of contraception. Social workers, in collaboration with parents and teachers, thus have a role in promoting the knowledge, skills and alternatives which will make young people's personal relationships less problematic and which may thus enhance their self-esteem.

Crime and delinquency have also in the last few decades been explained morally, psychologically and sociologically, with the concomitant responses of punishment, re-education, counselling, and group and community work, and attempts to reduce unemployment and urban deprivation. Research illuminates the potential and the flaws of all these responses and shows, above all, the limitations of single, over-simple explanations.

Another example of the complexities of the influences on behaviour widely regarded as self-damaging is found in the research of Hilary Graham (1993a and b) and others who vividly portray the poignant dilemmas of women for whom the only relief from struggles of parenting in poverty comes from smoking, the one thing which gives relief and which they have for themselves. In smoking, for a brief moment, these women have the illusion that their poverty is suspended and that they have joined the world of consumption.

Smoking by enabling mothers to cope promotes family welfare, but only by undermining individual health. It reflects in a particularly sharp way the conflicts that go with caring for health in circumstances of hardship.

(Graham, 1993a, p. 183)

Sustained analysis of such social and personal problems and of the impact of social policies would demand a lifetime spent in the social sciences, and for most social workers only a brief journey is possible. How, therefore, can social workers pursue a research-based understanding of the world in which they move, especially when, notoriously, many have little time or inclination for reading and, equally important, for weighing and interpreting evidence and conclusions? There is no easy response and responsibilities must be shared.

First, social workers, their teachers and managers must cultivate critical scepticism about their understanding and explanations of social problems. Are these received wisdom and does this wisdom have empirical support; and what is the quality of this analysis? If there seems little or no research-based evidence – but response and action cannot wait – what questions demand attention? In identifying such gaps in knowledge social workers can help set research agenda. Contemporary examples include fuller understanding of the real workings of markets – now perceived as the fastest freeway to economic prosperity and individual liberty – in the mixed economies in health and social care; a better understanding of the lives of very dependent people in the community, and a critical analysis of the meaning and realities of empowerment for the users of health and social care. These are all the policy fashions of the moment, sustained by rhetoric and bolstered by enthusiasm. Neither should get in the way of sober, critical assessment of their delivery in the real world; and central to this assessment must be the perspectives of users and their influence on research agenda, something which has so far largely been pursued in the field of disability (Oliver, 1991). This critical questioning and searching cannot be solely the task of practitioners. Their departments must encourage and support it through research sections whose job it is to keep in touch, review and summarize key research.

Researchers too have responsibilities to disseminate their work succinctly and in forms and publications accessible to practitioners and policy-makers. They also have another crucial service to perform as well in providing systematic review and reflection on what is known. These are not simply great intellectual endeavours; they are also practical acts of altruism because they relieve practitioners – and researchers too – of the impossible and onerous task of reading and critical analysis of the ever-burgeoning amount of research, of variable quality, which is relevant to social work. Excellent examples include Smith et al.'s (1994) account of effective probation practice; Ramon's (1991) reflections on the limitations of contemporary community care; Twigg's (1992) analysis of the different roles social workers thrust upon carers and Howe's (1993) account, from clients' perspectives, of the essentials of helpful counselling, whatever its 'school' or theoretical base. Smith and Rutter's (1995) outstanding synthesis of international research on the aetiology of the psycho-social disorders and delinquency of young people will provide, for many years, challenges to many contemporary explanations which focus on poverty, as well as pointers to the importance of family influences in their social context.

Determining the Impact of Social Work

A second important function for research is its contribution to the evaluation of the effectiveness of social work. There are many internal and external pressures for evaluation. These include:

- consumers' right to quality and choice;
- taxpayers' right to value for money;
- professionals' need to be accountable;
- increasing knowledge about impact; and
- the wish and need to improve services.

Social workers must embrace willingly the hard questions about the impact of what they do as individuals, agency members and as a profession. They must be able to respond to their own and others' enquiries about whether social work can make a demonstrable difference to the lives of those who receive it. They must derive more confidence from – and

make more widely known – the now well-established good news about the effectiveness of well-targeted and carefully planned social work. This evidence is readily accessible through the writings of Reid and Hanrahan (1982); Sheldon (1986); Videka-Sherman (1988); Macdonald et al. (1992) and Sinclair (1992); and from the summary reports of University of Stirling Social Work Research Centre studies.

Social workers in health, practitioners and researchers alike, should also take heart from being part of a huge wave of work which, not before time, is subjecting to critical scrutiny, the impact of political and managerial policies. Hospital closure

---

Three Questions

1 What are your three chief priorities for social work research?
2 With reference to one of these priorities what key research questions should be asked; and how might these be studied?
3 How can research, policy and practice be more closely integrated? (Use some real examples of research to discuss this question.)

---

programmes and their alternatives, care management, community-based health care, the promotion of choice, the discovery of carers' centrality to welfare, the expanding possibilities of care for people with dementia, the place of the multidisciplinary team, the primacy of the user, and the special role of lay and user help for people with shared experiences are but a few major contemporary preoccupations likely to endure at least for the next decade.

Some of these enthusiasms have been extensively researched but some appear to be prejudices given prominence through political expediency. They all attempt to deal with the enduring problems of the human condition –

problems of poverty, ill health, disability and of struggling and disintegrating relationships. The responses to such troubles are often both contentious and ill-resourced and social work, by its association with them, can reap the whirlwind. A critical analysis and defence must be research based if it is to have the authority which goes beyond anecdote, prejudice and individual experience. The still small voice of evaluative research must be heard amidst the wind and fire of politics. The next section addresses priorities important for those who carry out this research and those who use it.

Process and outcome and stakeholders

Research which evaluates effectiveness involves two different but closely related activities. To study effectiveness requires a focus on outcomes, both service and client based. To evaluate requires more than the identification of outcomes; it demands an assessment of their worth. This may well be judged differently by the many different stakeholders and interest groups for whom the outcomes of social work can be significant. These include those who receive services directly, their carers, managers, social workers, funders and taxpayers. Their different perspectives are crucial for holistic evaluation (Smith and Cantley, 1984). Process must also be studied to ensure programme integrity and to make replication possible. There is also substantial evidence that the manner in which social work is delivered can greatly affect its outcomes and can be perceived as an end in itself.

Most difficult of all, attempts must be made to relate process to outcome. The promise of experimental and cross-institutional designs to produce conclusive evidence of causation is often not fulfilled in practice; and they often present serious practical and resource problems. In trying to elucidate the relationship between intervention and

outcome, social work research must therefore use a range of methods which include measures before and after intervention and over time, comparison groups, and seeking the expert opinion of users about the effective components of the services they have received. Studies using these diverse approaches gain added strength when they are reviewed and compared, and their collective conclusions distilled. This demonstration of research as incremental is an important research task.

Finally, since the affairs of social work are so central to individual experience and social life, every study must retain a clear view of the significance and ordinary meanings of the problems confronted and the help given. Research questions and focus should not be so narrowed, in the interests of precision in data collection and analysis, that these realities are distorted and the research becomes incomprehensible to those whose lives and behaviour it is meant to illuminate.

Methodological pluralism

The consequence of such priorities must be a plurality of research methods and design. The contribution of an interaction of quantitative and qualitative methods is now well accepted (Brannen, 1993) but a range of research designs is also necessary if social work services are to be studied as they are, and if analyses of effectiveness are to be relatively easily incorporated into agencies' activities. This approach does not expect services will be planned to suit the needs of researchers or to make systematic comparison between one service and another a relatively routine and simple exercise. Practice and policy are rapidly evolving and changing, pressed by legislative changes, political priorities and resource constraints. Evaluative research which meets the tenets of social scientific enquiry is not high on the agenda of social work agencies. This is the reality which confronts researchers in social work, and which must be taken into account if most modes of social work practice are to be regarded as candidates for serious evaluation (Cheetham et al., 1992).

This context for social work research, and for research in other human services, (Daley et al., 1992) entails methodological pluralism which is flexible and pragmatic in its adaptation of research questions, designs and instruments to fit the subject of enquiry, the resources available and the interests of the audiences to be addressed, and which also allows feasible, systematic studies. There is, thus, no one research method which is always to be preferred for its potential to illuminate the impact of social work and no hierarchy of research methods. Research rigour is not the prerogative of any single method or design.

The Integration of Research with Policy and Practice

Discussions of the integration of research, policy and practice usually focus on the need for active dissemination addressed to a variety of audiences. Written and oral dissemination may be equally important, particularly in professional cultures where reading research literature, in any form, is not well established. However, even the most energetic dissemination will not ensure the integration of research policy and practice. The nature of their relationship is often complex (Booth, 1988). Politics, custom and crises are frequently stronger influences than the often tentative conclusions of research. Notable examples in Britain are recent developments in penal policy which emphasize custodial sentences and which fly directly in the face of decades of research evidence about more and less effective responses to offending. The closure of hospital social work

departments by local authorities, in favour of community-based social work for health problems, is a further perverse example given hospital social workers' proven cost-effectiveness in arranging expeditiously and humanely the discharge of vulnerable patients and their support in the community (Connor and Tibbitt, 1988).

There are some signs, however, that the receptiveness of the worlds of policy and practice to research may be changing (Richardson et al., 1990). This is certainly the British government's intention in the strong emphasis on the primacy of the utility and relevance of research, and its necessary close relationship with research users outlined in the White Paper on science and technology *Realising our Potential* (1993).

These aspirations are also taken up in a Department of Health report (1994) on research and the personal social services which concluded, perhaps a trifle optimistically that, while there is a reasonably well-established relationship between policy-makers and researchers, there is too large a gulf between practitioners and researchers. The report recommends various ways to increase the involvement of practitioners in research including their greater contribution to setting research agenda. It is sometimes assumed that practitioners have little interest in research and feel alienated from its purposes and processes.

Further Reading

1 Cheetham, J., Fuller, R., McIvor, G. and Petch, A. (1995) *Evaluating Social Work Effectiveness*, Buckingham: Open University Press.
2 Fuller, R. and Petch, A. (1995) *Practitioner Research; The Reflexive Social Worker*, Buckingham: Open University Press.
3 Sutton, C. (1987) *A Handbook of Research for the Helping Professions*, London: Routledge & Kegan Paul.

However, Smith (1995) has shown that a substantial minority, despite huge pressures upon them, are keen for more interaction with research and researchers and believe that this would enhance their practice.

Practitioner Research

One particularly effective method of developing research-minded practice is the development of practitioner research through small-scale projects chosen and carried out by practitioners, usually with the advice and support of academics. Such enterprises are increasingly being established within and outside Britain (Addison, 1988; Whittaker and Archer, 1989; Thyer, 1992; Connor, 1993; Hess and Mullen, 1995; Cheetham, 1995; Fuller and Petch, 1995; Fook, 1996; Kazi, 1996).

The Practitioner Research Programme at Stirling University provides one example. It is designed to demystify research and to help practitioners acquire the basic skills of evaluative research in the context of their chosen small study projects, to be completed within a year, which focus on their own or their immediate colleagues' work. The overall purpose is to promote an intimate, interactive relationship between thinking and action for people with no grounding in research and often very limited knowledge of social science. Programme participants report that, in addition to completing studies immediately relevant to their own work, the 'hands-on' experience of research has greatly increased their critical understanding of its contribution to policy and practice (Fuller and Petch, 1995).

Students, Social Workers and Research Enquiry

A principal argument of this chapter is that research can and should be an accepted component of social work practice. Research must, therefore, be firmly on the agenda of all levels of social work education. This does not need to entail the acquisition of research skills but it must involve appreciation of the potential and limitations of the most common research approaches. Social work education must also focus on what is known about effective practice. It must not be a supermarket where students and their supervisors choose according to whim and preference rather than evidence. The centrality of research for social work's proper understanding of the problems it confronts and of the most effective intervention is not universally accepted in increasingly crowded curricula. In Britain, there are, paradoxically, threats from the pressure for hands-on, skill-oriented social work training. Such competencies are to be desired but as techniques which stand alone from the real complexities of the arena and tasks of social work, or knowledge about their short and longer term effectiveness, they will be devices without a broader strategy, possibly open to manipulation by those who control social work. Social workers must be much more than competent technicians. They therefore need research which is accessible and useful.

This personal interpretation of the role of research in social work, which sees its functions as informing, challenging, changing and permeating the policy and practice of social work services, is intended to place research within the grasp of practitioners and to be an activity of researchers and practitioners in alliance. Experience shows this inclusive approach to the scope, methods and designs of research to be highly practical and increasingly influential.

References

Addison, C. (1988) *Planning Investigation Projects: a Workbook for Social Service Practitioners*, London:

National Institute for Social Work.

Booth, T. (1988) *Developing Policy Research*, Aldershot: Avebury.

Brannen, J. (ed.) (1993) *Mixing Methods, Qualitative and Quantitative Research*, London: Avebury.

Brannen, J., Dodd, K., Oakley, A. and Strong, P. (1994) *Young People Health and Family Life*, Buckingham: Open University Press.

Brown, G. W. (1987) 'Social factors in the development and course of depressive disorders in women: a review of a research programme', *British Journal of Social Work*, 17(6), 615–34.

Cheetham, J., Fuller, R., McIvor, G., Petch A. (1992) *Evaluating Social Work Effectiveness*, Buckingham: Open University Press.

Cheetham, J. (1992) 'Evaluating the effectiveness of social work: its contribution to the department of a knowledge base', *Issues in Social Work Education*, 12(1), 52–68.

Cheetham, J. (1995) 'Knowledge for practice: what is the effect of what we do?', in P. Hess and D. Mullen, *Practitioner Researcher Partnerships*, Washington: National Association of Social Workers.

Connor, A. and Tibbitt, J. E. (1988) *Social Workers and Health Care in Hospitals*, London: HMSO.

Connor, A. (1993) *Monitoring and Evaluation Made Easy*, London: HMSO.

Daley, J., MacDonald, I. and Willis, E. (eds) (1992) *Researching Health Care, Designs, Dilemmas, Disciplines*, London: Tavistock/Routledge.

Department of Health (1994) *Research and the Personal Social Services*, London: HMSO.

Fook, J. (1996) *The Reflective Researcher*, New South Wales: Allen and Unwin.

Fuller, R. and Petch, A. (1995) *Practitioner Research: The Reflexive Social Worker*, Buckingham: Open University Press.

Goldberg, D. and Huxley, P. (1992) *Common Mental Disorders: a Biosocial Model*, London: Routledge.

Graham, H. (1993a) *Hardship and Health in Women's Lives*, London: Harvester Wheatsheaf.

Graham, H. (1993b) *When Life's a Drag: Women Smoking and Disadvantage*, London: HMSO.

Hess, P. and Mullen, E. (1995) *Practioner–Researcher Partnerships*, Washington: National Association of Social Workers.

Horobin, G. (ed.) (1985) *Responding to Mental Illness*, London: Kogan Page.

Howe, D. (1993) *On Being a Client*, London: Sage.

Kazi, M. (1996) *Single Case Design in Social Work*, Aldershot: Avebury.

Macdonald, G., Sheldon, B. and Gillespie, J. (1992) Contemporary Studies of the Effectiveness of

Social Work, *British Journal of Social Work*, 22, 615–43.

Miller, B. C., Card, J. J., Parkoff, P. and Peterson, J. L. (ed.) (1992) *Preventing Adolescent Pregnancy*, London: Sage.

Oliver, M. (ed.) (1991) *Social Work, Disabled People and Disabling Environment*, Research Highlights in Social Work, 21, London: Jessica Kingsley.

Ramon, S. (ed.) (1991) *Beyond Community Care*, London: Macmillan/Mind.

Realising our Potential: a Strategy for Science, Engineering and Technology (1993), London, HMSO (Cm 2250).

Reid, W. J. and Hanrahan, P. (1982) 'Recent evaluations of social work: grounds for optimism', *Social Work*, 27, 328–40.

Richardson, A., Jackson, C. and Sykes, W. (1990) *Taking Research Seriously*, London: HMSO.

Rogers, A., Pilgrim, D. and Lacey, R. (1993) *Experiencing Psychiatry*, London: MacMillan/NIMH.

Sheldon, B. (1986) 'Social work effectiveness experiences: review and implications', *British Journal of Social Work*, 16, 223–42.

Sinclair, I. (1992) 'Social work research: its relevance to social work and social work education', *Issues in Social Work Education*, 2, 65–80.

Smith, G. and Cantley, C. (1984) 'Pluralistic evaluation', in J. Lishman (ed.), *Evaluation: Research Highlights*, vol. 8, London: Jessica Kingsley.

Smith, D., Raynor, P. and Vanstone, M. (1994) *Effective Probation Practice*, London: Macmillan.

Smith, D. and Rutter, M. (ed.) (1995) *Psycho-Social Disorders of Youth*, Oxford: Oxford University Press.

Smith, J. (1995) *Practitioners and Research*, University of Stirling: Social Work Research Centre.

Social Work Research Centre (SWRC) (1993) *Is Social Work Effective?*, University of Stirling: Social Work Research Centre.

Thyer, B. (1992) Promoting evaluation research in the field of family prevention in E. S. Morton and R. K. Grigsby (ed.) *Advancing Family Prevention Practice*, Newbury Park, CA: Sage.

Twigg, J. (1992) *Carers: Research and Practice*, London: HMSO.

Videka-Sherman, L. (1988) 'Meta-analysis of research on social work practice and mental health', *Social Work*, 33, 325–38.

Whittaker, D. S. and Archer, J. C. (1989) *Research by Social Workers: Capitalising on Experience*, London: CCETSW.

VI.2
A Quality-control Perspective
Ian Sinclair

Introduction

This chapter makes three related points. First, there are important variations in the quality of the various front-line units and professionals delivering social services. Second, the various mechanisms which might 'even up' performance (for example, market forces and inspection) typically fail to do so to any marked degree. Third, these mechanisms remain whatever their defects the only ones we have got for improving quality, and we need a sustained, long-term effort to ensure that they deliver the goods.

Existence of Variations

My interest in variations in quality was sparked by the first piece of social research in which I was involved. This focused on probation hostels and in many ways the most striking thing about these was the extraordinary variation in the degree to which the young people were involved in delinquent activities. Under different wardens (the places were run by husband and wife teams), the proportion of young men (in the male hostels) leaving prematurely as a result of an absconding or offence varied from 14 to 78 per cent.

These percentages were calculated on routine information available on over 4,000 young men over a period of ten years. Interestingly, the variations were not explained by differences in intake, or by the location, size, physical characteristics, or any other aspect

associated with the hostel other than its staff. Differences in the failure rates between successive wardens in the same hostel were as great as those between different wardens in different hostels. In short, these differences in outcome all seemed to boil down to the characteristics of the husband and wife teams who ran the hostels, together with a 'random effect' whereby waves of trouble could occur in even the best ordered establishment. Impressionistically it was not hard to see why this might be so – to quote from the warden who ran the least successful hostel, 'each boy has his breaking point and I find it'. Statistically it was possible to show that the characteristics of successful husband and wife teams approximated to those of parents of 17–21-year-old probationers who did not re-offend (Davies and Sinclair, 1971; Sinclair, 1971).

These findings on the importance of individuals in shaping the welfare of small residential establishments were complemented by other studies of residential care for young people carried out at around the same time. These studies confirmed the existence of major variations between establishments in the apparent quality of care. Establishments varied in the percentages of their young people who felt supported, in the numbers who were bullied, in the numbers running away, in the quality of talk between staff and young children, in the degree to which the rules seemed humane and child centred, and indeed in almost every aspect of the regimes and outcome which were studied. Progress was made in relating the outcomes of interest to characteristics of the establishment (e.g., the amount of autonomy possessed by the staff), so that it could be seen that the nature of the influence wielded by individual members of staff was itself a function of the overall organization. In small establishments such as probation hostels the immediate leader might be of paramount importance but this reflected the organizational context within which the wardens worked. In other establishments the position was more complex (see, e.g., Millham et al., 1975; Tizard et al., 1975).

It might have been expected that these findings on the variations between establishments would have been followed by an intensive attack on the problem of how overall quality might be achieved. This, however, did not occur and as Bullock and his colleagues have pointed out interest shifted to describing the careers of children in care rather than analysing the quality of their experience in it (Bullock et al., 1993). The possibility of the existence of similar differences among other kinds of unit (day centres for example) remained largely unexplored, but more recently there has been some evidence that large and interesting differences exist between old people's homes. These differ in staffing ratios, facilities, the mortality rates and frailty of their residents, and in the proportion of residents who knit or score highly on measures of happiness. There is, however, much less clarity on what produces these differences with a number of negative findings (notably in Booth's impressive 1985 study) and some evidence that in small private homes those in charge may exercise similar influence to that once wielded by wardens in probation hostels (Gibbs and Sinclair, 1992a).

A further feature of this field of research is the lack of interest in individual differences between practitioners who deliver a personal

Five Key Points

1   Research has shown wide variations in the effectiveness of social work, apparently caused by differences in the characteristics of individual· practitioners.

2   Strangely these findings have rarely been pursued: little further attempt has been made to determine how a more consistent performance might be achieved.

3   But we know that consumers are clear about the kind of social workers they want; and we know, also from consumer studies, that social workers do differ from each other – for example, in their reliability.

4   The various mechanisms designed to 'even up' performance (for example, market forces and inspections) typically fail to do so.

5   We need more research into variations in social work performance, the impact of organizational structures on practice and the relevance of training.

service. The importance given to the training of social workers and the calls for training for home care and residential workers suggest a general recognition that the way in which these individual workers perform their tasks is crucial. A recognition of differences in effectiveness is after all commonplace in the case of other professions. It is presumably the justification for the vast differences in salary paid to barristers, and for the large salaries of the captains of industry, and it is implicit in the reports that the death rate among comparable patients varies with the surgeon performing the operation. Yet in the case of social work hardly any studies have set out to look at differences in effectiveness between practitioners.

That said there is some evidence that individual differences in effectiveness are important. One line of evidence comes from consumer studies. Users in all client groups value, it seems, similar characteristics in their social workers. They want workers who keep appointments, understand the user's perception of the problem, are straight and not two-faced, are warm, and are efficient in getting services and benefits. Those who have home helps have analogous requirements for warmth, efficiency and sensitivity – they like friendly people who get the work done, understand the users' requirements for privacy and control over their environment, and do not gossip. So far no study has systematically set out to see whether some workers routinely get favourable comments in these respects while others get negative ones. Nevertheless, the quoted comments strongly suggest that workers do differ from each other (e.g., in reliability) (see Packman, 1986; Sinclair et al., 1989).

A variety of mechanisms exist which might be expected to even up these variations in performance. Broadly they can be grouped into those which rely on choice and market mechanisms, those which emphasize organizational approaches to ensuring quality control and assurance, and those which focus on the selection, training and professionalization of the individuals delivering service.

Choice and Market Mechanisms

Let us look first at choice and the market. Much hope is undoubtedly placed in these. In the new mixed economy of welfare the market is expected both to drive down costs and drive up quality. Within a very different tradition social workers have been expected to empower their clients, which would seem to imply giving them choices. Government exhortations are directed towards involving clients in case conferences and

enhancing 'consumer power' through complaints procedures and the provision of information on services and entitlements. How much hope can we place in these widely advertised nostrums?

The short answer to this question is that we do not know. And this is curious for if we are serious about enhancing quality we might be expected to be making every effort to see if we were succeeding in doing so. It is perhaps more curious if one reflects that there are reasons for thinking that the ability of users to choose between different providers of the same service (as against the ability to refuse particular kinds of service if offered) is limited.

The limitations referred to above are partly to do with principle and partly pragmatic. The difficulties of principle arise because users' wishes cannot always be paramount. In 'statutory' cases rights conflict. Bell (1996), for example, examined the effect on parental satisfaction of invitations to attend a case conference. She found as had other researchers that parents liked to be asked. However, the parents did not feel that they had influenced the decision, and there was no evidence that they did so. Parental satisfaction with social services was not related to involvement in the case conference but was related to whether their child had been removed from home.

More commonly users' wishes are considered within a framework of scarcity, and other pragmatic constraints. It would, for example, be unusual for a user to be allowed a choice of social workers or a choice of home care workers. In some cases users are able to choose between units but even in the case of what is probably the most notable of these – old people's homes – the limitations on choice are severe. In many parts of the country the number of homes is too few to allow realistic choice between them, choices are in any case often made for rather than by the future elderly resident, and the capacity of all concerned to make realistic choices on the basis of what they can see is heavily constrained (see, e.g., Weaver et al., 1985). And what is true of old people's homes is almost certainly true of other units (children's homes, day centres of various kinds, etc.) where resources do not typically allow choice and circumstances often conspire to ensure that choices are made before users have had sufficient time to reflect on the alternatives.

These reflections do not undermine the case for increasing consumer power through participation, the provision of information and encouragement to complain. They do, however, suggest limits to the degree to which these innovations will greatly improve the lot of the consumer. Providers are often in a position where if they do not provide the service no one else will and where they can argue that complaints of consumers reflect priorities providers cannot share. Few social services' units are closed down because consumers have been empowered to judge that the service is poor.

Organizational Control

If market forces are unlikely to provide uniform high performance what can be expected of the organizations which provide services themselves? Here hopes are expressed for the power of inspection, and the identification of explicit procedures and objectives.

Inspection, to take the first of these organizational prescriptions, seems clearly an idea whose time has come. The clientele of social services include the most vulnerable in society. Market forces seem unlikely to protect them. The private market in care provides itself a strong argument for inspection – for how else are we to be satisfied that public money is being well spent and that providers compete on quality as well as price? The logic of inspection with its insistence on goals, explicit standards and

a credible feedback mechanism relating performance to change seems impeccable. And an increase in inspectors seems as natural an answer to a scandal as an increase in police to a rise in crime.·

So it is sobering to think of the difficulties which inspectors must confront. The values against which they assess services conflict. Resources are often the key to performance but outside the control of the service providers they assess. Much that goes on in social welfare – the transactions of the social worker with her client or of the residential staff with an elderly person – are effectively invisible to outside parties and the more powerless the user the less they may wish to draw attention to

---

Three Questions

1 What are the appropriate criteria for judging a particular service?
2 What mechanisms are likely to ensure that these criteria are met?
3 How can systems of management and inspection contribute to this process rather than leading to defensive actions by staff and the diversion of scarce resources?

---

malpractice. Standards are hard to measure and while inspectors are willing to commit themselves to judgements of quality, one study suggests that their witness agrees very weakly with that of another inspector assessing the same home (Gibbs and Sinclair, 1992b). Attempts to concentrate on the measurable lead to long lists which themselves generate unreliability. And if strong action needs to be taken, there are often formidable reasons for not doing so – partly because of the difficulty of getting evidence which stands up in court, and partly for practical reasons such as lack of time and the need to ensure alternative arrangements for clients.

A further difficulty facing inspectors lies in the lack of any adequate account of what factors are key in assessing quality and what organizational features lead to a high quality service. Typically inspectors cover a wide variety of aspects of whatever they inspect – and no doubt some of this is highly relevant. At present, however, we do not know whether, for example, size of home or proportion of trained staff are important in producing a high quality children's home. (Research in which I am currently involved suggests that one is and one is not – but my own guess of which would be important was wrong.) Implicitly inspectors tend to pursue a theory of organization in which things go better if procedures are clear and written down, but there is no evidence that this is so in social services – indeed in residential care there is some evidence that things go a good deal better if staff are given considerable autonomy rather than being hemmed in with rules and regulations.

This lack of a theory makes it very hard to know whether protocols and procedures, and other methods of staff control make staff perform better or not. Clearly they have some value in protecting the organization, for they show that the managers have given thought to difficult situations and are not to be blamed when things go wrong. What remains uncertain is whether practice itself is improved.

Thus the use of organizational controls to produce good practice is bedevilled by the lack of evidence that they work. Inspection is not manifestly effective. The probation hostels which showed such great variations in outcome were supposed to be inspected at least twice a year by the then children's inspectorate and at least once by the then probation inspectorate without apparently producing a uniform level of performance. Subsequent scandals in which atrocious establishments have been visited by inspectors before the scandal broke do not suggest that efficacy has increased greatly since that date. As to procedural controls, the situation is that we do not know what impact they have on performance.

So Where Next?

The difficulties we have been discussing apply whether the aim is to improve overall performance through quality assurance or to avoid disasters through quality control. In what follows, however, we will stick to our title and the issue of quality control. The question is how standards can be defined, deviations from them assessed and action then taken. For the moment we will assume that these tasks have to be achieved through inspection, although as it will appear this is too simple a view of the matter.

Part of the solution is likely to lie in the scheduling and operation of inspections. Common sense would suggest that guarding against malpractice is more likely to be successful if 'risky' services are inspected more frequently than less risky ones. In identifying 'risk', lessons could perhaps be learnt from the field of child protection in that the difficulty may be less one of identifying bad practice than of ensuring that concerns about a situation are brought together in one place so that a pattern begins to emerge. In order for this to happen it would be necessary for the wide variety of those in contact with the service – users, relatives, staff, GPs, social workers and so on – to know what they can expect and where they can take their concerns. .

In carrying out inspections inspectors would then need to concentrate on key points (for research suggests that they get lost if standards are too numerous), to solicit a wide range of user opinion using postal questionnaires if necessary, to visit at times without appointment and to pursue initial concerns in a systematic manner. (For example, a high runaway rate from a children's home may simply suggest that the young people are particularly difficult or it may indicate a deeper malaise. To determine which applies an inspector would need to examine the intake, and to talk to the young people and staff about what was going on.)

Further Reading

1   Department of Health (1991) *Inspecting for Quality: Guidance on Practice for Inspection Visits in Social Services Departments and Other Agencies*. London: HMSO.
2   Donabedian, A. (1980) *The Definition of Quality and Approaches to its Assessment*, Ann Arbor: Michigan: Health Administration Press.
3   Kelly, D. and Warr, B. (eds) (1992) *Quality Counts: Achieving Quality in Social Care Service*, London: Whiting & Birch/Social Care Association.

If difficulties are identified, they have to be tackled. Ideally this takes place against a common framework in which all sides have agreed on the standards that are to be applied and that things are not going well. In practice there may well be differences of opinion on such matters. Successful action is then more likely if the inspector has been able to identify allies (e.g., external managers), if s/he has been even handed – not attributing to staff failures that arise through lack of resources – if there is a timetable for implementation and review, and if there are penalties for non-compliance which stop short of the draconian action of closure. Success must also be more likely if there is a coherence between inspection, management, training, registration and complaints. For it is unlikely that a single inspection will succeed, if the messages given by other parts of the organization differ from the inspector's report, or if

their proposals for extra resources or training can not be followed up.

In the longer run we require more research. For, if we are serious about improving performance we need to know in what way performance varies, what administrative tools (e.g., training or staff ratios) there may be to improve it, and what, at field level, are the characteristics that differentiate successful and unsuccessful performers. Without such knowledge inspectors will continue to conflate the relevant and the irrelevant, and managers will pursue expensive rules of thumb (e.g., over the improvements to be achieved by training) with no evidence that these improve their results.

References

Bell, M. (1996) 'An account of the experiences of 51 families involved in an initial child protection conference', *Child and Family Social Work*, 1(1), 43–57.
Booth, T. (1985) *Home Truths*, Aldershot: Gower.
Bullock, R., Little, M. and Millham, S. (1993) *Residential Care for Children: a Review of Research*, London: HMSO.
Davies, M. and Sinclair, I. (1971) 'Families, hostels and delinquents: an attempt to assess cause and effect', *British Journal of Criminology*, 11(3), 213–29.
Gibbs, I. and Sinclair, I. (1992a) 'Residential care for elderly people: the correlates of quality', *Ageing and Society*, 12(4), 463–82.
Gibbs, I. and Sinclair, I. (1992b) 'Consistency: a pre-requisite for inspecting residential homes for elderly people?' *British Journal of Social Work*, 22, 535–50.
Millham, S., Bullock, R. and Cherrett, P. (1975) *After Grace, Teeth*, London: Human Context Books.
Packman, J. (1986) *Who Needs Care? Social Work Decisions About Children*, Oxford: Blackwell.
Sinclair, I. (1971) *Hostels for Probationers*, London: HMSO.
Sinclair, I., Crosbie, D., O'Connor, P., Stanforth, L. and Vickery, A. (1989) *Bridging Two Worlds*, Aldershot: Avebury.
Tizard, J., Sinclair, I. and Clarke, R. (1975) *Varieties of Residential Experience*, London: Routledge & Kegan Paul.
Weaver, T., Willcocks, D. and Kellaher, L. (1985) *The Business of Care: a Study of Private Residential Homes for Old People*, Report no. 1, The Polytechnic of North London, Centre for Environmental and Social Studies in Ageing.

VI.3
Service Users' Perspectives
Suzy Croft and Peter Beresford

This discussion is concerned with the key critique of social work which is emerging from its recipients. Long hidden and largely ignored, it has grown in strength and visibility in recent years. Three of the key questions it raises are:

- what part have service users played in the development of social work?
- what part do they want to play?
- what kind of social work, if any, does this point to for the future?

The Dominant Social Work Discourse

Before we can move on to address these questions, we need to locate them in professional debates about social work. These have been clouded by an air of impending doom. They convey a strong sense of social work in retreat and decline. The talk is of 'the crisis of public, political and professional confidence which has come to dominate social work since the 1970s' (Clarke, 1993, p. viii) and the fear is that 'social work faces a troubled and uncertain future' (Langan, 1993, p. 164).

Concern has grown that social work and social services are increasingly used to implement authoritarian welfare policies and that social work education is under tightening bureaucratic control (Payne, 1994). Critics fear that social work has itself internalized the new right doctrines which are associated with the increasing poverty, social injustice and division which it is meant to counter

(Holman, 1993). At the same time, social work is seen as under constant attack from the media and political right (e.g., Marsland, 1993). It is not difficult to see the reasons for the anxiety and loss of confidence which have characterized late twentieth-century social work. The Griffiths Report, which underpinned the reshaping of community care, made no reference to social work. Under the new arrangements for community care, social work tasks were restructured as care management and a wide range of professions, including nurses and occupational therapists, were seen as equally qualified to undertake them. Under the Children Act, social workers were given new responsibilities for children in need, but no matching resources. Social work's preoccupation with child protection has been challenged by official research (Department of Health, 1995). Social work's fortunes have taken a sharp downward turn since the 1970s when it predominated in the massive expansion of personal social services.

There has been a search for a new direction for social work, away from market-led practice, to a more humane and humanistic model (Holman, 1993; Day, 1995); from a concept of social work based on aid to one based on development (Smale, 1995). But no clear route maps have been offered to show how social work is to reach these different destinations, or from where the support for them is to come. At the same time, the idea of 'empowerment' has come to the fore in social work, as it has in other human service professions, as a basis for increasing people's control over their lives. But critics have raised fundamental questions about it, suggesting that its dominant definition by professionals reflects their agendas rather than those of service users (Shemmings and Shemmings, 1995) and that it may have regulatory as well as liberatory implications, focusing narrowly on people taking responsibility for their own lives, instead of recognizing and challenging the constraints operating upon them (Baistow, 1994/5).

What Service Users have to say about Social Work

Service users have raised serious but different concerns about social work. They have highlighted its failings and expressed fundamental reservations about it. Organizations like Parents Against Injustice (PAIN), Voice for the Child In Care and the National Association of Young People In Care, have spotlighted the frequent failure of social work to safeguard service users' rights or meet their needs. Psychiatric system survivors report the same problem. As one said:

The dice are loaded so much in favour of what are statutory requirements of social workers when doing Approved Social Worker work. There are precious few opportunities . . . where the actual people who are being subject to, not so much having their rights and expectations guaranteed as statutory requirements, have a chance to talk back. The emphasis now is on statutory controls of social workers, not ensuring the rights of service users.

One of the paradoxes of legislation is that it gives people powers and responsibilities who are ambivalent about exercising them and because of this it is all too easy to become oblivious to the real struggles of someone from a personal and social point of view.

(Beresford, 1994, p. 84)

Five Key Points

1 Social work is increasingly marginalized publicly and politically, amid growing professional fears that it is tied to authoritarian welfare policies.

2 Social work service users have traditionally played little part in the development of social work.

3 Social work service users and their organizations highlight fundamental failings in social work policy and practice.

4 In their discussions and developments, social work service users highlight three themes and priorities for policy and practice: autonomy, participation and inclusion.

5 User-led social work, based on social work service users' priorities, provides a practical basis to restore social work to its traditional commitment to uphold service users' independence, rights and choices.

However, it is not only where social work's powers to restrict people's rights are applied that these difficulties arise. People's experience of social work has been equally problematic where it is intended to provide support. Social work has traditionally given low priority to work with older people, people with learning difficulties and disabled people (Warburton, 1982). Social work has been part of a system of social services based on a model which segregates and congregates disabled people, reinforcing their economic dependence rather than ensuring equal opportunities, access, choices and rights (Barnes, 1991). In a survey of disabled people, a disabled researcher spoke of 'one of the few people interviewed who received significant help from a social worker to move out of residential care' and concluded:

For most people, however, organising housing and personal assistance is very difficult and they received little help in doing this from social services professionals.

(Morris, 1993, p. 69)

Recipients of social work generally report little choice in practitioner or in the professional practice they experience. Conventional research reinforces this discouraging picture. Assessments are clouded by judgementalism and workers' preconceptions (Ellis, 1993). Despite the introduction of formal complaints procedures, there continue to be many problems in making a complaint and service users remain reluctant to complain (Simons, 1995). People's experience of community care remains patchy and uneven. For example:

Against individual experiences of good support and the kindness of particular care workers, must be placed accounts of unreliable and impersonal support.

(Henwood, 1995, p. 18)

Social work has continuing difficulties ensuring equal access, opportunities and outcomes for women, black people and members of minority ethnic groups as both service users and workers (Dominelli, 1988; Langan and Day, 1992). There doesn't seem to have been the pre-market golden age of social work for service users to which some expert commentators seem anxious to retreat. Instead the dominant pattern has been one of exclusion and paternalism, which Bill Jordan summed up as early as 1975 as the 'giving of second hand goods and second hand sympathy' (Jordan, 1975).

The Role of Service Users in Social Work

So far service users have played little part in the development of social work. They

have been allocated two overlapping roles. The first of these follows from the tradition epitomized and established by *The Client Speaks* (Mayer and Timms, 1970). This study was not, as has sometimes been assumed, a plea for more accountable or democratic social work. It was less 'the client' than the authors of the study who spoke. They were mainly interested in clients as a *data source* for researchers (Beresford and Croft, 1987). This tradition still thrives. More than two decades later, the role of service users in evaluating social work effectiveness is still seen mainly as one of providing information rather than helping to define or measure effectiveness (Cheetham, Fuller, McIvor and Petch, 1992).

Since *The Client Speaks*, there has been an attempt to extend the role of service users in social work through the idea of 'partnership' (Marsh and Fisher, 1992). But this has been undermined by a lack of clarity and agreement about the meaning and definition of partnership. The failure of its advocates to take sufficient account of conflict and inequalities of power and control has resulted in it carrying little credence among service users (Morris, 1993). Other critics argue that: 'even more curious is the notion that parents or carers accused of abusing a child are expected to relate as "partners" with those investigating the allegation' (Shemmings and Shemmings, 1995).

This leads us to the second role offered service users in social work and social services more generally – *getting involved*. The 1990s saw a new emphasis on 'user involvement'. This followed from the commitment of Conservative governments to a mixed economy of care and consumerist welfare; legislation like the Children Act and NHS and Community Care Act, including specific provisions for the involvement of service users; and pressure from service users and their organizations for more say in and control over their lives and services affecting them. User involvement has mainly focused on planning and management rather than social work practice itself. Service users have typically been drawn into formal consultative structures concerned with bureaucratic and administrative functions. The indications from both service users and independent research findings is that user involvement has been patchy and qualified, and its gains limited. Instead of social work practice being more explicitly participative, competing government priorities of 'value for money' and 'needs-led provision', have resulted in budget-driven rather than the promised user-centred services. Service users have more often experienced user involvement as stressful, diversionary and unproductive. While it has generally failed to include black people and members of minority ethnic groups on equal terms, service users and their organizations can expect to be criticized as 'unrepresentative' (Beresford and Campbell, 1994; Bewley and Glendinning, 1994; Henwood, 1995; Shemmings and Shemmings, 1995). As the Director of the British Council of Organisations of Disabled People said:

We're getting a bit fed up with being asked to participate in events which are meant to be about user involvement where on the day the professionals who are involved in organising these things and talking about user-involvement show very little evidence of being committed to it.
(Croft and Beresford, 1991, p. 71)

Policy and practice for user involvement have mainly been concerned with consultation and market research exercises, rather than with any shift in decision making or power (Croft and Beresford, 1990). Service users have been expected to feed into professional debates and developments. Thus service users' main role in the development of modern social work has remained essentially unchanged – to provide information first for researchers and subsequently for

social work agencies, policy-makers and professionals.

This is a role with which users of social services have expressed increasing dissatisfaction. It is based on a narrow, service-led approach to involvement which abstracts the contribution of service users. The conceptualization of user involvement has become heavily contested, reflecting the competing concerns of service providers and users. The former are primarily concerned with meeting the political, economic and managerial requirements of their agencies and services. The concerns of the latter are at once more personal and broader. They are committed to improving the *quality of their lives*, rejecting inappropriate provision which restricts what they can do and seeking appropriate support to live as they want to.

Three Questions

1 What part have service users played in the development of social work?
2 What part do they want to play?
3 What kind of social work, if any, does this point to for the future?

This has profound implications for the way service users see their involvement in social work and social services. They have shown an increasing frustration with demands to comment on the detail of existing arrangements. They do not see themselves in narrow terms as 'consumers' of social work or users of social services.

Service Users' Perspectives on Social Work

They have a different starting point. Disabled people and other social care service users have established their own powerful and growing movements. They have their own democratically constituted local, regional, national and international organizations. They have developed their own discussions, writings, arts, culture and forms of political action. They have developed their own world-view. In their struggle for anti-discrimination legislation in the UK, disabled people showed that they had become far more powerful politically than the social work profession which traditionally intervened to shape their individual lives.

Social work's commentators continue to look for solutions to social work's ills from among their own ranks (Day, 1995). But so far their track record for halting social work's decline is poor. Social care service users, on the other hand, are changing the terms of the social work debate. They are asking fundamental and important questions, like: why social work, what is it for, how is it to be accountable, what would it look like, and they are beginning to offer their own answers to all of these. They have developed new demands, models and theories which are having a growing impact on public policy and which point to the reconception and reconstruction of social work and social services. They place an emphasis on people's civil rights and the relation between the individual and society, and the service system and society.

Disabled people's social model of disability draws a distinction between people's impairment – the functional limitations which affect their bodies, and disability – and the oppression and discrimination they experience as a result of society's reaction to impairment. The social model of madness and distress emerging from psychiatric system survivors validates people's experience, feelings and perceptions, and highlights the social causes of people's distress, and the damaging and discriminatory psychiatric and social response to it.

In their discussions, social care service users constantly return to three key themes and priorities: *autonomy, participation* and *inclusion*. The disabled people's movement places an emphasis on independent living, but it has turned conventional ideas of independence, 'to stand on your own two feet', on their head. It has transformed 'independence' to mean autonomy instead of individualism – to have appropriate support to ensure people equal rights, choices and opportunities. Participation, the idea of speaking and acting for yourself and being part of mainstream society, lies at the heart of social care service user movements. Service users have highlighted the limitations of personal social services policy from both the political left and right. They have reported the failure of market solutions to meet need, and of paternalistic state prescriptions to ensure choice and equal opportunities, and pressed instead for *user-led* policy and provision. To ensure inclusion, they have stressed the need for:

- support for service users to be able to participate on equal terms;
- equity in the treatment of service users, regardless of age, class, race, disability, sexual identity or gender; and
- recognition of diversity, for example, people's different ways of communicating – non-verbally, in pictures, by signing or in minority ethnic languages.

Service users argue for social work and social services which reflect these commitments and which:

- are concerned with enabling people to be independent rather than maintaining them in dependence, focus on people's abilities rather than their incapacities, and support people to be autonomous;
- do not serve as a palliative for the failure of mainstream policies but instead are systematically related to broader needs-led social and

economic policies which include rather than marginalize groups like disabled people, lone parents and psychiatric system survivors, ensuring their access to education, training, child care and employment; and

- provide support rather than direction and are fully participative.

Service users also highlight the skills which are needed to achieve these objectives. In one development project they identified a wide range of skills which they felt were needed for helpful practice. Significantly, there was considerable agreement between different 'user groups' about these skills. They included seeing the individual as a whole person, not as a set of symptoms or problems; treating people as individuals, not as an anonymous group or class; treating people with respect; acknowledging the validity of their experience and views; providing them with full and accessible information; listening to what they say and asking them what they want; recognizing the need to meet them on their own terms and if possible on their own ground where they would feel more comfortable and relaxed. As one member of a self-advocacy organization of people with mental distress said:

I think a lot of it is basic consideration for people . . . It is treating people as individuals. Treat them as humans. It's all that sort of thing.
(Beresford and Trevillion, 1995)

The standards service users have begun to identify for social services workers, reflect similar priorities and concerns, and again there is great consistency from a wide range of service users. They stress:

courtesy and respect, being treated as equals and as individuals, and as people who make their own decisions; they value people who are experienced and well informed, able to explain things clearly

and without condescension and who 'really listen'; and they value people who are able to act effectively and make practical things happen.
(Harding and Beresford, 1996, p. 1)

Service users argue that they need to play a greater part in both the *socialization* and *practice* of social workers to achieve these new skills, standards and objectives. Strategies for the first include service users' involvement in social workers' selection and recruitment; the increased and systematic involvement of service user trainers and service user organizations in social work education and training (Beresford, 1994; Hastings and Crepaz-Keay, 1995), and the increased recruitment of disabled people and other service users as social workers (Hunter, 1990). There is already considerable experience to show the effectiveness and feasibility of all three. Routes to increasing service users' involvement in practice range from schemes ensuring service users an effective say in assessment, planning, recording and review, through to service users defining their own needs, putting together their own 'package of support' with the support of user-led advocacy and information services, and monitoring and evaluating the service they receive (Beresford and Harding, 1993).

The direct payments schemes 'created, designed, established and developed by disabled people' to achieve the goals of the independent living movement have

Further Reading

1 Beresford, P. and Croft, S. (1993) *Citizen Involvement: a Practical Guide for Change*, Basingstoke: Macmillan.

2 Lindow, V. (1994) *Self-Help Alternatives To Mental Health Services*, London: MIND publications.

3 Morris, J. (1993) *Independent Lives?: Community Care and Disabled People*, Basingstoke: Macmillan.

perhaps been the ultimate expression of the latter (Evans, 1995). Such schemes, now incorporated into legislation, enable people to choose and control the support they want. They have been demonstrated to be cost-effective and to increase the quality of disabled people's lives and the control they have over them (Zarb, Nadash and Berthoud, 1994).

The same desire for more appropriate, more participatory provision is embodied in the idea of collective 'user-led alternatives'. These are now being established by disabled people, psychiatric system survivors, people living with AIDS and other groups in many parts of the world, including the UK, Europe and USA. They offer training, employment, accommodation, counselling, information, advocacy, drop-in, asylum and other support services. They are rooted in the values and beliefs of service users rather than traditional dominant medical, and professional frameworks (e.g. Lindow, 1994).

Towards User-led Social Work

Service users' ideas, initiatives and demands add up to a coherent paradigm for social work, but how does it relate to social work's own agendas and aspirations? What distinguishes social work is that it operates at the junction of our personal lives and civil status. It is concerned with our selves and our personal relationships. It addresses both our psyche and our understanding of and dealings with the social world we inhabit. Thus it is concerned with the social and personal; the psychological and the public; the individual and the collective; and with the self and agencies affecting it. The social worker deals with the benefits agency and the housing department, as well as addressing people's innermost fears and desires. (S)he is concerned with the social, economic, sexual, political and cultural aspects of people's lives, as well

as the politics of welfare and of the state. The key recurring themes and goals of social work have been to enable people to live their lives independently, to negotiate conflict and safeguard people's rights.

This closely coincides with service users' concerns. Ironically their agenda comes closest to restoring social work to its original inspiration and challenging the narrow bureaucratic and regulatory role to which both its proponents and the political right have increasingly confined it. The latter have ignored valued and innovatory areas of social work, like work with people living with HIV and work in the hospice movement. Service users challenge the view of social work as a marginal special service for a separate 'disadvantaged' group and instead remind us of its relevance to all of us in those times and conditions of loss, impairment, distress, abuse, want and illness which are an inherent part of the human condition. The vision of social work which service users offer – as a universalist support service – not only represents a return to its first principles, it also unifies the concerns of social work and service users. By doing this, it helps offer to both a positive prospect for the future.

References

Baistow, K. (1994/5) 'Liberation and regulation? Some paradoxes of empowerment', *Critical Social Policy*, Issue 42, Winter, 34–46.

Barnes, C. (1991) *Disabled People in Britain and Discrimination: a Case for Anti-discrimination Legislation*, London: Hurst.

Beresford, P. (1994) *Changing the Culture. Involving Service Users in Social Work Education*, Paper 32.2, London: Central Council for Education and Training in Social Work.

Beresford, P. and Campbell, J. (1994) 'Disabled people, service users, user involvement and representation', *Disability And Society*, 9(3), 315–25.

Beresford, P. and Croft, S. (1987) 'Are we really listening', in T. Philpot (ed.), *On Second Thoughts: Reassessments of the Literature of Social Work*, London: Community Care.

Beresford, P. and Croft, S. (1993) *Citizen Involvement: a*

Practical Guide for Change, Basingstoke: Macmillan.

Beresford, P. and Harding, T. (eds) (1993) *A Challenge To Change: Practical Experiences of Building User-led Services*, London: National Institute for Social Work.

Beresford, P. and Trevillion, S. (1995) *Developing Skills For Community Care: a Collaborative Approach*, Aldershot: Arena.

Bewley, C. and Glendinning, C. (1994) *Involving Disabled People in Community Care Planning*, York: Joseph Rowntree Foundation and Community Care.

Cheetham, J., Fuller, R., McIvor, G. and Petch, A. (1992) *Evaluating Social Work Effectiveness*, Buckingham: Open University Press.

Clarke, J. (1993) *A Crisis In Care?: Challenges to Social Work*, Hertfordshire: Sage in association with the Open University.

Croft, S. and Beresford, P. (1990) *From Paternalism to Participation*, London: Open Services Project and Joseph Rowntree Foundation.

Croft, S. and Beresford, P. (1991) 'User views', *Changes: An International Journal of Psychology and Psychotherapy*, 9(1), March, 71–2.

Day, P. R. (1995) 'The turn of the tide: humanistic perspectives, social policy and social work', *Changes: An International Journal of Psychology and Psychotherapy*, 13(2), Wiley, 77–81.

Department of Health (1995) *Child Protection: Messages from Research*, London: HMSO.

Dominelli, L. (1988) *Anti-Racist Social Work*, Basingstoke: Macmillan.

Ellis, K. (1993) *Squaring The Circle: User and Carer Participation in Needs Assessment*, York: Joseph Rowntree Foundation/Community Care.

Evans, J. (1995) *Direct Payments and why they are Important: from being Dependent on Inappropriate Services to Becoming an Employer*, London, presentation to the Association of Metropolitan Authorities, 16 February.

Harding, T. and Beresford, P. (eds) (1996) *The Standards we Expect: What Service Users and Carers want from Social Services Workers*, London: National Institute for Social Work.

Hastings, M. and Crepaz-Keay, D. (1995) *The Survivors' Guide: To Training Approved Social Workers*, London: Central Council for Education and Training in Social Work.

Henwood, M. (1995) Measure for Measure, *Community Care*, 6–12 July, 18–19.

Holman, B. (1993) *A New Deal for Social Welfare*, Oxford: Lion Publishing.

Hunter, E. (1990) 'The right stuff', *Social Work Today*, 24 May, 16–17.

Jordan, B. (1975) 'Is the client a fellow citizen?' *Social Work Today*, 30 October.

Langan, M. (1993) 'New directions in social work', in Clarke, J. (ed.) *A Crisis in Care?*, London: Sage.

Langan, M. and Day, L. (eds) (1992) *Women, Oppression and Social Work*, London: Routledge.

Lindow, V. (1994) *Self-Help Alternatives to Mental Health Services*, London: MIND publications.

Marsh, P. and Fisher, M. (1992) *Good Intentions: Developing Partnership in Social Services*, York: Joseph Rowntree Foundation/Community Care.

Marsland, D. (1993) 'Social workers, the final folly of the sixties', *Daily Mail*, 21 June, p. 8.

Mayer, J. and Timms, N. (1970), *The Client Speaks*, London: Routledge & Kegan Paul.

Morris, J. (1993) *Independent Lives?: Community Care and Disabled People*, Basingstoke: Macmillan.

Payne, M. (1991) *Modern Social Work Theory: a Critical Introduction*, London: Macmillan.

Payne, M. (1994) 'The end of British social work', *Professional Social Work*, 5 February.

Shemmings, Y. and Shemmings, D. (1995) 'Defining participative practice in health and welfare', in R. Jack (ed.), *Empowerment in Community Care*, Hampshire: Chapman and Hall.

Simons, K. (1995) *I'm not Complaining but . . . Complaints Procedures in Social Services Departments*, York: Joseph Rowntree Foundation/Community Care.

Smale, G. (1995) *Social Services Departments: Aid or Development Agencies?*, presentation at: Social Justice: A Framework for Personal Social Services?, workshop discussion with Labour parliamentarians, National Institute for Social Work and British Association of Social Workers, House of Commons, London, 21 June.

Warburton, W. (1982) *What Social Workers Do: the Results in from the Case Review System Deployed by Three Social Services Teams*, Cambridge: Cambridgeshire Social Services.

Zarb, G., Nadash, P. and Berthoud, R. (1994) *Cashing in on Independence*, Derbyshire: British Council of Organisations of Disabled People Publications.

VI.4
A View from Central Government
Sir William Utting

I took up the new post of Chief Social Work Officer at the Department of Health and Social Security in 1976. The advertisement had said that the successful candidate would be 'the chief professional adviser to Ministers and the Department on social work and social services'. Almost identical wording headed the advertisement for my successor as Chief Inspector of Social Services at the Department of Health in 1991. Such continuity suggests the permanent nature of the central task of a chief professional officer in a government department.

All the responsibilities of a chief professional adviser cannot be discharged by an unsupported individual. I also headed the Social Work Service, later the Social Services Inspectorate. This expert body provided professional advice on all aspects of the personal social services, and also a systematic flow of structured information about the condition of those services throughout England. Another of my tasks – linking the Department with relevant service, professional, local government, voluntary and academic interests – placed me at the centre of a unique network of information.

What use did my colleagues and I make of this knowledge? In the first place, we were at the service of ministers and the Department in discharging their responsibilities for health and social security as well as for the personal social services. Established interdisciplinary methods of work and the seniority of my post meant that any large issues of policy were open to a social work contribution.

Those for the personal social services contained a heavy professional content. The fact that the Secretary of State answered to Parliament for the personal social services and also possessed powers of inspection and inquiry meant that operational problems and casework about individuals were constantly referred to the Department. Investigating and advising on these, many of which attracted public attention and concern, generated a heavy load of work for the Social Work Service and the Social Services Inspectorate. With this went a painstaking professional contribution to preparing and implementing new legislation, of which a decade of work leading up to the Children Act 1989 and its implementation is an outstanding example.

Secondly, and in the context of our primary obligation to ministers, our knowledge was available to colleagues and agencies in the field. We explained the background to policy initiatives, offered practical help in implementing them, focused advice from the Department and helped to avert crises. The Social Work Service and the Social Services Inspectorate also assessed and channelled information from the field to the Department, including feedback on current policies and news about service initiatives that might spark new developments. The Department's openness to the world outside Whitehall, and the success of the professional service in facilitating communication, meant that relationships between social services authorities and the Department remained strong throughout a long period of hostility between local and central government.

The professional associations – the Association of Directors of Social Services, the British Association of Social Workers and the Social Care Association – held positions of particular importance in this professional network. The first spoke with the collective experience of the local authority chief officers charged with delivering services to their local populations. BASW made an irreplaceable contribution to the professional content of policy. The Social Care Association stimulated progress in residential care, and its experienced leadership provided wise and consistent counsel.

The greatest barrier to effective communication for many people was their difficulty in understanding why and how government operated as it did. The business of government seemed unlike any other business they had encountered. Even people with extensive experience of the politics and processes of local government had difficulty in transferring relevant knowledge to the national level. Social workers, with their strong commitment to vulnerable groups in the community, had particular problems with an ethic which differed markedly from their own in serving the political objectives of a national government. Almost everybody had difficulty with the processes of government, which appeared to follow an alien logic in its selection of issues for short bursts of concentrated attention while apparently weightier matters were exiled to the long grass.

The realities of government at national level are daunting, if invigorating. Government pursues the best interests of all of the people, as interpreted by the dominant political party. Personal or professional values which cut across this objective are discounted or disregarded. Sectional, service and vested interests are viewed sceptically and questioned

Five Key Points

1 Contributing a social work perspective to national policy requires understanding and experience of the processes and politics of government.

2 The legal duties and powers for securing personal social services rest with local authorities, but four-fifths of the funding comes from central government.

3 Community Care and the Children Act will revolutionize the personal social services – if their intentions are carried through in practice.

4 Training is the single most important issue in the personal social services.

5 Government has unavoidable responsibilities for the social care of vulnerable groups and individuals.

ruthlessly. At the same time, ministers and civil service colleagues welcomed relevant and authoritative contributions on any aspect of social policy.

Political imperatives may light the touch-paper for government action, but it is fuelled by feasibility, timeliness and luck. Few of the large policy initiatives in the social services depended solely on thought and planning over a long period. The stately, repetitive rhythms of consultation which preceded the Children Act 1989 may constitute an exception, but even here the process was kick-started by a recommendation from one of the new Select Committees which coincided with a bid by the DHSS to clarify and rationalize the law relating to children. Thought and planning played a greater part in enabling opportunities to be exploited than they could in pursuit of an overarching strategy. Nevertheless, the Department kept a steady eye on the longer term of a decade hence in the intervals of dealing with the crisis of the moment: initially through regular reviews of policy, and later as the consequences of new policy developments unfolded.

The professional role can be illustrated

by briefly describing its contribution to three major developments: in the establishment of the Inspectorate, in social services training, and in community care. The DHSS, heavily influenced by the culture of the health service, had not been receptive to the concept of an Inspectorate for the social services. The mood in government changed in the 1980s, however, in particular towards obtaining better value for the money allocated to local government through the rate support grant. Government had previously taken a very relaxed view on this matter, regarding local authorities as independent in managing their resources, and requiring exceptional circumstances to justify using the Secretary of State's powers of inspection. The Financial Management Initiative in government, however, now required central departments to account for expenditure in all the programmes for which they were responsible. This caused the DHSS to reappraise its responsibilities for the social services, to clarify its objectives for them and to link these objectives to the allocation and use of national resources.

The role of the professional service immediately became more significant. It already helped to develop policy. But the expectations the FMI had of the Department required it to improve its evaluation of the effectiveness of local authority services, linked – if possible – with assessment of the efficiency with which resources were used. It was decided to adopt an inspectorial approach, adding these responsibilities to the traditional inspectorial functions of protecting vulnerable people and promoting good general standards of practice. Achieving acceptance of this was neither easy nor swift. Sceptics in central government suspected that an Inspectorate would write blank cheques for its colleagues in the field. Those in local government regarded it as the thin

end of a cost-cutting wedge. Both were eventually satisfied. SWS became the Social Services Inspectorate in 1985, with a broader remit and the capacity to recruit staff from other relevant backgrounds. It has succeeded in maintaining a genuine partnership with the local authority associations, preserving the detachment that inspectorial functions require, and pursuing the objectives of the Secretary of State.

Soon after its inception the Inspectorate also became responsible for leading work on the Department's policies for social services training. The first major issue it confronted was the proposal by the Central Council for Education and Training in Social Work to increase the period of qualifying training for social workers to three years. This had been long in preparation and was backed by almost all the relevant academic and professional interests. Against it were the anti-professional temper of the time, those to whom social work was anathema, those who felt that training was superfluous for people with common sense and some experience of life, those who wanted evidence that training improved performance – and the hard fact that it would cost an extra £40 million a year.

My own perspective was that two years' qualifying training was not enough to equip students for the full range of duties of social work in local authorities. I would have argued for a third year accumulated through post-qualifying training, rather than for a simple addition to qualifying training, but the issue for me then, as it is now, was *when* a third year could be achieved – not whether. There were, however, powerful arguments that the training agenda of the social services contained higher priorities than social work for any additional public expenditure that could be secured.

Successive reports and reviews, and the accumulated experience of SSI inspections, demonstrated that the social services workforce was grossly under-prepared by qualifying or other forms of training for the duties it was asked to undertake. Residential and domiciliary staff – almost entirely unqualified – were called upon to discharge complex tasks ranging from management to personal care. Community care and the Children Act required attitudinal change as well as the acquisition of new skills by large numbers of staff. Training was emerging as the single most important issue in the personal social services. How was this large workforce to be equipped for the challenges of the next decade? The great bulk of expenditure on training was already directed at social workers, 12 per cent of the workforce, who were consequently by some distance the best trained group. The merits of the case for extending their training – which in their own right were considerable – were overborne when placed in the context of the obviously greater needs of the majority of staff.

Such considerations led SSI to negotiate a government strategy for social services training between the seven central departments with a direct interest. This identified the needs of the workforce as a whole, and established the training support programme in order to target money from the centre on priorities for certain staff, client groups and special needs. Brokering the service, educational, financial and national interests of seven departments needed great skill and application by my colleagues, and securing a specific grant for training was exceptional in the face of the entrenched disapproval within government for such mechanisms. The strategy included improvements to social work training, but these fell far short of CCETSW's original proposals. It is greatly to the credit of the Central Council and its officers that they played so constructive a role in implementing the strategy. The Department's partnership with CCETSW was further

strengthened by more formal arrangements for reviewing training policies and accounting for resources.

Issues about community care recurred continually throughout my 15 years in central government. The client-based approach to policy in the DHSS had a number of advantages. Securing a distinctive identity for client groups played a major part in reducing the stereotyping to which all disabled people were subjected; explaining the difference between mental illness and mental handicap, for example, had been a necessary preliminary to any public statement on either subject. The Chronically Sick and Disabled Persons Act of 1970 established individual rights

---

Three Questions

1 What is the role of the state in meeting the need for social care?
2 Does government need professional advice in developing policy for the personal social services? How should this be provided?
3 What is the role of inspection in the personal social services and how is it best discharged?

---

to service for physically disabled people and triggered a sharp growth in services. The White Paper *Better Services for the Mentally Handicapped* capitalized on the more understanding public attitudes which followed scandals in long-stay hospitals. It produced an integrated national policy and rapid improvement in services. Its successor, *Better Services for the Mentally Ill*, appeared in 1975 – just in time to miss the grand period of growth in social services budgets.

Concentrating on client groups also meant that the complications of working with other government departments were reduced. Limiting objectives in work between departments almost always made them more achievable. The client group approach also led, however, to the differences between groups being emphasized at the expense of what they might have in common. A piecemeal approach meant that progress was uneven as between client groups, and common issues which required action by government as a whole – or even by the Department as a whole – were either not identified or could not be progressed. My awareness of these issues was stimulated by chairing a group of senior officials established to try to harmonize policies across the responsibilities of the DHSS. Achieving an integrated approach to social policy across government, even on some distinct issues, remains an unrealized ideal.

Community care policies had taken important steps forward in the 1970s. They moved at different speeds and in different ways; however, the 1980s ended with a higher proportion of old people in residential care than at the beginning of the decade, in spite of explicit policies of supporting them in their own homes. Attempts to integrate community care policies and to secure unified implementation foundered; the support and ingredients essential to success were missing. There was political opposition, scepticism that the policy was a cloak for cutting expenditure, and a host of vested interests fearing loss of responsibilities, jobs and status. The time was simply not ripe. A report by the Audit Commission criticizing the subvention of residential care through social security then stimulated government to invite Sir Roy Griffiths to review the position. His genius was to produce solutions which were also widely popular. The publication of his report in 1988 was followed by a crucial period of interdepartmental scrutiny and evaluation by officials, in which SSI played an important role. Cabinet consideration of the issues led to the acceptance of most of Sir Roy's recommendations, the White Paper

Caring for People, the relevant parts of the NHS and Community Care Act, and eventual full implementation on 1 April 1993.

Community care and the Children Act should revolutionize the personal social services. They required changes in philosophy, outlook and practice; the people needing and using social services are no longer the objects of municipal charity, but partners in a joint enterprise. As *Caring for People* said, 'Promoting choice and independence underlies all the Government's proposals.' Change was long overdue. The reorganizations of 1971 and 1974 had been largely administrative, through which the spirit of the Seebohm Report gleamed only fitfully. By the end of the 1980s it was plain that the only practical (and, it might be argued, moral) way forward was to ensure that the full resources of the community were mobilized in order to meet the growing need for personal and social care. This approach was foreshadowed by the then Secretary of State, Norman Fowler, in his speech at Buxton in 1984. It found fulfillment with the belated introduction of a coherent policy of community care almost ten years later.

Changes in the nature and role of government have caused corresponding changes in the Civil Service which affect the size and composition of the professional arm. The latter's contribution to policy remains indispensable, providing a framework of practical experience and detailed understanding of the human issues being discussed. It draws on substantial knowledge at national level of the political and administrative structures, the content, resources, delivery, methods, practice and staffing of the personal social services, and their relationship with health and other social services. A convincing professional contribution also depends upon individual credibility, in which factors such as personal authority and familiarity with the processes of government may be as important as the purely technical knowledge. Knowing how to apply what you know, through revolutions in political leadership and philosophy, changes in society, developments in the social services and shifts in the role of government itself, is perhaps the key.

Further Reading

1 Department of Health (1996) *Progress through Change: the Fifth Annual Report of the Chief Inspector Social Services Inspectorate 1995/96*, London: HMSO.
2 Department of Health (1989) *Caring for People: Community Care in the Next Decade and Beyond*, Cm 849, London: HMSO.
3 Social Services Policy Forum (1992) *Great Expectations . . . and Spending on Social Services*, London: National Institute for Social Work.

The role of government has indeed changed dramatically since I entered the Civil Service in 1976. The thesis that there was too much government attracted wide support. The frontiers of the state have rolled back, and comfortable assumptions about the scope and capacity of the Welfare State are continually questioned. Paradoxically, however, the field of social care is one in which the balance of evidence favours the state doing more, not less. Longer lives generally, and longer survival after disabling illness or accident, have created needs for personal care that far exceed those faced by earlier generations. At the same time the capacity of the family – the primary and proper source of care – has been impaired by reductions in size, the prevalence of divorce, increases in one parent families and the effects of poverty. There are now more people than ever before who must depend on the policies and indirect support of government if they are to have lives that come within bearable distance of the expectations of the majority of the population. The Secretary of State will continue to need his own inspectorial capacity in order to discharge the government's responsibility for protecting those growing numbers of people who cannot protect themselves, and to monitor how the major policies which government has promulgated for the personal social services are delivered in practice.

Part VII
Work Settings in Social Work

Introduction to Part VII

The settings in which social workers are employed are clearly defined in terms of their historical identity, but are subject to ever more rapidly changing circumstances brought about by legislation, policy development and research. Most established social workers assume a specialist mantle by virtue of their attachment to a unit defined by the nature of its clientele and the objectives of its practice. Although social work training remains largely generic, the skills needed, for example, in communication with children, in mental health, in family conciliation, in discharge planning and in the penal system all mean that the historic notion of a generic practitioner is probably now just that – a facet of history that came to the fore in the 1960s and 1970s, only to be overtaken by the pressure of events, the demand for specialist expertise and the very different kinds of skill that social workers need to employ in different settings. Increasingly there is a tendency for social workers in the hospital, the prison, and elsewhere, to see themselves as members of a multidisciplinary team with a unique contribution to make to the achievement of organizational goals.

VII.1
The Community Child Care Team
June Thoburn

There are few, if any, countries which do not have some form of state or local authority child and family welfare service, the scope of which will vary depending on the extent of more universalist provisions in the field of housing, income support, health care and education. In England and Wales the Children Act 1989 requires that local authority Social Services Departments provide a range of services for children 'who are unlikely to achieve or have the opportunity of achieving a reasonable standard of health or development without the provision of services under this Act' (Section 17 10a).

Parents and older children may refer themselves directly to Social Services Departments for assistance, or the department may be contacted by another agency. It is the responsibility of the community child and family social work team to publicize its existence and make known the services which are available to those who might be able to benefit from them. Once contacted, a social worker must assess whether any child in the household is 'in need' under the terms of the legislation and, in consultation with family members, work out how best the identified need can be met.

A second group of children, smaller in number but making greater demands on social work time is the group who are suspected of being in need of protective services because of maltreatment by a parent or carer, or because the parent is unable to protect the child from accidental or deliberate harm. In the UK the child protection system has three interlocking parts. In the first instance, the Children Act requires child and family social work teams to seek to prevent children from suffering maltreatment by use of the family support provisions available to all children in need. Secondly, there is a complex *formal* child protection administrative system which has been put in place over the years to facilitate a co-ordinated multidisciplinary response to children who may be suffering significant harm as a result of maltreatment. This system is described in the Department of Health guidance *Working Together* (Department of Health, 1991c). Although there is no clear evidence that more children are maltreated in the UK now than was the case in the recent or more distant past, a series of well-publicized cases in which children have been killed by their parents has led to a concentration of social work time and resources on cases of child abuse. The system has developed from being a co-ordinating process for protecting children from violent assault or life-threatening neglect to one which encompasses children harmed at home in a variety of ways. Neglect and emotional abuse of older children whose emotional rather than physical development is threatened increasingly figure in the child protection statistics.

Thirdly, if it becomes clear that compulsion is required to protect the child the social worker may apply to the Family Proceedings Court for either a Supervision Order or a Care Order. In some cases action in the criminal courts is taken against the person who is alleged to have maltreated the child but this is the responsibility of the police and Crown Prosecution Service, although the social worker may be required to give evidence or facilitate the collection of evidence from the child.

The practice of child and family social workers has been described, monitored and evaluated by a comparatively large number of researchers. These studies have been summarized in three Department of Health documents. The first two (Department of Health, 1985, Department of Health, 1991a) provide a portrait of child welfare practice in the provision of accommodation away from home for shorter or longer periods. The third, (Department of Health, 1995) gives an overview of the workings of the formal child protection system and of social work practice with children and their families where protection is an issue. These studies identify groups of children who regularly receive social work services. Packman (1986) describes three overlapping groups. The 'victims' are those who have been on the receiving end of less than adequate parenting which may have amounted to abuse. They are usually, though not always, younger children. The 'volunteered' group are those whose parents request services because they are unable to provide for their children adequately as a result of some combination of personal or interpersonal stresses, deprivation or disability, and who sometimes request that their children be placed away from home. These children also tend to be either in the younger age ranges or to have behaviour problems or disabilities. The 'villains' are older children whose behaviour is such as to cause concern either to their parents or to the authorities because of their difficult behaviour, delinquency, non-school attendance or other anti-social activities. Packman also points out that these are overlapping characteristics and that there is

Five Key Points

1 Child and family social workers are the 'general practitioners' of the child welfare system and are responsible for the provision of a flexible casework service.

2 Their daily work will be a mix of assessment, social care planning, and the direct provision of therapeutic service to children and families.

3 Children in need of services have been characterized as 'victims, volunteered or villains' – or any combination of all three.

4 Child protection and family support are two key objectives in this field.

5 Good practice today requires the social worker to operate in partnership with parents, children and substitute carers; the skilled technician must also be a skilled negotiator.

considerable scope for the social worker making the initial assessment to exercise discretion as to whether, for example, a case should be seen as a child protection ('victim') case or one in which the parent is under stress and seeking assistance and support ('volunteered'). Similarly, the troublesome child may be perceived as a 'villain' or 'volunteered' in that the troublesome behaviour might be attributed to wilful misbehaviour or to stresses in the family necessitating additional support.

All these studies show that the children most in need of additional child welfare services tend to come disproportionately from certain groups in society. Amongst those who are over-represented are children from single parent or reconstituted families; those who are badly housed and living in deprived areas, and those whose families subsist on incomes below the recognized poverty line. The parents and children tend to have more physical and mental health problems than the general population, and children of mixed racial parentage tend also to be over-represented.

Principles for Practice

Once the need for support or protection services has been established, the social worker is responsible for the provision of appropriate services to meet identified need. Before describing these services it is important to consider the principles which underlie practice. To work effectively as a child and family worker in the community the worker must apply the values, knowledge and skills required for all social work to fulfil the specific requirements of day-to-day practice. The principles for practice required by the Children Act and its Guidance (Department of Health, 1991b) are congruent with social work's values of respect for individuals, families and communities, with a commitment to maximize the rights and freedoms of children and parents and to give them as much choice as possible about the services to be offered. From these come five pointers for positive practice:

- Prevention (of family disintegration);
- Protection (of child and other vulnerable family members);
- Permanence (the importance of the child's sense of);
- Partnership (with family members and with other professionals); and
- Preparation (of the social worker and of family members before important meetings, courts, etc.)

These principles apply to work with colleagues in other agencies and professions; with self-help and interest groups within the community; or with parents and children in need of a service. The Children Act's emphasis on attempting to work in partnership with family members is congruent with social work's ethical requirement to treat people with respect and to maximize their opportunities for making their own decisions. The research of Thoburn et al. (1995), evaluating attempts to work in partnership and highlighting those practices which appear to be most successful in achieving this aim, has contributed to the Department of Health guidance on working in child protection cases *The Challenge of Partnership* (Department of Health, 1995).

The Knowledge Base

The knowledge required by the area child and family social worker in order to put together the most appropriate package of support, therapy and services is extensive (Thoburn, 1994). In addition, if the case comes to court the social worker will require research-based knowledge of the likely outcomes of alternative placements, since the court may not make an order unless convinced that the outcome of the plan proposed by the worker, if an order is made, is likely to be better for the child than if alternative measures are taken.

The Services Provided

There are many ways of looking at the range of services available. They may be considered in terms of therapeutic or supportive relationships, deeds or services and words or therapy (Thoburn, 1994). There is much evidence from mental health as well as child care research that the availability of emotional support is associated with lower levels of stress and more competent parenting. Ideally this will come from partners, family or friends but if these sources of support are not available the area team worker may wish to link the parents with a volunteer, a self-help group, or a relative may be encouraged to play a more supportive role. The Children Act 1989 has encouraged the growth of

Family Centres as sources of support to parents under stress (Holman, 1988; Gibbons et al., 1990; Gibbons, 1992; Cannan, 1994).

From research interviews with parents whose children were believed to be suffering or likely to suffer significant harm, it was concluded that a family casework service involving continuity of relationship with a social worker as well as the provision of practical help, and in some cases therapeutic work designed to achieve change, was particularly valued by those parents who were seeking help (Dartington, 1995; Thoburn et al., 1995). In the USA family preservation services in which the provision of a short-term but intensive relationship with a social worker plays an essential part, have been found to have positive results with some families in crisis whose difficulties were severe (Whittaker et al., 1990).

The Children Act 1989 lists the services which should be available to support families. They include the provision of day care and out-of-school care; help with recreational activities and holidays; the provision of respite accommodation in appropriate cases; practical help in the home, and assistance with laundry, for example if a child has a severe disability involving incontinence. Surveys (Aldgate et al., 1994) have shown considerable discrepancy in the way in which these provisions have been implemented. Some authorities have adopted a minimalist approach, whilst others provide a much wider range of services, from help to community groups to set up credit unions or food or clothing co-operatives on the one hand, to the provision of respite care or accommodation schemes at the other end of the continuum. Gibbons (1991) reports considerable satisfaction with the provision of practical assistance, day care, and voluntary befriending schemes.

An essential arm of a child welfare service is the provision of out-of-home care. In most agencies there will be a specialist resource team responsible for

recruiting, preparing and supporting the families who provide day care, through respite care, to long-term or adoptive homes. However, the area team social workers also undertake some of this work. They will most frequently be responsible for matching the child to the placement; for working with the natural parents and the child, and making arrangements for continued contact between them after placement; and for actually making the placement and providing support to the parents and the child throughout the separation. The 1989 Children Act makes it clear that the provision of accommodation is no longer something which should be avoided, but that it should be seen as an appropriate

---

Three Questions

1 How and why has the emphasis of child care practice changed in recent years?

2 In what way has child care policy been influenced by research results?

3 How far can the principle of partnership be taken in social work with families?

---

family support service in some cases. Respite care schemes for children with disabilities have been well established for some years, but the provision of this service for families under stress for other reasons is a comparatively recent development. Bradley and Aldgate (1994) show that parents under stress greatly value this form of support and assistance and offer suggestions about how respite care can best be arranged to maximize the benefits and minimize any distress to the child.

Research studies indicate that a range of methods may be appropriate and effective if care is taken to match the social work method used with the needs and wishes of the family members. If a parent is not requesting a service, as may be the case when an allegation of maltreatment is made which a parent denies, keeping the family fully informed of the protection process, and giving clear information about what may happen and the powers available to the agency, is likely to be the most effective approach. For those who are seeking help to make changes which they know to be necessary, a combination of a trusting relationship, practical help and the skilled use of appropriate social work methods will be needed. In more difficult cases where there are multiple and overlapping problems, short-term methods are unlikely to be successful unless they are provided episodically in the context of a longer term relationship either with an individual worker or a team of workers.

Thus, the daily work of a child and family area team social worker will be a mix of assessment, social care planning, and the direct provision of a social casework or therapeutic service to parents, children and close relatives either individually or in combinations. The mix will vary in each case. The social care planning role requires the worker to be particularly skilled as a negotiator, mediator and advocate. In more complex cases, especially those where there is a likelihood of significant harm to the child, skills at working with multidisciplinary groups will also be essential. The ability to work directly with children of different ages, and with parents who have a range of problems from material deprivation to mental ill-health or learning disability are essential. The recruitment, training and support of volunteers, who may provide support or advocacy, has become an increasingly important part of the work, the skills for which are close to those required for the recruitment and support of foster carers.

Organizational Issues

In developed as well as developing

countries the need for family support and child protection services is greater than the resources available. The community child and family social worker must therefore engage with the difficult question of prioritizing or rationing scarce resources. In some agencies priorities are determined by managers, usually with the source or nature of referral determining the order of priority. Most often, cases where there is any question of parental maltreatment will take precedence over other cases. This is the usual position in most UK local authority agencies with the unfortunate result that some children who are likely to suffer significant harm from other causes than parental maltreatment remain unhelped. These might include children who have been seriously assaulted but where the abuser is no longer living in the household, or even children in care who because of abuse or other reasons cannot return home. Unless a skilled social worker is allocated to help them to maintain links with their original family, and to work to secure an appropriate long-term placement for them, their chances of avoiding serious harm are very poor indeed. Another group whose needs are not being prioritized at the moment are children who care for seriously ill parents or those who have a mental health or other disability. Recent UK legislation requiring social services departments to assess the needs of carers, including children who care for a parent or other dependent adult, should ensure that their needs are given a higher profile through community care legislation, which will necessitate close co-operation between children and families teams and adult services teams.

It can be seen that the exercise of professional discretion is central to the work of child and family social workers. They are the 'general practitioners' of the child welfare system and retain responsibility for the assessment and reassessment of the needs of the child and

family, and for the provision of a varied
and flexible casework service. The results
of their decisions may be life enhancing
or life threatening. Although the decision
as to whether to remove a child from
home or return a child back home will
usually be supervised or sanctioned by
the Courts, the research is clear that it is
the social worker who has the major
influence on these decisions.

Conclusion

In the UK as in most countries, child and
family social work started as a service for
the placement of children who were
orphaned, maltreated or for some other
reason unable to live with their parents or
extended family. The logical move in the
1960s was to develop preventative
strategies to avoid the need for out-of-
home care. Initially the emphasis was on
prevention of a range of hazards which
led to child placement or family
breakdown. However, the emphasis soon
shifted to the prevention of delinquency,
shortly followed by a change in emphasis
to protection from physical and then
sexual abuse. A realization that children
in care could be abused by carers or by
the system designed to protect them led
in the 1970s and 1980s to a child rescue
philosophy and the move to place more
children permanently in substitute
families. However, research indicating
that around 90 per cent of children
leaving home will eventually return to
their parents or home communities,
pushed the emphasis in the Children Act
1989 back to prevention, now reframed as
'family support'. As a consequence of this
move enshrined in the Children Act 1989,
child care social workers and managers
are encouraged by government to reorder
their priorities. This is not without
opposition from child and family workers
themselves who have grown up during a
period when professional value and
status was more likely to lie in

competence in therapeutic methods, such
as family therapy, or specialist aspects of
the work, such as child abuse
investigation and assessment or
permanent family placement. The
partnership-based practice required by
the Children Act requires the skilled
delivery of therapeutic and protection
services but also emphasizes negotiation
skills, and takes away some of the power
of the professional worker to determine
the methods to be used. The clear
message from research backed by
legislation and guidance is that the skilled
technician must also be a skilled
negotiator. Child and family social work
went a long way along the path of
technical competence and practice
dominated by official procedures.
Consumer and outcome studies have
once again shown clearly that neither will
succeed either in engaging families or in
achieving positive outcomes for children
without the accurate empathy, warmth
and genuineness which have long been
known to be associated with effective
practice.

References

Aldgate, J., Tunstill, J. and McBeith, G. (1994)
   *Implementing Section 17 of the Children Act – the
   First 18 Months*, University of Leicester (see
   Annual Reports of Children Act for Summaries).
Bradley, M. and Aldgate, J. (1994) 'Short-term family
   based care for children in need', *Adoption and
   Fostering*, 18(4).
Cannan, C. (1994) *Changing Families: Changing Welfare*,
   Hemel Hempstead: Harvester Wheatsheaf.

Further Reading

1   Department of Health (1990) *The
    Care of Children: Principles and
    Practice in Regulations and
    Guidance*, London: HMSO.
2   Marsh, P. and Triseliotis, J. (eds)
    (1993) *Prevention and Reunification
    in Child Care*, London: Batsford.
3   Thoburn, J. (1994) *Child Placement:
    Principles and Practice*, Aldershot:
    Arena.

Dartington Social Research Unit (1995) *Child Protection and Child Abuse: Messages from Research*, London: HMSO.

Department of Health (1985) *Social Work Decisions in Child Care*, London: HMSO.

Department of Health (1989) *Introduction to the Children Act 1989*, London: HMSO.

Department of Health (1991a) *Patterns and Outcomes in Child Placement*, London: HMSO.

Department of Health (1991b) *The Children Act 1989: Regulations and Guidance*, London: HMSO.

Department of Health (1991c) *Working Together under the Children Act, 1989*, London: HMSO.

Department of Health (1995) *The Challenge of Partnership in Child Protection*, London: HMSO.

Gibbons, J., Thorpe, S. and Wilkinson, P. (1990) *Family Support and Prevention*, London: HMSO.

Gibbons, J. (ed.) (1992) *The Children Act 1989 and Family Support*, London: HMSO.

Holman, B. (1988) *Putting Families First: Prevention and Child Care*, London: Macmillan.

Jones, M. A. (1985) *A Second Chance for Families: Five Years Later: Follow-up of a Program to Prevent Foster Care*, New York: Child Welfare League of America.

Packman, J. (1986) *Who Needs Care?*, Oxford: Blackwell.

Thoburn, J. (1994) *Child Placement: Principles and Practice*, Aldershot: Arena.

Thoburn, J., Lewis, A. and Shemmings, D. (1995) *Paternalism or Partnership? Family Involvement in the Child Protection Process*, London: HMSO.

Whittaker, J. K., Kinney, J., Tracy, E. M. and Booth, C. (eds) (1990) *Reaching High-risk Families: Intensive Family Preservation Services*, New York: Aldine de Gruyter.

VII.2
The Hospital
Jo Connolly

The role of hospital social workers in acute and rehabilitation adult care has been radically affected by developments in health and social care policy. The evidence suggests that 'doing a good job under difficult circumstances' finds social work ideals thriving, interdisciplinary working a reality, new skills a challenge, client choice a possibility and the impact of social work intervention acknowledged as undeniably beneficial to both the host institution and patient care. Difficulties for practitioners arise from pressure of work and from the shift in emphasis of social work practice from being largely autonomous to being wholly accountable, and 'fitting in' hospital discharge planning around activities which straddle the purchaser–provider split.

Background

Changes in the wake of the NHS White Paper – *Working for Patients* (Department of Health, 1989b), include hospitals becoming 'provider units', in a quasi-market of health care provision. As with any contractual arrangement, their existence is dependent upon meeting the needs of 'purchasers' (District Health Authorities and GP fundholders). Acute hospital services are obliged to operate efficiently and contain costs – bed blocking is the antithesis of these objectives. Hence there is constant pressure on 'freeing' beds to make room for new admissions. Alongside changes in acute services, and in line with community care policy, long-stay beds

are being closed and erstwhile occupants decanted into nursing homes, residential homes or other facilities in the community as responsibility for continuing care shifts from health to social services.

Under the National Health Service and Community Care Act 1990, social services departments gained responsibility for the co-ordination of multidisciplinary assessment and financing of community care. Hospital discharge arrangements for those entering care and for those returning to the community are now seen as a major issue in the implementation of the reforms. Hospital social workers are in the front line of working together with other health care professionals in effecting discharge arrangements. Their new roles and responsibilities have been consolidated into the creation of a system of 'care management' in which the central tasks are:

1 assessment of the circumstances of the user, including any support required by carers;

2 negotiation of a care package in agreement with users, carers and relevant agencies, designed to meet identified need with available resources; and

3 implementation and monitoring of the agreed package, together with a review of outcomes and any necessary revision of services provided (SSI, 1990).

What is the reality of the reforms for

social work practitioners attached to adult hospital teams?

Social Workers or Bed Managers?

The medical imperative for early discharge often clashes with the aspirations of social workers to engage in 'traditional social casework'. Costing packages of care and negotiating contracts with others as service providers requires a different set of skills entirely and gives rise to the question: Is the care management/discharge planning role the prerogative of the professionally qualified social worker?

The construction of a system of care management/discharge planning with clearly defined objectives gives a purpose and rigour to 'social work' intervention which in the past was often lacking. Personal agendas, special interests and protracted casework meant that 'collectively' hospital social work intervention appeared unfocused with no measurable impact on clients.

The challenge of 'managing care' instead of cases is significant, linking the critical task of assessing need with the right of the person being assessed to contribute to that assessment and to be involved in decisions about the services to be delivered. It embodies social work principles but widens the resources.

The initial impact of the care management concept as it impinges on the social work role has been met with predictable reservation. Participants in a survey of hospital social workers (Davies and Connolly, 1995b) unanimously attested to a noticeable impact on practice, and in some cases thought their work wholly changed by its demands. They expressed apprehension about giving financial advice: some felt disinclined to intrude into clients' affairs and were anxious about 'getting it right'. Others found the increase in paperwork tiresome and the workload increased in terms of time spent helping and advising families about various options. They voiced misgivings about dealing with budgets for the first time and negotiating for services. Generally, however, there was a kind of stoic acceptance of the new responsibilities, 'I have a calculator in my drawer – something I didn't expect to need as part of the equipment of a social worker – I have to use it'. Burgeoning social work training curricula will doubtless reflect the need for additional skills and hopefully the 'calculator' will be upgraded to tailor-made computer software programmes. This would do much to cut down on the amount of time social workers report they are spending 'doing paperwork'.

Aside from apprehension about making mistakes there is real excitement generated as the positive benefits of care management become apparent. 'We have a lot more flexibility in arranging packages of care for people', 'It has become easier to meet care needs now we are commissioners'; 'We are empowering clients and giving them real choices'.

Central to discharge planning is direct work with clients: listening to patients' feelings, helping families acknowledge and cope with their situation and then plan for the future. While social workers' particular interests have largely been consigned to specialist posts or continue as extra curricula/out of hours activities, the interpersonal skills in line with much traditional social work activity are particularly vital in the assessment task.

More arbitrary is the role of 'counsellor' as a legitimate activity in the discharge planning process. Where it is understood to mean 'one-to-one contact' with a specific aim, usually time limited (for example bereavement counselling); it is a 'provider service' outside the remit of care management. However, counselling is not only a direct service dealing specifically with major change, but also part of the workers' repertoire of skills in helping patients to decide on needs and solutions in the context of immediate practical issues such as preparing for discharge (SSI, 1992a).

Practitioners need to protect themselves against risk of 'burn-out' as they balance the inexorable demands of discharge planning with best practice. There is a role for workload management in ensuring that demands are not unrealistic, or that they fail to reflect the unpredictably complex and time consuming nature of some discharge arrangements. It is a simple strategy with far-reaching effects: preventing work overload at the same time as providing practice accountability and a powerful management tool when competing for scarce resources.

So, is discharge planning social work or bed managing? Practitioners are quick to claim they are the ideal professionals and the domain rightfully belongs to them. The concept of care management is interfered with if some activities are separated out and assigned to others; the reality seems to be that 'the sum of the parts is larger than the whole'. The whole discharge planning process is a social work role; not one for unqualified bed managers. Social workers set standards and provide a framework for practice that is unique; their skills provide psychological support to clients and families by creating a facilitative climate in which they can adjust to the psycho-social impact of their physical/mental condition on themselves and their families, as well as guiding them on practical issues such as finance.

Interdisciplinary Working – the Reality

Community care assessments are not the responsibility of a single professional; they are multidisciplinary decisions. How professionals work together and communicate with each other, the 'characteristics of interdisciplinarity',

Five Key Points

1 Hospital discharge planning rightfully belongs to social workers.

2 Their roles and responsibilities have been consolidated through health and social care reforms.

3 Counselling and psychological support are incidental to the discharge planning process.

4 Social work, to be effective, must be compatible with the interdisciplinary setting in which it operates.

5 There is consensus among social workers themselves, health care colleagues and patients, and their carers about the indispensibility of social workers in effective discharge planning.

vary enormously. The institutional setting for hospital discharge planning adds some of its own distinguishing features.

Location

Hospitals are a major location of social services departments and social workers provide a unique and effective link between hospital and the community, and between health and social care agencies.

Much has been written about the wisdom, or otherwise, of social work's unconditional collaboration with the medical profession in hospitals (see Bywaters, 1986). Traditionally, arguments have been based on fear of medical domination over social work. The risk of being regarded as medical 'handmaidens' in hospital discharge planning must have receded apace with the introduction of reforms in health and welfare policy: hospital 'trust' status; the management of doctors; cost containment; clarification of social service department's responsibilities for, and their budgetary control of, community care. There has never been a better time, or climate, for hospital social workers, through regular contact and communication, to educate and influence health care colleagues about the social meaning of health.

Multidisciplinary arena

All care professionals are together and hospital social workers are in daily contact with health care colleagues. There are opportunities for formal and informal meetings. The most successful organizational arrangement, in terms of mutual professional satisfaction, is where the social worker is attached or assigned to a particular ward, visits regularly and is identified as a member of the multidisciplinary team.

Short-term intervention

Discharge arrangements may be simple or complex; involving intensive work or a simple telephone call. But the circumstances of patient/social worker contact are always triggered by hospital admission and usually end on the occasion of a review of the care package a few weeks after leaving hospital. There is no remit for long-term involvement with clients once they have returned to the community. It is inevitable that social workers combine a hospital ethos with their own professional commitment to a degree which makes them feel comfortable in the host environment.

Referrals

There are possibilities for influencing the source and type of social work referrals, and the timing and planning of intervention through direct case finding, and through contact with health colleagues in multidisciplinary ward teams. The social work role continues to be, at least partly, defined and redefined through contact with nurses and other health care professionals on the wards. Where a relationship is based on clear and regular communication and a mutual

professional regard, the expectation is that social workers use their professional judgement to negotiate a wide range of roles to do with patient welfare. At the other end of the scale, a working environment characterized by poor quality communication leaves nurses with little choice other than to define patients' social problems themselves and make referrals for certain tasks to be carried out.

Purchaser–provider?

Hospital social workers can no longer rely on home care managers to carry out home assessments on their behalf since the separation of purchaser and provider services. This is proving particularly difficult for social workers operating in rapid turnover settings like Accident and Emergency departments where the volume and pace of work is unpredictable. The loss of a proxy assessor in the community is also significant where the medical condition of individuals causes major changes in mental/physical functioning.

In terms of 'interdisciplinarity' a renegotiation of professional roles might already be providing a solution. Social workers and hospital occupational therapists (OTs) traditionally work in close tandem, with the OT being the link with the community, finding out if patients can cope at home and what type of services they need, while social workers concentrate on consulting with clients and carers.

Time-scales

Discharge protocols (jointly agreed between health and social services departments) set the planning process within a time-scale. The target time for patient discharge is just one measurement by which performance in hospitals is judged successful or otherwise. What this indicator fails to reflect is the different complexities of individual discharge arrangements and sometimes leads to a criticism of social workers working to 'different time-scales'.

Diverse professional perspectives have a potential for causing conflict. Good communication between disciplines at least informs each party of the other's concerns, and hopefully encourages mutual respect.

What these six factors serve to illustrate are that hospital social workers involved in discharge planning are undeniably working in a multidisciplinary setting. The prevailing circumstances impinge on interdisciplinary roles and relationships and show in mutual dependency and professional regard.

In discharge planning there is a need for someone to bring together the various inputs in order to ensure continuity of care for each patient. It is important that the co-ordinator has ready access to a wide range of resources and the status to negotiate for those services rather than just make referrals or respond passively to the demands of other professionals. Hospital social workers are in an ideal position to undertake these tasks effectively.

Impact of Hospital Social Work – the Evidence

Evidence from three studies provides a comprehensive portrayal of the beneficial contribution made by hospital social work to the smooth running of the hospital organization and to patient welfare.

1   Davies and Connolly (1995a) sought the opinions of doctors and senior nurses about the roles and functions of hospital social workers in a series of face-to-face interviews in one East Anglian Health Authority.

2   Connor and Tibbitt (1988) used a diary study, complemented by observations in their Scottish study, to illustrate the nature and contribution of hospital social work in two major patient/client groups – geriatrics and paediatrics.

3   The Social Services Inspectorate (1993) reported on interviews with 59 discharged hospital patients (elderly people and adults with physical disabilities and chronic ill-health) and 26 of their carers.

All three studies found that where hospital social workers play a pivotal role

---

Three Questions

1   Is there a future for hospital social workers as 'counsellors' on the wards?

2   Does successful interdisciplinarity inevitably depend on the personalities of individual professionals?

3   Is the professional profile of social work practitioners working with adults different to that of child care practitioners?

---

in multidisciplinary working, where there is good interdisciplinary collaboration and where they are hospital based and ward assigned (factors associated with a higher level of staffing), intervention results in better case finding, earlier referrals, better planning and more successful discharges. This has an effect of maximizing valuable medical resources through effective and efficient use of hospital beds and the prevention of bed blocking.

Early and appropriately organized discharge is mutually beneficial to hospital organization and patient alike. Once the acute stage of illness is past, the efficacious effect of in-patient care is quickly outweighed by concerns about increased risk of 'institutionalization', 'loss of social skills' and 'increased risk of infection'.

The findings demonstrate that social workers are in an ideal position to communicate with all the players in each set of discharge circumstances. They have knowledge of and skills in communication, advocacy, liaison and networking; they are able to access a wide range of resources and, as commissioners for Social Service Departments, they have the status to negotiate for these services.

It was thought by social workers that much of their work would simply have not been done, in their absence, by others. This declaration is corroborated by the findings of all three studies. The most frequently noted group of consequences were client-centred: for example, people would remain at risk, or the client's family would have to try and cope with an increased level of stress. Users and carers stated that things would have turned out differently if they had not had contact with the hospital social worker. Some believed that they would have found it very difficult to cope without their intervention. Studies (1) and (2) identified people who were the sole source of information about their own home circumstances: in their anxiety to get home there was a risk that they would underestimate their own problems or oversell the willingness or ability of relatives and neighbours to provide extra support. The SSI found that a significant minority of users and carers could have benefited from earlier intervention, particularly carers who were concerned about the user's future care. 'Even when it was judged unlikely that matters would not escalate in this way, delays in providing services could result in problems becoming more entrenched and thus more difficult [and often more expensive] to deal with' (p. 83).

Health care professionals working with hospital social workers overwhelmingly supported their presence on the wards; they recognize and respect their unique contribution to health and do not wish to have them supplanted by any other group. Criticisms concerned desirable staffing levels and organizational arrangements not the role of social workers *per se*. Although other professionals claimed they did share some of the tasks done by social workers such as providing emotional support to patients and their families, or obtaining information about new patients' home circumstances, they had neither the remit nor inclination to get involved in other areas of work done by social workers.

Study (3) found that 'in more complex situations where emotional and practical support were required, users and carers thought the hospital social work response tailored to individual need' (p. 23).

Doing a good job in changing and sometimes difficult circumstances could be the hallmark of social workers in any situation. In this respect, hospital social work in general, and discharge planning in particular, is no different; it has its difficulties and its compensations. What makes it unique is the setting in which health and social services come together in a multidisciplinary arena where each player has a contribution to make. The particular role of social work practitioners is to bring the objectives of care management in discharge planning to realization.

Further Reading

1   Bywaters, P. (1986) 'Social work and the medical profession – arguments against unconditional collaboration', *British Journal of Social Work*, 16(6), 661–7.
2   Butrym, Z. and Horder, J. (1983) *Health, Doctors and Social Work*, London: Routledge, Kegan & Paul.
3   Connor, A. and Tibbitt, J. (1988) *Social Workers and Health Care in Hospitals*, London: HMSO.

References

Bywaters, P. (1986) 'Social work and the medical profession – arguments against unconditional collaboration', *British Journal of Social Work*, 16(6), 661–7.

Connor, A. and Tibbitt, J. (1988) *Social Workers and Health Care in Hospitals*, London: HMSO.

Davies, M. and Connolly, J. (1995a) 'The social worker's role in the hospital', *Health & Social Care in the Community*, 3(5), 301–9, Blackwell Science Ltd., Oxford.

Davies, M. and Connolly, J. (1995b) 'Hospital social work and discharge planning: an exploratory study in East Anglia', *Health & Social Care in the Community*, 3(6), 363–71, Blackwell Science Ltd., Oxford.

Department of Health (1989b) *Working for Patients*, London: HMSO.

Department of Health (1990) *NHS and Community Care Act*, London: HMSO.

Social Services Inspectorate (1990) *Training for Community Care: a Strategy*, London: Department of Health.

Social Services Inspectorate (1992a) *Social Services for Patients I: Working at the Interface*, London: Department of Health.

Social Services Inspectorate (1992b) *Social Services for Hospital Patients II: the Implications for Community Care*, London: Department of Health.

Social Services Inspectorate (1993) *Social Services for Hospital Patients III: the User and Carer Perspective*, London: Department of Health.

VII.3
Probation
Peter Raynor

The probation service of the late-1990s is a rapidly changing environment for practitioners, and its inclusion in a general survey of social work settings is itself controversial: much more so now than it would have been ten years ago. Changes in penal policies and in the part the service is expected to play in their implementation have affected and sometimes conflicted with its traditional self-image and the preferred work culture of many of its staff. This chapter provides an overview of current functions and developments, and of some of the changes in thinking which have influenced recent and current practice. The sensitive question of whether probation is, or should be, a branch of social work is treated here as a partly empirical matter, to be illuminated by considering what probation officers do and where or how they can be effective, rather than as an *a priori* ideological issue; my hope is that this will avoid the tendency of some recent discussions to generate more heat than light.

What, then, is today's probation service like? In the mid-1990s 55 separate probation areas in England and Wales are overseen by Probation Committees consisting largely of magistrates, which will shortly be replaced by Probation Boards including a larger element of local authority and 'community' representation. All operate under regulations prescribed by the Home Office, which also provides by far the lion's share of the budget and monitors services through regular statistical returns and through Her Majesty's Inspectorate

of Probation. In theory a Committee which fails to ensure a satisfactory service can be disbanded and its area service run directly by the Home Office, but these powers have not yet been used. By March 1994 probation areas employed a total of about 20,000 staff including part-timers; of these about 8,100 were probation officers in various grades, equivalent to nearly 7,700 full-time officers (this compares to 5,900 at the end of 1983, representing 30 per cent growth in ten years, a rate of expansion which many public services would envy). By the end of 1993 just over half of probation officers were women: this included over 80 per cent of the part-time officers but only a minority of the managerial grades, a common employment pattern which has been described as a 'dual labour market' differentiated by gender (Barron and Norris, 1976). About 7 per cent of probation staff are recorded as 'belonging to an ethnic minority group' (Home Office, 1994), slightly higher than the corresponding proportion of the population but considerably less than, for example, the proportion of ethnic minority prisoners (Home Office, 1995a). The proportions among probation managers are a good deal lower: 1.6 per cent of chief probation officers and 3.3 per cent of senior probation officers in 1993.

These aggregate figures mask a good deal of diversity: for example, at the end of March 1994 the largest probation area, Inner London, had 667 probation officers while the Welsh rural county of Powys had 14. Although such huge differences of scale obviously have consequences for

structure and management (Inner London
in 1995 had a chief officer, three deputy
chiefs, 20 assistant chiefs and over 100
seniors, while Powys had a chief, one
assistant chief and two seniors) the core
tasks and methods of work of all
probation areas remain remarkably
similar with far less diversity of
procedures and practice than exists, for
example, among social services
departments. This contributes to a sense
of being a national service engaged in
common tasks despite a strong tradition
of local devolution in management. The
common tasks can be summarized as the
provision of pre-sentence reports for the
courts; the supervision of offenders
subject to community sentences such as
probation orders, community service
orders, combination orders and juvenile
supervision orders; the supervision of
offenders released from custodial
sentences, and contact with them during
their sentences; and the provision of
family court welfare services in
connection with separation or divorce
proceedings. Nearly 650 probation
officers work inside Prison Service
establishments. In 1992–3 total spending
on the probation service was £449 million,
compared with £1,623 million on prisons
and £5,980 million on the police
(Government Statistical Service, 1994).

In spite of a high degree of underlying
continuity in organization and functions,
many probation staff regard the last few
years as a time of unprecedented change
which has brought many new pressures
and stresses (see, for example, May, 1991).
Much of this is a reflection of wider
pressures facing all public services, which
are increasingly expected to demonstrate
value for money to politicians who may
be sceptical in principle about the role of
the State in public service provision. More
specific issues for the probation service
arise from its location within a criminal
justice system which has itself undergone
major changes in thinking and practice,
sometimes following each other with

Five Key Points

1 The core tasks of the probation
   service are to supervise offenders in
   the community and to provide pre-
   sentence reports to the courts.
2 The service is locally organized but
   centrally regulated, and the degree of
   central regulation has increased.
3 Many probation officers believe that
   increasing pressure towards
   standardization makes it more difficult
   to offer an individualized and helpful
   service.
4 Recent research shows that offenders
   can be supervised in ways that
   reduce offending, but much of the
   supervision currently offered is not
   fully informed by this research.
5 The future health of the probation
   service depends on demonstrating
   greater effectiveness and on securing
   public and political support for its
   special role in criminal justice.

bewildering rapidity. The 1991 Criminal
Justice Act aimed for the first time to set
down a consistent and rational basis for
all sentencing, based broadly on the
principle of 'just deserts' or punishment
proportionate to the seriousness of the
crime (rather than, for example, penal
'treatment' based on the personal
characteristics or expected future
behaviour of the offender) (Home Office,
1990). The role envisaged for the
probation service was the provision of
'community sentences', intended to
replace custodial sentences for all but the
most serious offenders, but the use of
phrases like 'punishment in the
community' led many probation officers
to fear that their traditional role of
helping offenders to sort out their lives
was under threat. Probation officers
pointed out that they had not been
trained to administer punishment but to
do social work. This was largely a
restatement of a long-standing and rather
unhelpful argument about the presumed

incompatibility of 'care' and 'control', both of which seem to be necessary and indeed inescapable components of probation work (see, for example, Raynor, 1985), but it tended to divert attention from many positive features of the Act. Further confusion resulted when many of these were modified or repealed as the Government of the day reverted to a more punitive and prison-centred policy in the Criminal Justice Acts of 1993 and 1994: many of the same probation officers who had condemned the 1991 Act now found themselves defending it against the new proposals.

Alongside these confusing twists and turns of policy, which in the late-1990s seem to owe more to electoral considerations than to new thinking about criminal justice and have led to a deluge of new and sometimes contradictory instructions and circulars to probation services, it is possible to identify some longer term changes which will almost certainly play a more important role in shaping the probation service of the future. These can best be considered under the two headings of accountability and effectiveness. Both of these modify the traditional perceived autonomy of practitioners, but in different ways.

Accountability: the Search for a Predictable Service

As well as general pressures in all public services towards greater centralized accountability and 'VFM' (Value for Money in audit-speak), there were specific reasons for the Probation Service to move in this direction. For example, the Green and White papers leading up to the 1991 Criminal Justice Act (Home Office, 1988, 1990) sought to redefine probation as a community-based punishment and considerations of proportionality required that when imposing such a sentence courts should

have a clear idea of what would be involved and what requirements and restrictions would be imposed on the offender. Although this approach led to many further questions (for example, did it imply punitive content in probation orders, or simply a new way of describing the limitation of liberty inherent in a requirement to report?) the main implication was clear: issues such as frequency of contact or, on occasion, absence of contact with probationers could no longer be left to the discretion of individual practitioners. Although some probation officers no doubt exaggerated the threat posed by a new political rhetoric designed for public consumption rather than for the professional audience, one practical outcome was certainly destined to make a substantial difference to their work. This was the development and publication of *National Standards for the Supervision of Offenders in the Community* (Home Office, 1992 and 1995b) which laid down required minimum expectations for all the main probation service tasks specifying, for example, minimum frequencies of contact; when and how enforcement action should be taken; and when a probation officer must refer to higher management for a decision.

The full effect of National Standards on the working practices of probation officers will take some years to assess, but what does seem clear is that many officers welcome them on the basis that they spell out for the first time the basic requirements of a 'good enough' performance. They have also become the routine yardstick for performance measurement in both national and local inspections. More worrying, in the view of many practitioners and some academics, has been their contribution to the growth of managerialism (see, for example, Nellis, 1995) and the implied impoverishment of the role of practitioners whose decisions would increasingly be based on following rules rather than on their own assessment of a situation. Some other developments point in a similar direction, such as the recent Home Office review of probation officer training which argued that for most officers a short period of employment-based training would be more appropriate than a two-year social work qualification (Dews and Watts, 1994).

Even more interesting from a penological point of view is the National Standards' focus on the form of supervision rather than its content: for example, they prescribe frequencies of contact at different stages of supervision, and even the precise circumstances and manner in which offenders should be warned about compliance, but they say nothing about what kind of supervision programme might contribute to the rehabilitation of offenders or the reduction of crime. The purpose of probation is defined as 'securing the rehabilitation of the offender, protecting the public from harm from the offender, or preventing the offender from committing further crimes' (Home Office, 1995b), but the connections between these purposes and the various rules and procedures are left implicit or taken for granted. The emphasis is on what is expected of officers and offenders in the way of compliance, rather than on how changes of attitude, behaviour or available opportunities might actually be brought about. More fundamentally, there is no obvious link between the Standards and the emerging body of evidence about effectiveness in supervision. National Standards are about accountability for processes rather than outcomes, when arguably the major challenge for contemporary probation services is to demonstrate that their work has some impact on the behaviour of offenders.

'What Works': towards an Effective Service

By the mid-1980s most probation officers in England and Wales had been trained and had developed their approach to practice against the background of a consensus that 'nothing works'. The major research reviews of the 1970s such as Lipton et al. (1975) and Brody (1976), or at least the summaries and simplifications available in secondary sources, had supposedly demonstrated that no form of custodial or non-custodial programme offered a realistic prospect of reducing offending. Probation officers tended to assume that crime was a consequence of social

---

Three Questions

1 Is the probation service part of social work, part of the criminal justice system, or both?
2 Can probation practice become more consistent without becoming less responsive to individual need?
3 How can the supervision of offenders become more effective in reducing re-offending?

---

disadvantages such as poverty, unemployment or discrimination, and that their main job was to avoid pointless and expensive prison sentences by providing 'alternatives to custody' or diversion from more coercive to less coercive sentences. This strategy had little to say about the content of supervision: if nothing worked better than anything else, the practitioner's individual preference was as good a guide as any. Paradoxically, much practice appeared still to be loosely based on counselling or psycho-dynamic models, while the task of providing constructive non-custodial punishment fell increasingly to the popular Community Service Order, managed by the Probation Service but supervised by staff who were not qualified as probation officers.

Probably the most influential attempt to articulate a coherent theoretical basis for probation practice during this period was the 'non-treatment paradigm' (Bottoms and McWilliams, 1979) based on principles of diversion from custody and the provision of constructive help to offenders in relation to self-identified social and personal problems. While this had the advantage of rejecting one-sided psycho-social diagnosis as the basis of supervision, it shared the pessimism of the 'nothing works' era in relation to outcomes and had little to say about the content of supervision. The 'just deserts' model which informed the development of the 1991 Criminal Justice Act was itself partly a product of 'nothing works': if no sentence is more effective than another, then the seriousness of the crime becomes the only criterion for choosing between sentences. However, the Act itself and the National Standards paradoxically contributed to the demand for a new approach. Faced with the expectation of more frequent contact and more demanding and purposeful approaches to supervision, probation services had to search for ideas about methods which could meet these requirements.

Some approaches based on structured programmes and social learning were already gaining ground in probation, derived, for example, from psychological approaches to offending behaviour (McGuire and Priestley, 1985) and from practice experience in probation day centres. However, the major challenges to 'nothing works' were emerging from American and Canadian research reviews (such as Lipsey, 1992; Andrews et al., 1990), from research in Scotland designed to inform a more effective approach to criminal justice (McIvor, 1990) and from evaluations of special programmes in England and Wales which seemed to be

having some impact on offending (for example, Raynor, 1988; Roberts, 1989). This material tended, broadly speaking, to favour structured programmes designed to influence attitudes and behaviour, which could be implemented consistently and evaluated. It gave little or no support to unstructured approaches such as relationship-based reactive counselling when applied to persistent or relatively serious offenders. A series of publications and 'What Works' conferences gave currency to these ideas (see, for example, McGuire, 1995), and some carefully designed and implemented programmes began to show modest positive results (Raynor and Vanstone, 1994).

Potentially, this emerging commitment to effectiveness may be the most significant current development in probation, but it also poses a number of problems. If evaluation of effectiveness, rather than simple adherence to National Standards, were to become the main yardstick of good practice, this could call aspects of the Standards into question. It would also require the development of the capacity and expertise for evaluation on a scale which the Service cannot yet deliver: the majority of probation innovations are still not adequately evaluated. Taking effectiveness seriously would also imply a different approach to ineffectiveness, and although some practice shows good results, the overall reconviction performance of probation orders in England and Wales is not much better than that of prison (Lloyd et al., 1994). Another recent study which measured the quality and effectiveness of probation officers' pre-sentence reports in the Crown Courts identified wide variation in quality, together with evidence that the better quality reports had more influence on the courts' decisions and led to more community sentences and fewer prison sentences (Gelsthorpe and Raynor, 1995). Evidence of this kind suggests a need for strategies to improve effectiveness, and does not sit easily with the idea that practice should be determined primarily by practitioners' preferences. If the Probation Service is in the business of crime reduction, which seems a legitimate public expectation of any criminal justice agency, the current changes of emphasis will need to continue and the Service which emerges from them will look different from the Service of ten years ago.

To return to a question raised briefly at the beginning of this chapter, will it then be doing social work, or something else such as correctional case management? To some extent this seems a metaphysical question which we cannot answer in the absence, still, of generally agreed definitions of social work. However, it seems clear that such a Service would be concerned for the interests of offenders, their communities and their victims. It would be seeking to resolve problems by influence rather than coercion. By working for the rehabilitation of offenders it would be promoting their reintegration in communities, which seems to be a major theme of the increasing amount of statutory after-care undertaken with released prisoners (Maguire et al., 1996). It could also serve to promote a more humanized and restorative approach to criminal justice as an alternative to unconstructive punishments (see, for example, Nellis, 1995). Wider concerns about social disadvantage would remain highly relevant, given the evidence that links higher offending rates with unemployment (Dickinson, 1993) and poverty (Wilkinson, 1994), but the Service needs also to address the more specific criminogenic factors which lead some people (mainly men) to offend far more than others in similar circumstances. Some offending has more to do with exploitation and abuse of power than with difficult circumstances, and the poor are disproportionately victimized by crime.

One recent graduate of a structured probation programme described what he had learned in these words (Lucas et al., 1992): 'It's made me realise . . . it's learnt me to put myself in other people's places if they'd been burgled . . . guilty's the word . . . it's out of order. It's opened my mind and I look at a subject from all different angles . . . not just jumping the gun. With problems I can clear them up more easily.' The probation area which offered this programme described the service's aim as 'helping offenders to help themselves to stop offending'. Is this social work? If it is, then probation officers are doing social work, but this is probably less important than the answers to other questions – such as whether they are helpful, whether they are effective, whether they contribute to the rehabilitation of offenders, and whether they help to improve both criminal justice and social justice.

References

Andrews, D. A., Zinger, I., Hoge, R. D., Bonta, J., Gendreau, P. and Cullen, F. T. (1990) 'Does correctional treatment work? A clinically relevant and psychologically informed meta-analysis', *Criminology*, 28, 369–904.

Barron, R. D. and Norris, G. M. (1976) 'Sexual divisions and the dual labour market', in D. Baker and S. Allen (eds), *Dependence and Exploitation in Work and Marriage*, London: Longman, pp. 47–69.

Bottoms, A. E. and McWilliams, W. (1979) 'A non-treatment paradigm for probation practice', *British Journal of Social Work*, 9, 159–202.

Brody, S. R. (1976) *The Effectiveness of Sentencing*, London: HMSO.

Further Reading

1 May, T. and Vass, A. (eds) (1996) *Working with Offenders: Issues, Contexts and Outcomes*, London: Sage.

2 McGuire, J. (ed.) (1995) *What Works: Reducing Reoffending*, Chichester: Wiley.

3 Raynor, P., Vanstone, M. and Smith, D. (1994) *Effective Probation Practice*, Basingstoke: Macmillan.

Dews, V. and Watts, J. (1994) *Review of Probation Officer Recruitment and Qualifying Training*, London: Home Office.

Dickinson, D. (1993) *Crime and Unemployment*, Cambridge: Department of Applied Economics.

Gelsthorpe, L. and Raynor, P. (1995) 'Quality and effectiveness in probation officers' reports to sentencers', *British Journal of Criminology*, 35, 188–200.

Government Statistical Service (1994) *Criminal Justice Key Statistics England and Wales 1994*, London: Home Office.

Home Office (1988) *Punishment, Custody and the Community*, Cm 424, London: HMSO.

Home Office (1990) *Crime, Justice and Protecting the Public*, Cm 965, London: HMSO.

Home Office (1992) *National Standards for the Supervision of Offenders in the Community*, London: Home Office.

Home Office (1994) *Probation Statistics England and Wales 1993*, London: Home Office.

Home Office (1995a) *The Prison Population in 1994*, Home Office Statistical Bulletin 8/95, London: Home Office.

Home Office (1995b) *National Standards for the Supervision of Offenders in the Community*, London: Home Office.

Lipsey, M. W. (1992) 'Juvenile delinquency treatment: a meta-analytic enquiry into the variability of effects', in T. D. Cook, H. Cooper, D. S. Cordray, H. Hartmann, L. V. Hedges, R. L. Light, T. A. Louis and F. Mosteller (eds) *Meta-analysis for Explanation*, New York: Russell Sage Foundation, pp. 83–127.

Lipton, D., Martinson, R. and Wilks, J. (1975) *The Effectiveness of Correctional Treatment*, New York: Praeger.

Lloyd, C., Mair, G. and Hough, M. (1994) *Explaining Reconviction Rates: a Critical Analysis*, London: HMSO.

Lucas, J., Raynor, P. and Vanstone, M. (1992) *Straight Thinking on Probation One Year On*, Bridgend: Mid Glamorgan Probation Service.

Maguire, M., Perroud, B. and Raynor, P. (1996) *Automatic Conditional Release: the First Two Years*, Home Office Research Study 156, London: Home Office.

May, T. (1991) *Probation: Politics, Policy and Practice*, Milton Keynes: Open University Press.

McGuire, J. (ed.) (1995) *What Works: Reducing Offending*, Chichester: Wiley.

McGuire, J. and Priestley, P. (1985) *Offending Behaviour*, London: Batsford.

McIvor, G. (1990) *Sanctions for Serious or Persistent Offenders*, Stirling: Social Work Research Centre.

Nellis, M. (1995) 'Probation values for the 1990s', *Howard Journal of Criminal Justice*, 34, 19–44.

Raynor, P. (1985) *Social Work, Justice and Control*, Oxford: Blackwell.

Raynor, P. (1988) *Probation as an Alternative to Custody*, Aldershot: Avebury.

Raynor, P. and Vanstone, M. (1994) 'Probation practice, effectiveness and the non-treatment paradigm', *British Journal of Social Work*, 24, 387–404.

Roberts, C. H. (1989) *Hereford and Worcester Probation Service Young Offender Project: First Evaluation Report*, Oxford: Department of Social and Administrative Studies.

Wilkinson, R. G. (1994) *Unfair Shares*, Ilford: Barnardo's.

Social work is not the main function of prisons. Not surprisingly, social workers in prisons often feel somewhat marginalized. They have to 'sell' what they can offer, not only to prison governors but also to the inmates. As in other total institutions, there is a danger that they are drawn into helping to run the place rather than helping individual prisoners. But social work has a great deal to offer in the prison setting.

Prisoners are isolated, deprived of their independence and privacy, often vulnerable and afraid. Many feel guilt about their offences, but it often seems as if nobody is interested in helping them to leave prison better people than when they first went inside. Probation officers and social workers cannot solve any of these problems, but they can help with them all. (In England, Wales and Northern Ireland, the probation service sends staff to work in prison probation departments. In Scotland, a similar service is provided by local social work departments. References to probation officers below should be taken to include Scottish prison social workers.)

Prison social work is generally an interdisciplinary endeavour. Although there are tensions between the different professions working in prisons, there is a good deal of common ground between them. In practice, probation officers often run groups jointly with psychologists, teachers and uniformed staff – and they liaise not only with these professions but with chaplains, governors, health workers and others inside the prison. They also maintain important links with their field-based colleagues and with professionals and voluntary agencies in the community. Increasingly, prison probation officers are case managers as well as caseworkers, brokering the provision of services to prisoners by outsiders.

Social work in prisons demands special skills and qualities. Staff need to be diplomatic, but must stoutly defend the values of their own agency and profession in the face of considerable and persistent hostility from prison staff. Many of them would say that prison probation officers need a thick skin – but they must also display the sensitivity and empathy needed by all social workers. They need considerable integrity. They must be clear about their own values, and prepared to challenge injustices. This is important in itself, and also in displaying professional independence from the prison service.

'Selling' Social Work in Prison

The governor of each prison has considerable discretion as to how social work services to prisoners are delivered. The statutory agencies which have traditionally had a monopoly now face competition from the voluntary and private sectors. The National Association for the Care and Resettlement of Offenders has won contracts to provide services in some prisons for example, and this trend is likely to increase. Prisons' expectations of probation teams inevitably changed in response to the prison privatization programme, requiring greater flexibility on the part of staff.

This involved senior probation officers in time-consuming negotiations about whether the probation service's contract would be renewed. On a more positive note, it also meant that team members had to be more responsive to meeting new needs and were encouraged to be imaginative about involving community agencies in service provision. Less constructively, privatization and the devolution of responsibilities to governors have changed the nature of the prison social work task in recent years. In some places, staff are in danger of becoming rather isolated, because some governors frown on them attending meetings and training events outside the prison, and find it difficult to see how such activities directly benefit the institution.

It has always been difficult to prove that social work is effective, in prisons as elsewhere (Raynor et al., 1994). The official view of the purpose of imprisonment has changed in the UK in recent decades (and the prison systems in Scotland and Northern Ireland have increasingly gone their own, rather different, ways). In England and Wales, the emphasis on rehabilitation and training has lessened since the 1980s. The Woolf Report urged a reappraisal of the purpose of the prison system, but the anticipated debate never really took place inside the prison service, which adopted a pragmatic strategy (Woolf and Tumim, 1991; Morgan, 1994). Some improvements were made to prison regimes, but increasing pressure of numbers meant that these were often short-lived. Politicians repeatedly claimed that 'prison works'. This encouraged sentencers to make more use of custodial sentences, and this led to severe overcrowding in prisons and a deterioration in prison regimes. Meanwhile the conditions for granting home leave were changed,

leading to a reduction in prisoners' links with the community (Williams, 1995).

Social work has little to contribute – and little wish to contribute – to the effectiveness of prisons if one takes the view that their primary purpose is to punish and humiliate their inmates. If, on the other hand, prisoners are there as a punishment, not *for additional punishment*, social work has an important role. Prison-based social workers can play a vital part in helping prisoners to maintain community contacts, preparing them for constructive activities after their release, and providing opportunities for reflection on their offending and planning for a better life. Social work is based upon a belief in the dignity and worth of all human beings, and in individuals' ability to change. This therapeutic optimism is a crucial factor in the lives of many prisoners who are tempted to give up hope. It is not unique to social work: it is shared in the prison setting by chaplains, psychologists and many individual members of other disciplines. But the prison probation officer personifies this hope, as has been the case since the first Prisoners' Aid Society workers went into British prisons in the late eighteenth century.

The social work presence in prisons has considerable symbolic importance. On the one hand, it might be used to argue that the system has a caring side, and so to lend it legitimacy (see Sparks, 1994). But the probation service has traditionally opposed the profligate use of custody, and it can build upon this record in engaging with prisoners. Clients are likely to trust independent social workers rather more than people like medical staff employed by the prison service, although many prisoners are suspicious of any staff member who carries keys (Williams, 1991).

Prison-based probation officers face a constant dilemma: how to avoid merely servicing the needs of the prison as an institution, and how to give proper priority to prisoners' needs. This is not new, but it is heightened by the contract culture and the pragmatism about the aims of imprisonment described above. Probation officers have suggested a number of partial solutions (see Williams, 1991; Smith, 1992; Dominelli et al., 1995), but the problem requires constant vigilance. It was no accident that Philip Priestley chose prison probation staff to illustrate his theory of 'role strain' – the tensions experienced by staff trying to carry out several, sometimes contradictory, tasks in an unsympathetic environment (Priestley, 1972).

What Social Work has to Offer in Prisons

Prison can be soul-destroying, even life threatening, for inmates and staff. The social work presence, and the service offered to individuals and groups of prisoners, can help to maintain their hope and self-esteem. Like the other professionals working inside, probation officers provide an advice and counselling service. Like the chaplaincy, they make links with colleagues outside, and so help inmates maintain important relationships with their families and communities. Often alongside the other professional groups, they run groups for inmates with specific problems, at particular stages in their sentences, and inside for particular types of offending. What is distinctive about the probation service is that it is independent of the prison service: its staff are answerable to chief probation officers in the community (if also to some degree to governors), and within certain limits they can guarantee to maintain confidentiality. They provide a service to all inmates – although the needs of those serving shorter sentences and on remand are often neglected in practice.

Although in theory the probation service could have been replaced by other

Five Key Points
1 Social work in prisons is marginalized – but important.
2 Prisons have social problems which are susceptible to social work help, which probation officers are well-placed to provide.
3 Social work values are difficult to put into practice in custodial settings, but prisoners trust probation officers more than other staff because of their perceived independence.
4 Particular personal qualities are needed for probation work in prisons. Perhaps the most important is the ability to form appropriate professional relationships with clients and colleagues.
5 Increasingly prison work is carried out in collaboration with members of other professions, including uniformed prison officers.

providers of social work services, conditions did not encourage this. The Home Office's National Framework for Throughcare (Home Office/Prison Service, 1994) assumed the involvement of probation officers. In any case, the established links between prison probation officers and their field colleagues would have been difficult and expensive for any other agency to duplicate.

Prison probation officers carry out a wide variety of tasks, drawing upon their social work training and their community contacts. In a typical day, a main grade officer might

- sift applications from prisoners and pass some of them on to a specially trained prison officer working on the wing, who will be able to deal with requests for overseas phone calls and other routine matters more quickly;
- attend a case conference of all the disciplines in the prison to consider the circumstances of a particularly

troubled client (for example in order to try and get a prisoner with severe mental illness transferred to hospital);
- return a number of telephone calls from probation officers, social workers and family members about individual clients;
- meet members of a black community organization from the nearby city to review the progress of a group they have been running in the prison for clients from their area;
- have lunch with one of the psychologists and take the opportunity to discuss the arrangements for the next course of the prison's Sex Offender Treatment Programme; and
- see eight inmates from the wing who have made applications for appointments, write up these interviews and start making telephone calls and dictating letters arising from them.

The individual interviews might involve a wide range of problems. In some cases, the uniformed 'SWIP' (Social Work in Prisons) officer may have found that apparently simple referrals involved complex problems, and passed them back to the probation officer. Mostly, the clients will be familiar and some will have attended for counselling over a period of weeks. Others will come to discuss issues arising in the course of groupwork. Wherever possible, opportunities will be taken to invite clients to address issues to do with their offending behaviour, and to take responsibility for dealing with their own problems.

It is often more effective to work with groups of clients: not only can more people be seen in this way, but they can learn from what they have in common with each other, and in longer term groups the dynamics of the group itself can be a powerful influence upon members' future behaviour (Fisher and Watkins, 1993). Probation officers are the largest group of staff involved in setting up and running groupwork in prisons, and the main types of group (according to Towl, 1995) are:

- offending behaviour,
- alcohol,
- drugs,
- anger management,
- lifers,
- social skills,
- sex offenders, and
- anxiety management (in order of frequency).

It is likely that in coming years, specific groups for sex offenders will increase in frequency. A National Sex Offender Treatment Programme began in prisons in the early 1990s, and probation officers have been heavily involved in this, although they have been critical of the content of the nationally prescribed programme and of the preparatory training (see Sabor, 1992; Sampson, 1994; Cowburn and Modi, 1995), which have been improved as a result.

Groupwork has often been undertaken without proper evaluation, both in prisons and in the field (Raynor et al., 1994; Towl, 1995). There is, however, an increasing concern in the social work profession to demonstrate the effectiveness of its interventions, and in the prison context, the huge investment of resources involved in the Sex Offender Treatment Programme has necessitated some systematic evaluation of its effectiveness. While the budget of the probation service remains constrained, it seems likely that groupwork with imprisoned offenders will continue to be an area of growth.

Probation Values in Prison

Social work values and the incarceration of offenders do not coexist easily. Many prison officers are hostile to the very presence of 'civilian' workers such as teachers and probation officers employed to assist prisoners. While this makes for an uncomfortable working environment, it also sets up opportunities for dialogue. It is important that these are taken at the local, personal level as well as at a macro-political level.

At a national level, there was an apparent consensus for a time in the late 1980s around the idea that prison 'makes bad people worse', and the 1991 Criminal Justice Act introduced arrangements consistent with a more parsimonious use of imprisonment. A change of Home Secretary, and of political direction, led only two years later to the bizarre assertion that 'prison works' and to policies based on that assumption which rapidly over-filled the prisons again. The probation service did its best to limit the damage, but the political forces involved were enormously powerful.

The values of the probation service may have been largely ignored during this period, but the damage limitation exercise was extremely important. High quality, anti-oppressive practice in preparing court and parole reports plays a vital role in preventing individual injustices. The legal requirement (in section 95 of the 1991 Act) upon criminal justice agencies to avoid improper discrimination gave legal force to policies previously developed by probation teams, and this work continues in prisons around the country.

Prison probation officers have done a great deal of useful work in exploring what it means to practise social work anti-oppressively in the prison context, and there is a wide range of resources available to inform such practice (see Williams, 1995). While accepting the inevitability, at least for the time being, of clients being unnecessarily imprisoned, probation officers are not required to collude with this injustice. While it is difficult to maintain an anti-custodial stance while actually working in a prison, it is a vital balancing act which prison

probation officers maintain with aplomb. Similarly, it is difficult to give due priority to the rights and needs of victims of crime when one's prime responsibility is to offenders, but it is essential that probation officers and social workers get this balance right. The alternative, which all agree to be unacceptable, is to work in a reactive, bureaucratic way and simply respond pragmatically to externally imposed change (Williams, 1992).

The essential values of probation work

Three Questions

1 How can probation officers gain and keep the trust of both prisoners and other prison staff?
2 How can social work be practised anti-oppressively in an oppressive total institution such as a prison?
3 If prison probation officers are to be trusted by their prisoner clients, how can they also work as part of the system which legitimates imprisonment?

in prisons have been summarized elsewhere (Williams, 1995). They include:

- opposition to custody and commitment to constructive ways of dealing with imprisoned offenders;
- opposing discrimination and promoting justice in prisons and in the community;
- protecting the confidentiality of information relating to clients, and

Further Reading

1 Towl, G. (1995) 'groupwork in prisons – a national survey', *Prison Service Journal*, 97, 5–8.
2 Williams, B. (1996) *Counselling in Criminal Justice*, Buckingham: Open University Press.
3 Woolf, L. J. and Tumim, His Honour Judge S. (1991) *Prison Disturbances April 1990*, Cm 1456, London: HMSO.

promoting openness in all dealings
with them;

- valuing and accepting clients,
offering a personal service based on
clients' own definition of problems,
whilst openly challenging their
offending;
- protecting victims and potential
victims of crime, in a way consistent
with clients' rights and needs
wherever possible; and
- promoting positive change through
the constructive use of professional
relationships.

There is no doubt that this represents an
ambitious and demanding professional
agenda for prison probation work. The
working environment is a difficult one,
and the clients are among the most
challenging and damaged people
probation officers have to work with.
Prison social work certainly offers a
challenge – and enormous variety and
interest – to probation officers with the
right approach and personal qualities.

References

Cowburn, M. and Modi, P. (1995) 'Justice in an unjust
context: implications for working with adult male
sex offenders', in D. Ward and M. Lacey (eds),
Probation: Working for Justice, London: Whiting &
Birch.
Dominelli, L., Jeffers, L., Jones, G., Sibanda, S. and

Williams, B. (1995) *Anti-racist Probation Practice*,
Aldershot: Arena.
Fisher, K. and Watkins, L. (1993) 'Inside Groupwork',
in A. Brown and B. Caddick (eds), *Groupwork with
Offenders*, London: Whiting & Birch.
Home Office/HM Prison Service (1994) *National
Framework for the Throughcare of Offenders in
Custody to the Completion of Supervision in the
Community*, London: Home Office.
Morgan, R. (1994) 'Imprisonment', in M. Maguire, R.
Morgan and R. Reiner (eds), *The Oxford Handbook
of Criminology*, Oxford: Clarendon.
Priestley, P. (1972) 'The prison welfare officer – a case
of role strain', *British Journal of Sociology*, 23(2),
221–35.
Raynor, P., Smith, D. and Vanstone, M. (1994) *Effective
Probation Practice*, London: Macmillan.
Sabor, M. (1992) 'The sex offender treatment
programme in prisons', *Probation Journal*, 39(1),
14–18.
Sampson, A. (1994) *Acts of Abuse: Sex Offenders and the
Criminal Justice System*, London: Routledge.
Smith, D. (1992) 'Social work in prisons', *Practice*, 6(2),
135–45.
Sparks, R. (1994) 'Can prisons be legitimate?', *British
Journal of Criminology*, 34, 14–28.
Towl, G. (1995) 'Groupwork in prisons – a national
survey', *Prison Service Journal*, 97, 5–8.
Williams, B. (1991) *Work with Prisoners*, Birmingham:
Venture.
Williams, B. (1992) 'Caring professionals or street-
level bureaucrats? The case of probation officers'
work with prisoners', *Howard Journal of Criminal
Justice*, 31(4), 263–75.
Williams, B. (1995) 'Probation values in work with
prisoners' in B. Williams (ed.), *Probation Values*,
Birmingham: Venture.
Woolf, Lord Justice and Tumim, His Honour Judge S.
(1991) *Prison Disturbances April 1990*, Cm 1456,
London: HMSO.

The Psychiatric Unit
Michael Sheppard

Mental Health Problems and the Psychiatric Unit

Two key features of service delivery – one policy and one organizational – provide the context for mental health social work practice. The policy of care in the community has led to the winding down and closure of psychiatric hospitals and an emphasis on community-based care delivery (Jones, 1988; Goodwin, 1990). The organization of that care delivery means that mental health problems are confronted in a wide variety of settings which provide social work bases: district teams, family centres, community mental health centres, hospitals and so on.

We can, however, distinguish between settings whose primary focus is on mental health and those which are not. Goldberg and Huxley (1992) have shown that as we go through the various filters to specialist hospital psychiatric services, (a) an ever higher proportion of individuals suffer mental illness, and (b) an increasing proportion is severe or psychotic. Thus clients received from an acute psychiatric ward will generally suffer (or have suffered) a mental illness. Hospital closure has been accompanied by a considerable spread of community mental health centres in recent years (Sheppard, 1991a). There is a limited amount of published data. The Lewisham project is the best documented in this respect, showing that the most frequent practice diagnoses for the crisis team were functional psychoses and neuroses, and for the more general walk in service, adjustment reactions, neuroses and personality disorders (Boardman et al., 1987).

A number of studies have been undertaken of social work settings whose primary focus is not mental health. These found between 25 and 66 per cent of area team clients were 'cases' (i.e., suffered mental illness) (Corney, 1984; Huxley and Fitzpatrick, 1984; Cohen and Fisher, 1987; Huxley et al., 1987). Sheppard's (1995a) study of child care social work found 45 per cent of mothers in deprived urban caseloads and 35 per cent of women in rural caseloads to suffer a depression of clinical severity. This figure may be above 50 per cent when children are in care (Quinton and Rutter, 1984; Isaac et al., 1986). In non-mental health settings, however, the extent of mental health problems is consistently underestimated. Very few clients are departmentally designated mental health cases (Corney, 1984; Huxley et al., 1987). Some studies have shown that social workers (Corney, 1984; Cohen and Fisher, 1987; Huxley et al., 1987), show no more than chance ability to diagnose correctly, while Sheppard (1995a) found a strong negative bias in the identification of depression by child care social workers: social workers were very unlikely to identify depression, *whether or not* the mother was depressed.

This may arise from ignorance, but also reflects social work perspectives. This approach towards mainstream psychiatry is borne from the essentially psycho-social orientation of social work and its humanist commitment (Sheppard, 1991a). Social workers are far from uncritical consumers of psychiatric orthodoxy, and their perspectives are bound to be influenced by the social science and humanist emphases of their training (Sheppard, 1991a, 1992a, 1992b, 1993a). Fisher et al. (1984) found a third of social workers considered the concept of mental health problems to be unhelpful in defining the condition of their clients. The rest expressed antipathy to the labelling effects of psychiatry and a dislike of the over-biological approach of doctors. On the whole social workers would initially attempt to explain client behaviour in terms of social–environmental factors, and the client's experiences. Only when an individual's behaviour became incomprehensible (cf. Coulter, 1973) were workers prepared to concede a mental health problem.

Four Key Areas of Practice

The widespread presence of mental health problems in social work settings is, then, accompanied by a limited, or variable, adherence to psychiatric concepts. This scepticism arises from the same source as that of their distinctive contribution to mental health problems: the psycho-social orientation of education and practice. This orientation is largely consistent with their role, but reflects also educationally influenced perspectives on mental health and illness, and organizational and legally determined responsibilities. These may be usefully divided into four: therapy/care provision, management, authority and interprofessional collaboration.

Therapy and Care

The development of care management has, to some extent distinguished areas formerly unified under social work into those of care management and provision (Sheppard, 1995a). However, it remains possible to identify distinctive roles and

skills for social workers based on their psycho-social orientation. Therapeutic work with clients remains significant, and with the closure of psychiatric hospitals much specialist mental health social work is liable to occur in community mental health settings/centres (CMHCs). CMHCs' distinctive characteristic is that they offer a 'direct access' community-based service, whereby not simply medical practitioners, but others, including other agencies and the general public, may make referrals. Ideally, they offer a multidisciplinary service, including social workers, community psychiatric nurses (CPNs), doctors and psychologists.

Happily, we know something of the conduct of practice in these settings. In a series of studies, including comparison with community psychiatric nurses, it has become clear that social workers offer a distinctive contribution, that its focus is psycho-social–interactionist, and that it reflects the reproduction in practice of its 'knowledge domain' (Sheppard, 1991a, 1992a, 1992b, 1993a, 1994a). This 'knowledge domain' has a number of characteristics. The knowledge orientation is fundamentally towards the social, with an accompanying emphasis on social science to provide the predominant categories with which to make sense of situations. The context for intervention is the domain of the psycho-social, involving developments in understanding from person-in-situation to ecological approaches. Its practice orientation involves the use of judgement, rather than some simplistic one-way application of formal knowledge, and its focus is presented in terms of needs or problems.

This distinctive approach is reproduced distinctively in practice. Compared with CPNs, social workers tend to define their clients more frequently in terms of social problems, even where mental health problems are present. They operate in a wider community context, with greater flexibility of action as between a focus on the individual, right up to a focus on outside professionals and agencies. They use a greater range of outside resources and do so more frequently. Social workers, furthermore, tend to identify a wider range of problems, have a wider repertoire of roles and undertake more activities than CPNs. This represents a coherent domain of practice which reflects their particular knowledge domain: a sense of theoretical or methodological cohesion in their practice which is distinctive to their professional knowledge and professional role.

This knowledge domain is complemented by their interpersonal or relationship skills. Social workers, compared with CPNs, have both a wider and deeper analysis and presentation of interpersonal skills as part of their formal knowledge base (Sheppard, 1991a). They are, furthermore, considered fundamental, relationship skills in many respects, providing the 'glue' which holds together disparate areas of practice. They are finally, operationalized rather better in social work. Evidence suggests (Sheppard, 1991a, 1992a, 1993a) that social work clients are more positive and less negative about social work intervention than CPN clients; that clients report more skills manifested by social workers than CPNs; that those skills are often of the more expert therapeutic kind and that they can at times have a considerable beneficial impact on clients.

Care Management

Social work involvement in the social care of individuals is increasingly mediated by care management, and mental health is no different in this respect (Sheppard, 1995b). Care management is the 'method of systematically linking the process of identifying and assessing need with the arrangement of monitoring and review of service provision' (Department of Health,

Five Key Points

1 Mental health problems are confronted in a wide variety of social work settings including those (e.g., child care) whose central focus is not mental health.
2 Where social workers are involved in specialist mental health settings they have a distinctive psycho-social practice incorporating interpersonal skills reflecting their formal knowledge base.
3 Social work training provides an excellent base for undertaking the care management role at the professional level.
4 A central aspect of mental health practice is the work of the Approved Social Worker, an authority role for which high levels of skill are required.
5 Mental health work involves interprofessional collaboration sometimes leading to conflict. An understanding of different professional perspectives is necessary in order to minimize this conflict.

1991). The care manager is expected to assess need, identify appropriate services and review and evaluate their provision. A key element (in theory) is the encouragement of client participation in all aspects of the care management process. However, the care manager is not herself a provider of services. The social worker acts as manager, rather than therapist. A mental health specific variant on this is the Care Programme Approach (Department of Health, 1990) targeted at discharged patients and those requiring continuing care to live within the community and avoid (re)admission to hospital care.

Social work, it has been argued, is well suited to the care managerial role (Johnson and Rubin, 1983) at the more complex professional level (Sheppard, 1995b). It is evident from its psycho-social focus that social work possesses a knowledge domain which is highly relevant to care management. It is the interactional dimension which allows for the focus on both individual strengths (and problems) and the social context and supports within which they occur. The focus of care management on mobilizing resources (human and practical) and their review and evaluation is, therefore, consistent with the central focus of social work 'knowledge domains'.

Care management is relatively new, and is being operationalized in different ways by different local authorities. In the context of hospital closure, it is of particular interest. Pilot projects have shown this method to be quite successful in moving long-stay mental hospital residents into the community (Challis and Davies, 1986; Challis et al., 1990; Knapp et al., 1992). A review of eight projects showed that many were able to live in ordinary housing, that they expressed positive attitudes about their residence, that many were able to make regular and full use of community services and that they were more able to exercise choice than when hospitalized (Knapp et al., 1992). They participated, furthermore, in a wider range and a new set of activities. However, there was no significant improvement in social skills, symptoms, social contacts or morale (neither, however, was there a deterioration).

Clearly care management provides a means for the important activity of establishing a community base for those previously in long-term hospital care. However, it will also impinge on other areas of practice involving a mental health component, for example, older people with mental health problems, or depressed mothers receiving child care social work help (Sheppard, 1993b, 1994b, 1994c, 1995a). The psycho-social approach which provides social work with a distinctive contribution to mental health work provides not simply an approach consistent with care management, but a

basis (potentially) for apparently distinctive areas of practice (e.g., child care and mental health) to be brought together in a manner appropriate for the needs of relevant groups.

Authority

The authority role is most apparent with the involvement of a group of social workers called Approved Social Workers (ASWs) in compulsory admission assessments under the Mental Health Act, 1983. Under this Act, an individual may be compulsorily admitted to mental hospital, where they are suffering a mental disorder; where such admission is in the interests of their own health or safety or for the protection of other persons (the 'health or safety' criteria); and where the individual is unwilling to enter hospital voluntarily. This may last, in the first instance, for up to six months.

This Act places a fearful responsibility upon ASWs. Assessments are carried on in private, away from the public gaze and the courts, and appeal (to Mental Health Review Tribunals) may only take place later. The use of compulsion clearly rests on the overriding importance of the needs of the patient. Equally, however, this power may reasonably be expected to be used fairly, precisely and impartially.

This is an issue of risk analysis. However, despite an appropriate use of the Act with many patients, two clear problems can arise. First, ASWs frequently appear to be imprecise in their analysis of the degree of risk with the result that the degree of danger presented by those admitted is not always clear. Second, at times different ASWs, assessing similar situations, make different decisions regarding admission – they are inconsistent (Sheppard, 1990). The reasons for this are complex, but essentially arise from the imprecision of the legislation itself, the lack of appropriate knowledge foundations, and a 'presumption of risk' which leads ASWs to err on the side of caution, admitting patients where the likely outcome is uncertain. The development and use of the Compulsory Admissions Assessment Schedule (CASH) (Sheppard, 1993c) showed that greater precision and consistency was possible if ASWs were supplied with an appropriate theoretical framework and this was operationalized for practice. For those who remain sceptical of the very idea of mental illness, these assessments will remain something for deep suspicion. However, for those who believe that some individuals will require such help from time to time, CASH provides an important step forward.

It does so in terms of social work's distinctive psycho-social knowledge and practice orientation. ASWs are capable of undertaking wide-ranging and flexible psycho-social assessments when considering an individual for compulsory admission (Sheppard, 1991b). This reflects the widely different social, economic and familial circumstances of those referred. In this, they both largely fulfil official expectations placed on them, and reflect their psycho-social orientation (DHSS, 1983; Department of Health, 1993). They most frequently examine past history of mental disorder, family relations and the availability of support and the patient's personal strengths and coping ability. Some limited evidence, furthermore (Sheppard, 1991c, 1992c, 1992d), suggests that general practitioners may be using compulsory admission assessments as a means for the social control of women, particularly those with children with 'familial problems' (i.e., with fulfilling conventional role expectations). ASWs play a clear part in the diversion of many of these women away from compulsory admission.

ASWs using CASH (Sheppard, 1993c) showed this psycho-social orientation married to a framework of risk analysis. This revealed further the distinctive characteristics of those compulsorily admitted. Those presenting a health hazard or threatening violence (who also had a mental disorder) were far more likely than others to be admitted, while those whose behaviour constituted minor social misdemeanours were far less likely to be admitted. Those with support which was both available and adequate were far less likely to be admitted than those without such support. The ASWs also operated a threshold of risk, where individuals were more likely to be admitted where a mental disorder was a central feature and serious disruption of social relations occurred. Where circumstances were as bad or worse than this, compulsory admission occurred; where less bad they did not.

Three Questions

1   To what extent are mental health problems a feature of social work in the non-mental health settings?

2   What contribution does social work have to make to the mental health team?

3   What skills do social workers need to collaborate with other mental health professionals?

Interprofessional Collaboration

Official publications always trumpet the merits of good interprofessional collaboration (DHSS, 1974, 1975, 1978), but experience shows us that the ideal is frequently far from realized. Part of this arises from organizational separation (e.g., between social services and NHS; Fisher et al., 1984) and a failure properly to understand the roles of organizationally separate occupations. Much, however, arises from an occupational rivalry, in which status, leadership and occupational 'territory' are in dispute between occupations such as social work, medicine and community psychiatric nursing (Sheppard, 1986, 1995c). This is exacerbated by the very 'knowledge domains' which give occupations their distinctive contribution to mental health work. Hence, while their psycho-social orientation provides considerable legitimation for social work involvement in mental health, this can create conflicts of perspective with GPs, who have a predominantly biophysical perspective (Huntington, 1981).

These differences are important, for considerable interprofessional animosity can develop with destructive consequences. For example, even where social workers are based at GP surgeries (attachment schemes), the success of collaboration depends on the already existing attitudes of GPs and social workers (Sheppard, 1987). The experience of attachment does not alter prior negative attitudes among GPs. Indeed, conflict is prevented by a technique of 'avoidance' by which GPs with little respect for social workers avoid contact, either by not referring or not collaborating once a referral is made (Sheppard, 1985). Other problems arise from limited conceptions of the social work role, with an emphasis amongst many doctors on social work as an essentially practical, resource mobilizing activity (Sheppard, 1983, 1984).

Doctors, furthermore, when making referrals for specialist psychiatric help, tend to refer to other doctors, rather than social workers or CPNs (Sheppard, 1994a). Where mental health social workers provide the focus for help, GPs initiate contact and collaboration very rarely. Unless the other profession (social worker, CPN, etc.) initiates contact no contact is likely to take place (Sheppard, 1992b). Where social workers do contact, it is purposeful contact i.e. it aims to achieve some action rather than simply give information. This contrasts with the more frequent CPN contact with GPs, which is primarily about information provision. This pattern is consistent with

an assumption of team leadership being made by GPs when dealing with non-medical personnel, an assumption noted in other contexts (Huntington, 1981).

Good collaboration remains a long-stated and important aim (DHSS, 1974, 1975, 1978; Department of Health, 1989). However, organizational separation, occupational rivalry, and most of all different ways of viewing problems, derived from different knowledge orientations provide barriers to such collaboration. Sheppard (1995c) has identified a number of factors which would improve collaboration: a more democratic equalitarian image of the multiprofessional team; recognition and tolerance of different frames of reference; awareness of different professional roles and an awareness of the nature and limits to individual professional skills.

Conclusion

It is apparent that all aspects of mental health social work are influenced by the particular educational-practice 'space' occupied by the profession, generally referred to as their psycho-social approach or interactional orientation. It is this which gives both distinctiveness and coherence to the social work enterprise in mental health, where a variety of occupations – CPNs, psychologists, psychiatrists, occupational therapists – vie for 'space' with which to justify their involvement. This approach is also, on the whole, consistent with their role (Sheppard, 1991a), and both legitimates social work involvement in care management, while providing them with 'professional level' skills (Sheppard, 1995b). However, there is a certain unease and distance from psychiatric orthodoxy which can make social work relations with other psychiatric professions – particularly doctors – sometimes awkward and conflictual. Social workers are emphatically not – nor should they be

– psychiatrists' 'poodles', and the difficulties engendered, in part, by differing perspectives, should be considered against the benefits provided by the particular approaches and skills offered by social workers.

Further Reading

1 Duggan, C., Williamson, A., Ritter, S. and Watkins, M. (ed.) (1996) *Multiprofessional Co-operation in Community Mental Health*, Sevenoaks: Hodder and Stoughton.
2 Sheppard, M. (1990) *Mental Health: the Role of the Approved Social Worker*, Sheffield: Sheffield University Press.
3 Ulas, M. (ed.) (1996) *Research Highlights in Mental Health Social Work*, London: Jessica Kingsley.

References

Boardman, A. P., Bouras, N. and Cundy, J. (1987) *The Mental Health Advice Centre in Lewisham*, London: NUPRD.

Challis, D., Chessum, R., Chesterman, J., Luckett, R. and Traske, K. (1990) *The Gateshead Community Care Scheme: Case Management in Health and Social Care*, PSSRU, University of Kent at Canterbury.

Challis, D. and Davies, B. (1986) *Case Management in Community Care*, Aldershot: Gower.

Cohen, J. and Fisher, M. (1987) 'Recognition of mental health problems by doctors and social workers', *Practice*, 3, 225–40.

Corney, R. (1984) 'The mental and physical health of clients referred to social workers in a local authority and general practice attachment scheme', *Psychological Medicine*, 14, 137–44.

Coulter (1973) *Approaches to Insanity*, London: Martin Robertson.

Department of Health (1989) *Caring for People: Community Care in the Next Decade and Beyond*, London: HMSO.

Department of Health (1990) Circular, *The Care Programme Approach for People with a Mental Illness*, HC (90) 23/LASSL (90) 11.

Department of Health (1991) *Purchase of Service*, London: HMSO.

Department of Health (1993) *Code of Practice, Mental Health Act 1983*, London: HMSO.

DHSS (1974) *Social Work Support for the Health Service: Report of the Working Party*, London: HMSO.

DHSS (1975) *Better Services for the Mentally Ill*, London: HMSO.

DHSS (1978) *Collaboration in Community Care: a Discussion Document*, London: HMSO.

DHSS (1983) *Mental Health Act, 1983: Memorandum*, London: HMSO.

Fisher, M., Newton, C. and Sainsbury, E. (1984) *Mental Health Social Work Observed*, London: George Allen and Unwin.

Goldberg, D. and Huxley, P. (1992) *Common Mental Disorders: a Bio Social Model*, London: Routledge.

Goodwin, S. (1990) *Community Care and the Future of Mental Health Service Provision*, Aldershot: Avebury.

Huntington, J. (1981) *Social Work and General Medical Practice: Collaboration or Conflict?* London: Allen and Unwin.

Huxley, P. and Fitzpatrick, R. (1984) 'The probable extent of minor mental illness in adult clients of social workers: a research note', *British Journal of Social Work*, 14, 67–73.

Huxley, P., Korer, J. and Tolley, S. (1987) 'The psychiatric "caseness" of clients referred to an urban social services department', *British Journal of Social Work*, 17, 507–20.

Isaac, B., Minty, E. and Morrison, R. (1986) 'Children in care: the association with mental disorder in the parents', *British Journal of Social Work*, 16, 325–39.

Johnson, P. and Rubin, A. (1983) 'Case management in mental health: a social work domain', *Social Work*, 28, 49–55.

Jones, K. (1988) *Experience in Mental Health*, London: Sage.

Knapp, M., Cambridge, P., Thomason, C., Beecham, J., Allen, C. and Darton, R. (1992) *Care in the Community: Challenge and Demonstration*, Aldershot: Ashgate.

Quinton, D. and Rutter, M. (1984) 'Parents with children in care – current circumstances and parenting', *Journal of Child Psychology and Psychiatry*, 25(2), 211-29.

Sheppard, M. (1983) 'Referrals from general practitioners to a social services department', *Journal of the Royal College of General Practitioners*, 33, 33–40.

Sheppard, M. (1984) 'General practitioners' use of social services', *Update: the Journal of Postgraduate General Practice*, 1431–9.

Sheppard, M. (1985) 'Communication between general practitioners and a social services department', *British Journal of Social Work*, 15, 25–42.

Sheppard, M. (1986) 'Primary health care workers' views about social workers', *British Journal of Social Work*, 16, 459–68.

Sheppard, M. (1987) 'Dominant images of social work: a British comparison of general practitioners with and without attachment schemes', *International Social Work*, 30(1), 77–91.

Sheppard, M. (1990) *Mental Health: the Role of the Approved Social Worker*, Sheffield: University of Sheffield Press.

Sheppard, M. (1991a) *Mental Health Work in the Community: Theory and Practice in Social Work and Community Psychiatric Nursing*, London: Falmer.

Sheppard, M. (1991b) 'Referral source and process of assessment: a comparative analysis of assessment for compulsory admission under the Mental Health Act, 1983', *Practice*, 5(4), 284–98.

Sheppard, M. (1991c) 'Social work, general practice and mental health sections: the social control of women', *British Journal of Social Work*, 21, 663–83.

Sheppard, M. (1992a) 'Client satisfaction, brief intervention and interpersonal skills', *Social Work and Social Science Review*, 3, 2, 124–50.

Sheppard, M. (1992b) 'Contact and collaboration with general practitioners: a comparison of social workers and community psychiatric nurses', *British Journal of Social Work*, 22, 419–36.

Sheppard, M. (1992c) 'General practitioners' referrals for compulsory admission under the Mental Health Act I: comparison with other GP mental health referrals', *Psychiatric Bulletin*, 16, 138–9.

Sheppard, M. (1992d) 'General practitioners' referrals for compulsory admission under the Mental Health Act II: the process of assessment', *Psychiatric Bulletin*, 16, 140–42.

Sheppard, M. (1993a) 'Client satisfaction, extended intervention and interpersonal skills in community mental health', *Journal of Advanced Nursing*, 18, 246–50.

Sheppard, M. (1993b) 'Maternal depression and child care: the significance for social work and social work research', *Adoption and Fostering*, 17(2), 10–17.

Sheppard, M. (1993c) 'Theory for approved social work: the use of the compulsory admissions assessment schedule', *British Journal of Social Work*, 23, 231–57.

Sheppard, M. (1994a) 'GP and informal network referrals to a community mental health centre: an examination of the pathway to psychiatric care', *Social Work and Social Sciences Review*, 4(3), 232–55.

Sheppard, M. (1994b) 'Maternal depression, child care and the social work role', *British Journal of Social Work*, 24, 33–51.

Sheppard, M. (1994c) 'Child care social support and maternal depression: a review and application of findings', *British Journal of Social Work*, 24, 287–310.

Sheppard, M. (1995a) *Maternal Depression in Clients of Social Workers and Health Visitors: a Rural and Urban Comparison*, Report for Devon Family Health Services Authority.

Sheppard, M. (1995b) *Care Management and the New Social Work: a Critical Analysis*, London: Whiting & Birch.

Sheppard, M. (1995c) 'Primary health care and the social organisation of interprofessional collaboration in mental health: lessons from general practice and social work', in C. Duggan, A. Williamson, S. Ritter and M. Watkins (ed.), *Multiprofessional Co-operation in Community Mental Health*, Sevenoaks: Hodder and Stoughton.

As a term community care has a chameleon quality, susceptible to differential interpretation by different stakeholders. An oft-quoted commentary from two decades ago remains valid:

To the politician, 'community care' is a useful piece of rhetoric; to the sociologist, it is a stick to beat institutional care with; to the civil servant, it is a cheap alternative to institutional care which can be passed to the local authorities for action – or inaction; to the visionary, it is a dream of the new society in which people really do care; to social services departments, it is a nightmare of heightened public expectations and inadequate resources to meet them.

(Jones et al., 1978, p. 114)

As a work setting, it can reflect equal diversity in terms of organizational structure. This can range from the individual with responsibility for community care within a generic team structure, through a variety of more specialist social work teams working with one or more of the community care groups, to the potentially inter-agency structure of the community mental health or community learning disability team (Ovretveit, 1993). The defining characteristic lies, therefore, not with the specific structure but with the groups of individuals whose needs are being targeted. Thus, there would be general agreement that community care embraces individuals with mental health problems, with learning or physical disabilities, with sensory impairment or head injuries, with alcohol, drug or HIV/AIDS related problems, or with dementia. Elderly people not already within the above

categories would be added, together with children and young people with special needs. Any individual may, of course, be within more than one group. Moreover, community care is most appropriately regarded as a continuum extending from the individual receiving domiciliary support in their own home to those requiring an intensively supported residential or nursing home placement.

Working with individuals from the various groups identified above has always been a part of social work practice (Payne, 1995). Community care has emerged, however, as a distinct area for focus with the shift from an assumption of institutional provision. Indeed community care policy in the 1980s and 1990s can be characterized as a series of potential shifts, encapsulated in the recommendations of the Audit Commission and Griffiths Reports (1986 and 1988) and in the provisions of the White Paper *Caring for People* (DoH, 1989) and the subsequent NHS and Community Care Act (1990). In addition to the shift in the balance of care from the more institutional to the more community base, shifts are envisaged:

- from a service-led to a needs-based response;
- from the local authority as provider to enabler of a mixed economy of provision;
- from central to devolved budgets;
- from a single service to multiple choice; and
- from a professionally determined to a user-led response.

Such shifts all feature within the key objectives for community care defined in the 1989 White Paper. Local authorities have been given the lead responsibility for ensuring that the needs of the community care groups are met, both individually and collectively. Key objectives of community care are:

- to promote the development of domiciliary, day and respite services to enable people to live in their own homes wherever feasible and sensible;
- to ensure service providers make practical support for carers a high priority;
- to make the proper assessment of need and good care management the cornerstone of high quality care;
- to promote the development of a flourishing independent sector alongside quality public services;
- to clarify the responsibilities of agencies and so make it easier to hold them to account for their performance; and
- to secure better value for taxpayers' money by introducing a funding structure for social care.

Behind the directives for this new pattern of response lies accumulating research-based evidence on the effectiveness of community-based provision across a range of care groups (Sinclair et al., 1990; Knapp et al., 1992; Robbins, 1993; Cambridge et al., 1994; Emerson and Hatton, 1994; Tinker et al., 1994). For frail, elderly people key findings include:

- significant reduction in need for institutional care;
- marked improvement in levels of satisfaction and well-being;
- lower levels of carer stress;
- no greater costs; and
- more flexible provision of services.

For individuals with mental health problems research has demonstrated:

- no increase in psychiatric symptomatology;
- no deterioration in either social functioning or behaviour and possibly some improvement in the longer term;
- no drift into homelessness/prison;
- enhanced quality of life; and
- preferred choice.

Across the majority of care groups, there is general agreement that individuals can be sustained in the community without deterioration in social functioning or symptomatology, and with enhanced quality of life. This is valid both for individuals discharged from long-stay hospitals as policy preferences support de-institutionalization, and for those, the large majority, who have always been supported in community settings. Cost comparisons for the two locations vary according to care group and according to dependency levels (Netten and Beecham, 1993). Only for individuals with dementia are there reservations about the extent to which community provision can suffice as dependency levels increase, not least because of the impact on informal carers. For individuals with dementia the major points to be noted are:

- carers wish to continue to care for as long as possible;
- caring for a person with dementia is a greater source of stress than caring for a person without dementia;
- caring for a person with moderate or severe dementia is a greater source of stress than caring for a person with mild dementia;
- a lack of well-being in carers is particularly associated with incontinence, disturbance at night and the need for constant supervision;
- male carers have higher levels of well-being than female carers; and
- whatever the number and type of

respite services used, the psychological distress of the carer lowers with admission to residential care.

In focusing on the needs of the community care groups, there was a particular desire to introduce more routinely into practice the principles of care (originally case) management which had been explored in pilot projects evaluated by the Personal Social Services Research Unit (Challis and Davies, 1986; Challis et al., 1990; Challis et al., 1995). Effective care management is seen as the mechanism through which the response to those with more complex needs can be co-ordinated.

Assessment and Care Management

In preparation for the implementation of the key features of the NHS and Community Care Act in April 1993, guidance concentrated on what were defined as the seven stages of care management (DoH, 1990; DoH SSI/SWSG, 1991a, 1991b). Despite assessment itself being one of these stages, there has been a tendency to refer to it as if it were a separate function. The seven stages identified are as follows:

1   publishing information,

2   determining the level of assessment,

3   assessing need,

4   care planning,

5   implementing the care plan,

6   monitoring, and

7   reviewing.

The organizational arrangements for these different stages of care management have been interpreted differently in different authorities. The guidance itself (DoH SSI/SSWG, 1991a) posited a wide

Five Key Points

1   Community care is not only or even primarily about closing institutions; the majority of community care users have always lived outwith the hospital.

2   Community care is not necessarily cheaper than the institutional alternative; all cost information must be treated with care to ensure comparability.

3   The needs of community care groups span the health/social care boundary; it is often difficult and inappropriate to separate out the various components.

4   Multidisciplinary working, including collaboration with GPs, is the key to the effective implementation of community care.

5   Users and carers should be regarded as active partners in care.

variety of potential models for both assessment and care management, nine local authority and a further six inter-agency models for assessment and ten for care management, half on an inter-agency basis. In practice, many would argue that there are as many different forms of care management as there are agencies; moreover arrangements continually evolve. It is useful, however, to draw a key distinction between care management as a distinct *role*, performed as a separate job by individuals appointed as care managers, and care management as a *task*, carried out by workers alongside other social work tasks. The location of care management within the local authority has led in the initial years to a tendency for care managers to be social workers but this is by no means a requirement and it remains to be seen how the recruitment pattern will evolve. There is, moreover, a potential opportunity not only to recruit a wider range of professionals to fulfil the function as local authority employees, but also to consider the desirability, in certain cases, of appointing a professional from another agency, for example health or the voluntary sector, as the care manager.

Specific Challenges

Contingent on the shifts outlined above, a number of challenges exist for those working in the community care setting.

Working collaboratively with other professionals

Many would argue that to isolate the social work function within community care is artificial. The defining feature of community care is its location at the junction of the health and social care divide. The needs of many of the community care groups fluctuate in terms of their definition as primarily health or social care based. At the same time there is redefinition of the entitlement of individuals to continuing NHS care, with profound implications in terms of the requirement upon individuals to pay for social care. As a result two areas of collaboration are of particular importance. The first relates to the interface with the hospital where the effective operation of discharge (and admission) protocols is essential to the management of individual cases across the boundary (Neill and Williams, 1992). The second features collaboration with the members of the primary health care team, both GPs and the range of nursing and other professionals (Owens et al., 1995). The necessity of such collaboration features both at the assessment stage and in the response to identified needs, where the specification of those contributions unique to each professional group and those which can be offered on a generic basis is of increasing importance.

The contribution of different professional groups to the needs of those with long-term mental health problems is a classic illustration. Some confusion has arisen from the specification of the

initially health-based Care Programme Approach targeted at this group alongside the local authority care management model. It is less important whether the key role be assumed by community psychiatric nurse or social worker provided that one individual clearly assumes responsibility, working collaboratively with other professional colleagues where their skills are complementary.

Equally important for the effective implementation of community care is collaboration with those involved in housing provision. The key role of housing has, somewhat belatedly, been acknowledged, with increasing sophistication in the separation of the housing and support elements in the care package.

Designing imaginative care packages

The transformation from a system led by available services to one responsive to individual need cannot be achieved overnight. Workers are being asked not only to operate according to new guidelines but to introduce new ways of thinking, a different mind set. The aspiration is that workers will respond imaginatively to the set of needs that are presented and fashion a response that utilizes a range of existing and innovative solutions. Responses may be constrained or encouraged by the strategies which have been adopted locally for the commissioning and purchasing of services. Block contracts and the use of lists of approved providers may limit the more imaginative response; those who can operate with greater freedom, spot purchasing with a devolved budget, for example, have access to a more flexible agenda for meeting need.

Operating within a mixed economy of care

A key feature of the community care reforms of the 1990 Act was to encourage a greater range of providers, most explicitly to shift the balance from the statutory to the independent sector. In England and Wales specific requirements were imposed as to the proportion of the care monies transferred from DSS to the local authority which were to be used for the purchase of services in the independent (voluntary or private) sector. The independent sector has always had a role in the provision of residential care; its contribution to domiciliary support, particularly from the private sector, is less developed (Leat, 1993; Wistow et al., 1994). Yet, the maximization of the potential offered by domiciliary support, for example through augmented home care schemes for the frail elderly, is the key challenge for the social worker operating in the community care field.

Working in partnership with informal carers

Estimates suggest that there are 6.8 million people in Britain involved in the care of a relative or friend who is elderly, ill or disabled. Towards the heavier end of the caring spectrum, 1.9 million are thought to be involved in substantial caring activities involving more than 20 hours a week (Twigg and Atkin, 1994). Recognition by the community care worker of the distinctive needs of the carer, including their right to their own assessment of need, together with an acknowledgement of both the contribution and the limitations of respite care (Levin et al., 1994) is essential.

Acknowledging the centrality of the user voice

There has been a steady acceleration of the directives to give due prominence to the voice of the service user (Parsloe and Stevenson, 1993). This is relevant both in the assessment and response to individual need, where choice in particular is an important feature, and in

the planning process at a more collective level (Osborn, 1991). Mechanisms for the effective involvement of users at the strategic level are constantly being pursued, most particularly as part of the community care planning process. It is essential to recognize, however, that there will be many different user voices, often in conflict. Finite resources, moreover, may necessitate prioritization. Particular vigilance needs to be exercised to ensure that all voices are heard, for example those from ethnic minority care groups (Atkin and Rollings, 1993).

Three Questions

1 What are the limits to community care?
2 How should individual needs be distinguished from wants?
3 Is there a distinctive role for the social worker within care management or should the care manager be recognized as a new professional?

Planning for identified need

The requirement that each local authority produce a community care plan for its area represents the first serious attempt at strategic planning within the social work arena. The needs of the population within an area are to be specified, together with the resources and the time-scale that will be deployed to meet those needs. Most

Further Reading

1 Bornat, J., Pereira, C., Pilgrim, D. and Williams, F. (eds) (1993) *Community Care: a Reader*, Basingstoke: Macmillan.
2 Malin, N. (1994) *Implementing Community Care*, Buckingham: Open University Press.
3 Means, R. and Smith, R. (eds) (1994) *Community Care: Policy and Practice*, Basingstoke: Macmillan.

importantly, the link between the
individual and the collective should be
forged through the aggregation of
unmet need recorded in individual
assessments. Only through such
linkage across components can the
catalysts which will trigger the 'cascade
of change' (Audit Commission, 1992) be
activated.

References

Atkin, K. and Rollings, J. (1993) *Community Care in Multi-racial Britain: a Critical Review of the Literature*, London: Social Policy Research Unit/HMSO.

Audit Commission (1986) *Making a Reality of Community Care*, London: HMSO.

Audit Commission (1992) *Community Care: Managing the Cascade of Change*, London: HMSO.

Cambridge, P., Hayes, L. and Knapp, M. (1994) *Care in the Community: Five Years On*, Aldershot: Arena.

Challis, D., Chessum, R., Chesterman, J., Luckett, R. and Traske, K. (1990) *Case Management in Social and Health Care: The Gateshead Community Care Scheme*, University of Kent, Canterbury: Personal Social Services Research Unit.

Challis, D., Darton, R., Johnson, L., Stone, M. and Traske, K. (1995) *Care Management and Health Care of Older People: the Darlington Community Care Project*, Aldershot: Arena.

Challis, D. and Davies, B. (1986) *Case Management in Community Care: an Evaluated Experiment in the Home Care of the Elderly*, Aldershot: Gower.

DoH (1989) *Caring for People: Community Care in the Next Decade and Beyond*, Cm 849, London: HMSO.

DoH (1990) *Caring for People: Community Care in the Next Decade and Beyond – Policy Guidance*, London: HMSO.

DoH SSI/SWSG (1991a) *Care Management and Assessment: Managers' Guide*, London: HMSO.

DoH SSI/SWSG (1991b) *Care Management and Assessment: Practitioners' Guide*, London: HMSO.

Emerson, E. and Hatton, C. (1994) *Moving Out: the Impact of Relocation from Hospital to Community on the Quality of Life of People with Learning Disabilities*, London: HMSO.

Griffiths, R. (1988) *Community Care: an Agenda for Action*, London: HMSO.

Jones, K., Brown, J. and Bradshaw, J. (1978) *Issues in Social Policy*, London: Routledge & Kegan Paul.

Knapp, M., Cambridge, P., Thomason, C., Beecham, J., Allen, C. and Darton, R. (1992) *Care in the Community: Challenge and Demonstration*, Aldershot: Ashgate.

Leat, D. (1993) *The Development of Community Care by the Independent Sector*, London: Policy Studies Institute.

Levin, E., Moriarty, J. and Gorbach, P. (1994) *Better for the Break*, London: HMSO/NISW.

Neill, J. and Williams, J. (1992) *Leaving Hospital: Elderly People and their Discharge to Community Care*, London: NISW/HMSO.

Netten, A. and Beecham, J. (eds) (1993) *Costing Community Care*, Aldershot: Ashgate.

Osborn, A. (1991) *Taking Part in Community Care Planning*, Leeds: Age Concern Scotland/Nuffield Institute for Health.

Ovretveit, J. (1993) *Coordinating Community Care: Multi-Disciplinary Teams and Care Management*, Buckingham: Open University Press.

Owens, P., Carrier, J. and Horder, J. (1995) *Interprofessional Issues in Community and Primary Health Care*, Basingstoke: Macmillan.

Parsloe, P. and Stevenson, O. (1993) *Community Care and Empowerment*, York: Joseph Rowntree Foundation.

Payne, M. (1995) *Social Work and Community Care*, Basingstoke: Macmillan.

Robbins, D. (ed.) (1993) *Community Care: Findings from Department of Health Funded Research 1988–1992*, London: HMSO.

Sinclair, I., Parker, R., Leat, D. and Williams, J. (1990) *The Kaleidoscope of Care: a Review of Research on Welfare Provision for Elderly People*, London: HMSO.

Tinker, A., McCreadie, C., Wright, F. and Salvage, A. (1994) *The Care of Frail Elderly People in the United Kingdom*, London: HMSO.

Twigg, J. and Atkin, K. (1994) *Carers Perceived: Policy and Practice in Informal Care*, Buckingham: Open University Press.

Wistow, G., Knapp, M., Hardy, B. and Allen, C. (1994) *Social Care in a Mixed Economy*, Buckingham: Open University Press.

Foster Care and Adoption
John Triseliotis

The informal care of children by people who are not their parents is as old as the history of humankind. Formal arrangements, however, sanctioned by legislation are of a more recent origin, especially in the case of foster care. From antiquity onwards, a close relationship always existed between levels of poverty and the numbers of children requiring substitute care outside their families. In Britain too, the history of both foster care and adoption has been closely associated with that of the Poor Law, and with the policies and practices of the philanthropic, mostly religious organizations, that mushroomed during the second half of the nineteenth century.

Whilst it is difficult to pin-point the exact origins of formal fostering by public and voluntary bodies, it would be safe to link it to the 'wet nursing' system that originated in France around the fifteenth century and introduced in Britain by the so-called Foundling hospitals during the early part of the eighteenth century. The system did not spread to older children, especially in England in contrast to Scotland, until after about 1860 mainly because of fears that it would undermine the deterrent element of the Poor Law.

Though adoption has a much longer history, compared to foster care, nevertheless the legally sanctioned adoption of children in Britain is barely more than 70 years old. If foster care has its main roots in the wet nursing system and the Poor Law, modern adoption has its origins in the foster care system of the last century. Adoption legislation was not passed in England until 1926 and in Scotland until 1930. This delay had mainly to do with attitudes to inheritance, non-marital births, and ideas about heredity and bad blood (see Triseliotis, 1995a). Until the 1970s, much of adoption work was in the hands of voluntary adoption societies before the initiative passed on to local authorities, for reasons to be explained later.

The evolutionary history of adoption and fostering is one of overlaps, leading sometimes to ambiguities and confusion about purpose, expectations, roles and relationships. These have recently increased mainly as a result of the kind of children requiring substitute family care and the type of families responding. A number of social services (work) departments have been responding to these developments by setting up joint Family Finding Teams whose main job is to recruit, prepare and support new families, some of which are approved for foster care and others for adoption, depending on preferences. When it comes to the placement of older and problematic children, much of the preparation, training and post-placement support required has many commonalities between the two groups. The children's needs, circumstances and preferences eventually determine whether adoption or foster care will be pursued. Yet clear boundaries between these two institutions are essential, especially the intended temporary nature of most fostering.

The Evolution of Foster Care

Foster care is an umbrella-type term that covers a wide variety of arrangements in which a child is cared for temporarily in a family, not their own, for an allowance or a fee. Fostering can be public or private, for short, medium or long periods, or it can be used for assessment or remand purposes.

Mainstream fostering, as understood today, was introduced by the Children Act 1948, which also provided for the setting up of Children's Departments, the precursors of present-day social services. The Act also broke all previous connections between child care and the Poor Law, though many would claim, that some of the Poor Law attitudes are still with us. Unlike the pre-1948 period when fostering was mostly a long-term arrangement, the Act came to look upon it mainly as a temporary service to children and families in need. However, the implementation of this idea proved more problematic. Subsequent studies were to show that besides high levels of foster care breakdowns, much confusion and ambiguity, among both practitioners and foster carers, continued to surround its practice. As an example, many foster carers and social workers were unclear about the purpose of each placement and many carers continued to look upon the children as their own. Though fostering was initially used for young and non-problematic children, nevertheless breakdowns would sometimes reach up to 50 per cent within a three-year period (Parker, 1966; George, 1970; Holman, 1975; Berridge and Cleaver, 1987).

The early 1970s witnessed a new phase in the evolution of foster care with the introduction of what came to be known as 'specialist' or professional fostering. This form of fostering came to be used either to divert children from institutions or to get them out of there and place them with families. The philosophy that informed it was associated with the notions of community care and normalization that were new in the 1970s. Besides viewing specialist fostering as being for the most troubled and troublesome children, its other key features were:

- its contractual nature;
- time limited with an average of two years;
- the payment of a fee to foster carers;
- the training and preparation of carers;
- the preparation of children before placement; and
- the provision of post-placement support to foster carers and children alike. (see Hazel, 1981 and Shaw and Hipgrave, 1983)

The first experimental scheme was set up in Kent in the early 1970s and its first evaluation some years later provided promising results. Similar schemes were subsequently set up in many other parts of the country, but the original rates of success were only infrequently repeated (Triseliotis, 1989; Berridge, 1995; Biehal et al., 1995; Triseliotis et al., 1995c.). The high breakdown rates found by recent studies are not accidental and some of the reasons include:

- low recruitment leading to poor matching;
- far more problematic children presenting many challenging problems;
- lack of agreement on the aims and outcomes of each placement;
- inadequate monitoring of outcomes and changing needs;
- unsystematic approach to the training, preparation and post-placement support of carers, and the preparation and support of children.

Achieving continuity and stability in foster care is very elusive, but when it works, it seems to offer a lot to the children involved.

Another unresolved issue concerns the kind of role fostering should play in the placement of teenagers. One view is that most teenagers in care prefer residential homes (Kahan, 1979; Berridge, 1985) whilst another is that very difficult teenagers can successfully be fostered (Hazel, 1981; Hudson and Galloway, 1989). Findings from a recent study (Triseliotis et al., 1995b) suggest that teenagers and their parents, for valid reasons to them, are split half and half between those favouring foster homes and those preferring children's homes. According to the same study, the teenagers' needs appeared to be responsive to a combination of care measures, rather than to either/or solutions.

In spite of the move towards the professionalization of foster care, the number of those fostering, about 32,000, has remained constant over the last 25 years. However, over the same period the percentage of those fostering has gone up from 32–62 per cent, mainly because of a significant fall in the number of children looked after by local authorities (Department of Health, 1994). Because most children placed in foster care are psychologically damaged, requiring skilled care, a number of local authorities in order to improve recruitment and retainment, and perhaps meet the competition of the growing private foster care sector, are now treating all their foster carers as specialists with appropriate rewards.

The organizational arrangements for fostering and adoption services across the country seem to vary, but an accurate picture is lacking. Following the recent moves towards greater forms of specialization within the social services and the introduction of 'purchaser–provider' structures, some authorities have also been disbanding their Family Finding Teams. Studies are mixed about the kind of structure that promotes better foster care outcomes, but Jones and Bilton (1994) are critical of the introduction of the 'purchaser–provider'

Five Key Points

1　The placement of older and more problematic children for adoption, along with the practice of more open forms of adoption, have narrowed the differences between foster care and adoption, especially long-term foster care.

2　For about 50–60 per cent of the children foster care works well, depending on the type of fostering experienced. Foster care lasting for less than three months is the most successful.

3　The adoption of children under about the age of nine, including those who are adopted inter-country and/or transracially, works well and often very well but failures are high for children who are older at placement and more problematic.

4　Specialist fostering and the viewing of foster carers as professionals has opened new dimensions to the practice of foster care.

5　The structure and organization of the services seem important for the recruitment, training, deployment and retention of carers, but little is known about it.

---

structure claiming that daily care providers often have the best insight into children's needs and artificial separation from care managers is likely to be unhelpful (p. 54).

A Child for a Home or a Home for a Child?

Since the enactment of adoption legislation, three distinct periods can be recognized in the evolution of adoption in Britain. Between the two Great Wars, adoption was largely frowned upon and was practised mainly by the working classes, who it was thought were not too bothered by issues of heredity, bad blood and inheritance. Furthermore, adoption then was not confined to infants but to older children and sometimes included children with handicaps and disabilities. Except for the post-1970s, this was possibly the nearest that adoption policy and practice came to be offering a home for a child, than the other way round.

From about the early 1950s to the early 1970s a dramatic change took place in the practice of adoption, no doubt reflecting a change in social attitudes. For a number of reasons, adoption became very popular among the middle classes. It came to be seen as largely providing a child to childless couples, whilst also being seen as a solution to the problem of non-marital births. Those from the 'lower' classes now had to be content with adopting so-called 'marginal' children, that is those whose pedigree appeared to be suspect. Adoption during this period was justly described as being practised largely in the interests of the adopters, that is a child for a home (see Triseliotis, 1970; Triseliotis and Russell, 1984).

Adoption policy and practice during this period was also greatly influenced by Bowlby's (1951) studies highlighting the harmful effects on children of separations and institutionalization. Bowlby went further suggesting that the adoption of children over about the age of two should be avoided. This reinforced an earlier recommendation by a government committee urging adoption agencies to avoid the placement of children with handicaps, disabilities or with suspect social backgrounds (Horsbrugh Report, 1937).

The end of the 1960s signalled a new phase in adoption policy and practice reversing earlier approaches. Because of the wider availability of contraception, easier abortion, improved services to single mothers and the lowering of stigma attached to non-marital births an increasing number of single mothers kept their children. As a result, the adoption of infants and of very young children by

non-relatives, fell sharply from around 21,000 in 1969 to around 4,500 in the early 1990s. Following from this development, the attention of adoption agencies turned towards what came to be known as children with 'special needs', that is older children, often emotionally damaged or having mental and physical handicaps.

The theoretical underpinning for the move to place such children came from a number of sources, including Rowe and Lambert's study (1973) highlighting the large numbers of children in care without permanent arrangements. Furthermore, new research now was suggesting that, given an enabling family environment, older children could overcome earlier psychological adversities and do almost as well as those adopted as infants (Kadushin, 1970; Tizard, 1977; Triseliotis and Russell, 1984). At the same time, other studies were also suggesting that psychological parenting was a reality thus encouraging people to adopt (Goldstein et al., 1973; Triseliotis, 1973; Schaffer, 1990).

Unlike the rest of northern and western Europe and, to a degree, North America, British agencies and practitioners took a stance against inter-country (and transracial) adoption, preferring to concentrate instead on the placement of own country special needs children. Moving children from the care system into adoptive homes proved also to be an attractive option to social services departments who otherwise would have faced many years of funding residential or foster care placements. This move shifted also much of adoption work from voluntary societies into the hands of local authorities leading to the closing of many societies.

It cannot be denied that the move to place children with special needs in permanent adoptive homes has met with a high level of success and thousands of children have secured families 'for ever'. A large body of new knowledge and skills has also been developed, mainly in relation to the preparation, matching and support of adoptive families and children (Triseliotis et al., 1996). Apparently this new know-how, which according to studies is vital to the stability and success of placements, is not being uniformly applied by agencies, particularly so with regard to post-placement support (Hughes, 1995; McGhee, 1995).

However, studies also suggest that the gains outlined above, were achieved at some cost. For example, a number of adoptive families took on more than they expected, finding some children very problematic and very demanding. Some children, too, experienced new disruptions in their lives with all the unhappiness that it involved. Studies suggest that especially for children placed when under the age of nine, stability in the arrangements can be as high as 85–90 per cent but the breakdown rates for older children are much higher, reaching sometimes 50 per cent. In fact there is a close association between increasing age and higher breakdown rates. Obviously increasing age is often accompanied by higher levels of disturbance (see Thoburn, 1990; Borland et al., 1991; Fratter et al., 1991). It is suggested that because many of the older children currently requiring adoptive families, appear to be more psychologically damaged, than before, agencies are being much more cautious about their placement. The emerging practice is to place such children either with permanent foster carers or with foster carers with a view to adoption, if everything goes well.

Mistakes have also been made in the past when placing children with special needs. They include:

- the revivalist approach with which the policy was pursued;
- the introduction of time limits;
- the use of the law to assume parental rights and thus stop parental access before placing the children with new families; and

- the severance of important emotional links between older children and their birth families.

The main issues that are likely to continue to dominate adoption policy and practice include:

- the placement of some very psychologically damaged children;
- inter-country adoption;
- own race or transracial placements;
- adoption by lesbians and homosexuals;
- the provision of alternative orders to adoption;
- adoption with contact; and
- post-placement support.

In conclusion, both fostering and

Three Questions

1   Should all foster carers be treated as 'professionals' and receive a fee for their services?
2   Consider the psychological aspects of adoption as these relate to each member of the adoption triangle.
3   Discuss the arguments and empirical evidence referring to own race and transracial placements.

---

adoption are complex activities, especially now, because they involve some very emotionally damaged children. Both institutions are experiencing some similar and also different concerns and challenges which are likely to continue into the twenty-first century. They include:

- the recruitment of new families to foster or adopt some very 'damaged' and problematic children at a time when an increasing number of families are themselves being reconstituted, having to care for children from more than one relationship;
- more uniform and better developed

and informed preparatory and matching methods;
- the improved training of foster and adoptive parents in skills dealing with the handling of problematic behaviours;
- the organization of more uniform post-placement support services; and
- the development of skills to manage open forms of adoption.

Further Reading

1 Brodzinsky, M. D. and Schechter, D. M. (1990) *The Psychology of Adoption*, Oxford: Oxford University Press.
2 Triseliotis, J., Hundleby, M. and Shireman, J. (1996) *Adoption: Policy and Practice*, London: Cassell.
3 Triseliotis, J., Sellick, C. and Short, R. (1995) *Foster Care: Theory and Practice*, London: Batsford.

References

Berridge, D. (1985) *Children's Homes*, Oxford: Blackwell.
Berridge, D. (1995) *Foster Care: a Research Review*, London: Department of Health.
Berridge, D. and Cleaver, H. (1987) *Foster Home Breakdown*, Oxford: Blackwell.
Biehal, N., Clayden, J., Stein, M. and Wade, J. (1995) *Leaving Care Schemes*, London: HMSO.
Borland, M., O'Hara, G. and Triseliotis, J. (1991) Permanency planning and disruption in Lothian Region', in Scottish Office, *Adoption and Fostering*, Edinburgh: Scottish Office.
Bowlby, J. (1951) *Maternal Care and the Growth of Love*, Geneva: World Health Organisation.
Department of Health (1994) *Children Act Report 1993*, London: HMSO.
Fratter, J., Rowe, J., Sapsford, D. and Thoburn, J. (1991) *Permanent Family Placement*, London: British Agencies for Adoption and Fostering.
George, V. (1970) *Foster Care*, London: Routledge & Kegan Paul.
Goldstein, J., Freud, A. and Solnit, A. J. (1973) *Beyond the Best Interests of the Child*, New York: Free Press.
Hazel, N. (1981) *A Bridge to Independence*, Oxford: Blackwell.

Holman, R. (1975) 'The place of fostering in social work', *British Journal of Social Work*, 5(1), 3–29.
Horsbrugh Committee (1937) *Departmental Committee on Adoption Societies and Agencies*, London: Cmd 5499.
Hudson, J. and Galloway, B. (1989) *Specialist Foster Care: A Normalising Experience*, New York: Haworth Press.
Hughes, B. (1995) *The Development of Post-Placement Services*, London: Department of Health.
Jones, A. and Bilton, K. (1994) *The Future Shape of Children's Services*, London: National Children's Bureau.
Kadushin, A. (1970) *Adopting Older Children*, New York: Columbia University Press.
Kahan, B. (1979) *Growing up in Care*, Oxford: Blackwell.
McGhee, J. (1995) 'The consumers' view of a post placement support project: consultancy and training initiatives', Edinburgh: privately circulated paper.
Parker, R. (1966) *Decision in Child Care*, London: Allen and Unwin.
Rowe, J. and Lambert, L. (1973) *Children Who Wait*, London: British Agencies for Adoption and Fostering.
Schaffer, H. R. (1990) *Making Decisions About Children: Psychological Questions and Answers*, Oxford: Blackwell.
Shaw, M. and Hipgrave, T. (1983) *Specialist Fostering*, London: Batsford.
Thoburn, J. (1990) *Success and Failure in Permanent Family Placement*, Aldershot: Avebury.
Tizard, B. (1977) *Adoption: a Second Chance*, London: Open Books.
Triseliotis, J. (1970) *Evaluation of Adoption Policy and Practice*, the University of Edinburgh Dept. of Social Administration.
Triseliotis, J. (1973) *In Search of Origins*, London: Routledge & Kegan Paul.
Triseliotis, J. (1989) 'Foster care outcomes: a review of research findings', *Adoption and Fostering*, 13(3), 5–16.
Triseliotis, J. (1995a) *Adoption: Evolution or Revolution*, in British Agencies for Adoption and Fostering, Selected BAAF Seminar Papers 1994/5, London: BAAF.
Triseliotis, J., Borland, M., Hill, M. and Lambert, L. (1995b) *Teenagers and the Social Work Services*, London: HMSO.
Triseliotis, J., Hundleby, M. and Shireman, J. (1996) *Adoption: Policy and Practice*, London: Cassell.
Triseliotis, J. and Russell, J. (1984) *Hard to Place*, London: Heinemann/Gower.
Triseliotis, J., Sellick, C. and Short, R. (1995c) *Foster Care: Theory and Practice*, London: Batsford.

Divorce Court Welfare

Adrian L. James

Social work in the context of family breakdown and divorce has seen major changes since the 1970s reflecting changes in the social and legal contexts in which divorce occurs. However, there has also been a fundamental reconceptualization of court welfare work which has been only partly in response to these developments.

The Social and Legal Context of Divorce

There is a complex web of social, demographic, economic and political factors which have contributed to the rapid changes in British society during the latter half of this century. The powerful imagery and ideologies which surround marriage and the family, which serve to shape attitudes about them and about marital breakdown and divorce, have also had an impact on these changes and the often heated debate which has accompanied them (James and Wilson, 1986; Goldthorpe, 1987; Burgoyne et al., 1988; Phillips, 1988; Stone, 1990; Allan, 1991).

Such processes are reflected in changing patterns of family formation and an increasing diversity of household structures (Kiernan and Wicks, 1990; Utting, 1995). These are partly a consequence of the incidence of divorce which has increased more than fourfold since 1965 (from 38,000 decrees absolute granted to a new peak of 165,000 in 1993, an increase which takes no account of the breakdown of relationships between unmarried couples) and which is one of the most obvious effects of this continuing social upheaval. Such changes have had major implications for court welfare practice, not least amongst which is that increasingly it has had to address the broader issue of family breakdown rather than divorce.

From the 1930s, largely by an accident of history, the probation service has been the main statutory provider of social work services to the courts, and to families experiencing family breakdown and divorce, since when there have been a number of significant changes in the law relating to divorce (see James and Hay, 1993). The current legal framework for divorce was introduced by the Divorce Reform Act, 1969. This introduced 'irretrievable breakdown' as the sole ground for divorce, based on the proof of one or more of five facts – adultery, cruelty, desertion, two years' separation with the respondent's consent, and five years' separation. However, partly because it became evident that court hearings in such cases served no obvious function, but also (and perhaps more importantly) out of a desire to reduce the growing burden on the civil legal aid budget of matrimonial costs, the streamlined 'special procedure' was introduced by the Matrimonial Causes Act 1973 and eventually extended to all undefended petitions, with legal aid being restricted to disputes over ancillary matters. These changes probably did more to alter the nature of the divorce process than any substantive change introduced by the 1969 Act since as a consequence, divorce became primarily an administrative process.

These many and diverse developments were reflected in the work of the probation service. Its work as the largest marriage-guidance agency plummeted by 75 per cent between 1961 and 1973 (James and Hay, 1993, p. 24), whilst the number of requests from courts to investigate matters relating to the welfare of children and prepare welfare reports increased by 400 per cent during the same period (James, 1988). This trend has continued since then, with a total of 33,768 welfare reports having been prepared in 1993 (Home Office, 1994a).

At the same time as these developments were taking place, dissatisfaction was growing with the constraints imposed by the legal process on the social and psychological processes of relationship breakdown. The nature of the adversarial legal process, particularly with the increasing use being made of allegations of unreasonable behaviour to substantiate claims of irretrievable breakdown in order to secure a swift divorce, was coming under increasing attack for exacerbating the conflict between couples seeking divorce and thereby inflicting even greater damage on children unfortunate enough to be caught up in the process.

Against this background, and as a consequence of a growing interest in the concept of conciliation – helping couples to reach agreements in order to reduce the conflict associated with divorce – first mooted by the Finer Committee in 1974 (James, 1990), a process of redefining substantial elements of both the legal process of divorce and the social work contribution to this began (see Fisher, 1990). With the growing interest in and development of voluntary conciliation services (drawing extensively on the experience of mediation in the USA), court welfare officers also increasingly began to question the limitations of a role defined solely in terms of 'investigating and reporting' and to experiment with some of the ideas and practices being developed by conciliators and family therapists working with divorcing families (James and Hay, 1993).

Although in some areas, with the

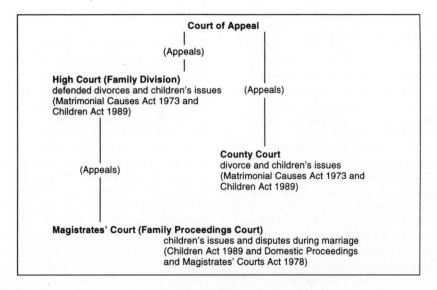

Figure VII.8.1   Courts dealing with divorce and children's issues in England and Wales.

encouragement and co-operation of courts, conciliation was formally offered as a service by welfare officers, this was not a universal development and wide variations in local practice began to emerge. This was partly because of a wide range of initiatives by practitioners at a local level, but also because of a general lack of management of such developments at a time when senior probation managers were preoccupied by managing the development of their principal area of responsibility, that of working with offenders. In addition, a particular problem faced by welfare officers was the absence of any statutory responsibility for or authority to undertake conciliation. As a consequence of this, and occasionally trenchant judicial criticism of perceived failures of welfare officers to investigate adequately and to provide courts with the information they required, much of this settlement-seeking work was covertly incorporated into the report writing function.

The Welfare of the Child and the Children Act 1989

The introduction of the Children Act 1989 led to major changes in the legal context of social work with families experiencing divorce. The Act took a significant step towards creating a family jurisdiction, although it fell short of creating a family court *per se*. Under the Act, children's issues, such as residence and contact with parents, can be dealt with in magistrates' family proceedings courts, county courts or the High Court, while undefended divorce petitions and related children's issues, which constitute the large majority of divorce cases, are dealt with mainly by the county courts (see figure VII.8.1). Thus the bulk of the cases concerning children's issues which require social work intervention are brought before local magistrates' and divorce county courts.

Five Key Points

1 There has been a transition from thinking about parents having rights over their children to their having responsibilities for them.

2 There has been a change of focus for court welfare work from marriage-saving to that of child-saving.

3 As a consequence of the many changes, the lack of pro-active management, and the many initiatives at grass-roots level, there are now large variations in court welfare practice in different parts of the country.

4 There has been growing concern, evident in successive changes in the law and procedures relating to divorce, about the increasing burden of the costs associated with the rising number of divorces.

5 As a consequence of all of these changes, there has been a fundamental reconstruction of the concept of children's welfare in divorce and of divorce court welfare, with increasing emphasis on mediation in helping parents to reach agreements concerning their children's future.

More importantly, the Act is based on certain clearly articulated principles (see figure VII.8.2), all of which endorse in various ways the further development of approaches which seek to maximize family autonomy and parental responsibility, involvement and agreement, in order to minimize harm to children. Thus, even though s. 1(3) of the Act makes explicit the criteria by which the welfare of children is to be judged (which welfare officers must, therefore, consider when preparing reports), and this has resulted in much greater prominence being given to children's wishes and feelings, where parents are in agreement the principle of family autonomy prevails over the

- *The welfare principle* – courts must treat the child's welfare as the paramount consideration in all questions about his or her upbringing.
- *The principle of parental responsibility* – in the interests of the child, parents retain responsibility for their children, even after separation.
- *The principle of parental involvement* – in exercising their responsibilities, parents should be as fully involved as possible in making decisions relating to the upbringing of their children.
- *The principle of positive intervention* – courts shall not make orders unless satisfied that it will be a positive contribution to the interests of the child.
- *The principle of minimal delay* – delay in court proceedings is generally harmful to a child and must be kept to a minimum.

Figure VII.8.2   Principles underpinning the Children Act 1989.

paramountcy of the child's welfare (Parry, 1994).

In addition, changes to the Probation Rules in 1992 and the introduction of National Standards (Home Office, 1994b) both endorsed the use of mediation (now the preferred term because of confusion surrounding the meaning and use of the term 'conciliation'). Increasingly, therefore, the social work contribution to the judicial task of ensuring that paramountcy is given to the welfare of children in divorce has come to be defined in terms of reducing conflict and encouraging parents to agree about the arrangements to be made for the upbringing of their children (James, 1995).

Although so far court welfare work has been discussed as the preserve of the probation service and its family court welfare officers, the Act also confirmed the existing powers of the courts to involve other social work agencies. Under s. 7, for example, courts may ask for a welfare report to be prepared by the probation service, the social services department or any other agency which the court thinks appropriate, whilst family assistance orders may also be made under s. 16 to either the probation service or to the social services department.

However, because of the many changes in court welfare work and government concerns about variations in this, National Standards introduced for family court welfare work (Home Office, 1994b) apply to *any* agency preparing welfare reports for the courts and not just the probation service. Thus, social work involvement in divorce must be understood more broadly, although the nature and extent of this broader involvement is hard to determine for whilst social services departments do undertake welfare reports and the supervision of family assistance orders, little is known about this.

Future Developments

Of even greater significance, however, are the proposals for the reform of the law relating to divorce which led to a Green Paper (Lord Chancellor's Department, 1993), White Paper (Lord Chancellor's Department, 1995) and the Family Law Act, 1996. Although it is clear that a significant factor behind these changes was concern about the increasing costs of divorce in terms of the legal aid bill, they also reflect many of the issues referred to above and, in particular, are a response to widespread public criticism of the current law, widespread concern to encourage amicable resolution of problems arising from divorce whilst minimizing the harm caused to children, and support for the retention of the irretrievable breakdown of marriage as the sole ground for divorce.

The reforms have a number of key elements. Those wishing to initiate the divorce process are required to attend a session at which information will be given concerning the divorce process, its impact on children, the costs involved, and the availability of various services (including marriage guidance, mediation and legal advice). This is seen as an important element in developing a new and more constructive approach to the problems of marital breakdown and divorce. Three months later, one or both parties can file a statement indicating that they believe their marital relationship has broken down, after which a 'cooling-off' period lasting fifteen months where children are involved will ensue. This is intended both to demonstrate that the marital relationship has broken down irretrievably and to give the couple time to resolve the practical consequences of any ensuing divorce. After this period has elapsed, the parties will be able to apply for a divorce or separation order.

The changed model clearly reflects a move towards a more informal, administrative system of divorce, but it also clearly reflects many of the principles embodied in the Children Act 1989 and represents an endorsement of mediation and many of the developments which have been at the heart of the revolution in court welfare work. It also clearly acknowledges the need for a much wider range of social work services for families contemplating divorce, including both statutory and independent-sector agencies.

Main Themes and Issues

The development of court welfare work has been complex and has reflected

changes in both the social and legal contexts of divorce. However, certain trends are apparent which seem likely to continue to shape these developments.

The first of these is the growing move away from the notion of parental rights over their children to that of parental responsibility for them (Eekelaar, 1991). This has brought with it a growing concern about children's rights and the need for social workers to take full account of their wishes and feelings when preparing reports for the courts.

Secondly, and closely associated with this, has been the move away from marriage-saving as the focus for court

---

Three Questions

1 Which agency and which government department should be responsible for the court welfare service?

2 Who is the client in the context of divorce court welfare work? – the parents? the child(ren)? the family? the courts?

3 What services should be available for parents and children experiencing family breakdown through divorce, who should provide them and should the same services be available in all areas?

---

welfare work to that of child-saving. This trend, in conjunction with the first, has witnessed the decline in a predominantly investigative approach to welfare reporting and facilitated the growth of mediatory, family-focused approaches as the favoured social work method for both obtaining information for the courts and for ensuring that the best interests of the child are provided for. This has echoed the more broadly-based interest in and growth of voluntary, independent mediation services.

Thirdly, as this redefinition has taken place, so have variations in local practices increased, raising important questions about what services should be available to parents and children in divorce. Although the introduction of National Standards for court welfare work may bring about a greater degree of uniformity, as the role of social work in divorce continues to be redefined, such variations and the questions to which they give rise seem likely only to increase, raising further dilemmas and challenges for policy-makers, managers and practitioners alike.

The fourth theme, which has permeated many of these developments, has been the growing burden of the costs associated with the increasing number of divorces. Certainly the proposals for reform were presented as a means of trying to stem the rising tide of divorce and there has been some re-awakening of interest in marriage-saving as evidence concerning the potentially negative impact of divorce on children accumulates (see, for example, Cockett and Tripp, 1994; Kelly, 1993). However, although the proposed reforms promote marriage-saving as an objective and mediation is presented as being the most effective way of dealing with marriages which cannot be saved (by reducing parental conflict in order to enhance parental responsibility and to protect children), the shift to what will become a primarily administrative rather than judicial process has been heavily informed by the need to reduce costs. Since it seems unlikely that there will be a sudden or substantial reversal of the current divorce trends, and since the costs associated with divorce will continue to be high, the search for the cheapest methods of delivering divorce and related social work services seems unlikely to cease.

The fifth and most recent trend, which reflects the impact of the others, is the redefining of the role of social work in divorce. Not only has this increasingly been reconstructed in terms of mediation, with a focus on the family as opposed to

the parties to the divorce, but as a consequence of this and of the recent changes, it can no longer be seen as the sole preserve of the court welfare officer or, indeed, of the statutory sector. In view of this, and the increasingly central and politically sensitive role which the probation service is being given in working with offenders in the community, the responsibility of the probation service for court welfare work is beginning to look increasingly anomalous.

Further Reading

1   Fisher, T. (ed.) (1990) *Family Conciliation Within the UK: Policy and Practice*, Bristol: Family Law.
2   James, A. and Hay, W. (1993) *Court Welfare in Action: Practice and Theory*, Hemel Hempstead: Harvester Wheatsheaf.
3   Robinson, M. (1993) *Family Transformation Through Divorce and Remarriage*, London: Routledge.

References

Allan, G. (1991) *Family Life*, Oxford: Basil Blackwell.
Burgoyne, J., Ormrod, R. and Richards, M. (1988) *Divorce Matters*, Harmondsworth: Penguin.
Cockett, M. and Tripp, J. (1994) *The Exeter Family Study: Family Breakdown and its Impact on Children*, Exeter: University of Exeter Press.
Eekelaar, J. (1991) 'Parental responsibility: state of nature or the state of the state?', *Journal of Social Welfare and Family Law*, No. 1, 37–50.
Fisher, T. (ed.) (1990) *Family Conciliation Within the UK: Policy and Practice*, Bristol: Family Law.
Goldthorpe, J. (1987) *Family Life in Western Society*, Cambridge: Cambridge University Press.
Home Office (1994a) *Probation Statistics, England and Wales, 1993*, London: Home Office.
Home Office (1994b) *National Standards for Probation Service Family Court Welfare Work*, London: Home Office.
James, A. (1988) ' "Civil Work" in the probation service', in R. Dingwall and J. Eekelaar (eds) *Divorce Mediation and the Legal Process*, Oxford: Clarendon Press.
James, A. (1990) 'Conciliation and social change', in T. Fisher (ed.) *Family Conciliation Within the UK: Policy and Practice*, Bristol: Family Law.

James, A. (1995) 'Social work in divorce: welfare, mediation and justice', *International Journal of Law and the Family*, 9, 256–74.

James, A. and Hay, W. (1993) *Court Welfare in Action: Practice and Theory*, London: Harvester Wheatsheaf.

James, A. and Wilson, K. (1986) *Couples, Conflict and Change*, London: Tavistock.

Kelly, J. (1993) 'Current research on children's postdivorce adjustment', *Family and Conciliation Courts Review*, 31(1), 29–49.

Kiernan, K. and Wicks, M. (1990) *Family Change and Future Policy*, York: Joseph Rowntree/FPSC.

Law Commission (1990) *Family Law: Ground for Divorce*, Law Com. No. 192, London: HMSO.

Lord Chancellor's Department (1993) *Looking to the Future: Mediation and the Ground for Divorce*, Cm 2424, London: HMSO.

Lord Chancellor's Department (1995) *Looking to the Future: Mediation and the Ground for Divorce – The Government's Proposals*, Cm 2799, London: HMSO.

Parry, M. (1994) 'Children's welfare and the law: the Children Act 1989 and recent developments – Part 2', *Panel News*, 7(3), 4–11.

Phillips, R. (1988) *Putting Asunder: a History of Divorce in Western Society*, Cambridge: Cambridge University Press.

Stone, L. (1990) *The Road to Divorce: England 1530–1987*, Oxford: Oxford University Press.

Utting, D. (1995) *Families and Parenthood: Supporting Families, Preventing Breakdown*, York: Joseph Rowntree Foundation.

Part VIII
The Placement Tradition in Social Work Training

Introduction to Part VIII

Social work trainers have been unambiguously committed to the importance of supervised practice learning for half a century. Long before community physicians were required to go on placement into a doctor's surgery during their medical school training, it was part and parcel of the social workers' world that as much as half of their learning experience would be spent, not in the classroom, but face to face with the reality of the world of the client. An emphasis on the importance of this process has continued to grow and two key elements in it are here reflected: the role of the practice teacher, and the need for the student to demonstrate professional competence prior to qualification. The experience of social work in the development of practice-learning techniques is widely acknowledged, and interesting moves are afoot in the establishment of parallel systems in related professions; this, in turn, will facilitate improvements in the increasingly important world of interdisciplinary communication and practice.

VIII.1
The Role of the Practice Teacher
Gwyneth Boswell

The content and process of social work education have changed rapidly over the last three decades. The theory and practice of social work, once treated as if they were two separate entities, have gradually become more synthesized, and agency/college partnerships have developed, culminating in requirements for joint social work training programme provision (CCETSW, 1991a). Alongside this gradual evolution, the role of the practice teacher known, in days gone by, as the student supervisor, has also changed significantly. In particular, practice teaching has moved from engaging students in a rather vague quasi-personal growth process (Wijnberg and Schwartz, 1977) to the point where it is, in some cases, a near-precise professional art. Between the years 1967 and 1995, when much of this change was in play, the author was first a social work (probation option) student, later a singleton practice teacher, later still manager of a specialist student training unit, and subsequently a student tutor and director of a practice-teaching award programme. Thus, there is an extent to which this chapter, which chronicles the development of the practice-teaching role, will be semi-autobiographical based on almost 30 years of reflection and participation in the learning, teaching and practice of social work.

Whatever form it took, the practice component of qualifying social work training always assumed major importance for the students undertaking it. Ask any social worker or probation officer to recount something memorable about their own training and the chances are that they will refer to a placement rather than to a lecture or an essay (Wright and Davies, 1989). Purposeful, competent social work results from a sound blend of knowledge and practice experience. The first practice placement, in particular, constitutes a real test for students as to whether they can relate to and help service users in the way they believed they could when they applied for social work training; and whether they will merit credibility in the eyes of their colleague professionals. Acquiring the knowledge base and writing about it at the college end is potentially safer and more protected than applying it in the uncertain and unpredictable world of social work practice. Thus, it is crucial for students to be placed for support, development and accountability purposes with a practice teacher whom they can trust to recognize and build on their strengths, gently to identify and improve upon their weaknesses, and generally to help consolidate their confidence and competence as social workers.

The role of the practice teacher in qualifying social work training has enduringly been the provider of necessary and appropriate learning experiences which furnish students with the opportunity to demonstrate their ability in the practice of social work. The ways in which these experiences are provided have, however, changed considerably over time. Following the example of their earlier American counterparts, those involved in social work activity in the UK, during the pre-

and post-Second World War years, had moved on from reaction to the structural problems arising from the Depression, to thinking in terms of psychological and social casework techniques (Boswell, 1982). When social work training courses based in higher education establishments began to open up widely during the 1960s and 1970s, practice experience formed a significant proportion of training. Student supervisors were self-selecting and tended to be people who were seen as experienced and skilled caseworkers. Without formal training in the practice teacher role, it was inevitable that they would transfer their existing casework skills to the supervisor/student relationship. Indeed, such literature as was available suggested that those involved in training for the professions should adopt just such a transfer of learning process (Towle, 1954; Grose and Birney, 1963). Many parallels were perceived between the client/social worker and student/supervisor relationship such as the casework principles of, for example, 'individualization' and 'purposeful expression of feelings/controlled emotional involvement' set out by Biestek (1961). This therapeutic mode, in which student supervisors identified students' problems as located in their personal development and utilized supervision as a form of 'treatment' for these deficiencies, was experienced negatively by many students and was later categorized by North American researchers as an 'objectionable supervisory style' (Rosenblatt and Mayer, 1975). Continuing this endorsement of the casework/student supervision parallel, however, Kent suggested:

There is something of teaching and helping in both casework and supervision; caseworkers often fail to recognize how much they teach their clients about themselves and their environment. Because much of casework is teaching and because much of supervision is enabling, experienced practitioners

Five Key Points

1 The practice component of social work training tends to constitute the most memorable learning experience for pre-qualifying students.
2 The role emphasis of the practice teacher has changed over time from agent of personal growth to assessor of practice competence.
3 The practice teacher's enduring task has been to provide necessary and appropriate learning experiences which furnish students with the opportunity to demonstrate their ability in the practice of social work.
4 Agency and practice teacher accreditation has brought about a shift from the management of placements to the strategic management of practice teaching as a specialist activity.
5 Good quality, empowering practice teaching facilitates the transfer of learning, the assessment of core skills and the integration of self-evaluation and consumer feedback.

can transfer the knowledge and skill which they have acquired in the field and bring it to bear in understanding the process of supervision.
(Kent, 1969, pp. 2–3)

Although Kent went on to differentiate between student social workers and clients, it is clear that the notion either of the social worker as teacher of the client or the supervisor as teacher of the student was seen as unproblematic. Awareness of power relations and the steps which could be taken to vary power balances, the interrelation of the teaching and learning processes in adult education generally, were not yet developed in the way that they came to be during the 1980s (Butler and Elliott, 1985; Gray and Gardiner, 1989).

Alongside the casework relationship model of student supervision went the apprenticeship model of learning. This meant that the student learned primarily from the appointed supervisor via the mode which came to be known as 'sitting with Nellie'. In other words, the student shadowed her/his supervisor in order to learn at firsthand how social work was done. Apprenticeship meant that the supervisor had to model good casework both in her/his practice and in the relationship with the student. Although modelling is a concept which remains popular in practice teaching it has broadened out from the responsibilities placed upon a single professional to 'get it right' to long-arm and team responsibility settings where the student is likely to observe a variety of models from a range of professionals and be encouraged to develop in the way appropriate to her/him as an individual. Apprenticeship in its heyday worked well to the extent that student and supervisor could survive constant 'togetherness' respecting and allowing for each other's roles.

My own most vivid memories of studenthood in my early twenties within the apprenticeship-learning mode extend to three particular instances, all of which occurred within settings where the casework relationship was treated as a sacred cow and the skills of those who were student supervisors therein were spoken of in hushed, reverential tones. The first instance was when a male supervisor, said to be highly experienced in marital work, brutally interrogated in my presence a woman client (who had come with marriage problems), about her early relationship with her father and reduced her to tears by the end of the session. Triumphantly he told me this was a breakthrough and not to be afraid of asking the hard questions. Privately I thought she would not keep her next appointment. She never came again.

The second instance was when a female supervisor, said to be skilled in working with adolescents, interviewed, in my presence, a young male offender in his home with his parents. Slightly to my

surprise, she behaved rather as she did in supervision with me – that is to say that she spoke hardly at all. I knew about pregnant pauses and fruitful silences, but after an hour of little else the boy was visibly yawning and his parents angry and confused. In both these situations I had found myself identifying with the reaction of the clients but feeling bemused, as if I had failed to appreciate what my supervisors had really achieved in these settings, because both I and their colleagues assumed that they were consummate social workers.

In the third instance my (male) supervisor and I visited a 'well-known' family in the neighbourhood one evening. The situation became fraught and the father of the family pulled out a knife. My supervisor remained completely calm and quietly indicated that I and the man's wife should leave the room which we did slowly, entering the adjoining kitchen where, through the hatch, we could hear everything that was said. I listened in awe as my supervisor quietly and gradually diffused the man's anger and took the knife off him. Soon after, we were able to leave the house and head to the nearest pub to settle our nerves. By then he had assumed icon status for me and could do no wrong thereafter. These varying states of disappointment and awe, having as much, of course, to do with the expectations and impressionability of the student as with the skill or otherwise of the supervisor, were actually unproductive and rather closed ways to learn, depending little on the honest exchange of reactions and feelings. Like most supervisory styles the apprenticeship model with its casework overtones had something to offer, but applied wholesale it could be both restrictive and developmentally inhibiting. As Brandon and Davies (1979) and Syson and Baginsky (1981) reported, it was usually also short on specifying objectives and desired professional outcomes, so that neither student nor supervisor was always sure what was being assessed or by what means.

Practice teaching continued in its somewhat amorphous role during the early 1970s, though by this time in the UK the Central Council for Education and Training in Social Work (CCETSW) had been established to provide a system of regulation and validation for social work training. Although increased numbers of social workers and probation officers were coming into their professions via the new Certificate of Qualification in Social Work (CQSW), their newly organized employing agencies had little time to afford to the learning needs of students on placement; and a paucity of guidance was, at this time, offered to practice teachers by CCETSW. As a singleton practice teacher myself during the early 1970s, I recall inventing objectives and assessment criteria as I went along, a process which, remarkably from current perspectives on the need for accountability, was questioned neither by managers nor students.

By the early 1980s, documents published by CCETSW were beginning to offer a limited amount of guidance on the subject of the process and outcome of social work training. Much of this guidance remained unspecific but, interestingly, placed emphasis on the earlier popular notion of transferred learning though in relation to students' rather than practice teachers' ability to do this (CCETSW, 1981, 1983). The complexity of this process, as applied to social work, however, had yet to be fully recognized and was first done so most usefully in 1985 by Butler and Elliott who set out a conceptual framework to facilitate the transfer of learning (Butler and Elliott, 1985). This was a device which encouraged the search for common elements in differing situations, enabling the student to engage in learning by bringing forward these links and implementing them in a new context, thus acquiring an applied social work

skill. Transfer of learning has continued to have bedrock status and, gradually increasing in sophistication as a concept, became a required competence both for the Diploma in Social Work (DipSW) (CCETSW, 1991a, 1995a) and the Practice Teaching Award (CCETSW, 1991b, 1995b) which will receive further attention later in the chapter.

A notable exception to the *ad hoc* evolution of practice teaching during the three decades in question was the development of student units whose teaching, for the first time, offered specialist supervision to students on placement (Curnock, 1975). Those

---

Three Questions

1 How can a social work student's 'necessary and appropriate learning experiences' best be identified within the placement setting?

2 What is the most effective means by which to enable students to monitor and evaluate their own performance as social workers?

3 What are the arguments for and against agencies continuing to invest scarce resources into a high quality practice element of social work education?

---

working in such units had the luxury of time to develop good practice in identifying skills to be learned and methods of assessing them. As a manager of a Probation training unit, I was fortunate to be involved with colleagues in the development of a set of eight core skills which, it was found, met the requirements of probation practice but also transferred appropriately to other social work settings. The document in which these core skills were enshrined has long since disappeared into obscurity, but so wholly useful and applicable did I find it as a specialist student supervisor that it is indelibly printed on my memory. Having mentally employed this list of eight core skills ever since to make sense of what I, in a variety of roles, was doing and expecting of students, I reproduce it here in all its simplicity.

Table VII.1.1 The core skills of social work.

Service User
1 Communication
2 Assessment
3 Intervention

Organization
4 Understanding of agency function
5 Workload management
6 Professional relationships
7 Record/letter/report writing
8 Use of supervision

Relating the set of skills set out in table VIII.1.1 to developing and assessing the work of a probation student (for example) a practice teacher requires evidence:

1 That a student can *communicate* sensitively and purposefully with an offender in order to obtain relevant information.

2 That a student can *assess* the reasons for the offending accurately (i.e., apply theory).

3 That a student can apply the assessment to employ the most effective means of *intervention* with the offender (i.e., apply method).

4 That a student can understand the *function* of the agency in the criminal justice system.

5 That a student can *manage a workload* in a way which prioritizes and balances offender and agency needs.

6 That a student can act in accordance with the agency function by making appropriate *professional relationships* both within and beyond the organization.

7 That a student can *write comprehensible documents* appropriate to the agency's function and credible to recipients.

8 That a student can *use supervision* in an open way to build on strengths, improve on weaknesses and continue the process of learning.

The role of the practice teacher in furthering these skills would be explicitly to define the purpose of the activity; to impart or provide sources of relevant knowledge; to foster and develop an understanding of values and policies on which agency practice is based; and to provide a range of opportunities and training materials for skills development. The means of acquiring evidence – for example, supervisory discussion, record/report scrutiny, direct observation, audio/videotape interviews, colleague/service user feedback – would be specified as would the student's access to feedback from these exercises. Where the student demonstrated skills underpinned by relevant knowledge and appropriate values she or he would be deemed overall competent in practice (rather than, as is now the case, competent in a range of competence areas). In a field characterized by vagueness and uncertainty for so long, these were very solid, even if not yet perfected, processes to adopt. Many practice teachers and scores of students were the beneficiaries.

The late 1980s saw an acceleration of thinking and development in pre-qualifying social work training in the UK. Following a number of official inquiries criticizing social workers' risky and uninformed practice, notably the

Beckford Report (1985), and long periods of consultation with interested bodies, a minimum period of three years training for social workers and probation officers was recommended (CCETSW, 1987). This was ultimately rejected by the government but, together with other groups working on improving practice learning during the 1980s, had spawned concrete ideas about standards of performance both for students and for practice teachers. The notion of accreditation of agencies, training courses and practice teachers was introduced (CCETSW, 1987) and ratified in 1989. In respect of practice teachers this meant that a position was being reached where DipSW students would only be placed with those who had gained the CCETSW Practice Teaching Award. This Award could be acquired either via a taught programme of at least 150 hours duration; or via a portfolio route, where experienced practice teachers accredited under transitional arrangements could submit a portfolio, drawing on their experience of student supervision and selecting their learning opportunities according to perceived gaps. Following their receipt of the Award, their agency would accredit them, usually for a period of five years in the first instance.

CCETSW's system of approval of agencies for practice learning (CCETSW, 1991b) was an attempt to raise employers' awareness of the importance of providing DipSW students with high quality placements. Agencies themselves had to submit evidence to CCETSW demonstrating that they met the required standard for support, recognition and monitoring of practice teachers within their organization. Consequently the emphasis within agencies has shifted from the management of placements to the management of practice teaching – towards quality instead of the focus on quantity identified by research in the early 1990s (Thompson and Marsh, 1991). As a result, practice teaching has begun to

move from the margins to inclusion within agency financial and management systems, and in planning and training processes as a legitimate mainstream activity which merits resources such as workload relief. Practice teachers are coming in from the cold. No longer does their activity survive purely as a result of personal enthusiasm and commitment over and above the call of duty; it is becoming part of a planned strategy which includes the consideration of staff members' professional development.

Assisted, to an extent, by the rules and requirements set out for the DipSW (CCETSW, 1991a), practice teachers have been afforded increasing clarity about what it is that students are required to demonstrate on placement and how evidence about their ability may be obtained. Ideas about the assessment of practice competence have become much more sophisticated (Evans, 1990). The developing notion of practice curriculum (Doel, 1987; Phillipson et al., 1988; CCETSW, 1993) has aided the understanding of the levels of performance which may be required at key stages in the practice-learning process, though much work remains to be done in this area. However, the idea of a social work competence as a catch-all composite of skills, knowledge and values remains an awkward and impracticable instrument with which to furnish the average practice teacher who

Further Reading

1   Schon, D. (1988) *Educating the Reflective Practitioner*, London and San Francisco: Jossey Bass.
2   Shardlow, S. and Doel, M. (1996) *Practice Learning and Teaching*, London: Macmillan.
3   Yelloly, M. and Henkel, M. (eds) (1995) *Learning and Teaching in Social Work: Towards Reflective Practice*, London and Bristol; Pennsylvania: Jessica Kingsley.

seeks intelligibility above all. Additional problems are that competences quickly become dated, are increasingly likely to become political and are prescriptive making little allowance for the professional discretion and reflective, critical faculty with which students crucially need to become equipped (Hayman, 1993). Social work activity is, most of all, a dynamic, risk-taking process, constantly open to review and redefinition which depends for its success on the continued refinement of the fundamental skills of communication, assessment and intervention (Boswell, 1995). Practice teachers, whilst in some ways liberated by the concrete expectations of competence lists, are in other ways constricted by the limitations these lists impose on the simple process of the narrative, telling the story of the student's development on placement, which naturally includes coverage of the progressions outlined above.

The competence dilemma is, however, somewhat less problematic within the Practice Teaching Award since the onus is on practice teachers themselves to direct their own learning and provide evidence of their own ability. Within a climate of participative learning towards the acquisition of competence, most Award programmes provide, as a baseline, inputs on adult learning, anti-discriminatory practice teaching, placement management, supervision, assessment and evaluation, and integrating theory and practice. Candidates are helped to apply these rather abstract notions to the requirements they will have to meet and to the evidence of their performance which their portfolios will have to demonstrate (CCETSW, 1995b). Most portfolios, as well as containing a written report from the candidate's own practice assessor also include a written report from the candidate's most recent student and a self-evaluation from the candidate herself/himself. This requirement for both the consumer and candidate's own view is in advance of the DipSW report requirements, though some practice teachers, as advocated in Evans' coherent model of practice teaching (Evans, 1993), view both as good practice and routinely include them in their reports of students' performance. All of these processes are instrumental in sharing out the power in adult learning, a process which received little attention within the earlier, mainly didactic, apprenticeship model of practice teaching.

In summary, this chapter has sought to chronicle some of the changes in the role of the practice teacher as social work education has developed and increased in sophistication over the last three decades. It has shown how the certainty of growth and apprenticeship models of student supervision gradually evaporated into something of a vacuum which ultimately came to be replaced by more concrete systems, placing the practice teacher in the role of provider of learning opportunities, based on the sharing of power within learning processes. The concrete systems brought complexities of their own for the hard-pressed practice teacher for whom it is suggested that three practices hold good in the provision of lucid, empowering student-learning opportunities. These are the transfer of learning, the assessment of core skills and the integration of self-evaluation and consumer feedback. Such practices can be developed and drawn upon to further practice teaching as a credible, purposeful activity which employs all relevant means to bring high quality practice into the culture of social work.

References

Beckford Report (1985) *The Report of the Panel of Inquiry into the Circumstances Surrounding the Death of Jasmine Beckford*, Middlesex: London Borough of Brent.

Biestek, F. (1961) *The Casework Relationship*, London: Allen and Unwin.

Boswell, G. R. (1982) *Goals in the Probation and After-*

Care Service, unpublished Ph.D. thesis, Liverpool University.

Boswell, G. R. (1996) 'The essential skills of probation work', in T. May and A. Vass (eds) *Working With Offenders: Issues, Contexts and Outcomes*, London: Sage.

Brandon, J. and Davies, M. (1979) 'The limits of competence in social work: the assessment of marginal students in social work education', *British Journal of Social Work*, 9, 295–347.

Butler, B. and Elliott, D. (1985) *Teaching and Learning for Practice*, Aldershot, Vermont: Gower, Community Care Practice Handbooks.

CCETSW (1981) *Revised Guidelines* (Supplement to Paper 15.1 (1977) *Guidelines for Courses leading to the Certificate of Qualification in Social Work*), London: CCETSW.

CCETSW (1983) *Review of Qualifying Training Policies*, (Paper 20), London: CCETSW.

CCETSW (1987) *The Qualifying Diploma in Social Work: a Policy Statement*, (Paper 20.8), London: CCETSW.

CCETSW (1991a) *Rules and Requirements for the Diploma in Social Work* (2nd edn), (Paper 30), London: CCETSW.

CCETSW (1991b) *Improving Standards in Practice Learning* (2nd edn), (Paper 26.3), London: CCETSW.

CCETSW (1993) *Improving Practice Teaching and Learning*, Northern Curriculum Development Project, London: CCETSW.

CCETSW (1995a) *Rules and Regulations for the Diploma in Social Work* (revised edn), (Paper 30), London: CCETSW.

CCETSW (1995b) *Assuring Quality in Practice Teaching*, London: CCETSW.

Curnock, K. (1975) *Student Units in Social Work Education*, Paper 11, London: CCETSW.

Doel, M. (1987) *The Practice Curriculum*, Sheffield University.

Evans, D. (1990) 'Assessing students' competence to practise in college and practice agency', *Improving Social Work Education and Training* 3, London: CCETSW.

Evans, D. (1993) 'A model of practice teaching', *NOPT Newsletter* 7, July.

Gray, J. and Gardiner, D. (1989) 'The impact of conceptions of "learning" on the quality of teaching and learning in social work education', *Issues in Social Work Education*, 9 (1 & 2), 74–92.

Grose, R. F. and Birney, R. C. (eds) (1963) *Transfer of Learning*, New York: Van Nostrand.

Hayman, V. (1993) 'Re-writing the job: a sceptical look at competences', *Probation Journal*, 40(4), 180–3.

Kent, B. (1969) *Social Work Supervision in Practice*, Oxford, London, Edinburgh, New York, Toronto, Sydney, Paris, Braunschweig: Pergamon Press.

Phillipson, J., Richards, M. and Saunders, D. (1988) *Towards a Practice-led Curriculum*, London: NISW.

Rosenblatt, A. and Mayer, J. E. (1975) 'Objectionable supervisory styles: students' views', *Social Work (USA)*, 20(3), 184–9.

Syson, L. and Baginsky, M. (1981) *Learning to Practise*, Study 3, London: CCETSW.

Thompson, S. and Marsh, P. (1991) *Practice Teaching Management*, Research Report, Department of Health.

Towle, C. (1954) *The Learner in Education for the Professions, as seen in Education for Social Work*, Chicago: University of Chicago Press.

Wijnberg, M. H. and Schwartz, M. C. (1977) 'Models of student supervision: the apprentice, growth and role systems models', *Journal of Education for Social Work*, 13(3), 107–13.

Wright, A. and Davies, M. (1989) 'Becoming a probation officer: through training and into practice', *Skills, Knowledge and Qualities in Probation Practice*, Research Report 2, Norwich: Social Work Monographs, University of East Anglia.

VIII.2
Demonstrating Competence in Social Work
Dave Evans

The process of assessment in social work education is located firmly in a wider socio-political context (Murphy and Torrance, 1988). The student seeking to demonstrate competence and gain a professional award is giving tacit support to the professionalization of social work. The teacher who passes or fails a student participates in the profession's attempt to guarantee its standards to a wider, often sceptical, society.

The political act of passing or failing a student entails an exercising of power and where power is exercised, there is always the possibility of discrimination. Research (de Souza, 1991; Evans, 1991) suggests that the experience of discrimination in assessment is more widespread than assessors might generally wish to acknowledge: on grounds such as gender, age, race, religion and class. With such potential it is important that assessment systems in social work education are based upon sound principles (Evans, 1991; Shardlow and Doel, 1993; Brown and Knight, 1994).

Three principles seem particularly crucial. Firstly, there should be *clarity of purpose*. Rowntree (1987) suggests six overlapping purposes for assessment, of which two central ones are: learning, for both the assessor and the assessed; ensuring standards of entry into the profession. A second important principle is *clarity of process*. Both assessors and assessed need a detailed awareness of what is being assessed and how judgements are being made. Research (Evans, 1991) suggests that both participants often lack this clarity. Finally,

the assessment system should be *congruent with the educational aims and methods*. Social work is a complex activity learned through a wide range of processes and requiring a similar range of assessment methods. Moreover, the assessment system needs to be clearly compatible with social work values.

Professional Competence

As a central concept in assessment during the 1980s and 1990s, competence also has a political context. Its origins in the UK can perhaps be seen in the attack by the Manpower Services Commission in the 1970s on apprenticeships, replacing the notion of 'time serving' with competency (Murphy and Torrance, 1988). The concept was also endorsed in the New Training Initiative (DoE, 1981), recognizing the need for a competent workforce which would increase the UK's economic competitiveness.

The Training Agency (1988) has provided one of the most influential definitions of competence for the 1990s:

Competence is a wide concept which embodies the ability to transfer skills and knowledge to new situations within the occupational area. It encompasses organisation and planning of work, innovation and coping with non-routine activities. It includes those qualities of personal effectiveness that are required in the work place to deal with co-workers, managers and customers.

This view of occupational competence has had a number of strengths. Firstly, it has emphasized effective performance in the workplace: the practice component in social work education. Secondly, it has led to the production of clear, overt assessment criteria for a growing number of occupations, including social work. Thirdly, the process of developing occupational competences, outlined by Micklewright (1992), requires collaboration at a national level thus producing a general consensus to inform assessment, as occurred in social work in 1994.

However, a number of writers (Ashworth and Saxton, 1990; Evans, 1991; Bines, 1992; Kemshall, 1993; Brown and Knight, 1994; Yelloly, 1995) have indicated significant weaknesses in this view of competence, including:

An over-emphasis on behaviour and performance and insufficient stress on cognitive abilities.

A constraining focus on an uncritical and narrow training for an existing job.

The reductionist tendency to delineate a list of specific criteria and hence lose a more holistic view of the worker.

The use of a consensual process to produce occupational competences which may omit or diminish less powerful views held, for example, by women or black people.

A tendency to be over-individualistic when effective work often requires team work and partnership.

The first competences to be developed were for vocational occupations. Although social work education has progressively aligned itself with the competence movement (CCETSW, 1989, 1990, 1995), the suspicion has remained concerning the appropriateness of the concept 'competence' for what Winter (1992) terms the 'higher status occupations'. This raises an important

Five Key Points

1. Assessment in social work education is a political act.

2. Three key principles in assessment are: clarity of purpose, clarity of process, congruence with educational aims and methods.

3. Social work professional competence comprises: a repertoire of knowledge skills and values, effective practice, higher order learning skills and development through time.

4. The process of standard setting involves both the exercise of judgement and a process of collaboration.

5. Valid assessment methods which place professional practice at the heart of the assessment system need further development.

question:

What is the nature of competence in a profession such as social work?

A number of models of professional competence appear in the literature (Benner, 1984; Schon, 1987; Evans, 1991; Winter, 1992; Eraut and Cole, 1993; Jones and Joss, 1995). From these, it is possible to develop a model with four major components: (1) a repertoire upon which the professional worker draws, (2) professional practice, (3) higher order cognitive skills, and (4) career progression or time (see figure VIII.2.1).

1. The repertoire contains not only the required knowledge, skills and values elaborated in the literature (CCETSW, 1995) but also attributes appropriate to the professional worker as a whole person (Jones and Joss, 1995). Winter (1992) includes an emotional dimension in his model, indicating that appropriate attributes for social work might include

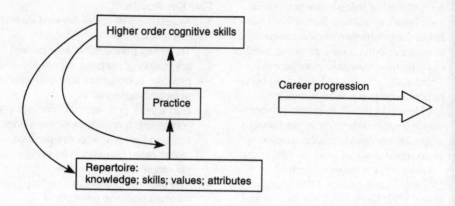

Figure VIII.2.1 A model of professional competence.

warmth, empathy, emotional maturity. Other attributes might include commitment, integrity and creativity. This repertoire will be drawn on for all practice contexts that the worker encounters. It therefore represents a potential which is broader than the actual. A key issue for professional education, therefore, is to determine exactly how much broader.

2   Practice comprises the entire range of activities performed by the professional worker, both direct work with service users and indirect work, and including internal judgement and decision making as well as observable behaviours.

3   The higher order cognitive skills enable the professional to learn about their practice to adapt it, and develop it in changing contexts. These skills can be seen to form in part the knowledge through communicative action (Henkel, 1995), which contrasts with the knowledge as objective reality which forms part of the repertoire. They include (i) skills for employing the repertoire in practice such as: relating theory and research to practice; transfer of

learning, and (ii) skills for developing the repertoire such as: critical reflection on practice; evaluating practice outcomes; effective use of supervision, consultancy and other dialogue; study skills.

4   This fourth dimension allows for the way in which professionals can change and adapt their higher order cognitive skills through time (Benner, 1984) as they become more experienced. The qualifying social worker and experienced practitioner may make different use of or attach different weight to study skills and reflective skills.

The implications of this model for assessment include the need to:

Observe practice at one point in time.

Explore the subset of knowledge, skills, values and attributes which informed that practice.

Explore the existence of a broader set of knowledge, skills, values and other attributes.

Observe practice at other points in time.

Explore the processes of learning which have led to changes in practice from one point in time to another..

Criteria and Standards

The Training Agency has promoted the development of occupational competence across an ever-widening range of occupations. Their commonly accepted notion of 'occupational standards', however, begs an important question. Does the delineation of a competence necessarily entail a statement of standard? Some writers (Evans, 1991; Winter, 1992) suggest it does not. They suggest that while national processes may delineate the dimensions to be examined, the individual assessor will still have to make a professional judgement of standard. A helpful analogy is with the dimension of heat which can be measured (by thermometer) to determine a particular standard, i.e. temperature (figure VIII.2.2).

It is useful, therefore, to distinguish the dimension, or criterion, for assessment from the standard achieved.

The history of social work education has seen a process of making overt the criteria for assessment, particularly in the practice placement (Morrell, 1980). Not only do overt, agreed criteria make the task of the assessors easier and more comparable, they can also help to combat the discrimination which already disadvantaged students may experience in the assessment process (Evans, 1991; Brown and Knight, 1994).

However, the process of agreeing overt criteria through consensus in social work has had the disadvantage of a proliferation of criteria. The Certificate in Qualification in Social Work (CCETSW,

---

Three Questions

1 What is the nature of competence in a profession such as social work?
2 Which are the most important criteria in judging a student?
3 How can practice teachers develop their range of valid and reliable assessment methods?

1977) specifies 12 broad areas for assessment. However, two later versions of the Diploma in Social Work (CCETSW, 1989, 1995) have approximately 120 criteria each.

The difficulty for the assessor and the student has become how to determine which criteria are the most important.

Three strategies could help resolve this difficulty. One would be to be aware of those criteria which most usually lead to student failure. Two investigations (Morrell, 1980; Syson and Baginsky, 1981) produced a short list for practice assessment: making relationships; understanding and helping clients; learning and developing; commitment to

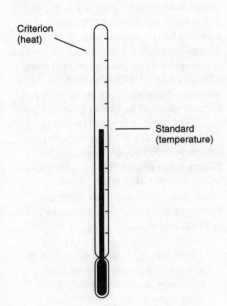

Criterion (heat)

Standard (temperature)

Figure VIII.2.2   Criterion and Standard.

the job; working effectively in the agency; and personal qualities. It would undoubtedly be useful for such investigations to be updated.

A second strategy might involve reference to a model of professional competence, possibly giving differential weight to the higher order cognitive skills, the professional practice and the repertoire of knowledge, skills, values and attributes. A final strategy would be for less powerful people in the assessment system to discover the preferred criteria of more powerful people. This requires dialogue and initiative: students will need to discover from internal assessors; and internal assessors from external assessors.

However, criteria are not of themselves sufficient in assessment. The judgement of standard will be made on the basis of three processes: understanding factors within the student's performance; referring to situations outside the student's performance; seeking consensus. The student's performance may be judged intrinsically to be of a sufficient standard if it is at an appropriate level, demonstrated with sufficient frequency, and across a wide enough range of contexts (Evans, 1991).

There are three main situations outside a given student performance to which the assessor or the student can refer to make judgements of standard. One is a sense of norm, be it of the student year group, of beginning social workers or of team colleagues. Norm-referencing has some dangers, however, since many assessors have had limited access to norms or skewed experience of them. It is risky for assessors to use themselves as a norm, since practice teachers, particularly those who have a CCETSW award, may have higher standards than other 'good enough' practitioners.

A second situation which can be referred to is the student's previous performances. It is interesting to note that practice teachers appear to favour self-

referenced assessment (Brandon and Davies, 1979; Morrell, 1980; Williamson et al., 1989). Not only does this give important indirect evidence of effective higher order cognitive skills but it can encourage student's motivation and confidence. However, it does only indicate a relative change in standards and not the attainment of an absolute minimum.

A final reference point in judging standards is a model. Evans (1991) and Brown and Knight (1994) both advocate the value of models, which are concrete and demonstrable as opposed to norms which are abstract and hypothetical. Students can seek out good enough examples of reports, running records, interviews and the like, and practice teachers can propose them.

The judgement of standard is not, however, the province of one person. Several writers (Paley, 1987; Evans, 1991; Brown and Knight, 1994) have suggested that standards are set through a process of consensus and agreement throughout the professional body. This process entails two or more people having access to the same evidence. At its simplest it involves the practice teacher in a discussion with at least one other internal assessor: for example, the second opinion advocated by CCETSW (1989). Likewise, two-way discussion can occur between the two external assessors required by CCETSW (1989, 1995) and between internal and external assessors. Practice Assessment Panels and Assessment Boards often extend this process into a wider group. Other methods of broadening the consensus include training courses for practice teachers and external assessors.

The process of standard setting can be summarized as involving both the exercise of judgement and a process of collaboration.

Methods and Processes of Assessing

The above discussion of criteria and standards presupposes that the evidence of the student's performance is available. Students and practice teachers must ensure the availability of evidence through a range of methods, some of which are specified by CCETSW (1989, 1995). However, choice of methods is of considerable significance, since without the appropriate method, a given criterion may not be accurately targeted. Continuing an earlier analogy, we would be unlikely to judge someone's temperature accurately if we used a barometer.

Much of the literature on methods (Gibbs et al., 1986; Evans, 1991) concentrates on the attempt to gain an objective view of the student and their abilities. However, the literature (Rowntree, 1987; Evans, 1991) also indicates that assessment necessarily entails the subjective process of getting to know people. If this process is conducted in too analytical, cold and critical a style the student may begin to under-perform through a lack of confidence or attempt to withhold important information.

There are two main concepts which can help both assessors and assessed in the process of seeking increased objectivity: 'reliability' and 'validity'. Reliability concerns the issue of consistency in measurement. Consistency can be achieved when:

Different assessors agree with each other.

Different assessment methods give the assessor the same result (Shardlow and Doel's, 1993, 'triangulation').

One assessor using the same method on different occasions confirms the same opinion.

All three forms of reliability can increase anti-oppressive practice in assessment: a second or third assessor can counteract the prejudice of the first; different methods will show different student strengths; frequent evidencing can help counteract the prejudice formed from initial encounters.

'Validity' concerns the issue of ensuring that assessors assess what they actually intend to assess. If the goal is to assess students' ability to practise social work then methods which take the assessor to the heart of this activity can be seen as more valid. Thus if the assessor wishes to assess the student's ability to engage with service users, the student's self-report would be a less valid method than observation or feedback from the service user. If, however, the criterion for assessment was the student's ability to reflect accurately and critically on their practice, self-report would be a more valid method.

There are a number of methods which can increase the validity of evidence available and are elaborated in more detail elsewhere (Evans, 1991). Direct access to practice can give highly valid evidence of the process of practice performance as CCETSW have recognized (1989, 1995). It can be sought in four main ways – observation, co-work, live supervision and tape recordings. All four have different strengths and weaknesses and it is unfortunate that CCETSW (1995) only

Further Reading

1   Brown, S. and Knight, P. (1994) *Assessing Learners in Higher Education*, London: Kogan Page.
2   Evans, D. (1991) *Assessing Students' Competence to Practise*, London: CCETSW.
3   Rowntree, D. (1987) *Assessing Students: How Shall We Know Them?* (2nd edn), London: Harper and Row Ltd.

recognize two of the four. Moreover, they seem not to recognize the strengths of audio-taping (Evans, 1991), since they only appear to support video-taping.

A rigorous evaluation of the outcome of student's practice can give a further dimension of validity: something has or has not happened as a result of the student's practice. Service user feedback has particular strengths in terms of validity: not only does it give evidence of the outcome of the practice (a 'satisfied' consumer or otherwise), it can also give strong evidence about the process of the practice from a crucial subjective source.

The practice-based assignment (Evans, 1991; Evans and Langley, 1996) which incorporates a tape of practice plus the student's planning for and evaluation of that practice contributes two sources of validity. Not only does it give evidence of the processes of practice performance, but it also incorporates evidence of the student's higher order cognitive skills in planning for and reflecting on that practice.

Brown and Knight (1994) suggest that there has been a trend from reliability towards validity, but that reliability will still retain its significance for nationally accepted awards. Increased validity in assessing social work practice brings with it increased ethical issues of confidentiality and service user choice which require thoughtful and sensitive handling.

Two other principles should inform the choice of assessment methods. One is fairness. There is some evidence (Evans, 1991) to suggest that written methods of assessment can discriminate against students on grounds of class, ethnic origin and educational experience. The principle of fairness would also suggest the need for a wide range of assessment methods (Rowntree, 1987; Evans, 1991; Brown and Knight, 1994) since different students will do better with different methods.

Another important principle is

students' involvement, as adult learners, in the assessment system. Not only can students be involved in choosing assessment methods, but also they can make a major contribution in two specific methods: peer and self-assessment. Several writers (Gibbs et al., 1986; Rowntree, 1987; Evans, 1991; Brown and Knight, 1994) advocate the learning potential of these two methods. Additionally, they provide important evidence of the higher order cognitive skills of analysing, evaluating and reflecting on practice.

A further important process in assessment is the giving and eliciting of feedback. This is not directly related to the demonstration of competence by the student. However, it can promote a climate in which students have a greater confidence to demonstrate their competence and which students often complain is absent (Evans, 1991). Moreover, it helps fulfil the learning purpose of assessment. Gibbs et al. (1986) give an excellent summary of the main requirements for feedback, including:

- keeping the time short between student's work and the feedback;
- summarizing comments;
- balancing positives and negatives, indicating which is which;
- indicating ways of improving;
- using oral feedback and dialogue with the student;
- encouraging students to ask for feedback;
- giving affective as well as cognitive feedback; and
- giving oral feedback on initial attempts at practice.

Conclusion

Throughout this chapter, the position of the assessor and the assessed have been outlined. It has been recognized for some time (Brandon and Davies, 1979; Morrell,

1980) that it is the responsibility of the student to demonstrate competence. However, CCETSW and the internal and external assessors of its validated programmes also have responsibilities: firstly to seek to understand the nature of competence in social work and secondly to ensure that sound judgements are made about competence on the basis of appropriate evidence. If the assessment system itself can demonstrate its competence to the wider community, the quality of social work practice may be indicated to others and further assured.

References

Ashworth, P. D. and Saxton, J. (1990) 'On "competence" ' *Journal of Further and Higher Education*, 14(2).

Benner, P. (1984) *From Novice to Expert*, New York: Addison Wesley.

Bines, H. (1992) 'Issues in Course Design', in H. Bines and D. Watson (eds), *Developing Professional Education*, Buckingham: SRHE and Open University Press.

Brandon, J. and Davies, M. (1979) 'The limits of competence in social work: the assessment of marginal students in social work education', *British Journal of Social Work*, 9, 295–347.

Brown, S. and Knight, P. (1994) *Assessing Learners in Higher Education*, London: Kogan Page.

CCETSW (1977) *Guidelines for Courses leading to the Certificate of Qualification in Social Work, CQSW*, (Paper 15.1), London: CCETSW.

CCETSW (1989) *Rules and Requirements for the Diploma in Social Work* (Paper 30), London: CCETSW.

CCETSW (1990) *The Requirements for Post Qualifying Education and Training in the Personal Social Services* (Paper 31), London: CCETSW.

CCETSW (1995) *Rules and Requirements for the Diploma in Social Work* (Paper 30, revised), London: CCETSW.

de Souza, P. (1991) 'A review of the experiences of black students in social work training', in CCETSW (eds), *One Small Step towards Racial Justice*, London: CCETSW, pp. 148–79.

DoE (1981) *A New Training Initiative: a Programme for Action*, Cmnd 8455 London: HMSO.

Eraut, M. and Cole, G. (1993) 'Assessment of competence in higher level occupations', *Competence and Assessment*, 21, 10–14.

Evans, D. (1991) *Assessing Students' Competence to Practise*, London: CCETSW.

Evans, D. and Langley, J. (1996) 'Practice-based assignments: social work education as a case study'. Paper presented at the Higher Education Capability Conference.

Gibbs, G., Habeshaw, S. and Habeshaw, T. (1986) *53 Interesting Ways to Assess Your Students*, Technical and Educational Services Ltd.

Henkel, M. (1995) 'Conceptions of knowledge and social work education', in M. Yelloly and M. Henkel (eds) *Learning and Teaching in Social Work*, London: Jessica Kingsley.

Jones, S. and Joss, R. (1995) 'Models of professionalism', in M. Yelloly and M. Henkel (eds), *Learning and Teaching in Social Work*, London: Jessica Kingsley.

Kemshall, H. (1993) 'Assessing competence: scientific process or subjective inference?', *Social Work Education*, 12(1), 36–45.

Micklewright, J. (1992) 'Industrial standards – is there a rational consensus?' *Competence and Assessment: Compendium 2*, Department of Employment.

Morrell, E. (1980) 'Student assessment: where are we now?', *British Journal of Social Work*, 10, 431–42.

Murphy, R. and Torrance, H. (1988) *The Changing Face of Educational Assessment*, Milton Keynes: Open University Press.

Paley, J. (1987) 'Social work and the sociology of knowledge', *British Journal of Social Work*, 7, 169–86.

Rowntree, D. (1987) *Assessing Students: How Shall We Know Them?* (2nd edn), London: Harper and Row Ltd.

Schon, D. (1987) *Educating the Reflective Practitioner*, San Francisco: Jossey Bass.

Shardlow, S. and Doel, M. (1993) 'Examination by triangulation: a model for practice teaching', *Social Work Education*, 12(3), 67–79.

Syson, L. and Baginsky, M. (1981) *Learning to Practise*, London: CCETSW.

Training Agency (1988) *Developments of Assessable Standards for National Certification. Guidance Note 3: the Definition of Competences and Performance Criteria*, Sheffield: Training Agency.

Williamson, H., Jefferson, R., Johnson, S. and Shabbaz, A. (1989) *Assessment of Practice – A Perennial Concern?* Cardiff, University of Wales, College of Cardiff Social Research Unit.

Winter, R. (1992) *Outline of a General Theory of Professional Competence*, unpublished paper, Anglia Polytechnic University.

Yelloly, M. (1995) 'Professional competence and higher education', in M. Yelloly and M. Henkel (eds), *Learning and Teaching in Social Work*, London: Jessica Kingsley.

Name Index

Subject Index

abortion, 334
abuse of women, 42–8
acceptance, 181–3
accommodation, 154–5
accountability of social work, 34, 46, 137, 178, 184, 261, 276, 306–7, 351
actualizing tendency, 179
adolescence, 88–96, 100
adoption, 85, 142, 293, 331–6
adultery, 105
advocacy, 162, 164
aftercare, 136
ageism, 46, 163, 238, 243
agency-function, 352
agents of the state, 28
alternatives to custody, 307
Alzheimer's disease, 112
    see also dementia
ambiguity in social work, 10, 13–17, 20, 28–9, 33, 121, 123
anger management, 350
anorexia nervosa, 95
anti-custodialism, 128
anti-discriminatory practice, 130–1, 238–44, 276, 315
anti-oppressive practice, 17, 229, 315, 361
anti-racism, 251
anxiety, 135–6
anxiety disorders, 211
apprenticeship mode of training, 349–50, 354, 356
approved social workers (ASWs), 320–1
assessment
    in child care, 141–3, 145, 152, 290, 291, 294, 338
    in cognitive–behavioural therapy, 204-5, 210
    in community care, 20, 327–9
    in family therapy, 192
    in feminist practice, 246
    for hospital discharge, 297–9
    in mental health, 133–4, 137, 236, 319–21
    in network analysis, 215, 218–21
    in probation, 127, 129
    in social work, 10, 16, 21, 172, 241, 243
    in social work training, 352, 354, 356-3

associative principle, 18, 19
attachment, 75–8, 80, 82, 84, 106, 140
attachment schemes, 322
attempted suicide, 94–5
Audit Commission, 284
authority, 320–1
autonomy, 276–7

behavioural methods, 129, 202–11
behaviour problems in childhood, 81, 82, 88–96, 145
benefit trap, 155, 156
bereavement, 160
birth families, 144, 145, 293, 335
black child development, 98–101
black identity and self-concepts, 50–5, 98–101
black psychology, 50–5, 98–101
black service users, 16, 50–5, 131
black social workers, 250
bonding, 75
boundaries with the client, 69
breast milk, 74

care and control, 306
caregivers and infants, 74–8, 80–6
care management, 136, 297–8, 301–2, 319–20, 327, 333
Care Orders, 290
care planning, 142–4, 154, 221–2, 267, 294, 327, 329–30
Care Programme Approach, 319, 328
carers, 20, 43–4, 161–3, 215, 217, 221, 222, 248, 294, 297, 302, 326, 329
case conferences, 148, 151, 268, 313, 314
case management, 136
casework, 36, 136, 141, 297
CCETSW, 282, 283, 351, 353, 354, 363
cell replication, 111
changing behaviour, 128, 129, 141, 181, 187, 202–11, 227, 228, 293, 307–9
Charity Organisation Society, 118–22, 124
child abuse, 17, 20, 43, 44, 141, 144, 148–52, 274, 290, 291, 294
childbirth, 58, 59, 106